ASP.NET AJAX in Action

ASP.NET AJAX
in Action

ALESSANDRO GALLO
DAVID BARKOL
RAMA KRISHNA VAVILALA

MANNING
Greenwich
(74° w. long.)

For online information and ordering of this and other Manning books, please visit
www.manning.com. The publisher offers discounts on this book when ordered in quantity.
For more information, please contact:

Special Sales Department
Manning Publications Co.
Sound View Court 3B   fax: (609) 877-8256
Greenwich, CT 06830   email: orders@manning.com

Manning Publications Co.   Copyeditor: Tiffany Taylor
Sound View Court 3B   Typesetter: Gordan Salinovic
Greenwich, CT 06830   Cover designer: Leslie Haimes

ISBN 1-933988-14-2
Printed in the United States of America
1 2 3 4 5 6 7 8 9 10 – MAL – 13 12 11 10 09 08 07

To those who wait

     —A.G.

To my wife and best friend, Emily

       —D.B.

To my parents, for making me who I am!

        —R.K.V.

brief contents

contents

ix

foreword

ASP.NET is used daily by millions of professional developers world-wide. It runs some of the most successful websites and applications in the world, and every day thousands of new developers begin learning ASP.NET for the first time—supported by an incredible developer community of books, blogs, user groups, forums, and developer websites.

Our goal with ASP.NET AJAX is to enable developers to easily build great ASP.NET applications that fully leverage the power of the browser, and which deliver a smoother and more interactive experience for end users. ASP.NET AJAX works with all modern browsers, and allows you to easily build great web applications that work cross-platform on all operating systems. ASP.NET AJAX 1.0 is available as a free, fully supported download for ASP.NET 2.0. It will be built into the standard .NET setup package starting with the .NET Framework 3.5 release of ASP.NET.

There are several things that I think distinguish ASP.NET AJAX. The first is the productivity it delivers. ASP.NET AJAX can be used to very quickly add common AJAX behavior and functionality to an application with very minimal code. If you want smoother page updates and richer client-UI behaviors, there isn't another AJAX framework out there that makes it easier.

What is great about ASP.NET AJAX is that it also scales to advanced scenarios. You can use the ASP.NET AJAX client-side JavaScript library to build clean, encapsulated JavaScript that makes asynchronous network callbacks to the server to build extremely rich UI (for an example of this visit: http://www.pageflakes.com). This ability to start simple, but then go deep, using a core AJAX programming model that is nicely integrated into ASP.NET, ends up being extremely powerful, and is one that enables developers to build great next-generation web applications.

ASP.NET AJAX in Action provides an excellent guide to learning and mastering all of the functionality that ASP.NET AJAX provides, and in particular it does a great job of explaining its more advanced features. Alessandro, David, and Rama are ASP.NET AJAX experts and share their experiences and insights throughout the book. They will help teach you how to fully leverage ASP.NET AJAX and build robust web applications faster and better than ever before.

Enjoy!

SCOTT GUTHRIE
General Manager, Developer Division
Microsoft Corporation

foreword

Why is Ajax important? What makes a set of technologies that were invented a decade ago suddenly relevant? Don't we have easier ways to write rich applications? And aren't some of those already cross-platform? Wasn't the deployment problem solved long ago, making web applications less and less relevant?

Those are legitimate questions—yet all the planets seem to have aligned for Ajax right now.

First, the browser wars are finally over and even Internet Explorer is firmly steered toward standards compliance. This means that it has become possible, at last, to write truly cross-browser applications with a little help from Ajax toolkits, effectively ironing-out any last differences.

Second, JavaScript, long considered a toy language, has evolved (in its usage at least). Most of the engineering techniques that are a given in other languages are finally available for JavaScript, thanks in part to the flexibility of the language and in part to advances in tooling and IDEs.

Third, HTML and CSS as semantic and layout description languages are still one of the most relevant options. No other rendering technology associates such a low price of entry with the same developer friendliness and flexibility.

Finally, the technology is not disruptive and this may be its most compelling advantage. With Ajax, you can use what you already know about web technologies and incrementally improve your applications.

This is what ASP.NET AJAX is about: start with what you know and learn as you go, improving your toolset along the way. Our intention was to make it as easy as possible for you to start and then to take you as far as you're ready to go.

Alessandro, David, and Rama are among the best specialists in those technologies and they're going to take you on an exciting ride. You'll learn from the pioneers in this field what you need to know to write solid JavaScript, HTML, and CSS and how to exploit ASP.NET AJAX to its full potential. The authors of this book have more combined knowledge about and experience with Ajax than almost anyone else in the industry—and they're about to share that treasure with you.

BERTRAND LE ROY, PH.D.
Software Design Engineer, ASP.NET team
Microsoft Corporation

preface

Every book tells a story—even a book about web programming. This story begins in the summer of 2005, at the Professional Developer Conference (PDC) in Los Angeles. It was there that Microsoft gave us our first preview of *Atlas*, the original codename for ASP.NET AJAX. Excited about its promise, we immediately jumped at the opportunity to play around with the young and evolving framework. In the beginning (and we still do this today), we flocked to the forums, blogs, and user groups to learn, and in the process shape, the latest technology.

When Manning approached us about collaborating on this book, it seemed like a natural progression, considering all the time we had invested in learning about the framework. Our goal was to provide the reader with the tools for becoming a well-rounded ASP.NET AJAX developer. To us this meant becoming proficient in JavaScript, authoring Ajax-enabled controls, and understanding how to enrich ASP.NET applications through a collection of best practices and patterns. Along the way, we wanted to display our enthusiasm for what makes ASP.NET AJAX unique by sharing the lessons we had learned from the .NET community, our everyday jobs, and from Microsoft.

What makes *ASP.NET AJAX in Action* special (perhaps even irreplaceable) is its approach to explaining in detail how to use and understand the framework. Beginning with simple examples, we slowly progress to more complex, real-world scenarios that challenge the reader to master the technology and raise his or her skill level.

With the book now complete, our "story" has been told and we believe that we've achieved our goal in delivering a unique and thorough guide to ASP.NET AJAX. As you explore the book, it is our hope that you will become inspired to build the rich and intuitive applications that users expect today.

acknowledgments

We'd like to thank everyone at Manning, especially our publisher, Marjan Bace; our acquisitions editor, Mike Stephens; and our development editor, Nermina Miller, for their continuous support and help with many aspects of the manuscript. Thanks also to the others at Manning who worked with us in different stages of the project: review editor Karen Tegtmayer, webmaster Gabriel Dobrescu, and not least of all project editor Mary Piergies. Special thanks to copy editor Tiffany Taylor, proofreader Elizabeth Martin, design editor Dottie Marsico, and typesetter Gordan Salinovic. We'd like to also acknowledge the invaluable feedback and dedication of our technical editor Joe Stagner, whose support and encouragement greatly contributed to the success of the book.

A very special thank you to Scott Guthrie of Microsoft and Bertrand Le Roy of Microsoft for writing the forewords to our book. Finally, we also thank the many reviewers of the manuscript: Irena Kennedy, Walter Myers, Darren Neimke, Eric Pascarello, Lucas Carlson, Radhakrishna M.V., Berndt Hamboeck, Kazi Manzur Rashid, Mark Mrachek, Curt Christianson, Mohammad Azam, Al Harding, Omar AL Zabir, Sonu Kapoor, Steve Marx, Dave Glover, and Abe Semaan.

ALESSANDRO GALLO
This is my first book, and I've put my time, passion, and soul into writing it. Now that it's done, I can say that writing a book is tough. This would have been impossible to accomplish without the help of the people who contributed to its conception and development.

Working with David and Rama has been an amazing experience. It was an absolute pleasure working with you guys! I'm also grateful to those who dedicated their time and energy to read and comment on the manuscript: David Anson, Ronald Buckton, Sonu Kapoor, Bertrand Le Roy, Steve Marx, and Joe Stagner.

A special thank-you to Luis Abreu for all the help and suggestions he provided during the many hours spent discussing ASP.NET AJAX, since the first CTP release of "Atlas." *Muito obrigado Luis!*

And I can never say thank you enough to Valentina for her patience, enthusiasm, and love.

DAVID BARKOL

Writing this book has been a rewarding and challenging experience. Although it took more time that one could possibly justify, working with Alessandro and Rama has been an absolute pleasure. I'm truly proud of what we've produced together as a team and the friendship we've created in the process.

I would like to thank everybody at Neudesic for their technical expertise and support, especially Samir Patel, Jason Jung, Tim Marshall, Parsa Rohani, Anthony Ferry, and Ashish Agarwal. An extended thank-you goes out to Mickey Williams, Steve Saxon, and Phil Scott for influencing my career and providing me with invaluable advice and encouragement.

Thanks to our reviewers, who provided us with much-needed feedback and support that greatly influenced our book. I would like to particularly thank Irena Kennedy, Walter Myers, and Joe Stagner from Microsoft for their magnanimous contributions and assistance during the review process.

Most important, I would like to thank my wife Emily and two daughters Miranda and Madeline, for inspiring me to do my best every day. The sacrifices they made prove what a wonderful family I have and how lucky I am to have them.

RAMA KRISHNA VAVILALA

It has been an extreme pleasure to work with Alessandro and David. I consider myself very fortunate and blessed for all the support and understanding I received from them. Special thanks to our editor Michael Stephens for believing in all of us and in this project.

I would like to acknowledge the support my family has shown to me during the writing of the book. Thank you, Radhika, for all the hard work and understanding; and thanks, Shreya, for not troubling me too much while I was writing.

My friend Nishant Sivakumar, who had just been through the book-writing ordeal, was generous enough to share tips and tricks with me. Thanks, Nish!

Last but not least, I also thank the people who participate in the online forums www.asp.net and www.codeproject.com. I have learned a lot from them.

about this book

Almost one year has elapsed since the release of the 1.0 version of ASP.NET AJAX. With the buzz created by the Ajax paradigm, the framework has gained a strong popularity among ASP.NET developers. The official ASP.NET AJAX website provides video tutorials, online documentation, and discussion forums. With all these resources available, one might think that a book would have little to contribute.

Our opinion is different. It's true that the online documentation acts as a good, general reference. It's also true that you can search the ASP.NET forums for the latest tips and tricks.

We believe that a strong comprehension of the new concepts and development techniques that ASP.NET AJAX brings to ASP.NET is fundamental in order to become proficient with the framework. What is the client page lifecycle? How does a partial postback work? Why do you need to write an Ajax-enabled control? One of the goals of this book is to explain how things work in ASP.NET AJAX. We also wanted to provide as much code as possible to show how to implement common Ajax scenarios with the help of ASP.NET AJAX.

Each chapter tries to explain the *why*s and *how*s of the concepts covered. We believe that simple examples are the way to go, so the reader can quickly start coding without losing the focus on ASP.NET AJAX concepts. Once the main concepts have been assimilated, we challenge the reader with more advanced examples.

We believe that Ajax development is client-oriented. As a consequence, *six* chapters of the book are entirely dedicated to the *client-centric* development model. Two of these chapters cover features that will be embedded in the next versions of the framework, and are currently provided as CTP (Community Technical Preview) material. Both the client-centric and the server-centric development models are discussed in great detail. As result, this book aims at giving you a deep and comprehensive knowledge of the ASP.NET AJAX Extensions framework.

Who should read this book?

This book is targeted at ASP.NET developers who want to master the ASP.NET AJAX Extensions. Even if we wrote this book with the beginner and intermediate developers in mind, the advanced developer could benefit from it, due to the new concepts and programming techniques brought to the ASP.NET world by the ASP.NET AJAX framework.

A little knowledge of the Ajax paradigm and the JavaScript programming language is desirable in order to fully understand the material presented in the book, but we do provide a good amount of background material in order for you to quickly become familiar with the concepts involved if you are a novice. We'd like to stress the fact that this book is specific to the ASP.NET AJAX framework, which is an implementation of many common Ajax patterns. Consequently, you won't find a general and comprehensive discussion about Ajax and its techniques and patterns. If you're new to the Ajax world, we strongly recommend reading an additional book about general Ajax concepts that is a framework-agnostic book. We particularly enjoyed reading *Ajax in Action,* written by Dave Crane, Eric Pascarello, and Darren James and published by Manning in October 2005.

Roadmap

This book is divided into four parts and is intended to guide you from the initial stages of developing with ASP.NET AJAX all the way to becoming an expert.

Part 1, which spans chapters 1–6, covers the basics of ASP.NET AJAX and its two development models, the server-centric development model and the client-centric development model. In these chapters, you'll roll up your sleeves and become familiar with the essentials of Ajax programming and the ASP.NET AJAX infrastructure. You'll learn about the components that make up the framework and how to use it effectively to enhance web applications.

Part 2 encompasses chapters 7–10 and goes deep into the development models by covering advanced scenarios and techniques. Prior to this, we'll lay the groundwork for understanding the fundamentals of ASP.NET AJAX programming; but in this part it's time to apply those lessons against challenging, real-life situations.

Part 3 is chapters 11 and 12. It highlights a set of features knows as the ASP.NET Futures. Here, we examine what is on the horizon for ASP.NET AJAX.

Part 4 consists of chapter 13. This chapter will help you become an ASP.NET AJAX master by implementing some of the most common Ajax patterns using the skills acquired from the previous chapters.

The approach we decided to follow in this book provides concepts and code rather than a reference manual. For this reason, we strongly recommend that you read all the chapters, because each chapter is built on the previous one and the complexity increases gradually. If you intend to focus on a specific development model, the following table suggests a possible division of the material covered in the book.

Chapter	Title	Client-centric developer	Server-centric developer	ASP.NET AJAX master
1	Introducing ASP.NET AJAX	X	X	X
2	First steps with the Microsoft Ajax Library	X		X
3	JavaScript for Ajax developers	X		X
4	Exploring the Ajax server extensions		X	X
5	Making asynchronous network calls	X	X	X
6	Partial-page rendering with UpdatePanels		X	X
7	Under the hood of the UpdatePanel		X	X
8	ASP.NET AJAX client components	X		X
9	Building Ajax-enabled controls		X	X
10	Developing with the Ajax Control Toolkit		X	X
11	XML Script	X		X
12	Dragging and dropping	X		X
13	Implementing common Ajax patterns	X	X	X

Chapter 1 introduces Ajax and the ASP.NET AJAX extensions to the ASP.NET developer. Together with the foundations and the terminology, we present the server-centric and client-centric development models. With the client-centric model, you can develop Ajax applications by leveraging DHTML and JavaScript without relying on the ASP.NET server technology. With the server-centric model, you can take advantage of ASP.NET capabilities to combine client functionality with ASP.NET server controls.

After we've established the foundations and provided a whirlwind tour of features, chapters 2 and 3 cover the Microsoft Ajax Library, which is the client portion of the ASP.NET AJAX framework. In chapter 2, we'll explain some basic concepts such as the application model and the client page lifecycle, as well as provide an overview of all the features provided by the library. In chapter 3, we'll focus specifically on object-oriented programming with JavaScript and the Microsoft Ajax Library. After reviewing the basics of the JavaScript language and JSON, we'll go deep into the object-oriented constructs provided by the Microsoft Ajax Library.

Chapter 4 tackles a common scenario that many ASP.NET developers will encounter: upgrading an existing ASP.NET application to ASP.NET AJAX. In this chapter, you'll learn how a new collection of server controls called the *Ajax server extensions* can help you gracefully and easily enhance an existing application.

After some reinforcement about the server-centric model in the previous chapter, chapter 5 delves into a key pillar of Ajax development: the ability to make asynchronous network requests from the browser to the server. In this thorough chapter, we cover in detail topics such as working with ASP.NET Web Services, ASP.NET application services such as authentication and profile, and the bridge technology.

The next few chapters focus primarily on the UpdatePanel control and the partial-page rendering mechanism. Beginning with chapter 6, we explain how to use the UpdatePanel correctly and efficiently. Chapter 7 unveils how the partial-page rending mechanism works under the hood and provides insight into how you can take more control of the application during the process.

In chapter 8, we'll return to the Microsoft Ajax Library to examine the client component model. With this model, which is similar to the one used in the .NET framework on the server side, you can create components using JavaScript. Components let you easily encapsulate and reuse portions of client-side code, and they simplify the development of Ajax-enabled server controls.

We cover Ajax-enabled controls in chapter 9, which explains how to combine client components with ASP.NET server controls in order to enrich them with client functionality. In this chapter, you'll learn how to build extenders and script controls, the two new categories of server controls introduced by ASP.NET AJAX.

Chapter 10 is dedicated to the Ajax Control Toolkit, which is the biggest collection of Ajax-enabled controls available at present. The Toolkit is an open-source project owned by Microsoft and open to contributions from the community. In the chapter, we'll discuss some of the Ajax-enabled controls shipped with the Ajax Control Toolkit. We'll also introduce the Toolkit API for developing Ajax-enabled controls, as well as the Animation framework for easily creating animations and visual effects.

Chapters 11 and 12 explore the future of ASP.NET AJAX. We'll cover in detail some of the features that will be included in the next versions of ASP.NET AJAX. These features are, at present, shipped as evaluation code in a separate package called ASP.NET Futures. In chapter 11, we'll cover XML Script, which is a declarative language, similar to the ASP.NET markup code, used for instantiating client components in a web page. You can use it to execute complex client-side code without writing a single line of JavaScript. Chapter 12 is dedicated to the drag-and-drop engine, which makes it possible to drag and drop DOM elements in a web page. In this chapter, you'll build a drag-and-drop–enabled shopping cart from scratch by leveraging both the client-centric and the server-centric development models.

Finally, chapter 13 shows you how to implement some of the most common and useful Ajax patterns using the ASP.NET AJAX framework. In addition to implementing classic patterns such as drag-and-drop widgets and logical navigation, we've decided to give space to coding patterns as well. Chapter 13 covers advanced scenarios such as writing debug versions of script files and extending the Microsoft Ajax Library to become even more productive with JavaScript.

Appendixes A and B are dedicated to the setup of the tools needed to install and use ASP.NET AJAX. Appendix A covers the installation of both the ASP.NET AJAX framework and the Ajax Control Toolkit. It also shows you how to install the Visual Studio templates and how to add server controls to the Visual Studio Toolbox. A section is dedicated to the installation of the AdventureWorks database, which is used in some of the examples presented in the book.

Appendix B covers some of the tools that are a must-have for an Ajax developer. It explains how to install and use Firebug to debug web applications in the Firefox browser. You'll also learn how to install and use Web Development Helper and Fiddler to access the browser's console and debug HTTP traffic. The final section shows you how to configure Visual Studio 2005 for the purpose of debugging the JavaScript code.

Typographical conventions

The following typographical conventions appear throughout the book:

- Technical terms are introduced in *italics*.
- Code examples and fragments appear in a `fixed-width` font.
- Namespaces and types, as well as members of these types, also appear in a `fixed-width` font.
- Many sections of code have numbered annotations that appear in the right margin. These numbered annotations are discussed more fully following the code.

In the book, we use special paragraphs to highlight topics for further exploration of ASP.NET AJAX and the .NET Framework. Here's an example:

NOTE These paragraphs provide additional details about the .NET Framework or sources of additional information accessible from the Internet. The URL addresses shown in these paragraphs were valid as of August 1, 2007.

Source code downloads

All source code for the programs presented in *ASP.NET AJAX in Action* is available to purchasers of the book from the Manning website. Visit the site at www.manning.com/gallo or www.manning.com/ASPNETAJAXinAction for instructions on downloading the code.

Author Online

Free access to a private Internet forum, Author Online, is included with the purchase of this book. Visit the website for detailed rules about the forum, to subscribe to and access the forum, to retrieve the code for each chapter and section, and to view updates and corrections to the material in the book. You are invited to make comments, good or bad, about the book, ask technical questions, and receive help from the authors and other ASP.NET AJAX programmers. The forum is available at the book's website at www.manning.com/gallo or www.manning.com/ASPNETAJAXinAction.

Manning's commitment to readers is to provide a venue where a meaningful dialogue among individual readers and among readers and the authors can take place. It isn't a commitment to any specific amount of participation on the part of the authors, whose contribution remains voluntary (and unpaid). So please keep the questions and comments interesting!

Alessandro can be contacted directly at modulino@gmail.com or through his blog at aspadvice.com/blogs/garbin.

David can be contacted directly at david.barkol@neudesic.com or through his blog at weblogs.asp.net/davidbarkol.

Rama can be contacted directly at rama.vavilala@gmail.com.

about the authors

ALESSANDRO GALLO is a Microsoft MVP in the Visual ASP/ASP.NET category and a .NET developer/consultant with a primary focus on ASP.NET application design and development. He is a contributor for the Ajax Control Toolkit project, owned by Microsoft. Alessandro has been developing with ASP.NET AJAX since the first CTP. He won the Grand Prize at the Mash-it-up with ASP.NET AJAX contest held by Microsoft in 2006. Alessandro lives in Sassari, a small city on the beautiful Italian island of Sardinia.

DAVID BARKOL is a Principal Consultant for Neudesic, one of Microsoft's leading .NET professional service firms and a Gold Certified Partner. At Neudesic, David specializes in providing custom .NET solutions that leverage the Microsoft technology platform. A frequent speaker at code camps and .NET user groups in Southern California, David is also an MCSD in .NET and avid urban hang-glider. David resides in tropical La Palma, California, with his wife Emily and two daughters Miranda and Madeline.

RAMA KRISHNA VAVILALA is Chief Technical Architect at 3C Software. He is the brain behind Impact:ECS™, the leading enterprise cost-management solution for manufacturers in vertical markets ranging from textiles to semiconductors to food processors. He has over a decade of wide-ranging experience from developing desktop applications using MFC, Windows Forms, and WPF, to developing Microsoft Office Solutions, to developing Ajax-powered web applications. He lives in Atlanta with his wife Radhika and his daughter Shreya.

about the title

By combining introductions, overviews, and how-to examples, the *In Action* books are designed to help learning and remembering. According to research in cognitive science, the things people remember are things they discover during self-motivated exploration.

Although no one at Manning is a cognitive scientist, we are convinced that for learning to become permanent it must pass through stages of exploration, play, and, interestingly, retelling of what is being learned. People understand and remember new things, which is to say they master them, only after actively exploring them. Humans learn in action. An essential part of an *In Action* guide is that it is example-driven. It encourages the reader to try things out, to play with new code, and explore new ideas.

There is another, more mundane, reason for the title of this book: our readers are busy. They use books to do a job or to solve a problem. They need books that allow them to jump in and jump out easily and learn just what they want just when they want it. They need books that aid them *in action*. The books in this series are designed for such readers.

about the cover illustration

The figure on the cover of *ASP.NET AJAX in Action* is "Le Béarnais," or an inhabitant of the region of Béarn in Southwestern France. The region is known for its contrasts, encompassing both valleys and mountains, that extend to the Pyrenean frontier with Spain.

The illustration is taken from a French travel book, *Encyclopedie des Voyages* by J. G. St. Saveur, published in 1796. Travel for pleasure was a relatively new phenomenon at the time and travel guides such as this one were popular, introducing both the tourist as well as the armchair traveler to the inhabitants of other regions of France and abroad.

The diversity of the drawings in the *Encyclopedie des Voyages* speaks vividly of the uniqueness and individuality of the world's towns and provinces just 200 years ago. This was a time when the dress codes of two regions separated by a few dozen miles identified people uniquely as belonging to one or the other. The travel guide brings to life a sense of isolation and distance of that period and of every other historic period except our own hyperkinetic present.

Dress codes have changed since then and the diversity by region, so rich at the time, has faded away. It is now often hard to tell the inhabitant of one continent from another. Perhaps, trying to view it optimistically, we have traded a cultural and visual diversity for a more varied personal life. Or a more varied and interesting intellectual and technical life.

We at Manning celebrate the inventiveness, the initiative, and the fun of the computer business with book covers based on the rich diversity of regional life two centuries ago brought back to life by the pictures from this travel guide.

Part 1

ASP.NET AJAX basics

The first part of the book sets the foundations of ASP.NET AJAX. Chapter 1 introduces the main Ajax concepts and terminology. In this chapter, we'll also take a whirlwind tour of the features in ASP.NET AJAX that will be covered throughout the book.

The subsequent chapters discuss the primary development models used in ASP.NET AJAX programming. We present the client-centric programming model in chapters 2 and 3. Reading these chapters will provide you with the skills you need to write object-oriented JavaScript code using the Microsoft Ajax Library.

Chapter 4 takes a break from the client-script to introduce the Ajax server extensions-a server-centric solution for ASP.NET developers. In this chapter, you'll enhance an existing ASP.NET application with the controls and features of the ASP.NET AJAX framework. This pattern is continued in chapter 6, where we offer a thorough explanation of how to use the ScriptManager control for partial-page rendering. In between, chapter 5 focuses on one of the fundamental pillars of Ajax: making asynchronous calls. This chapter unveils how asynchronous calls to the server are invoked from the browser.

Introducing ASP.NET AJAX

In this chapter:

- An overview of Ajax programming
- The ASP.NET AJAX architecture
- The client-centric development model
- The server-centric development model
- A tour of ASP.NET AJAX

Ajax has revolutionized the way users interact with web pages. Gone are the days of frustrating page refreshes, losing your scroll position on a page, and working in the redraw-refresh paradigm of traditional web applications. In its place is the next generation of web applications: Ajax applications, whose characteristics include smoother page updates; continuous, fluid interaction; and visually appealing, rich interfaces.

The term *Ajax*, which stands for Asynchronous JavaScript and XML, was coined to describe this new approach to web development. Although most users aren't familiar with the acronym, they're certainly familiar with its benefits. Sites like Google Maps, Live.com, and Flickr are just a few examples of recent applications that are leading the way through this new frontier. Each of them offers slightly different services, but all share the same goal: to provide a rich user experience that is personalized, engaging, and supported across all major browsers.

Unfortunately, *using* these next-generation web applications is far more trivial than *authoring* them. Ajax applications require a different approach to thinking about web solutions. This paradigm shift requires more discipline and knowledge of client-side scripting along with the conscious decision to deliver a smarter and more intuitive application to the browser. In addition, although it's been around for a while, Ajax is still relatively new to web developers, and techniques for patterns, guidelines, and best practices are still being discovered and refined. To assist in this transition, the Microsoft ASP.NET AJAX framework encapsulates a rich set of controls, scripts, and resources that empowers you to more easily craft the next generation of web applications.

The goal in this introductory chapter is to get you started on developing applications with the ASP.NET AJAX framework. To whet your appetite, we'll go through a whirlwind tour of the most basic and commonly used components and follow up with a few quick examples that demonstrate their use. Subsequent chapters examine each of these components in more detail and reveal how things work under the hood. But before you can discover the ASP.NET AJAX framework, you must first understand what Ajax is and how we got here.

1.1 What is Ajax?

Ajax is an approach or pattern to web development that uses client-side scripting to exchange data with a web server. This approach enables pages to be updated dynamically without causing a full page refresh to occur (the dream, we presume, of every web developer). As a result, the interaction between the user and the application is uninterrupted and remains continuous and fluid. Some consider this approach to be a technology rather than a pattern. Instead, it's a combination of related technologies used together in a creative way.

The result of bringing these technologies together is nothing new. Techniques for asynchronous loading of content on the Web can be dated as far back as Internet Explorer 3 (also known as the Jurassic years of web development) with the introduction of the IFRAME element. Shortly after, the release of Internet Explorer 5 introduced the XMLHttpRequest ActiveX object, which made possible the exchange of data between the client and server through web browser scripting languages.

> **NOTE** Some credit remote scripting as the precursor to Ajax development. Prior to the XMLHttpRequest object, remote scripting allowed scripts running in a browser to exchange information with a server. For more about remote scripting, read http://en.wikipedia.org/wiki/Remote_Scripting.

Even with the release of the XMLHttpRequest object, and with applications like Outlook Web Access taking advantage of these techniques, it wasn't until the release of Google Maps that Ajax was noticed by the masses.

You now have a high-level understanding of Ajax and how it came to be, but we haven't discussed the technologies that make up the pattern or how the ASP.NET AJAX framework fits into the picture. It's important that we spend a little more time fully explaining how Ajax works and discussing the technologies that form it.

1.1.1 Ajax components

As we previously mentioned, the Ajax programming pattern consists of a set of existing technologies brought together in an imaginative way, resulting in a richer and more engaging user experience. The following are the main pillars of the Ajax programming pattern and the role they play in its model:

- *JavaScript*—A scripting language that is commonly hosted in a browser to add interactivity to HTML pages. Loosely based on the C programming language, JavaScript is the most popular scripting language on the Web and is supported by all major browsers. Ajax applications are built in JavaScript.

- *Document Object Model (DOM)* —Defines the structure of a web page as a set of programmable objects that can be accessed through JavaScript. In Ajax programming, the DOM is leveraged to effectively redraw portions of the page.

  Cascading Style Sheets (CSS)—Provides a way to define the visual appearance of elements on a web page. CSS is used in Ajax applications to modify the exterior of the user interface interactively.

  XMLHttpRequest—Allows a client-side script to perform an HTTP request. Ajax applications use the XMLHttpRequest object to perform asynchronous requests to the server as opposed to performing a full-page refresh or postback.

> **NOTE** The name of the XMLHttpRequest object is somewhat misleading because data can be transferred in the form of XML or other text-based formats. The ASP.NET AJAX framework relies heavily on a format called JavaScript Object Notation (JSON) to deliver data to and from the server. Examples of JSON and how the ASP.NET AJAX framework uses it are scattered throughout this book. You can find a more thorough explanation of JSON in chapter 3.

Listing the technologies is easy; but understanding how they work together, complement each other, and deliver a better user experience is the objective. Figure 1.1 illustrates how these technologies interact with one another from the browser.

In an Ajax-enabled application, you can think of JavaScript as the that holds everything together. When data is needed, the XMLHttpRequest object is used to make a request to the server. When the data is returned, the DOM and CSS are leveraged to update the browser's user interface dynamically.

> **TIP** You can find a collection of Ajax design patterns at http://ajaxpatterns.org.

To see this in action, visit the maps page on the Windows Live site at http://local.live.com (see figure 1.2). Notice the interactive map and how clicking and dragging the map updates the contents on the page without causing a full page refresh to occur. The tiles for the map are retrieved in the background via the

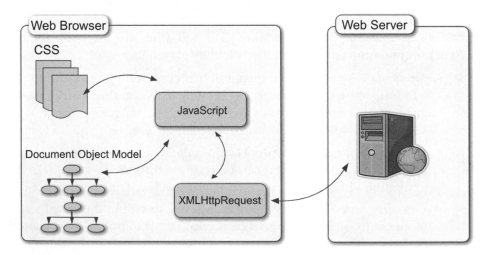

Figure 1.1   Ajax components. The technologies used in the Ajax pattern complement each to deliver a richer and smarter application that runs on the browser.

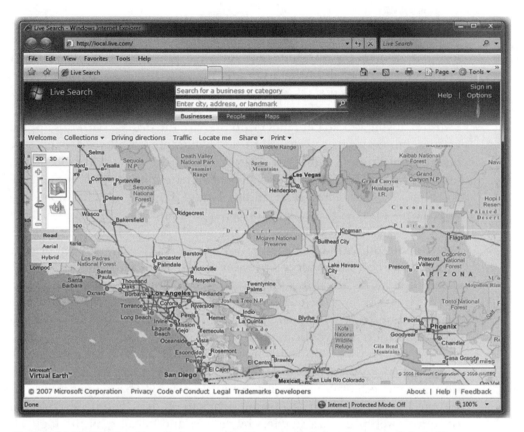

Figure 1.2   The Windows Live site is an excellent example of what can be accomplished with the ASP.NET AJAX framework.

XMLHttpRequest object; the user is granted continuous interaction with the application in the process. Take some time to discover what the site has to offer, and note how fluid and responsive the page actions appear. Using the ASP.NET AJAX framework, these are the types of intuitive and interactive applications that you'll build throughout this book.

The maps on Live.com rely heavily on retrieving data asynchronously so users can continue to interact with the applications. This key pattern is perhaps the most important thing to understand about Ajax.

1.1.2   Asynchronous web programming

The *A* in Ajax stands for *asynchronous*; this is a key behavior in the Ajax programming pattern. *Asynchronous* means not synchronized or not occurring at the same time. To better understand this, let's take a real-life example. If you go to Star-bucks and walk up to the counter, you present the cashier with your order (a tall, iced café mocha for David, in case you were wondering). The cashier marks an empty cup with details of the order and places it into a queue. The queue, in this instance, is literally a stack of other empty cups that represent pending orders waiting to be fulfilled. This process decouples the cashier from the individuals (*baristas*, if you want to get fancy) who prepare the drinks. With this approach, the cashier can continue to interact with the customers while orders are being pro-cessed at a different time—asynchronously. In the end, Starbucks maximizes its output and significantly improves the customer experience.

Now, let's examine what things would be like with a more traditional approach—in a synchronous process. If only one person were working in the shop that day, they would have to take on the chores and responsibilities of both the cashier and barista. A customer would place an order, and the next customer would be forced to wait for the previous order to be completed before they could place their own. This less efficient process is how traditional web applications work: They take away the continuous interaction and force users to wait for a par-ticular action to be completed. Figure 1.3 demonstrates the flow of a traditional web application in a synchronous manner.

Normally, a user action such as clicking a button on a form invokes an HTTP request back to the web server. The server then processes the request, possibly doing some calculations or performing a few database operations; and then returns back to the client a whole new page to render. Technically, this makes a lot of sense—web pages are stateless by nature, and because all the logic about the application typically resides on the server, the browser is just used to display the interface. The server goes through the entire page lifecycle again and returns to

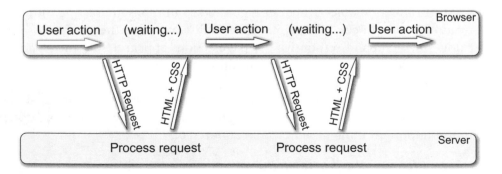

Figure 1.3 Traditional web applications behave in a synchronous manner and take away all interaction from the user during HTTP requests.

the browser the HTML, CSS, and any other resources it needs to refresh the page. Unfortunately, this doesn't present the user with a desirable experience. Instead, they're exposed to a stop-start-stop pattern where they temporarily (and unwillingly) lose interaction with the page and are left waiting for it to be updated.

NOTE   In ASP.NET, when a form posts data back to itself (or even to another page), it's called a *postback*. During this process, the current state of the page and its controls are sent to the server for processing. The postback mechanism is relied on to preserve the state of the page and its server controls. This process causes the page to refresh and is costly because of the amount of data sent back and forth to the server and the loss of interaction for the user.

An Ajax-enabled application works differently, mainly by eliminating the intermittent nature of interaction with the introduction of an Ajax agent placed between the client and server. This agent communicates with the server asynchronously, on behalf of the client, to make the HTTP request to the server and return the data needed to update the contents of the page. Figure 1.4 demonstrates this asynchronous model.

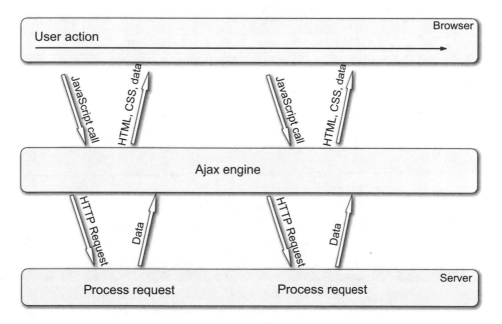

Figure 1.4   The asynchronous web application model leverages an Ajax engine to make an HTTP request to the server.

Notice that in the asynchronous model, a call originating from JavaScript is made to the Ajax engine instead of the server to retrieve and receive data. At the core of the Ajax engine is the XMLHttpRequest object, which we'll look at next to solidify your understanding of how Ajax works.

1.1.3 The XMLHttpRequest object

The XMLHttpRequest object is at the heart of Ajax programming because it enables JavaScript to make requests to the server and process the responses. It was delivered in the form of an ActiveX object when released in Internet Explorer 5, and it's supported in most current browsers. Other browsers (such as Safari, Opera, Firefox, and Mozilla) deliver the same functionality in the form of a native JavaScript object. Ironically, Internet Explorer 7 now implements the object in native JavaScript as well, although differences between browsers remain. The fact that there are different implementations of the object based on browsers and their versions requires you to write browser-sensitive code when instantiating it from script. Listing 1.1 uses a technique called *object detection* to determine which XMLHttpRequest object is available.

Listing 1.1 Instantiating the XMLHttpRequest object

```
var xmlHttp = null;

if (window.XMLHttpRequest) { // IE7, Mozilla, Safari, Opera, etc.
   xmlHttp = new XMLHttpRequest();
} else if (window.ActiveXObject) {
   try{
   xmlHttp = new ActiveXObject("Microsoft.XMLHTTP"); //IE 5.x, 6
   }
   catch(e) {}
}
```

Now that the object has been instantiated, you can use it to make an asynchronous request to a server resource. To keeps things simple, you can make a request to another page called Welcome.htm, the contents of which are shown in listing 1.2.

Listing 1.2 Welcome.htm

```
<!DOCTYPE html PUBLIC "-//W3C//DTD XHTML 1.0 Transitional//EN"
   "http://www.w3.org/TR/xhtml1/DTD/xhtml1-transitional.dtd">
<html xmlns="http://www.w3.org/1999/xhtml" >
<head>
    <title>Welcome</title>
</head>
```

```
<body>
    <div>Welcome to ASP.NET AJAX In Action!</div>
</body>
</html>
```

Welcome.htm is pretty minimal and contains some static text welcoming you to the book. You make the asynchronous request with a few more lines of code that you wrap in a function called sendRequest (see listing 1.3).

Listing 1.3 Sending an asynchronous request

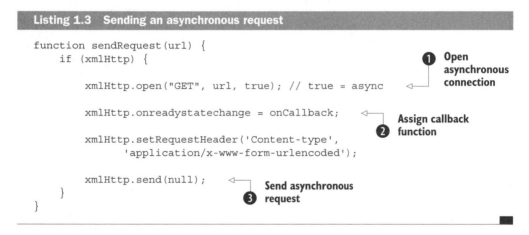

```
function sendRequest(url) {
    if (xmlHttp) {

        xmlHttp.open("GET", url, true); // true = async          ❶ Open
                                                                    asynchronous
                                                                    connection

        xmlHttp.onreadystatechange = onCallback;            ❷ Assign callback
                                                               function
        xmlHttp.setRequestHeader('Content-type',
                'application/x-www-form-urlencoded');

        xmlHttp.send(null);          ❸ Send asynchronous
    }                                   request
}
```

The sendRequest method takes as a parameter the URL to which you'll be making an HTTP request. Next, it ❶ opens a connection with the asynchronous flag set to true. After the connection is initialized, it ❷ assigns the onreadystatechange property of the XMLHttpRequest object to a local function called onCallback. Remember, this will be an asynchronous call, which means you don't know when it will return. A callback function is given so you can be notified when the request is complete or its status has been updated. After specifying the content type in the request header, you call the ❸ send method to transmit the HTTP request to the server.

Starbucks part 2

If you go back to the earlier Starbucks example, the open command is similar to placing the order, and the send command is like the order being placed in the queue. The callback function is the unique name associated with your order—typically your name. Another interesting tidbit is that in IE, only two connections can be opened at a time, which is the equivalent of having two cashiers available to take the orders.

When the status of the request changes and the callback function is invoked, the final step is to check the status and update the user interface with the contents returned from Welcome.htm (see listing 1.4).

Listing 1.4   The callback function gets called every time the ready state changes for the asynchronous request.

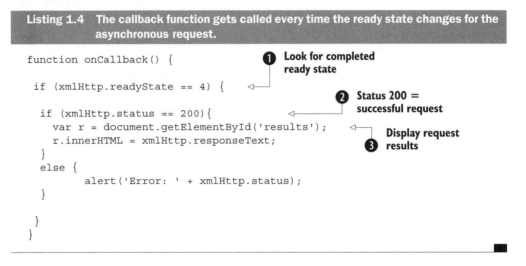

```
function onCallback() {                          ❶ Look for completed
                                                    ready state
 if (xmlHttp.readyState == 4) {   ◄───┘

                                                 ❷ Status 200 =
                                                    successful request
  if (xmlHttp.status == 200){   ◄──────────
    var r = document.getElementById('results');  ◄──
    r.innerHTML = xmlHttp.responseText;             Display request
  }                                              ❸ results
  else {
        alert('Error: ' + xmlHttp.status);
  }

 }
}
```

The status of the request is returned in the `readyState` ❶ property of the XMLHttpRequest object. The value 4 indicates that the request has completed. Next, the response from the server ❷ must be checked to confirm that everything was successful. Status code 200 is designated in the HTTP protocol to indicate that a request has succeeded. Finally, the `innerHTML` of a `span` element is updated to reflect the contents in the response ❸. Listing 1.5 shows the complete code for this example.

Listing 1.5   Using the XMLHttpRequest control to asynchronously retrieve data

```
<%@ Page Language="C#" AutoEventWireup="true"
   CodeFile="XmlHttpRequest.aspx.cs"
   Inherits="CH_01_XmlHttpRequest" %>
<!DOCTYPE html PUBLIC "-//W3C//DTD XHTML 1.0 Transitional//EN"
   "http://www.w3.org/TR/xhtml1/DTD/xhtml1-transitional.dtd">

<html xmlns="http://www.w3.org/1999/xhtml" >
<head runat="server">
    <title>ASP.NET AJAX In Action - XMLHttpRequest</title>
</head>
<body>
    <form id="form1" runat="server">
    <div>
        <span id="results">Loading...</span>
```

```
    </div>
    </form>

<script type="text/javascript">

var xmlHttp = null;

window.onload = function() {

    loadXmlHttp();
    sendRequest("Welcome.htm");
}

function loadXmlHttp() {

  if (window.XMLHttpRequest) { // IE7, Mozilla, Safari, Opera
    xmlHttp = new XMLHttpRequest();
  } else if (window.ActiveXObject) {
    try{
      xmlHttp = new ActiveXObject("Microsoft.XMLHTTP"); //IE 5.x, 6
    }
    catch(e) {}
  }
}

function sendRequest(url) {
    if (xmlHttp) {

        xmlHttp.open("GET", url, true); // true = async

        xmlHttp.onreadystatechange = onCallback;

        xmlHttp.setRequestHeader('Content-type',
                'application/x-www-form-urlencoded');

        xmlHttp.send(null);
    }
}

function onCallback() {

  if (xmlHttp.readyState == 4) {

    if (xmlHttp.status == 200){
     var r = document.getElementById('results');
     r.innerHTML = xmlHttp.responseText;
    }
    else {
     alert('Error: ' + xmlHttp.status);
    }
```

```
      }
    }

    </script>
    </body>
    </html>
```

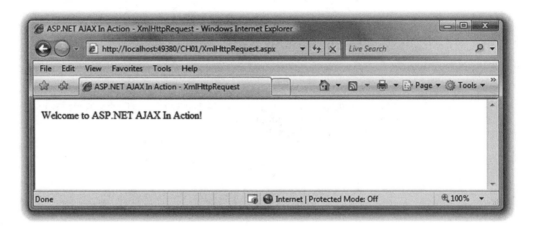

Figure 1.5   A simple asynchronous request to another page

Figure 1.5 shows the output that results when you execute the example code.

The example we just walked through demonstrates how to leverage the XMLHttpRequest object to make a simple asynchronous HTTP request to another page on the server. When the request is completed, you display the results on the page by dynamically updating the contents of one of its UI elements—a span. There is a lot more to the XMLHttpRequest object that we didn't cover; we barely scratched the surface. The point of this exercise was to introduce you to the basics of the Ajax programming pattern. You should recognize some of the issues that arise with Ajax development, such as cross-browser compatibility and the need for a lot of *plumbing* code to execute requests to the server. This takes us into the next section, which discusses other issues and complexities in Ajax development.

1.1.4 Ajax development issues

Without a toolkit or framework to leverage, developing Ajax-enabled applications is no trivial task. Several development issues arise, the most obvious of which is browser compatibility. Aside from the different implementations of the XMLHttp-Request object, each browser also implements a slightly different version of the

DOM. Keeping up with changes between browsers and managing browser detection can be a tedious and error-prone process. One of the goals of a toolkit or framework is to abstract away the complexities and discrepancies between browsers so you can use a simple and consistent set of APIs to perform the same operations.

Another challenge is the requirement for a strong grasp of the JavaScript language. JavaScript isn't inherently a complex language; however, many ASP.NET developers lack expertise in it. In addition, JavaScript doesn't offer the object-oriented, type-safe features that .NET developers have grown accustomed to with C#, VB.NET, and other .NET languages. Concepts such as inheritance, interfaces, and events can be simulated in JavaScript but are left to you to implement. Without a framework, this portion of JavaScript remains for you to master in order to make any progress. Debugging and the lack of support for client-scripting languages in integrated development environments (IDEs) adds to the complexity and challenges.

By now, you probably see the direction we're headed: In almost every case, it's wiser to leverage a framework or toolkit when developing Ajax-enabled applications rather than deal with these complexities on your own. We're certain there are simple situations where coding something quickly with the XMLHttpRequest object can get the job done, but this book's aspirations are much greater. With that said, it's time to look at ASP.NET AJAX and what it has to offer as a framework and library.

1.2 ASP.NET AJAX architecture

The ASP.NET AJAX framework enables developers to create rich, interactive, highly personalized web applications that are cross-browser compliant. At first glance, you may think this sounds like another way of saying that the framework is an Ajax library. The truth is, it's primarily an Ajax library, but it offers many other features that can increase the productivity and quality of your web applications. This will make more sense once we examine the architecture, shown in figure 1.6.

The first thing you may notice about the architecture of the ASP.NET AJAX framework is that it spans both the client and server. In addition to a set of client-side libraries and components, there is also a great deal of support on the server side, with ASP.NET server controls and services.

We'll explore both sides of the framework heavily throughout the book, beginning with the client framework.

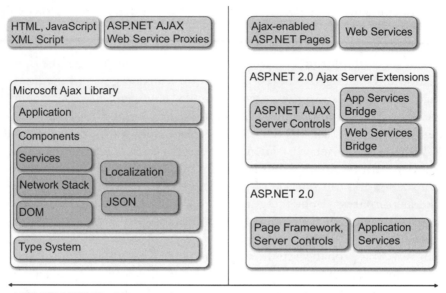

Figure 1.6   The ASP.NET AJAX architecture spans both the client and server.

1.2.1 Client framework

One of the nice things about the client framework is that the core library isn't reliant on the server components. The core library can be used to develop applications built in Cold Fusion, PHP, and other languages and platforms. With this flexibility, the architecture can be divided logically into two pieces: the client framework and the server framework. Understanding how things work in the client framework is essential even for server-side developers, because this portion brings web pages to life. At the core is the Microsoft Ajax Library.

Microsoft Ajax Library

As we stated previously, the heart of the client framework is the *Microsoft Ajax Library,* also known as the *core* library. The library consists of a set of JavaScript files that can be used independently from the server features. We'll ease into the core library by explaining the intentions of each of its pieces or layers, beginning with its foundation: the *type system.*

> **NOTE**   In previous versions of ASP.NET AJAX, when it had the codename *Atlas,* the core library was referred to as the *Client Script Library.*

The goal of the type system is to introduce familiar object-oriented programming concepts to JavaScript—like classes, inheritance, interfaces, and event-handling. This layer also extends existing JavaScript types. For example, the String and Array types in JavaScript are both extended to provide added functionality and a familiarity to ASP.NET developers. The type system lays the groundwork for the rest of the Ajax core library.

Next up in the core library is the *Components* layer. Built on top of the type system's solid foundation, the Components layer does a lot of the heavy lifting for the core library. This layer provides support for JSON serialization, network communication, localization, DOM interaction, and ASP.NET application services like authentication and profiles. It also introduces the notion of building reusable modules that can be categorized as controls and behaviors on a page.

This brings us to the top layer in the library: the *Application* layer. A more descriptive title is the *application model*. Similar to the page lifecycle in ASP.NET, this layer provides an event-driven programming model that you can use to work with DOM elements, components, and the lifecycle of an application in the browser.

HTML, JavaScript, and XML Script

ASP.NET AJAX-enabled web pages are written in HTML, JavaScript, and a new XML-based, declarative syntax called *XML Script*. This provides you with more than one option for authoring client-side code—you can code declaratively with XML Script and imperatively with JavaScript. Elements declared in XML Script are contained in a new `script` tag:

```
<script type="text/xml-script">
```

The browser can detect the `script` tag but doesn't have a mechanism for processing the `xml-script` type. Instead, the JavaScript files from the ASP.NET AJAX framework can parse the script and create an instance of components and controls on the page. Listing 1.6 provides a snippet of how XML Script is used to display a message after the page has loaded.

Listing 1.6 XML-Script: a declarative alternative for developing Ajax-enabled pages

```
<script type="text/xml-script">
  <page xmlns="http://schemas.microsoft.com/xml-script/2005">
    <components>
      <application load="page_load" />        ◁⎯┐  Hook application
    </components>                            ❶  load event
  </page>
</script>
```

```
<script type="text/javascript">
 function page_load(sender, e){
   alert("Hello from XML-Script!");
 }
</script>
```

❷ **Handler for load event** ⟵

In this example, a JavaScript function called ❶ page_load is declaratively attached to the load event in the page lifecycle. Executing this page invokes the ❷ page_load function after the load event to display a message box on the client.

> ## ASP.NET Futures CTP
>
> XML Script and some other features in the framework are delivered in a separate set of resources called the *ASP.NET Futures*. These features are currently in the Community Technology Preview (CTP) status. CTP reflects the current state of a product that is still undergoing possible changes. In this case, the ASP.NET Futures CTP is an extension of the core ASP.NET AJAX framework that will eventually be migrated into the core package. The good news is that we'll cover XML Script and other features in great detail throughout the book so nothing is left out.

Why choose XML Script over JavaScript or vice versa? Sometimes the answer comes down to your preference; some developers prefer the elegance of a markup language over script, but others feel more comfortable and in control coding only JavaScript. These approaches can coexist, and both have pros and cons that we'll discuss in their respective chapters of the book.

ASP.NET AJAX service proxies

The client framework offers the ability to call web services from JavaScript via a set of client-side proxies that are generated from the server. These proxies can be leveraged much like a web reference in managed .NET code.

> **NOTE**   A *proxy* is a class that operates as an interface to another thing—in this case, a web service. For more on the proxy pattern, visit the Wikipedia page at http://en.wikipedia.org/wiki/Proxy_pattern.

We'll take a more thorough look at how this works later in the chapter. If this is something you'd like to know more about now, feel free to jump to chapter 5, where we discuss working with services and making asynchronous calls in greater detail.

Now that you have a high-level understanding of the client framework, let's move on to the server framework to complete your understanding of the overall architecture.

1.2.2 Server framework

Built on top of ASP.NET 2.0 is a valuable set of controls and services that extend the existing framework with Ajax support. This tier of the server framework is called the *ASP.NET AJAX server extensions*. The server extensions are broken into three areas: server controls, the web services bridge, and the application services bridge. Each of these components interacts closely with the application model on the client to improve the interactivity of existing ASP.NET pages.

ASP.NET AJAX server controls

The new set of server controls adds to the impressive arsenal of tools in the ASP.NET toolbox and is predominantly driven by two controls. The first of these controls is the *ScriptManager*, which is considered the brains of an Ajax-enabled page. One of the many responsibilities of the ScriptManager is orchestrating the regions on the page that are dynamically updated during asynchronous post-backs. The second control, named the *UpdatePanel*, is used to define the regions on the page that are designated for partial updates. These two controls work together to greatly enhance the user experience by replacing traditional post-backs with *asynchronous postbacks*. This results in regions of the page being updated incrementally rather than all at once with a full page refresh.

The remaining components of the server extensions are services that bridge the gap between the client and server.

Web services bridge

Typically, web applications are limited to resources on their local servers. Aside from a few external resources, like images and CSS files, applications aren't granted access to resources that aren't in the scope of the client application. To overcome these hurdles, the server extensions in the ASP.NET AJAX framework include a *web services bridge* that creates a gateway for you to call external web services from client-side script. This type of technology will be handy when we look at how to aggregate or consume data from third-party services.

Application services bridge

Because ASP.NET AJAX is so tightly integrated with ASP.NET, access to some of the application services like authentication and profile can be added to an existing application almost effortlessly. This feature enables tasks like verifying a user's credentials and accessing their profile information to originate from the client script. This isn't entirely necessary, but it adds to the overall user experience.

Now that you have a general idea of what pieces form the framework, we can begin to examine how they're leveraged effectively. This leads to the examination of two development scenarios.

1.2.3 Client-centric development model

The flexible design of the architecture naturally provides two development scenarios. The first scenario is primarily implemented on the client side and is known as the *client-centric development model*. The second is developed mainly on the server side and is identified as the *server-centric development model*. It's worth taking some time to understand how these models work and when to use each of them.

In the client-centric model, the presentation tier is driven from the client-script using DHTML and JavaScript. This means a smarter and more interactive application is delivered from the server to the browser when the page is first loaded. Afterward, interaction between the browser application and the server is limited to retrieving the relevant data necessary to update the page. This model encourages a lot more interactivity between the user and the browser application, resulting in a richer and more intuitive experience. Figure 1.7 illustrates the client-centric development model.

The client-centric model is also ideal for *mashups* and applications that wish to fully exploit all the features DHTML has to offer.

> **NOTE**   A *mashup* is a web application that consumes content from more than one external source and aggregates it into a seamless, interactive experience for the user.

You'll build a simple mashup in chapter 5, once you've delved deeper into the networking components of the framework. In the meantime, Pageflakes.com provides an excellent example of the rich content mashups can consume (see figure 1.8).

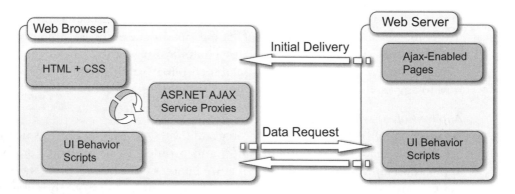

Figure 1.7   The client-centric development model is driven by a smarter and more interactive application that runs on the browser.

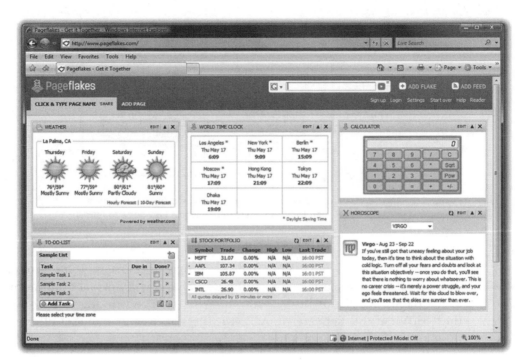

Figure 1.8 Pageflakes is a great example of how a mashup application consumes data from multiple resources to enrich the user experience.

An application like Pageflakes relies heavily on user interaction. In addition, the page needs to be light, effective, and mindful of system resources. For these reasons, a client-centric approach is the preferred model.

1.2.4 *Server-centric development model*

In the server-centric model, the application logic and most of the UI rationale remain on the server. Incremental changes for the UI are passed down to the browser application instead of the changes being made from the client-side script. This approach resembles the traditional ASP.NET page model, where the server renders the UI on each postback and sends back down to the browser a new page to render. The difference between this model and the traditional model in ASP.NET is that only the portions of the UI that need to be rendered are passed down to the browser application, rather than the whole page. As a result, interactivity and latency are both improved significantly. Figure 1.9 illustrates the nature of the server-centric development model.

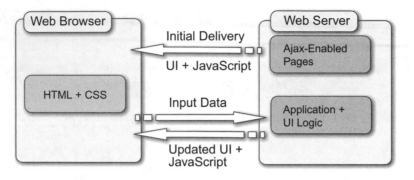

Figure 1.9 The Server-Centric Development model passes down to the browser application portions of the page to update instead of a whole new page to refresh.

This approach appeals to many ASP.NET developers because it grants them the ability to keep the core UI and application logic on the server. It's also attractive because of its transparency and ability to behave as a normal application if the user disables JavaScript in the browser. When you're working with controls like the GridView and Repeater in ASP.NET, the server-centric model offers the simplest and most reliable solution.

1.2.5 ASP.NET AJAX goals

After examining the architecture and features in the framework, you can easily deduce the goals and intentions that ASP.NET AJAX sets out to accomplish:

- *Easy-to-use, highly productive framework*—The main objective is to simplify the efforts of adding Ajax functionality to web applications. This is accomplished by providing a rich client library and a comprehensive set of server controls that are easy to use and integrate into existing applications.

- *Server programming model integration*—Server controls provide ASP.NET developers with a familiar paradigm for developing web applications. These controls emit the JavaScript needed to Ajax-enable a page with little effort or knowledge of JavaScript and the XMLHttpRequest object.

- *World-class tools and components*—Components and tools built on top of the framework not only extend the framework but also provide the development community with a rich collection of tools to leverage and build on. This includes tools for debugging, tracing, and profiling.

- *Cross-platform support*—Support for Internet Explorer, Firefox, Safari, and Opera extracts away the hassle of dealing with browser differences and discrepancies.

These goals are what you'd expect from a framework: simplicity, extensibility, community involvement, and powerful tools. Let's start using the framework!

1.3 ASP.NET AJAX in action

So far in this chapter, we've touched on the XMLHttpRequest object and some of the Ajax patterns used when developing richer, more interactive web applications. We've also examined the ASP.NET AJAX architecture and the different development scenarios that rationally emerge from its design. It's time to apply some of this knowledge and walk through a few quick applications that demonstrate how to build pages with ASP.NET AJAX.

The following sections move rather quickly, because they're intended to give you a whirlwind tour of the framework. Subsequent chapters will dissect and explain each of the topics more carefully. Let's begin the tour.

1.3.1 Simple server-centric solution

As you sit comfortably in your cubicle, reading your daily emails, the all-mighty director of human resources appears before you and demands that you build a web application immediately (a situation akin to a Dilbert cartoon strip). The request is for an application that gives the user the ability to look up the number of employees in each department of the company. After presenting you with his demands and an impossibly short timeline, the HR director retreats to headquarters as you hastily begin your new assignment.

The first step in every ASP.NET web development endeavor is creating the initial website. To get started, launch Visual Studio 2005 (or the free Visual Web Developer 2005), and select the ASP.NET AJAX-Enabled Web Site template from the New Web Site dialog (see figure 1.10). This creates a site that references the ASP.NET AJAX assembly System.Web.Extensions.dll from the Global Assembly Cache (GAC). It also generates a complex web.config file that includes additional settings for integration with the ASP.NET AJAX framework.

The initial site created from the template is all you need for this example and for a majority of ASP.NET AJAX applications that you'll build.

> **TIP** Details on how to install and configure the ASP.NET AJAX framework on a development machine are explained in appendix A. All examples in this book can also be built with the Visual Web Developer Express edition. For simplicity, we'll defer to *Visual Studio* when we mention the development environment.

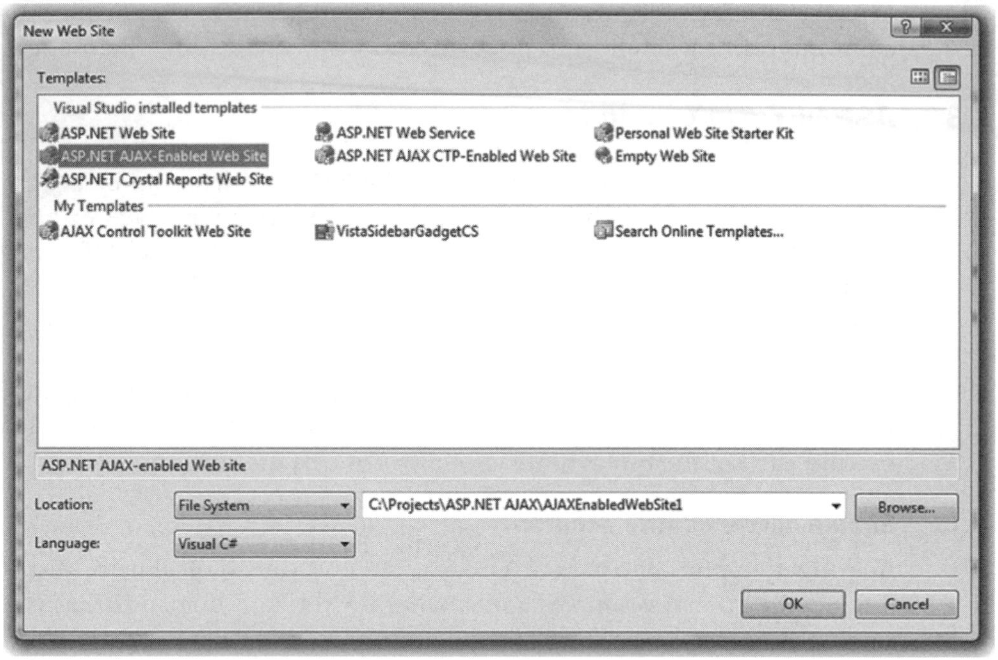

Figure 1.10   The ASP.NET AJAX-Enabled Web Site template creates a website that references the ASP.NET AJAX assembly and configures the web.config file for Ajax integration.

For the employee lookup logic, create a simple class called `HumanResources.cs`, and copy the code in listing 1.7.

Listing 1.7   A simple class that returns the number of employees in a department

```
using System;
public static class HumanResources
{
    public static int GetEmployeeCount(string department)
    {
        int count = 0;
        switch (department)
        {
            case "Sales":
                count = 10;
                break;

            case "Engineering":
                count = 28;
                break;

            case "Marketing":
```

```
            count = 44;
            break;

        case "HR":
            count = 7;
            break;

        default:
            break;
    }

    return count;
    }
}
```

The `HumanResources` class contains one method, `GetEmployeeCount`, which takes the department name as a parameter. It uses a simple `switch` statement to retrieve the number of employees in the department. (To keeps things simple, we hard-coded the department names and values.)

When you created the new website, a default page named Default.aspx was also generated. Listing 1.8 shows the initial version of the page.

Listing 1.8   Default page created by the ASP.NET AJAX-Enabled Web Site template

```
<%@ Page Language="C#" AutoEventWireup="true"
  CodeFile="Default.aspx.cs" Inherits="_Default" %>

<!DOCTYPE html PUBLIC "-//W3C//DTD XHTML 1.1//EN"
  "http://www.w3.org/TR/xhtml11/DTD/xhtml11.dtd">
<html xmlns="http://www.w3.org/1999/xhtml">
<head runat="server">
    <title>Untitled Page</title>
</head>
<body>                                           ScriptManager
    <form id="form1" runat="server">                control
     <asp:ScriptManager ID="ScriptManager1" runat="server" />   <───┘
     <div>
     </div>
    </form>
</body>
</html>
```

What's different in this page from the usual default page created by Visual Studio is the addition of the ScriptManager control. We briefly defined the ScriptManager earlier in the chapter as the brains of an Ajax-enabled page. In this example, all you need to know about the ScriptManager is that it's required to Ajax-enable a page—it's responsible for delivering the client-side scripts to the browser and managing the partial updates on the page. If these concepts still sound foreign, don't worry; they will make more sense once you start applying them.

As it turns out, creating the application requested by HR is fairly trivial. Listing 1.9 shows the markup portion of the solution.

Listing 1.9   Setting AutoPostBack to true causes a postback and invokes the server-side code.

```
                                            Invoke postbacks on each update  ❶
<div>
  <asp:ListBox AutoPostBack="true" runat="server" ID="Departments"  ⊲┘

  OnSelectedIndexChanged="Departments_SelectedIndexChanged">    ⊲┐  Register
      <asp:ListItem Text="Engineering" Value="Engineering" />    ❷  handler
      <asp:ListItem Text="Human Resources" Value="HR" />
      <asp:ListItem Text="Sales" Value="Sales" />
      <asp:ListItem Text="Marketing" Value="Marketing" />
  </asp:ListBox>
</div>
<br />
<div>                                              ❸  Label for
    <asp:Label ID="EmployeeResults" runat="server" />   ⊲┘   results
</div>
```

A ListBox is used to display the catalog of departments to choose from. The Auto-PostBack property of the control is initialized to ❶ true so that any selection made invokes a postback on the form. This action fires the SelectedIndexChanged event and calls the ❷ Departments_SelectedIndexChanged handler in the code. At the bottom of the page is a Label control where ❸ the results are displayed. To complete the application, you implement the UI logic that looks up the employee count for the selected department in the code-behind file (see listing 1.10).

Listing 1.10   Retrieve the employee count and update the UI when a new department has been selected.

```
protected void Departments_SelectedIndexChanged(object sender,
                                                EventArgs e)
{
  EmployeeResults.Text = string.Format("Employee count: {0}",
    HumanResources.GetEmployeeCount(Departments.SelectedValue));
}
```

When the application is launched and one of the departments is selected, it should look like figure 1.11.

Figure 1.11   The employee-lookup application before adding any Ajax support

The program works as expected: Selecting a department retrieves the number of employees and displays the results at the bottom of the page. The only issue is that the page refreshes each time a new department is chosen. Handling this is also trivial; you wrap the contents of the form in an UpdatePanel control (see listing 1.11).

Listing 1.11   UpdatePanel control, designating page regions that can be updated dynamically

```
<asp:UpdatePanel ID="UpdatePanel1" runat="server">
 <ContentTemplate>
  <div>
   <asp:ListBox AutoPostBack="true" runat="server" ID="Departments"
     OnSelectedIndexChanged="Departments_SelectedIndexChanged">
     <asp:ListItem Text="Engineering" Value="Engineering" />
     <asp:ListItem Text="Human Resources" Value="HR" />
     <asp:ListItem Text="Sales" Value="Sales" />
     <asp:ListItem Text="Marketing" Value="Marketing" />
   </asp:ListBox>
  </div>
  <br />
  <div>
   <asp:Label ID="EmployeeResults" runat="server" />
  </div>
 </ContentTemplate>
</asp:UpdatePanel>
```

Content that can be updated dynamically

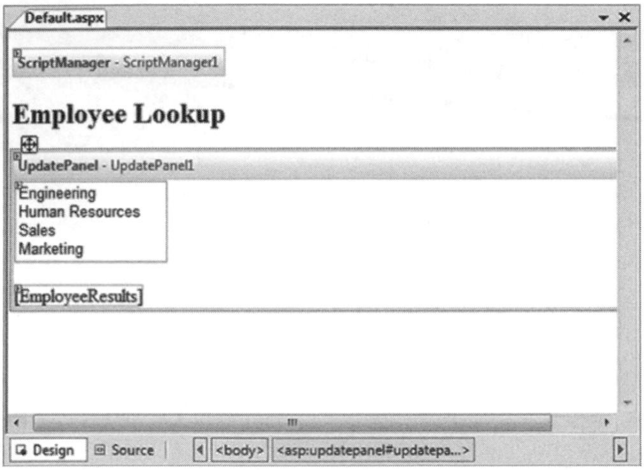

Figure 1.12
Using the Design view in Visual Studio provides a visual alternative to editing the layout and elements on the page.

As an alternative, figure 1.12 shows what the solution looks like from the Design view in Visual Studio.

By default, content placed in the `ContentTemplate` tag of the UpdatePanel control is updated dynamically when an asynchronous postback occurs. This addition to the form suppresses the normal postback that most ASP.NET developers are accustomed to and sends back to the server an asynchronous request that delivers to the browser the new UI for the form to render.

What do we mean when we say *asynchronous postback*? Most ASP.NET developers are familiar with only one kind of postback. With the UpdatePanel, the page still goes through its normal lifecycle, but the postback is marked as being *asynchronous* with some creative techniques that we'll unveil in chapter 7. As a result, the page is handled differently during the lifecycle so that updates can be made incrementally rather than by refreshing the entire page. For now, you can see that adding this type of functionality is simple and transparent to the logic and development of the page.

The next time you run the page and select a department, the UI updates dynamically without a full page refresh. In summary, by adding a few new server controls on the page you've essentially eliminated the page from reloading itself and taking away any interaction from the user.

1.3.2 *UpdateProgress control*

You show the application to the director of human resources, who is impressed. However, he notices that when he goes home and tries the application again, with a slow dial-up connection, it takes significantly longer for the page to display the results. The delay in response time confuses the director and initially makes him wonder if something is wrong with the application.

Before the introduction of Ajax, a page being refreshed was an indication to most users that something was being processed or that their actions were accepted. Now, with the suppression of the normal postback, users have no indication that something is happening in the background until it's complete. They need some sort of visual feedback notifying them that work is in progress.

The UpdateProgress control offers a solution to this problem. Its purpose is to provide a visual cue to the user when an asynchronous postback is occurring. To please the HR director, you add the following snippet of code to the end of the page:

```
<asp:UpdateProgress ID="UpdateProgress1" runat="server">
  <ProgressTemplate>
    <img src="images/indicator.gif" />  Loading ...
  </ProgressTemplate>
</asp:UpdateProgress>
```

When you run the application again, the visual cue appears when the user selects a new department (see figure 1.13).

If you're running this application on your local machine, chances are that the page updates fairly quickly and you may not get to see the UpdateProgress control working. To slow the process and see the loading indicator, add to the code the `Sleep` command shown in listing 1.12.

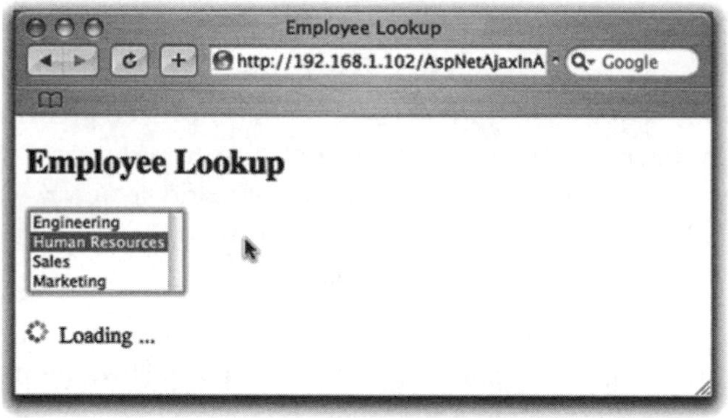

Figure 1.13   It's generally a good practice to inform users that work is in progress during an asynchronous update.

Listing 1.12   Adding a Sleep command to test the UpdateProgress control.

```
protected void Departments_SelectedIndexChanged(object sender,
                                                EventArgs e)
{
  EmployeeResults.Text = string.Format("Employee count: {0}",
    HumanResources.GetEmployeeCount(Departments.SelectedValue));

  System.Threading.Thread.Sleep(2000);        ⟵  Testing
}                                                  only
```

WARNING   Don't call the Sleep method in production code. You use it here only for demonstration purposes so you can see that the UpdateProgress control is working.

When used effectively with the UpdatePanel, the UpdateProgress control is a handy tool for relaying visual feedback to the user during asynchronous operations. We discuss best practices throughout the book; in this case, providing visual feedback to the user is strongly encouraged.

1.3.3   *Simple client-centric example*

The server-centric approach is appealing because of its simplicity and transparency, but it has drawbacks as well. Ajax development is more effective and natural when the majority of the application is running from the browser instead of on the server. One of the main principles of an Ajax application is that the browser is supposed to be delivered a smarter application from the server, thus limiting the server's role to providing only the data required to update the UI. This approach greatly reduces the amount of data sent back and forth between the browser and server.

To get started with the client-centric approach, let's add a new web service called HRService.asmx. For clarity, deselect the Place Code in Separate File option in the Add New Item dialog, and then add the service.

TIP   A common best practice would be to define an interface first (contract first) and to keep the logic in a separate file from the page. However, this example keeps things simple so we can remain focused on the Ajax material.

Next, paste the code from listing 1.13 into the web service implementation to add support for looking up the employee count.

Listing 1.13 Adding attributes to the class and methods

```
using System;
using System.Web;
using System.Web.Services;                        ❶ Namespace for
using System.Web.Services.Protocols;                 script services
using System.Web.Script.Services;        ◄────┐
                                              ┌── ❷ Declare service for
[ScriptService]                          ◄────┘      scripting support
[WebService(Namespace = "http://tempuri.org/")]
[WebServiceBinding(ConformsTo = WsiProfiles.BasicProfile1_1)]
public class HRService  : System.Web.Services.WebService {

    [ScriptMethod]                          ◄────┐
    [WebMethod]                                  ┌── Declare method for
    public int GetEmployeeCount(string department) ❸   scripting support
    {
        return HumanResources.GetEmployeeCount(department);
    }
}
```

First, note the ❶ using statement for the System.Web.Script.Services name-space. This namespace is part of the core ASP.NET AJAX framework that encapsulates some of the network communication and scripting functionality. It's not required, but it's included to save you a little extra typing. Next are the new attributes adorned on the ❷ class and ❸ method declarations of the web service. These attributes are parsed by the ASP.NET AJAX framework and used to determine what portions of the service are exposed in the JavaScript proxies. The ScriptMethod attribute isn't required, but you can use it to manipulate some of a method's settings.

If you view the ASMX file in your browser but append */js* to the end of the URL, you get a glimpse of the JavaScript proxy that is generated for this service. Figure 1.14 shows the generated JavaScript proxy that is produced by the framework after decorating the class and methods in the web service.

In chapter 5, we'll spend more time explaining what the proxy generates. In the meantime, if you glance at the proxy, you'll notice at the end the matching call to the service method GetEmployeeCount. This gives the client-side script a mechanism for calling the web methods in the service. The call takes a few extra parameters that you didn't define in the service.

With a web service ready to go, you can create a new page for this solution. Start by adding a new web form to the site, called EmployeeLookupClient.aspx. The first requirement in adding Ajax support to the page is to include the Script-Manager control. This time, you'll also declare a service reference to the local web

Figure 1.14   The framework generates a JavaScript proxy so calls to a web service can be made from the client-side script.

service, to generate the JavaScript proxies for the service that you can now call from in the client-side script (see listing 1.14).

Listing 1.14   Adding a service reference, which will generate the JavaScript proxies

```
<asp:ScriptManager ID="ScriptManager1" runat="server">
    <Services>
        <asp:ServiceReference Path="HRService.asmx" />
    </Services>
</asp:ScriptManager>
```

Reference for JavaScript proxies

To complete the declarative portion of the solution, copy the code shown in listing 1.15.

Listing 1.15 Markup portion of the client-centric solution

```
<div>
    <select id="Departments" size="5">
        <option value="Engineering">Engineering</option>          ❶ List of
        <option value="HR">Human Resources</option>                   departments
        <option value="Sales">Sales</option>
        <option value="Marketing">Marketing</option>
    </select>
</div>
<br />
<div>
    <span id="employeeResults"></span>
    <span id="loading" style="display:none;">                      ❷ Visual feedback
        <img src="images/indicator.gif" alt="" />                    during data
          Loading ...                                       retrieval
    </span>
</div>
```

Because you aren't relying on any of the business or UI logic to come from the server, you can use normal HTML elements on the page instead of the heavier server controls. This includes a select element for the list of ❶ departments and a ❷ span element to display visual feedback to the user when retrieving data from the server. To make this page come to life, add the JavaScript shown in listing 1.16.

Listing 1.16 The script portion of the employee lookup application

```
<script type="text/javascript">
<!--

 var departments = null;

Sys.Application.add_load(page_load);                    ❶ Register load and
Sys.Application.add_unload(page_unload);                   unload events

function page_load(sender, e){
 departments = $get("Departments");                    ❷ Register
 $addHandler(departments, "change", departments_onchange);  change
}                                                          event

function page_unload(sender, e){
 $removeHandler(departments, "change", departments_onchange);
}
                                     Release change event ❸
function departments_onchange(sender, e){
 $get("employeeResults").innerHTML = "";
 $get("loading").style.display = "block";
```

```
      var selectedValue = departments.value;
      HRService.GetEmployeeCount(selectedValue, onSuccess);    ◁┐
    }                                                  Call JavaScript proxy  ❹

  function onSuccess(result){
    $get("loading").style.display = "none";
    $get("employeeResults").innerHTML = "Employee count: " + result;
    }                                                    Display results  ❺

//-->
</script>
```

Note the functions registered with the application model for the ❶ load and unload events in the browser. If you recall from the earlier overview of the core library, the client framework provides a page lifecycle similar to the ASP.NET lifecycle. In this case, you use the load event as an opportunity to ❷ register a handler for any changes to the list of departments. In addition, you use the unload event to responsibly ❸ remove the registered handler.

Here's something new: commands that begin with $. These are shortcuts or alias commands that are eventually translated to their JavaScript equivalents. For example, $get is the same as document.getElementById. This little touch comes in handy when you're being mindful of the size of your JavaScript files. It also provides an abstraction layer between browser differences.

This brings us to the registered handler that's invoked each time the user selects a new department from the user interface. When this happens, you make a ❹ call to the web service to retrieve the employee count:

```
  HRService.GetEmployeeCount(selectedValue, onSuccess);
```

The first parameter in the call is the selected department in the list. The second parameter is the name of a callback function that is called when the method returns successfully. When the call ❺ returns, the user interface is updated dynamically. Running the application produces an output similar to the previous server-centric example.

1.4   Summary

In this chapter, we began with an introduction to Ajax and the XMLHttpRequest control. We then moved to the ASP.NET AJAX framework and examined its architecture and goals. Keeping things at an upbeat pace, we delved into the framework with examples for both client-side and server-side development. As a result, you may have felt rushed toward the end of the chapter. Fortunately, the remaining chapters will investigate and clarify each portion of the framework in much more detail.

This chapter was intended to whet your appetite for what the framework can accomplish. You should now have a high-level understanding of how ASP.NET AJAX empowers you to quickly and more easily deliver Ajax-enabled applications.

Succeeding chapters will build on this foundation by going deeper into both the client- and server-side portions of the framework. The next chapter begins our discussion of the client-side framework by examining the Microsoft Ajax Library and how it simplifies JavaScript and Ajax development.

First steps with the
Microsoft Ajax Library

In this chapter:

- Overview of the Microsoft Ajax Library
- The Application model
- The abstraction API for working with the DOM
- JavaScript extensions

In the age of Ajax programming, web developers need to be more JavaScript proficient than ever. You must accomplish a long list of tasks in an Ajax-enabled page and coordinate activities on the client side. For example, you need the ability to access server resources, process the results quickly, and maintain smooth webpage interactivity. The need for programming patterns that build robust and maintainable code is also on the rise. In a nutshell, a consistent client-side programming environment that works on all modern browsers is essential.

This chapter is the first one dedicated to the Microsoft Ajax Library, which is written on top of JavaScript and constitutes the client portion of the ASP.NET AJAX framework. In the tour of the basic framework components in chapter 1, you began to write code using the library's syntax. This chapter will provide more examples and give you a comprehensive overview of the library's features.

2.1 A quick overview of the library

The Microsoft Ajax Library provides a rich set of tools for managing nearly every aspect of client development. The library isn't just a simple framework for sending asynchronous requests using the XMLHttpRequest object. Instead, one of its main goals is to bring to the client side many coding patterns familiar to .NET developers. Such .NET flavors include the possibility of exposing multicast events in JavaScript objects and leveraging a component model on the client side. The library also enhances the JavaScript language's type system and lets you write client code using object-oriented constructs like *classes* and *interfaces*. In addition, you can easily access local web services using JavaScript and deal with the ASP.NET application services, such as membership and profile, from the client side. Nonetheless, this is just a taste of the goodies provided by the library.

2.1.1 Library features

The Microsoft Ajax Library is rich in features, which we've grouped into logical categories. Because we can't explore all of them in a single chapter, the following list shows how the features are distributed in the book's various chapters:

- *Application model*—When you enable the Microsoft Ajax Library in a web page, an Application object is created at runtime. In section 2.2, you'll discover that this object takes care of managing the client lifecycle of a web page, in a manner similar to what the Page object does on the server side. The Application object hosts all the client components instantiated in the web page and is responsible for disposing them when the page is unloaded by the browser.

- *Components*—The Microsoft Ajax Library brings to the client side a component model similar to that provided by the .NET framework. You can create *visual* or *nonvisual* components, depending on whether they provide a UI. In chapter 8, which is entirely dedicated to the client component model, you'll see also how visual components can be associated with Document Object Model (DOM) elements.

- *JavaScript extensions*—As you'll see in chapter 3, the library leverages the object model provided by JavaScript by introducing an enhanced type system that supports reflection and object-oriented constructs like classes, interfaces, and enumerations. In addition, the built-in JavaScript objects have been extended to support methods commonly found in .NET classes.

- *Compatibility*—Section 2.3 covers the *abstraction API*, which is a set of client methods for writing code that runs smoothly in all the supported browsers. This API abstracts common operations performed on DOM elements, such as handling events and dealing with CSS and positioning.

- *Ajax*—The library isn't exempt from providing a communication layer for sending asynchronous HTTP requests using the XMLHttpRequest object. Chapter 5 is entirely dedicated to the networking layer.

- *Application services*—By using the Microsoft Ajax Library, ASP.NET developers can deal with the authentication, membership, and profile providers on the client side. You can interact with the providers through proxy services by writing JavaScript code in the page.

- *Partial rendering*—The UpdatePanel control, introduced in chapter 1, makes it possible to update portions of the page's layout without refreshing the whole UI. This mechanism, called *partial rendering*, is leveraged on the client side by an object called the PageRequestManager. In chapter 7, when we discuss what happens under the hood of the UpdatePanel, we'll explain how the Microsoft Ajax Library participates in the partial-rendering mechanism.

Some of the features in the ASP.NET Futures package are interesting, and we decided to cover them in this book. Chapter 11 is dedicated to XML Script, a declarative language—similar to the ASP.NET markup language—used to create JavaScript objects without writing a single line of JavaScript code. Chapter 12 talks about how to perform drag and drop using the Microsoft Ajax Library.

Before proceeding, let's establish a couple of conventions relative to the terminology we'll use throughout the book. JavaScript is an object-oriented language; but, unlike C# or VB.NET, it doesn't support constructs like classes and namespaces. Nonetheless, as you'll see in chapter 3, you can manipulate JavaScript functions in interesting ways to simulate these and other object-oriented constructs. For this reason, when talking about client JavaScript code, we often borrow terms such as *class, method, interface*, and others from the common terminology used in object-oriented programming. For example, when we talk about a *client class*, we're referring to a class created in JavaScript with the Microsoft Ajax Library.

We're ready to start exploring the library. The first step is learning how to load the library's script files in a web page.

2.1.2 Ajax-enabling an ASP.NET page

The Microsoft Ajax Library is organized in client classes contained in namespaces. The root namespace is called `Sys`. The other namespaces are children of the root namespace. Table 2.1 lists the namespaces defined in the library and the type of classes that they contain.

Table 2.1   Namespaces defined in the Microsoft Ajax Library. The root namespace defined by the library is called `Sys`

Namespace	Content
`Sys`	Base runtime classes, Application object
`Sys.Net`	Classes that belong to the networking layer
`Sys.UI`	Classes for working with components and the DOM
`Sys.Services`	Classes for accessing ASP.NET services like profile, membership, and authentication
`Sys.Serialization`	Classes for JSON serialization/deserialization
`Sys.WebForms`	Classes related to partial page rendering

The Microsoft Ajax Library consists of multiple JavaScript files loaded by the browser at runtime. These files are embedded as web resources in the System.Web.Extensions assembly, which is installed in the Global Assembly Cache (GAC) by the Microsoft ASP.NET AJAX Extensions installer.

As you already know from chapter 1, the library files are automatically loaded into an ASP.NET page as soon as you declare a ScriptManager control. Therefore, every Ajax-enabled ASP.NET page must contain a ScriptManager control:

```
<asp:ScriptManager ID="TheScriptManager" runat="server" />
```

Table 2.2 lists the script files that make up the Microsoft Ajax Library, along with the description of the functionality they provide.

Table 2.2   The Microsoft Ajax Library features are distributed across multiple JavaScript files.

Filename	Features
MicrosoftAjax.js	The core library that contains the JavaScript extensions, the type system, classes for the object-oriented patterns, the communication layer, classes for creating components, and classes for dealing with the browser's DOM
MicrosoftAjaxTimer.js	Contains the client timer component used by the Timer server control
MicrosoftAjaxWebForms.js	Contains classes for supporting the partial-update mechanism used by the UpdatePanel server control

The Microsoft Ajax Library is written in pure JavaScript, so it isn't tied to the ASP.NET framework. If you want to work with the library without using ASP.NET, you need to reference the script files with `script` tags in the web page. However, the script files in the ASP.NET AJAX installation directory don't include some resources files needed by the library at runtime. For this reason, you need to download the Microsoft Ajax Library package, which includes all the library files and the resource files; it's available for download at the ASP.NET AJAX official website (http://ajax.asp.net).

All the library files are provided in *debug* and *release* versions. The debug version facilitates the debugging of the script files. It contains comments and takes advantage of a number of tricks that make debuggers happy. For example, it avoids using anonymous JavaScript functions to show more informative *stack traces*. In addition, calls to functions are *validated* to ensure that the number and types of parameters are those expected. The debug version of a library file is slower and bigger than the release version; the release version is compressed, comments are removed, and validation doesn't take place. This results in faster and considerably shorter code.

Let's examine the options you have to load the desired version of a script file.

2.1.3   *Script versions*

You can load the desired version of a script through the ScriptManager control. You can also load debug and release versions of custom script files. Debug and release versions are distinguished by the file extension: The debug version has the extension .debug.js, and the release version has the normal .js extension.

To load either the debug or the release version, you have to set the `ScriptMode` property of the ScriptReference control that references the script file in the ScriptManager. For example, suppose you want to load the release version of a custom script file called MyScriptFile.js, stored in the ScriptLibrary folder of the website. Here's how the ScriptManager control will look:

```
<asp:ScriptManager ID="TheScriptManager" runat="server">
    <Scripts>
        <asp:ScriptReference Path=" ~/ScriptLibrary/MyScriptFile.js"
                    ScriptMode="Release" />
    </Scripts>
</asp:ScriptManager>
```

Because the `ScriptMode` property is set to `Release`, the script file loaded in the page is MyScriptFile.js. If you set the value of the property to `Debug`, the MyScript-File.debug.js file is loaded.

> **NOTE** Regardless of whether you're loading the debug or release version, the name of the script file in the `Path` attribute must always be that of the release version.

The `ScriptMode` attribute can take one of the following values:

- `Auto`—The name of the script file to load matches the one specified in the `Path` property. This is the default value.
- `Inherit`—The ScriptManager control infers the name of the script file from the compilation mode of the website, as configured in the web.config file. If you're running in `debug` mode, the ScriptManager loads the file with the .debug.js extension. Otherwise, it loads the file with the .js extension.
- `Debug`—The ScriptManager loads the debug version of the script file.
- `Release`—The ScriptManager loads the release version of the script file.

In chapter 13, we'll explain some techniques used to develop a debug version of a custom script file.

After this quick overview of the Microsoft Ajax Library, let's examine some of the features in more detail. In the next sections, we'll discuss the foundations of the library: the Application model and the client page lifecycle.

2.2 The Application model

A web application is made up of pages. Because ASP.NET pages follow an object-oriented model, each page is modeled with an instance of the Page class, which encapsulates a hierarchy of controls. Controls follow the *page lifecycle*, which is a set of processing steps that start when the Page instance is created and consists of multiple, sequential stages. In the initial stages, like *Init*, controls are instantiated and their properties are initialized. In the final stages, *Render* and *Dispose*, the HTML for the page is written in the response stream, and all the controls and resources, as well as the Page instance itself, are disposed.

> **NOTE** To learn more about the ASP.NET page lifecycle, check the MSDN documentation at http://msdn2.microsoft.com/en-us/library/ms178472.aspx.

Imagine that the web page has completed its lifecycle on the server side. The Page instance and the controls raised their events, and you handled them to inject the custom application logic. The HTML for the page is ready to be sent down to the browser. If you enabled the Microsoft Ajax Library, a new lifecycle starts on the client side. As soon as the browser loads the main script file, MicrosoftAjax.js, the client runtime creates a global JavaScript object—the Application object—and stores it in a global variable called Sys.Application.

This new object becomes the brains of a web page in the browser. Despite its name, it plays a role similar to the Page object on the server side. Once the Page object is done on the server side, the processing on the client side is delegated to Sys.Application, as illustrated in figure 2.1.

The introduction of a global Application object in the browser isn't meant to revolutionize the way you write the client code. The goal is to achieve consistency between the programming models used on both the server and client sides. The main objectives of Sys.Application are as follows:

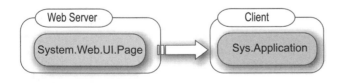

Figure 2.1
On the server side, an ASP.NET page is represented by an instance of the Page class. In a similar manner, on the client side, you have the global Sys.Application object.

- *Providing a centralized place to execute the client code*—This goal is reached by defining a custom page lifecycle on the client. As you'll see in a moment, the client page lifecycle starts when the browser loads the page and ends when the user navigates away from the page or the page is reloaded. When each stage in the lifecycle is entered, the Application object raises a corresponding event.

- *Hosting the client components instantiated in the page*—Once instantiated, client components become children of the Application object and can be easily accessed through the Application object. Also, they're automatically disposed by the Application object when the web page is unloaded by the browser.

Client components and the client-page lifecycle are the key concepts we'll dissect in the following sections. Let's start by illustrating the concept of a client component. Then, we'll focus on the client-page lifecycle and the events raised by the Application object.

2.2.1 Client components

Let's say you need a hierarchical menu for navigating the pages of a website. Whether it's written in C# or JavaScript—assuming it isn't poorly designed—you usually don't have to know anything about the logic used to render the menu. Instead, you only have to configure the menu and instantiate it in the page. If you also need the same menu in a different page, you perform similar steps to include and initialize it. The point is, the code should be packaged into a single, configurable object that can be reused in another application.

The primary tenet behind components is code reusability. Components implement a well-defined set of interfaces that allows them to interact with other components and to be interchanged between applications. Thanks to the base interfaces, the code encapsulated by components can change at any time without affecting the other processing logic.

The Microsoft Ajax Library provides specialized client classes that simplify the authoring of client components. The group of classes related to component development is called the *client component model* and closely mirrors the model in use in the .NET framework. In this way, you can write component-oriented client applications using JavaScript code.

We'll explore the nuts and bolts of client components in chapter 8. For now, it's enough to treat a client component as a black box that encapsulates reusable client logic and exposes it through methods, properties, and events, as shown in figure 2.2. You've already met your first component: the Application object introduced in the previous section. In the following section, we'll explain how the Application object and client components interact during the client-page lifecycle.

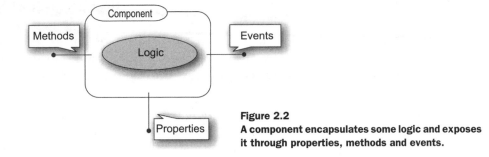

Figure 2.2
A component encapsulates some logic and exposes it through properties, methods and events.

2.2.2 Client-page lifecycle

Previously, we pointed out the Application object acts on the client side like the counterpart of the Page object. The Page object manages the lifecycle of a web page on the server side, and the Sys.Application object accomplishes the same task on the client side. The client lifecycle of a web page is much simpler than the server lifecycle of an ASP.NET page. It consists of only three stages: *init, load,* and *unload.* When each stage is entered, the Sys.Application object fires the corresponding event—init, load, or unload.

As shown in the activity diagram in figure 2.3, the client-page lifecycle starts when the browser loads a page requested by the user and ends when the user navigates away from the page. Let's examine the sequence of events in more detail.

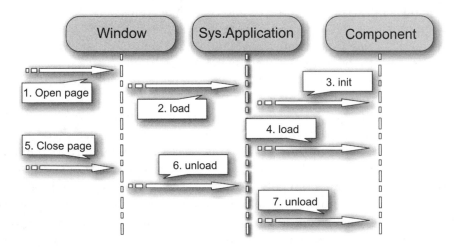

Figure 2.3   The client-page lifecycle starts when the browser loads a web page. The Sys.Application object is responsible for hooking up the events raised by the window object and, in turn, firing its own events. Client components are created during the init stage and disposed automatically in the unload stage.

When the browser starts loading a web page, the DOM's window object fires the load event. This event is intercepted by the Application object, which, in turn, starts initializing the Microsoft Ajax Library's runtime. When the runtime has been initialized, Sys.Application fires the init event. During the init stage, all the client components you want to use should be instantiated and initialized. As you'll discover in chapter 8, client components are instantiated using a special function called $create and are automatically hosted by the Application object.

After the creation of components is complete, Sys.Application fires the load event. This stage provides you with an opportunity to interact with the components created in the init stage. This is also the best place to attach event handlers to DOM elements and perform data access—for example, using the techniques for sending asynchronous requests that we'll illustrate in chapter 5.

When the user navigates away from the page or reloads it, the unload event of the window object is intercepted by Sys.Application, which in turns fires its own unload event. At this point, all the resources used by the page should be freed and event handlers detached from DOM elements.

The events raised by the Sys.Application object and, in general, by client components are different from the events raised by DOM elements. In chapter 3, we'll explain how to expose events in JavaScript objects. The event model used by the Microsoft Ajax Library is similar to the model used by the .NET framework: Events support multiple handlers and can be subscribed and handled in a manner similar to the events raised by ASP.NET server controls.

It's not difficult to deduce that one of the objectives of the Microsoft Ajax Library is bringing .NET flavors to the client side. The Application object, client components, events, and client-page lifecycle are the foundations of the Microsoft Ajax Library. They let ASP.NET developers use familiar development patterns even when writing JavaScript code. Before we go any further, let's take a moment to reinforce what you've learned by putting together a simple program.

2.2.3 *"Hello Microsoft Ajax!"*

This example illustrates how to write a simple program with the Microsoft Ajax Library. Because we've discussed the Application object and the client-page lifecycle, we'll show them in action in a page. The quickest way to start programming with the Microsoft Ajax Library is to create a new Ajax-enabled website using the Visual Studio template shipped with ASP.NET AJAX. See appendix A for instructions on how to install the Visual Studio template. The template creates a new website and adds a reference to the System.Web.Extensions assembly and a properly configured web.config file. In addition, it creates a Default.aspx page with a ScriptManager control already in it. To run the following example, open the Default.aspx page and insert the code from listing 2.1 in the page's form tag.

Listing 2.1   Code for testing the client-page lifecycle

```
<script type="text/javascript">
<!--
    function pageLoad() {
        alert("Page loaded!");
        alert("Hello Microsoft Ajax!");
    }

    function pageUnload() {
        alert("Unloading page!");
    }
//-->
</script>
```

The code in listing 2.1 is simple enough for a first program. It consists of two Java-Script functions, `pageLoad` and `pageUnload`, embedded in a `script` tag in the markup code of the web page. In the functions, you call the JavaScript's `alert` function to display some text in a message box on screen.

The names of the functions aren't chosen at random. Provided that you've defined them in the page, the Microsoft Ajax Library automatically calls the `page-Load` function when the load stage of the client page lifecycle is entered. The `pageUnload` function is automatically called when the unload stage is reached.

When you run the page, the code in `pageLoad` is executed as soon as the load stage is entered. Figure 2.4 shows the example up and running in Internet Explorer. To see what happens during the unload stage, you can either press the F5 key or navigate away from the page.

Figure 2.4
The "Hello Microsoft Ajax!" program
running in Internet Explorer

The pageLoad function

When you're using the Microsoft Ajax Library, the pageLoad function is the best place to execute the client code. Handling the window.load event isn't safe because the library handles it to perform the runtime initialization. It's always safe to run the code during the load stage of the client-page lifecycle, because the runtime initialization is complete, all the script files referenced through the ScriptManager control have been loaded, and all the client components have been created and initialized.

If you want to detect the init stage, you have to do a little more work. Declaring a `pageInit` function won't have any effect. Instead, you have to write an additional statement with a call to the `add_init` method of Sys.Application, as shown in listing 2.2.

Listing 2.2 Handling the `init` event of Sys.Application

```
Sys.Application.add_init(pageInit);

function pageInit() {
    alert("Entered the Init stage!");
}
```

The `add_init` method adds an event handler for the `init` event of Sys.Application. The event handler is the `pageInit` function you passed as an argument to the method. The Application object also has `add_load` and `add_unload` methods, which add event handlers to the `load` and `unload` events, respectively. However, the `pageLoad` and the `pageUnload` functions offer a way to execute code during the load and unload stages of the client page lifecycle.

The init stage is typically used to create instances of the client components you use in the page. However, we won't deal with it until chapter 8, where we'll explain the nuts and bolts of client components. The majority of the client code, including attaching event handlers to DOM elements and sending Ajax requests, can be safely executed in the `pageLoad` function.

Now that you've written your first program, let's focus on the client code a little more. Web developers use JavaScript primarily to access a web page's DOM. The DOM is an API used to access a tree structure built from a page's markup code. The following sections explore how to use the Microsoft Ajax Library to program against the browser's DOM.

2.3 *Working with the DOM*

When a browser renders a page, it builds a hierarchical representation (called the *DOM tree*) of all the HTML elements like buttons, text boxes, and images. Every element in the page becomes a programmable control in the DOM tree and exposes properties, methods, and events. For example, an `input` tag with its `type` attribute set to `button` is parsed into a button object with a `value` property that lets you set its text. The button can also raise a `click` event when it's clicked. The ability to manipulate DOM elements makes the difference between static and dynamic HTML pages. It's possible to change the behavior of the UI elements at any time, based on the user's inputs and interactions with the page.

But this is where life gets tricky. Almost all browsers implement the DOM programming interface differently. In some cases, there are differences between versions of the same browser. This means a dynamic page that works on one browser may stop working on another browser and complain about JavaScript errors. At this point, you're forced to duplicate the code to work around the browser incompatibilities.

The Microsoft Ajax Library addresses this serious problem by providing an *abstraction API* whose purpose is to abstract common operations made on DOM elements, such as handling their events and working with CSS. As we'll explain, the API frees you from having to know which functions are supported by the DOM implementation of a particular browser. It takes care of calling the correct function based on the browser that is rendering the page.

2.3.1 *The abstraction API*

The Microsoft Ajax Library lets you access the DOM in a manner independent from the browser that renders the page. The abstraction API consists of the methods exposed by two client classes: `Sys.UI.DomElement` and `Sys.UI.DomEvent`. The first one abstracts a DOM element, and the second represents the event data object that DOM event handlers receive as an argument.

Using this model, you prevent the code from dealing directly with the browser's API. Instead, you call methods defined in the Microsoft Ajax Library, which takes care of calling the correct function based on the browser that is currently rendering the page. Figure 2.5 illustrates this concept by showing how the DOM calls in a script file can be made through the `Sys.UI.DomElement` and `Sys.UI.DomEvent` classes.

For example, suppose you want to hook up an event raised by a DOM element. Instead of checking whether a browser supports an `attachEvent` rather than an `addEventListener` method, you can call the `addHandler` method of the

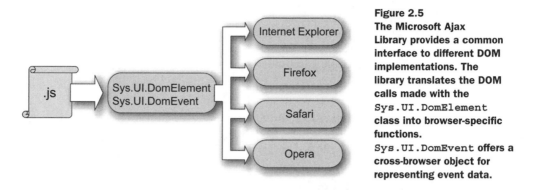

Figure 2.5
The Microsoft Ajax Library provides a common interface to different DOM implementations. The library translates the DOM calls made with the `Sys.UI.DomElement` **class into browser-specific functions.** `Sys.UI.DomEvent` **offers a cross-browser object for representing event data.**

`Sys.UI.DomElement` class. Then, it's up to the Microsoft Ajax Library to call the correct function based on the detected browser.

You know that Firefox passes the event object as an argument to the event handler, whereas Internet Explorer stores its custom event object in the `window.event` property. If you use the abstraction API, the same cross-browser event object is always passed as an argument to the event handler. Thanks to the cross-browser event object, you're also freed from the pain of dealing with different properties that describe the same event data.

To give you confidence using the API, let's work on an example that explains how to use some of the methods provided to handle an event raised by a DOM element. Later, we'll address CSS and positioning.

2.3.2 *A dynamic, cross-browser text box*

One of the main uses of JavaScript is to check and validate user input before a web form is submitted to the server. To perform this task, you often have to write client logic that limits the values a user can enter in a text field. As an example, suppose you want a user to enter some text in a text box. The requirements say that the text must contain only letters—no digits. To implement this task, you must access the text-box element, handle its `keypress` event, and filter the text typed by the user. Listing 2.3 shows how this task can be accomplished using the Microsoft Ajax Library. Notably, the resulting code runs in all the browsers supported by the library.

Listing 2.3 A text box that accepts only letters

```
<div>
    <span>Please type some text:</span>
    <input type="text" id="txtNoDigits" />
</div>

<script type="text/javascript">
```

```
<!--
    function pageLoad() {
        var txtNoDigits = $get('txtNoDigits');          Access text
                                                         box element

        $addHandler(txtNoDigits,                         Attach event
            'keypress', txtNoDigits_keypress);           handler
    }

    function pageUnload() {
        $removeHandler($get('txtNoDigits'),
            'keypress', txtNoDigits_keypress);           Detach event
    }                                                    handler

    function txtNoDigits_keypress(evt) {
        var code = evt.charCode;
                                                         Handle keypress
        if(code >= 48 && code <= 57) {                   event
            evt.preventDefault();
        }
    }
}
//-->
</script>
```

As you know, the code in the pageLoad function is executed as soon as the load stage of the client page lifecycle is entered. The function body contains calls to the $get and $addHandler methods.

> ### Shortcuts
>
> As we explained in chapter 1, functions prefixed with the character $ are aliases or shortcuts used to access methods with longer names. This saves you a little typing. Even if it seems like a minor detail, using shortcuts is useful for obtaining shorter code and smaller JavaScript files. Table 2.3 lists some of the shortcuts defined in the Microsoft Ajax Library together with the longer name of the associated method.

The first method called in pageLoad is $get, which gets a reference to a DOM element. $get accepts the ID of a DOM element and returns a reference to it. You can also pass a reference to a DOM element as the second parameter. In this case, the method searches an element with the given ID in the child nodes of the provided DOM element.

Table 2.3   Shortcuts for common methods defined in the abstraction API

Shortcut	Method Name	Description
`$get`	`Sys.UI.DomElement.getElementById`	Returns a reference to a DOM element
`$addHandler`	`Sys.UI.DomElement.addHandler`	Adds an event handler to an event exposed by a DOM element
`$removeHandler`	`Sys.UI.DomElement.removeHandler`	Removes an event handler added with `$addHandler`
`$addHandlers`	`Sys.UI.DomElement.addHandlers`	Adds multiple event handlers to events exposed by DOM elements and wraps the handlers with delegates
`$removeHandlers`	`Sys.UI.DomElement.removeHandlers`	Removes all the handlers added with `$addHandler` and `$addHandlers`

The second method, $addHandler, adds an event handler for an event raised by a DOM element. The first argument is a reference to the element that exposes the event you want to subscribe. The second argument is a string with the name of the event. The third argument is the JavaScript function that handles the event. The syntax of $addHandler is illustrated in figure 2.6. Note that the string with the name of the event must not include the prefix on.

You can remove the handler added with $addHandler at any time by passing the same arguments—the element, the event name, and the handler—to the $removeHandler method. It's a good practice to always dispose event handlers

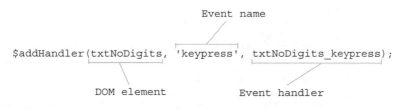

Figure 2.6   Syntax for the `$addHandler` method, used for attaching a handler to an event raised by a DOM element

added to DOM elements. You do so to prevent memory leaks in the browser that could slow the application and cause a huge performance drop. As in listing 2.3, a good place to use $removeHandler is in the pageUnload function, which is called just before the browser unloads the web page.

In the previous example, the handler for the text box's keypress event is the txtNoDigits_keypress function. The handler is called as soon as a key is pressed in the text field. As you can see, the first argument passed to the txtNoDigits _keypress function, evt, is an instance of the Sys.UI.DomEvent class. The main characteristic of this object is that it contains the event data and exposes the same properties in all the supported browsers.

> **NOTE** The $addHandler method uses a private function to subscribe the event. When the private handler is executed, the browser-specific event object is converted into a Sys.UI.DomEvent instance. At this point, the original event handler passed to $addHandler is called with the Sys.UI.Dom-Event instance as an argument, in place of the original event object.

Among the various properties of the event object, charCode returns the code of the typed character. The preventDefault method is invoked to avoid the execution of the default action for the subscribed event. In the example, this prevents characters whose code corresponds to a digit from being displayed in the text box. Table 2.4 lists all the properties of the cross-browser event object.

Table 2.4 Properties of the Sys.UI.DomEvent class, which provides a cross-browser object that contains the event data for DOM events

Property	Value
rawEvent	Underlying event-data object built by the current browser
shiftKey	True if the Shift key was pressed
ctrlKey	True if the Ctrl key was pressed
altKey	True if the Alt key was pressed
button	One of the values of the Sys.UI.MouseButton enumeration: leftButton, middleButton, rightButton
charCode	Character code for the typed character
clientX	During a mouse event, the x coordinate of the mouse location relative to the client area of the page
clientY	During a mouse event, the y coordinate of the mouse location relative to the client area of the page

Table 2.4 Properties of the `Sys.UI.DomEvent` class, which provides a cross-browser object that contains the event data for DOM events *(continued)*

Property	Value
target	Element that raised the event
screenX	During a mouse event, the x coordinate of the mouse location relative to the computer screen
screenY	During a mouse event, the y coordinate of the mouse location relative to the computer screen
type	Name or type of the event (like click or mouseover)
preventDefault()	Prevents execution of the default action associated with the event
stopPropagation()	Prevents the event from propagating up to the element's parent nodes

Changing the layout of DOM elements is one of the main tasks in dynamic HTML pages. For example, features like animations, scrolls, and drag and drop rely on the positioning and the style of DOM elements. Let's return to the `Sys.UI.DomElement` class to examine a group of methods related to CSS and positioning.

2.3.3 CSS and positioning

The `Sys.UI.DomElement` class provides a group of methods for performing common tasks related to CSS and positioning. If you pass a DOM element and a string with the name of a CSS class to the `addCssClass` method, you add the class to the list of CSS classes associated with an element. If you pass the same arguments to the `removeCssClass` method, you remove the class from the list of associated CSS classes.

If there's one thing that highlights the incompatibilities between the various implementation of the DOM, it's positioning. Due to the different ways in which the many parameters related to the box model are computed, making a UI look the same in multiple browsers can be a real challenge.

> **The box model**
>
> The box model describes the layout of DOM elements in a web page through a set of parameters implemented in CSS. You can read a good article about the box model at http://www.brainjar.com/css/positioning/.

The Microsoft Ajax Library tries to mitigate this issue by providing methods that take into account bugs and different algorithms for computing the position and bounds of DOM elements. To retrieve the location of an element, you write a statement like the following:

```
var location = Sys.UI.DomElement.getLocation(element);
```

The `getLocation` method takes a reference to a DOM element and returns an object with two attributes, x and y, which store the left and top coordinates of the element relative to the upper-left corner of the parent frame:

```
var top = location.y;
var left = location.x;
```

The `setLocation` method accepts the x and y coordinates (specified in pixels) and sets the element's position using the `left` and `top` attributes of its `style` object. In this case, the element's location is set based on the positioning mode of the element and its parent node. Consider the following statement:

```
Sys.UI.DomElement.setLocation(element, 100, 100);
```

If the parent node of `element` has a specific positioning mode (for example, `rel-ative` or `absolute`), then its location—by CSS rules—is set relative to the parent element and not to the parent frame.

If you need to know the *bounds* of an element—its location and its dimensions—the `Sys.UI.DomElement.getBounds` method takes a reference to a DOM element and returns an object with four attributes: x, y, `height`, and `width`.

The main goal of the abstraction API isn't to increase differences by adding a new group of methods to learn and remember; the objective is to offer a consistent programming interface to the browser's DOM. When the Microsoft Ajax Library evolves and adds support for new browsers, the code written with the API will continue to work as before. This is possible because under the hood the library takes care of all compatibility issues.

It's time to leave the abstraction API, but your work with the DOM isn't over. Handling DOM events is one of the most common tasks when scripting against a web page. In the next sections, we'll introduce two useful methods for implementing callbacks and *delegates* in JavaScript. We'll show how you can use them to make DOM event-handling easy and straightforward.

2.3.4   *Client delegates*

Think of a button on an ASP.NET page or on a Windows Forms form. When the user clicks the button, the Button object realizes this and raises a `click` event, which implicitly means, "Hey, someone clicked me, but I'm just a Button. What should happen now?" In the .NET framework, objects use a delegate to invoke one or multiple methods responsible for processing the event.

NOTE To learn more about delegates in the .NET framework, browse to the following URL: http://msdn.microsoft.com/msdnmag/issues/01/04/net/.

To implement a similar pattern in JavaScript, the Microsoft Ajax Library provides a method called `Function.createDelegate`, which accepts two arguments and returns a new function—let's call it the *client delegate*. The first argument is the object that will be pointed to by `this` in the client delegate. The second argument is the function that you want to invoke through the client delegate.

When you invoke the client delegate, it calls the function you passed previously. The difference is that now, `this` points to the object you passed as the first argument to `createDelegate`.

To understand why a client delegate is useful, recall what happens when you add a handler to an event raised by a DOM element. In the handler, `this` always points to the element that hooked up the event, which determines the *scope* you can access. Using a client delegate lets you access—through the `this` keyword—a different object than the DOM element that hooked up the event.

Listing 2.4 demonstrates how to use a client delegate to handle the `click` event of a button element. In the event handler, you can access a variable stored in a different scope.

Listing 2.4 Using a client delegate to handle a DOM event

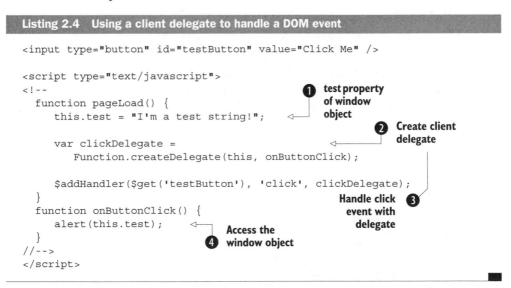

```
<input type="button" id="testButton" value="Click Me" />

<script type="text/javascript">
<!--
  function pageLoad() {
    this.test = "I'm a test string!";          ❶ test property
                                                   of window
                                                   object
    var clickDelegate =                         ❷ Create client
        Function.createDelegate(this, onButtonClick);    delegate

    $addHandler($get('testButton'), 'click', clickDelegate);
  }                                             ❸ Handle click
  function onButtonClick() {                       event with
    alert(this.test);          ❹ Access the        delegate
  }                               window object
//-->
</script>
```

The ❷ clickDelegate variable stores a client delegate that ❸ invokes the onBut-tonClick function. In the function, this points to the object passed as the first argument to createDelegate. Because pageLoad is a global function, this points to the global object, which will be accessible in the ❹ onButtonClick function. To demonstrate this, you alert the value of the ❶ test variable, which was added to the window object in the first statement of the pageLoad function. If you try to pass the onButtonClick function—instead of the client delegate—to the $addHandler method, you'll notice that the test variable is undefined, because this now points to the button element that raised the click event.

The Function.createDelegate method is useful because you don't have to store in a global variable—or even in a DOM element—the context that you want to access in the event handler. Plus, the Microsoft Ajax Library provides two methods for subscribing to multiple DOM events, creating delegates for them, and disposing both the delegates and the handlers automatically. These methods are accessed through the $addHandlers and $clearHandlers shortcuts.

2.3.5 *$addHandlers and $clearHandlers*

The main advantage of using $addHandlers and $clearHandlers is to avoid the error-prone (and boring) job of creating client delegates, attaching handlers, and then performing the reverse task, all multiplied by the number of events you're subscribing. For example, the following statement automatically creates the client delegates for the click and mouseover events of a button element:

```
$addHandlers(buttonElement, { click:onButtonClick,
        mouseover:onMouseOver }, this);
```

The first argument passed to $addHandlers is the DOM element. The second parameter is an object for which each property is the name of an event, and whose value is the event handler. The last parameter is the *owner* of the handler, which determines the context under which the event handler is executed. Usually you pass this, which lets you access—in the handler—the object that subscribed to the event.

If you need to detach all the event handlers from the element, you can do so with a single statement:

```
$clearHandlers(buttonElement);
```

Note that the $clearHandlers method detaches all the event handlers attached with $addHandler and $addHandlers. It also disposes all the delegates created with the $addHandlers method.

NOTE Browsers can leak memory if event handlers aren't correctly detached from DOM elements. For this reason, it's important to always detach all the event handlers and dispose all the delegates when a client object is cleaned up or the whole page is unloaded.

You don't always need to switch the scope of an event handler to access the information you need. Often, it's enough to access a context object where you've stored only the references that may be useful during the processing of the event. In this case, a better approach is to handle a DOM event using a callback function.

2.3.6 *Callbacks*

The Microsoft Ajax Library provides a method called `Function.createCallback`, which you can use to create a callback function that an object can invoke at any time. The main purpose of `Function.createCallback` is to call a function with a *context* provided by the object that created the callback. The context is an object that, usually, contains application data that otherwise wouldn't be accessible in the method, because they belong to a different scope. Just like client delegates, callbacks are useful for processing DOM events. The code in listing 2.5 shows how you can access, in a DOM event handler, a custom object created in the `pageLoad` function.

Listing 2.5 Using a callback to handle a DOM event

```
<input type="button" id="myButton"
       value="Time elapsed since page load" />

<script type="text/javascript">
<!--
    function pageLoad() {
        var context = { date : new Date() };          ← ❶ context
                                                           object
        var clickCallback =
            Function.createCallback(onButtonClick, context);   ❷ Create
                                                                 callback

        $addHandler($get('myButton'), 'click', clickCallback);   ←
    }                                                            Attach handler to click event ❸

    function onButtonClick(evt, context) {
        var loadTime = context.date;
        var elapsed = new Date() - loadTime;           ❹ Access event
                                                           object and
        alert((elapsed / 1000) + ' seconds');             context
    }
//-->
</script>
```

The ❶ context variable stores the time at which the pageLoad function was invoked. You want to access this information in the function that handles the button's click event. To do that, you ❷ create a callback that points to the onButtonClick function. In the Function.createCallback method, you specify the function to invoke and the context object. ❸ Then, you pass the callback to the $addHandler method. ❹ When the onButtonClick function is called, the context object is added to the list of arguments, just after the event object.

Callbacks and delegates are nice additions to the set of features you can leverage when programming against the DOM with the Microsoft Ajax Library. But in the Ajax age of web applications, interacting with the DOM is just a small portion of the tasks the client code should accomplish. You need features and tools that simplify everyday programming with JavaScript. In the following sections, we'll explore some of the classes that the Microsoft Ajax Library provides to increase productivity on the client side.

2.4 Making development with JavaScript easier

Since the first versions of JavaScript, developers have started writing libraries to leverage the base functionality provided by the language. Every new library or framework that sees the light—and lately, this seems to happen on a monthly basis—aims at increasing the productivity of JavaScript developers by offering a set of tools that makes it easier to design, write, and debug the client code. As you may have guessed, the direction taken by the Microsoft Ajax Library is to achieve the same goals by bringing some of the .NET coding patterns to the client side. Let's look at some of the client classes provided by the library, starting with the enhancements made to the built-in JavaScript objects. Later, we'll talk about browser detection and client-side debugging.

2.4.1 The String object

String manipulation is one of the most common tasks in everyday programming. JavaScript comes with a String object that contains various methods for dealing with strings. However, some frequently desired methods such as format and trim aren't in the list. The good news is that the Microsoft Ajax Library extends—at runtime—the String object to make it more similar to the counterpart class in the .NET framework. For example, one of the methods added to the client String object is format. You can use numbered placeholders like {0} and {1} to format strings using variables, just as you do on the server side:

```
alert(String.format("This code is running on {0} {1}",
    Sys.Browser.agent, Sys.Browser.version));
```

The Sys.Browser object can be used to get information about the browser that loaded a page. We'll return to browser detection in section 2.4.4. In the meantime, look at table 2.5, which lists the new methods added to the JavaScript String object.

Table 2.5   Methods added to the JavaScript String object

Method	Description
endsWith	Determines whether the end of the String object matches the specified string.
format	Replaces each format item in a String object with the text equivalent of a corresponding object's value.
localeFormat	Replaces the format items in a String object with the text equivalent of a corresponding object's value. The current culture is used to format dates and numbers.
startsWith	Determines whether the start of the String object matches the specified string.
trim	Removes leading and trailing white space from a String object instance.
trimEnd	Removes trailing white space from a String object instance.
trimStart	Removes leading white space from a String object instance.

An object familiar to .NET developers is the *string builder*. A string builder is an object that speeds up string concatenations because it uses an array to store the parts instead of relying on temporary strings. As a consequence, a string builder is orders of magnitude faster than the + operator when you need to concatenate a large number of strings.

2.4.2   *Sys.StringBuilder*

The Sys.StringBuilder class closely resembles the System.Text.StringBuilder class of the .NET framework. In JavaScript, it's common to build large chunks of HTML dynamically as strings and then use the innerHTML property of a DOM element to parse the HTML. Even if it isn't a standard DOM property, innerHTML is orders of magnitude faster than the standard methods for manipulating the DOM tree. Listing 2.6 shows how to use an instance of the Sys.StringBuilder class to format the URL of a web page and display it on a label. Instances of client classes are created with the new operator in the same way as JavaScript custom objects. We'll return to client classes and other object-oriented constructs in chapter 3.

Listing 2.6   Example using the `Sys.StringBuilder` class

```
<span id="urlLabel"></span>

<script type="text/javascript">
<!--
    function pageLoad(sender, e) {                        Create instance of
        var sb = new Sys.StringBuilder();          ◁──┘  StringBuilder

        sb.append('<h3>You are now browsing: ');
        sb.append('<b><i>');
        sb.append(window.location);
        sb.append('</i></b></h3>');

        var myLabel = $get('urlLabel');
                                                          Inject HTML chunk
        urlLabel.innerHTML = sb.toString();        ◁──┘  in span element
    }
//-->
</script>
```

To add the various parts to the final string, you pass them to the append method. When you're done, you call the toString method to get the whole string stored in the StringBuilder instance. The Sys.StringBuilder class also supports an appendLine method that adds a line break after the string passed as an argument. The line break is the escape sequence \r\n, so you can't use it when building HTML. Instead, you write something like this:

```
sb.append('<br />');
```

You can use the isEmpty method to test whether a StringBuilder instance doesn't contain any text. The following if statement performs this check and, if the StringBuilder isn't empty, clears all the text using the clear method:

```
if(!sb.isEmpty()) {
    sb.clear();
}
```

When the number of strings to concatenate is larger, the string builder becomes an essential object to avoid huge performance drops. The Sys.StringBuilder class relies on an array to store the strings to concatenate. Then, it uses the join method of the String object to perform the concatenation and obtain the final string.

Arrays are probably one of the most used data structures in programming. JavaScript provides a built-in Array object that the Microsoft Ajax Library extends with methods commonly found in the .NET Array class.

2.4.3   *The Array object*

In JavaScript, an *array* is an ordered collection of values that can be of different types. The built-in Array object exposes many methods to deal with arrays, but the Microsoft Ajax Library extends it so it looks and feels similar to the Array object of the .NET framework. Table 2.6 lists the new methods added to the Array object, together with their descriptions.

Table 2.6   Extension methods added to the JavaScript Array object

Method	Description
add	Adds an element to the end of an Array object
addRange	Copies all the elements of the specified array to the end of an Array object
clear	Removes all elements from an Array object
clone	Creates a shallow copy of an Array object
contains	Determines whether an element is in an Array object
dequeue	Removes the first element from an Array object
forEach	Performs a specified action on each element of an Array object
indexOf	Searches for the specified element of an Array object and returns its index
insert	Inserts a value at the specified location in an Array object
parse	Creates an Array object from a string representation
remove	Removes the first occurrence of an element in an Array object
removeAt	Removes an element at the specified location in an Array object

All the new methods added to the Array type act as *static* methods. As we'll clarify in chapter 3, one of the ways to extend an existing JavaScript object is to add a method directly to its type. As a consequence, the new method can be called directly on the type rather than on a new instance. This is similar to static methods in C# and shared functions in VB.NET; in practice, the usage is the same in JavaScript. In listing 2.7, you create an array and play with some of the new methods introduced by the Microsoft Ajax Library.

Listing 2.7   Some of the new methods added to the Array object

```
<script type="text/javascript">
<!--
    function pageLoad(sender, e) {
        var arr = new Array();

        Array.add(arr, 3);                              Add
        Array.addRange(arr, [4, 5, "Hello World!"]);    items

        Array.removeAt(arr, arr.length - 1);        ◁──┐ Remove last
                                                         item
        var sum = 0;
        Array.forEach(arr,
            function(item) { sum += item; });         ┐ Compute
                                                        sum of items
        alert(sum);
                                    ┌── Clear
        Array.clear(arr);       ◁──┘   array
    }
//-->
</script>
```

The first thing that .NET developers may notice is that methods have familiar names. The code in listing 2.7 could have been written using the standard methods of the built-in Array object. On the other hand, the Microsoft Ajax Library combines or renames them to achieve, wherever possible, consistency between server-side and client-side classes.

As we said previously, the new methods added to the Array object are static. For example, the addRange method is called as Array.addRange and accepts two arguments: the array instance on which you're working, and an array with the elements you want to add to the instance. The reason for having static methods is that the JavaScript for/in construct, if used to loop over the elements of an array, would return any methods added to the Array object. This happens because the for/in construct loops through the properties of a generic object. On the other hand, static methods aren't returned if you use for/in to loop over an array instance.

An interesting new method is Array.forEach, which loops through an array and processes each element with the function passed as the second argument. The example uses Array.forEach with a simple function that computes the sum of the integers in the array.

Often, web applications have a much wider scope than a company's intranet. Many are websites that can be browsed by virtually any corner of the world. However, different cultures have different ways to represent data such as dates, numbers, and currencies. It's important for applications to be aware of these differences and take *globalization* and *localization* into account.

2.4.4 Globalization

On the server side, ASP.NET does a great job at globalization by providing a group of objects that store information about different cultures. For example, you can rely on specific CultureInfo objects to set a culture for the web application. These objects contain all the settings relative to a particular culture, such as date and number formats.

Such infrastructure isn't available on the client side, where you usually have to elaborate your custom strategy or, worse, renounce it to implement globalization. Luckily, the Microsoft Ajax Library makes enabling globalization on the client side a piece of cake. If you set the EnableScriptGlobalization property of the ScriptManager control to true, the CultureInfo object relative to the current culture (set on the server side) is serialized using the JSON data format and then sent to the browser at runtime.

The serialized object is stored in the Sys.CultureInfo variable and contains two child objects: InvariantCulture and CurrentCulture. These objects contain the settings relative to the invariant culture and the current culture as set on the server side. The serialized CultureInfo object is used in conjunction with a group of new methods added to the Date and Number objects by the Microsoft Ajax Library.

The Date object provides formatting capabilities and localized parsing. You can format date instances by passing a format string to the format method, like so:

```
var date = new Date();
var formatString =
    Sys.CultureInfo.CurrentCulture.dateTimeFormat.LongDatePattern;

alert(date.format(formatString));
```

This code snippet uses the CurrentCulture object to obtain a standard format string, but you could also use a custom format string.

> **NOTE** If you need more information about standard and custom format strings for date and numbers, visit http://msdn2.microsoft.com/en-us/library/427bttx3.aspx and http://msdn2.microsoft.com/en-us/library/97x6twsz.aspx.

The format method uses the Sys.CultureInfo.InvariantCulture object to produce a string with the formatted date. If you want to use the CurrentCulture object, you have to pass the format string to the formatLocale method:

```
alert(date.formatLocale(formatString));
```

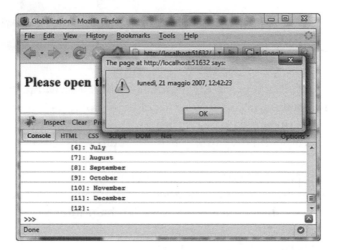

Figure 2.7
A `Date` instance can be formatted using the current culture as set in an ASP.NET page on the server side.

Figure 2.7 shows how a `Date` instance is formatted in the Italian culture (`it-IT`). Similar rules are used for parsing strings that contain date representations. The `Date.parseInvariant` method parses a string representation of a date using the InvariantCulture object. On the other hand, the `Date.parseLocale` method takes advantage of the CurrentCulture object.

The `Number` object has been extended with similar methods. You have `format` and `localeFormat` methods to format `Number` instances using the invariant culture or the current culture, as set on the server side. Similarly, the `parse` and `parseLocale` methods are responsible for parsing a string with a number representation using the desired culture settings.

> **NOTE** You can browse the MSDN documentation for globalization and localization at http://msdn2.microsoft.com/en-us/library/c6zyy3s9.aspx.

In addition to globalization, the ASP.NET AJAX framework provides support for localization. You can think of localization as the translation of a page into a particular culture: Client resources like JavaScript files and strings can now be localized from the client, not just the server. Chapter 4 will walk you through how this is attainable.

Now that you know how to deal with the enhanced JavaScript object, let's focus on the common tasks performed in everyday programming with JavaScript. Since web developers started scripting against web pages, browser detection has played a major role, especially due to the incompatibilities in the JavaScript implementations of different browsers.

2.4.5 *Browser detection*

The Microsoft Ajax Library extracts information about the browser that is rendering the page from the DOM's navigator object. This information is stored in an object called Sys.Browser, which you can use to perform browser detection on the client side. To see browser detection in action, the code in listing 2.8 displays a message with the name and the version of the detected browser.

Listing 2.8   Using the Sys.Browser object to perform browser detection

```
<script type="text/javascript">
<!--
  function pageLoad(sender, e) {
    var browser = String.format("Your browser is {0} {1}",
      Sys.Browser.name, Sys.Browser.version);

    alert(browser);
  }
//-->
</script>
```

The name and agent properties of the Sys.Browser object contain the browser's name and the current version. Figure 2.8 shows how this information is displayed in a message box in the Opera browser.

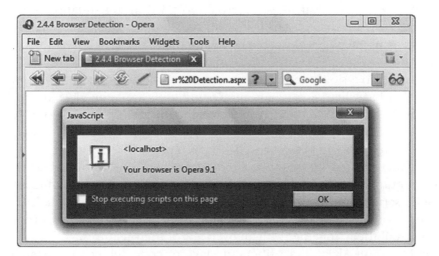

Figure 2.8   You can use the Sys.Browser object to perform browser detection at runtime.

Sometimes it's useful to take an action only if a particular browser is detected. In this case, you can test against the object returned by Sys.Browser.agent. For example, add the following statement in listing 2.8, after the call to the alert function:

```
if(Sys.Browser.agent == Sys.Browser.InternetExplorer) {
    alert('This message is displayed only on Internet Explorer!');
}
```

As you can easily verify, the message box in this code is displayed only in Internet Explorer. You can also test the Sys.Browser.agent property against Sys.Browser.Firefox, Sys.Browser.Opera, and Sys.Browser.Safari.

Performing browser detection is a small step toward the goal of writing client code that runs smoothly and behaves as expected in all the browsers you're targeting. Ajax web applications have introduced the need to dedicate even more time to debugging. The following sections will examine the tools available for debugging JavaScript code. We'll also discuss how the Microsoft Ajax Library can help you improve your debugging experience and handle errors.

2.4.6 *Debugging*

Debugging JavaScript code has never been the most exciting experience for a web developer. On one hand, browsers don't have embedded debuggers and often provide cryptic error messages that give no clue what went wrong. On the other hand, JavaScript continues to lack a real development environment, and almost all the debuggers are available as external tools. Given this situation, it shouldn't come as a surprise that one of the preferred debugging techniques has always been displaying messages on screen by calling the alert function at the right time in the code.

The situation is slowly getting better. All the modern browsers have a JavaScript console that logs client errors, and interesting tools are being developed. Among these, Firebug for Firefox and Web Development Helper for Internet Explorer have proven to be must-have tools for Ajax developers. These tools integrate with the browser and let you inspect and debug web pages directly in the browser. The next version of Visual Studio (codename "Orcas") will provide a real development environment for JavaScript, with features such as improved debugging and IntelliSense in script files. This book's Resources section points you to the URLs where you can download some of these tools. Also, Appendix B contains instructions on how to install them, together with an overview of their features.

The Microsoft Ajax Library offers support for code debugging through a class called Sys.Debug. This class exposes methods for logging messages to the browser's console and dumping client objects. To log a message to the console, you can call the `Sys.Debug.trace` method anywhere in the code, passing a string with the message as an argument:

```
Sys.Debug.trace("I'm a debug message.");
```

You can also dump an object by passing it to the `Sys.Debug.traceDump` method. An object dump displays all the properties of an object, together with their values, and can be helpful during debugging. The following example logs to the console the properties of the object returned by the `getBounds` method of the `Sys.UI.DomElement` class:

```
Sys.Debug.traceDump(Sys.UI.DomElement.getBounds(document.body));
```

Figure 2.9 shows the logged messages in the Firebug console of the Firefox browser. If you prefer to see the messages directly on the page area rather than in the JavaScript console, declare a `textarea` element with an ID of `TraceConsole`, like so:

```
<textarea id="TraceConsole" rows="30" cols="50"></textarea>
```

In this way, all messages passed to `Sys.Debug.trace` are displayed in the `textarea` element.

If you consider the two main tasks performed by Ajax applications—updating portions of the page layout and performing data access in the background—it's clear that a relevant part of the application logic consists of sending asynchronous HTTP requests to the server. For this reason, there's an increasing need for Ajax developers to monitor what happens during data transfers and to inspect the content of the requests and responses sent during the life of a web page.

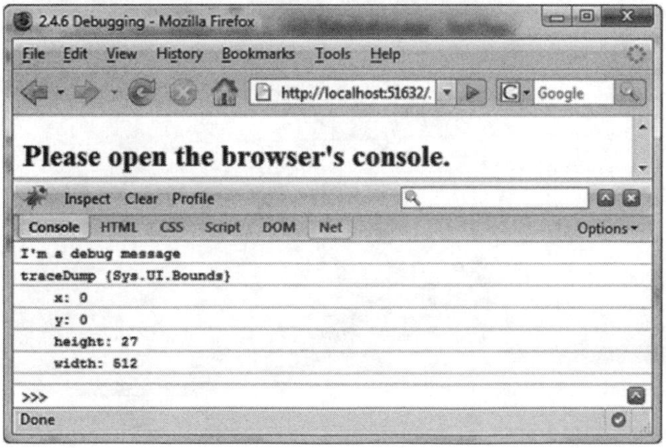

**Figure 2.9
Debug messages logged to the
Firebug console in Firefox**

For example, a response that never arrives may suggest that you have problems related to server availability or to network latency. On the other hand, receiving a response with a status code of 500 indicates that something went wrong on the server. In chapter 5, we'll develop techniques for detecting errors during HTTP transactions; but in some cases you need to inspect the headers or the payload of a request or a response.

HTTP debugging is provided by some of the tools recently available to Ajax developers. Fiddler, Firebug for Firefox, and Web Development Helper for Internet Explorer offer this kind of functionality. Figure 2.10 shows a request traced using the Fiddler tool.

Web Development Helper was developed by a member of the ASP.NET team and provides specific functionality for inspecting the content of a response sent during partial rendering. You'll see this tool in action in chapter 7, where we'll go under the hood of the `UpdatePanel` control and the partial rendering mechanism.

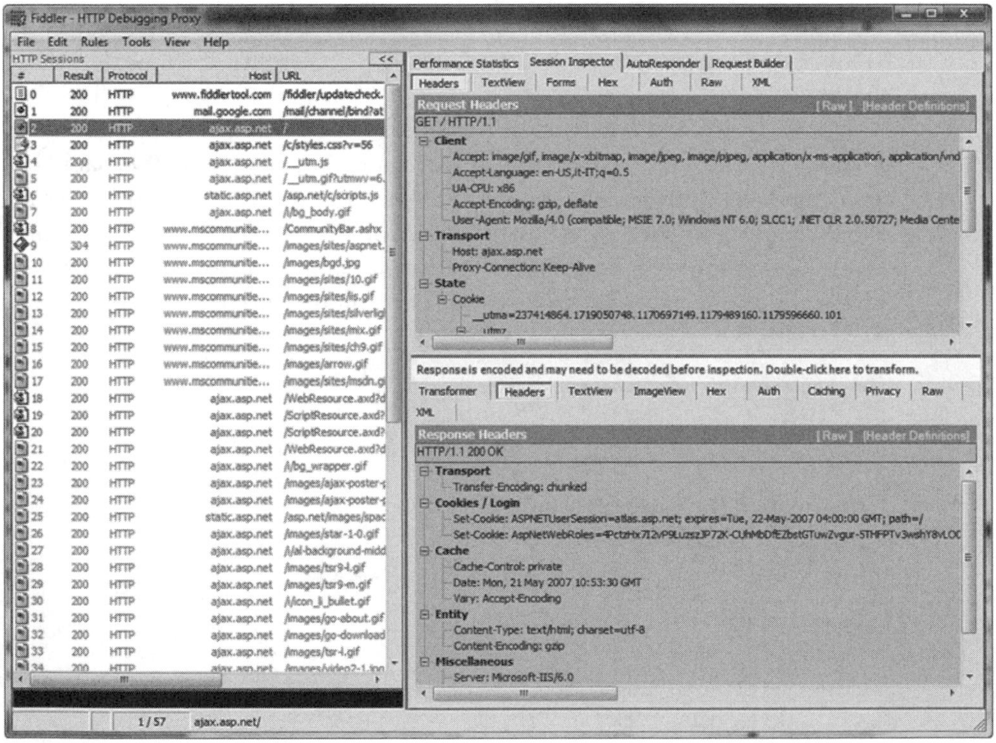

Figure 2.10 Fiddler is a free tool that lets you debug HTTP traffic.

Appendix B contains walkthroughs for configuring these tools and getting them up and running in a few minutes.

We'll end our discussion of debugging by returning to code. If debuggers do their best to help developers spot errors, we should ask what we can do—as programmers—to make debugging code easier. A good practice is to always raise meaningful and well-documented errors, as we'll explain in the next section.

2.4.7 *Typed errors*

In the .NET framework, you can raise either built-in or custom errors by leveraging the Exception class. For example, if you try to access an element beyond the bounds of an array, an exception of type IndexOutOfBoundsException is thrown at runtime. The purpose of this and the other typed exceptions is to carry information about the errors that occur at runtime.

To work with and detect exceptions, a programming language usually provides a special construct. For example, C# and VB.NET let you wrap a portion of code in a try-catch block. The catch block detects exceptions that are raised in the code encapsulated in the try block.

On the client side, JavaScript supports the try-catch construct and uses the built-in Error object as the base type to provide information about errors that occur at runtime. The Microsoft Ajax Library extends the Error object to make it possible to create typed exceptions on the client side. For example, to signal that a function lacks an implementation, you do the following:

```
function doSomething() {
    throw Error.notImplemented();
}
```

The notImplemented method throws a *client exception* that you can detect using a try-catch block. In general, an error can be raised anywhere in the code using the JavaScript throw keyword. To catch the error, you have to wrap the call to doSomething with a try-catch block:

```
function pageLoad() {
    try {
        doSomething();
    }
    catch(e) {
        alert(e.message);

        Sys.Debug.traceDump(e);    ⊲── Dump error object
    }                                  to console
}
```

Every Error object captured in a catch block has a message property that indicates the nature of the error. Figure 2.11 shows the exception message displayed with a call to the alert function. If you run the previous example with the browser's console opened, you can also see a dump of the Error object captured in the catch block. Interestingly, the Error object also has a stack property that returns a string with the stack trace.

Note that, in the message box in figure 2.11, the error raised by calling Error.notImplemented() is reported as an exception of type Sys.NotImplementedException. The information about the exception type is stored as a string in the name property of the Error object. As a consequence, you can use the string returned by the name property to identify a particular exception in a catch block, as in the following code:

```
try {
    doSomething();
}
catch(e) {
    if(e.name == "Sys.NotImplementedException") {
        // Handle this particular exception.
    }
}
```

NOTE   To browse the list of exception types defined by the Microsoft Ajax Library, consult the official documentation topic at http://ajax.asp.net/docs/ClientReference/Global/JavascriptTypeExtensions/ErrorTypeExt/default.aspx.

You can create custom exception types using the Error.create method. This method accepts two arguments: a string with the name of the exception type that the custom error represents, and a custom object whose properties are added to the Error object returned by Error.create. As a general rule, the custom object should contain at least a name property with the name of the exception type. Listing 2.9 shows an example of a custom error type created with the Microsoft Ajax Library.

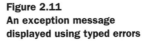

Figure 2.11
An exception message
displayed using typed errors

Listing 2.9 A custom error type created with the `Error.create` method

```
<script type="text/javascript">
<!--
    Error.myCustomError = Error.create('This is my custom exception
        message.',
      {
        name : 'Sys.MyCustomException',
        additionalInfo : 'Additional information about the error.'
      }
    );
```
> Custom properties attached to error object

```
    function pageLoad() {
        try {
            throw Error.myCustomError;
        }
        catch(e) {
            Sys.Debug.traceDump(e);
```
> Dump error object to console

```
            alert(e.name + '\r\n' + e.message +
                '\r\n' + e.additionalInfo);
```
> Format error info

```
        }
    }
//-->
</script>
```

This listing defines a `Sys.MyCustomError` exception by using the `Error.create` method. The first argument passed to the method is the exception message. The second argument is an object with two properties: `name` and `additionalInfo`. The `name` property always contains a string with the exception type. The `additionalInfo` property is a custom property that should contain additional information about the error. If you need to add more properties, you can do so by expanding the object passed to the `Error.create` method.

The method returns a new function that you store in the `Error.myCustomException` property. This function raises the client exception. You call it in the `pageLoad` function, in the `try` block. In the `catch` block, you access the Error object and display the exception message in a message box onscreen. You dump the contents of the Error object in the browser's console. Note that you're able to access the `additionalInfo` property supplied in the custom object.

2.5 *Summary*

The Microsoft Ajax Library isn't just a library for performing Ajax requests. Instead, it provides a full featured framework for easily writing complex JavaScript applications. In this chapter, we have given a high-level overview of the library's features and explained the Application model, together with the concepts of client components and client page lifecycle.

One of the goals of the Microsoft Ajax Library is to make possible writing code that runs without incompatibilities in all the supported browsers. We have explored the compatibility layer, which is implemented with an abstraction API that turns library calls into browser-specific calls. The abstraction API takes into account DOM event handling, CSS, and positioning. Furthermore, the Microsoft Ajax Library allows you to easily create callbacks and client delegates in order to handle DOM events.

The Microsoft Ajax Library extends the built-in JavaScript objects to make them more similar to their .NET counterparts. The String object now offers formatting capabilities, and arrays can be easily manipulated. Furthermore, the Date and Number objects are enhanced to support globalization and localization. The library also provides a set of objects to perform common tasks in JavaScript applications, from fast string concatenations to browser detection and support for debugging.

In the next chapter, you will see how the Microsoft Ajax Library makes it easier to program in JavaScript using object-oriented constructs such as classes, interfaces, and enumerations.

JavaScript for Ajax developers

Established in 1995 and initially integrated into the Netscape Navigator browser, JavaScript was capable of validating web-page user input without refreshing. Microsoft later packaged its own version, JScript, in Internet Explorer 3.0. In the following years, the language evolved, and developers began using it in conjunction with the Document Object Model (DOM) for Dynamic HTML pages. In 1998, the language was standardized as ECMAScript to facilitate the release of different versions.

Some JavaScript characteristics (weak typing, prototyping, the use of first-class functions), although typical for functional languages, may scare a programmer who works mostly with an object-oriented language like Java or C#. On the other hand, JavaScript has been used effectively to write complex and extraordinary client controls. You'll soon discover why JavaScript is now the language of choice among Ajax developers.

This chapter will explain how the Microsoft Ajax Library enhances JavaScript's object-oriented model. In the first section, we'll review some of the language's most important concepts, focusing on objects and functions. After an overview of the JSON data format, we'll study Microsoft Ajax Library's enhanced type system. By the end of the chapter, you'll be able to write object-oriented code using JavaScript, perform reflection, and expose events on client objects.

3.1　Working with objects

JavaScript is a true object-oriented language. The notion of an *object* in JavaScript is different from that in object-oriented languages such as C# and VB.NET. Objects in JavaScript aren't instances of classes, because JavaScript doesn't support the notion of a *class*. Instead, you obtain the structure—or template—of an object by manipulating a special, native object called the *prototype*, which you'll encounter in section 3.1.5.

A JavaScript object is nothing more than a collection of name and value pairs called *properties*. Usually, this kind of structure is also called a *dictionary* or an *associative array*. JavaScript provides also an *array* data type, which is a collection of values of different types. A major role in the language is played by *functions*, which are objects like dictionaries or arrays. Functions are probably the most powerful objects provided by JavaScript; they're responsible for its great power and flexibility. In the following sections, we'll do an overview of objects, arrays, and functions, which are the foundations of the JavaScript language.

3.1.1 Objects

To create a generic object, you can take two different approaches. First, you can use the new operator in conjunction with the Object type, as in the following code:

```
var book = new Object();
```

As you'll discover in section 3.1.4, the new operator is useful when you want to create custom objects using a function as a constructor. In the previous statement, the new operator is syntactic sugar, because an object is usually created with an object literal, like so:

```
var book = {};
```

The object literal {} represents a sort of *empty* object. We'll discuss the various JavaScript literals in detail in section 3.1.7. Once you've created an object, you can take advantage of an important characteristic of the language: You can expand objects at any time by adding new properties to them. This is different from what happens in class-based languages such as C# and VB.NET, where the structure of an object is specified in a class and instances can't be modified at runtime.

To add a property to an object, you need to access it and assign a value. You can do this anywhere in the code, at any time. If the property doesn't exist, it's automatically created at runtime. The following code shows how to add a property called title to the book object you created before:

```
book.title = 'ASP.NET AJAX In Action';
```

As we said previously, objects in JavaScript are collections of name and value pairs. To demonstrate, you can add a property to an object using an indexed notation, as if you were accessing a collection such as an array or a hash table. The following is another way to add a title property to the book object:

```
book['title'] = 'ASP.NET AJAX In Action';
```

You can loop over an object's properties by using the for-in construct. This construct is similar to the foreach construct of C#. For example, the following code displays the name and values of the properties of the book object:

```
for(var property in book) {
    alert('Name: ' + property + ', Value: ' + book[property]);
}
```

In this code snippet, the property variable holds, at each iteration, a string with the name of a property of the object. As result, book[property] returns the value of that property. The name and value of each property are displayed using the JavaScript's alert function, which displays a string in a message box on screen.

Values assigned to properties, such as strings, numbers, or Boolean values, expose properties and methods that can be accessed at runtime. For example, the value of the `title` property of the book object is of type String. It exposes methods such as `toUpperCase`, which converts a string to uppercase:

```
var stringToUpper = book.title.toUpperCase();
alert(stringToUpper);
```

Similar properties are exposed by the built-in Number and Boolean types, which represent numbers and Boolean values, respectively.

Next, we'll examine one of the most used data structures: arrays.

> **NOTE** You can find a quick reference to the JavaScript data types and their properties and methods at http://www.w3schools.com/jsref/default.asp.

3.1.2 Arrays

Another fundamental and widely used data type is the array. In JavaScript, an *array* is an ordered collection of values that can be of different types. You access values by specifying their position in the array using classic indexed notation. As with objects, you can create an array using two different approaches. The first is to use the new operator in conjunction with the Array type:

```
var arr = new Array();
```

However, arrays are usually created with an array literal. The array literal `[]` represents an empty array, as in the following code:

```
var arr = [];
```

To add elements to an array, you can use indexed notation, just as you do to add properties to JavaScript objects:

```
arr[0] = 'AJAX';
arr[1] = 3;
arr[2] = false;

var firstElement = arr[0];    ⟵ ⌐ Access first
alert(firstElement);              element of array
```

Playing with JavaScript arrays is like playing with arrays in the .NET framework. But JavaScript arrays are more similar to generic lists in .NET 2.0: You can add new elements to an array at any time. An array can also hold elements of different types, such as strings, numbers, Boolean values, objects, and child arrays.

> **NOTE** JavaScript arrays are sparse. That is, no space is allocated for unused elements.

Now, let's discuss what's probably the most powerful object that JavaScript provides: the *function*. The ability to manipulate functions as objects lets you create custom objects and simulate object-oriented constructs like classes, interfaces, and enumerations.

3.1.3 *Functions*

When a language treats functions as objects, it's said to support *first-class* functions. This means functions can be instantiated, returned by other functions, stored as elements of arrays, assigned to variables, and so on. A function represents a portion of executable code and, at first look, seems similar to a method of an object in a classic object-oriented language such as Java, C#, or VB.NET.

As an example, here's the code for a function called add that returns the sum of its arguments:

```
function add(a, b) {
    return a + b;
}
```

Because JavaScript is a loosely typed language, you don't need to specify the type of the arguments or the type of the returned value (if any). All the information about types is inferred at runtime. As a consequence, if the arguments a and b passed to the add function are numbers, the returned value is their sum. If, on the other hand, a and b are strings, the result is the concatenation of the two strings. If the arguments are of different types, strange things may happen, and an error may be raised at runtime. In chapter 13, we'll discuss a technique called *parameter validation*, which the Microsoft Ajax Library uses to check that the arguments passed to a function are of the expected types.

First-class functions can be assigned to an object's properties. The following code creates a calculator object and then assigns two functions to the object's add and multiply properties:

```
var calculator = {};

calculator.add = function(a, b) {
    return a + b;
}

calculator.multiply = function(a, b) {
    return a * b;
}
```

As shown in this example, you can declare a function without specifying a name. A function with no name is called an *anonymous function*. Interestingly, assigning an anonymous function to a property lets you invoke it through the property itself:

```
var sum = calculator.add(3, 5);          sum holds 8    product holds 15
var product = calculator.multiply(3, 5);
```

Note that this code treats the add and multiply properties as if they were the names of the functions they hold. Accessing a property that holds a function is similar to invoking a method of an object. For this reason, a JavaScript function stored in a property of an object is called a *method.*

Let's continue our discussion of JavaScript functions by introducing two important topics. The first concerns the *scope* of a function: the context that you can access inside it. The second is another powerful characteristic of functions: the ability to bind them to an environment.

The scope of a function

In JavaScript, every function is executed as a method of an object. But which object? A quick answer is, the object pointed to by the this keyword in the body of the function. This doesn't seem strange; but life isn't that easy. The original question is somehow still unanswered. Which object is referenced by this in a function?

Without going into too much detail, let's determine which object is pointed to by this in the three cases you'll encounter most often when programming in JavaScript:

- A simple JavaScript function declared in the page is called a *global function.* In the body of a global function, the this keyword references the *global object.* In the HTML Document Object Model (DOM), the window property of the global object is the global object itself. In a global function, this points to the window object.

- A function that handles a DOM event is called a *DOM event handler.* In the body of an event handler, the this keyword references the DOM element that hooked up the event. If you subscribe to the click event of a button element, for example, the object pointed to by this in the event handler is the button element. Again, if you have a div element with an event handler for the click event, and a span element inside of that, clicking the span will make the click event bubble up. Even though the span really triggered the event, this points to the div element to which the event handler was attached.

- A function used in conjunction with the new operator is called a *constructor*. In JavaScript, constructors are one of the preferred approaches to creating custom objects, as we'll discuss in section 3.1.4. In the body of a constructor, the this keyword references the newly created instance. If the newly created instance defines methods, the this keyword inside the methods points to the instance itself.

Knowing which object is referenced by this in a function is fundamental in order to determine which variables, objects, and properties you can access in the body of the function. In chapter 2, we discussed client delegates, which make it possible to change the object referenced by this in a function. To make things even more interesting, JavaScript functions can be *nested* and even *bound* to a scope.

Closures

One of the characteristics of JavaScript functions is that they can be nested. This means you can declare a function *in* another function. Consider the following code:

```
function parent(arg) {
    var testVariable = "I am a test variable.";


    function child() {
        alert(arg + testVariable);      A child
    }                                   function

                         Call child
    child();      ⟵——|  function
}
```

This code defines a function called parent, which declares a local variable called testVariable. In the parent function, you declare the child function. The child function can access, in its body, the testVariable and arg variables that are defined outside its body. The last statement of the parent function invokes the child function, which should display the values of the variables in a message box on screen. This is what happens if you invoke the parent function this way:

```
parent("Yes, ");
```

Calling the parent function this way produces the results shown in figure 3.1.

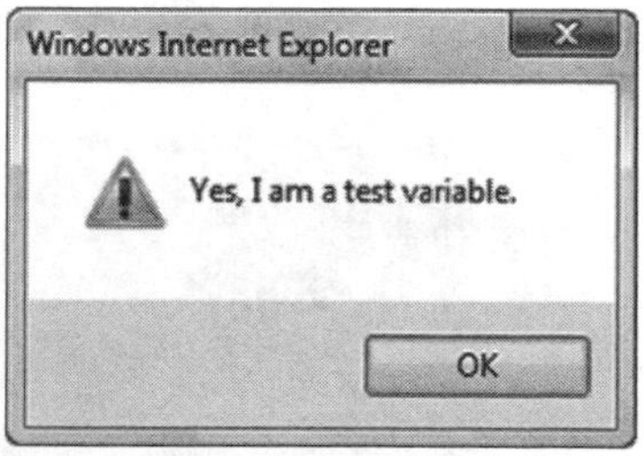

Figure 3.1 Calling a parent function that invokes a child function

What's happening here? JavaScript functions are always bound to a scope, or an *environment*. As a consequence, child functions can access the scope of the parent function, including its local variables and the parameters passed to it. But the real, powerful thing is that if you make the parent function return its child function, the local variables continue to "live" outside the parent function. To demonstrate the power of such a feature, let's rewrite the parent function as shown in listing 3.1.

Listing 3.1   Creating a closure by returning an inner function

```
function parent(arg) {
    var testVariable = "I am a test variable.";

    function child() {                          A child
        alert(arg + testVariable);              function
    }
                                 Return child
    return child;      ⟵──┘      function
}
```

This time, instead of invoking the `child` function, the `parent` function returns it. The curious thing is that even when the `parent` function has returned, its local variables continue to exist and can be accessed in the `child` function. To verify this, you have to call the `parent` function and then invoke the returned `child` function:

```
var child = parent("Yes ");

child();
```

Surprisingly, a child function can access the variables of the parent function even if they were declared as local variables. The scope of the child function remains bound to the local variables of its outer function. Whenever this happens, you can proudly say that you've created a *closure*.

Currying

In listing 3.1, the child function displays a message on screen using two parameters defined in the scope of the parent function: arg and testVariable. Nonetheless, you can call the child function without supplying any parameters to it: You have transformed a function that takes multiple parameters into a function that takes fewer (zero in this case) parameters. This technique is known as currying.

Understanding closures and dealing with them can be difficult at first, because the most used object-oriented languages don't support them. But closures have interesting applications; for example, the `Function.createDelegate` method illustrated in chapter 2 in section 2.3.4 is an application of closures. If you program in .NET using C# 2.0, then you may have heard of *anonymous methods*, which can't be called closures but that implement a similar technique.

NOTE   If you want to know more about C# anonymous methods, browse to http://msdn2.microsoft.com/en-us/library/0yw3tz5k.aspx.

So far, we've demonstrated that JavaScript functions are powerful objects, but you can do much more. For example, you can use functions to create custom objects, as you'll see in the next section.

3.1.4 *Creating custom objects*

In section 3.1, you saw how JavaScript objects can be created as dictionaries with name and value pairs. Each pair represents a property of the object and the value of the property. This approach may be less comfortable for developers acquainted with the mechanisms of class-based object-oriented languages. In such languages, you typically specify the structure of an object in a class, and then you create instances of the class using the new operator. If you want to use a similar approach in JavaScript, it's possible to define a function and use it in conjunction with the new operator to create custom objects. In this case, the function is called the *constructor,* and it's used to define the properties of the new object. Following this approach, listing 3.2 shows how to declare the constructor for a Cat object.

Listing 3.2   The constructor for a Cat object

```
function Cat() {
    this._name = '';
    this._age = 0;
}
```

A JavaScript function acts as a constructor when you use it together with the new operator. The following statement creates a new object using the Cat function as the constructor:

```
var cat = new Cat();
```

The new operator creates a new object and invokes the constructor. In the body of the constructor, this points to the newly created object. For this reason, accessing the properties of the this parameter in the Cat function is equivalent to adding properties to the new object. The use of the new operator causes the constructor to implicitly return the newly created object. As result, the cat variable in the previous statement holds an object with two properties: _name and _age.

A convention for private properties

Often, some properties of an object are prefixed with an underscore—as is the case with _name and _age—to suggest that they should be considered private. However, this remains a naming convention only because properties of objects can't have a private scope. Despite what happens in Java or C#, where you can use the private modifier to prevent external objects from accessing a member of a class, in JavaScript the properties of an object are always publicly accessible. By using closures, you can treat local variables defined in a function as private members. But the convention offers a number of advantages, including the ability to inspect members from a debugger.

Every JavaScript object has a property called prototype that returns a reference to an internal object called *the prototype*. The prototype object plays a major role in JavaScript because it's used to define the template of an object and to implement inheritance.

3.1.5 *The prototype object*

In a JavaScript object, the purpose of the prototype object is to hold all the properties that will be inherited by all the instances. The prototype object defines the structure of an object, in a manner similar to what is done with classes in many object-oriented languages. In the previous section, you saw how a function—the constructor—can be used to create custom objects and to add properties to the instances. Listing 3.3 shows how you can use the constructor's prototype object to add additional properties and methods to instances.

Listing 3.3 Expanding the prototype object to define an object's initial structure

```
function Cat() {
    this._name;
    this._age;
}
Cat.prototype.speak = function() {
    alert("Meeeeooow!");
}
```

In listing 3.3, you access the prototype of the `Cat` function and add a `speak` method. The `speak` method calls the `alert` function to display a string with the voice of a (hungry) cat. What are the consequences of adding a method to the prototype object of the constructor? First, whenever you create an object with the `new` operator and the `Cat` constructor, the new instance inherits the `speak` method, as shown in the following code:

```
var cat = new Cat();
cat.speak();
```

Second, all references to objects and arrays added to the prototype object are *shared* between all the instances.

> **TIP**   Never store objects or arrays in the prototype object, unless you want to share them across all instances. Instead, store references to objects or arrays in the constructor. This way, each instance has its own copy of the object.

Adding methods to the prototype object is safe, because you're sharing the same function objects between different instances. This can yield some advantages in terms of memory used to store multiple instances, because you're sharing the same function objects. But accessing functions in the prototype is slightly slower than accessing them in the constructor, because they're searched first in the current instance and then in the prototype. A common approach is to declare members in the constructor and methods in the prototype object; this is the approach we'll follow in this book.

Now that we've introduced the prototype object, we'll examine object extensibility. In the next section, we'll recap the most common ways of adding properties to JavaScript objects.

3.1.6   *Extending a JavaScript type*

In the previous sections, we explained how to add properties to objects. JavaScript's dynamic features let you add a property to an object at any time by accessing a nonexistent property and assigning it a value, as shown in the following code:

```
var book = {};
book.title = 'ASP.NET AJAX in Action';
book.publisher = 'Manning';
```

In addition, you can extend instances of the built-in types by adding new properties to them. For example, you could expand an object of type `String` as follows:

```
var str = new String();
str.createdOn = new Date();
```

In this code, treating the String type as a constructor returns an object of type String. You add a createdOn property that returns a Date object containing the date when the string was created.

A second way to add a property to an object is to do so before an instance is created. You can do this using a constructor and its prototype object, as we explained in sections 3.1.4 and 3.1.5. For example, the following code shows how to define an object with two properties x and y, using a Point constructor:

```
function Point() {
    this.x = 0;
    this.y = 0;
}
Point.prototype.setLocation = function(x, y) {
        this.x = x;
        this.y = y;
}
```

By using the Point constructor in conjunction with the new operator, you get back an object with the properties and methods defined in the constructor and in the prototype object:

```
var p = new Point();
p.setLocation(3, 6);
```

Usually, properties of objects are accessed through instances. Sometimes, though, it's desirable to access methods through the type rather than through an instance, as you do with *static* or *shared* methods in C# and VB.NET. Creating static methods in JavaScript is easy because you add a property to the type or the constructor, as in the following example:

```
Date.now = function() {
    return new Date();
}
```

Here, you extend the built-in Date object with a now method that you can use to retrieve the current date and time. The now method is invoked directly on the Date type rather than on an instance:

```
var dateTime = Date.now();
```

You encountered static JavaScript methods when we talked about the extended Array object in chapter 2. Now, we'll introduce literals, which are notations for representing values. In JavaScript, you can use literals to represent nearly every data type, including objects, arrays, and functions. Having a good knowledge of JavaScript literals will enable you to write compact, elegant, fast code.

3.1.7 *Literals*

In programming languages, a *literal* is a notation for representing a value. For example, "Hello, World!" represents a *string literal* in many languages, including JavaScript. Other examples of JavaScript literals are 5, true, false, and null, which represent an integer, the two Boolean values, and the absence of an object, respectively. JavaScript also supports literals for objects and arrays and lets you create them using a compact and readable notation. Consider the following statements which create an object with two properties called firstName and lastName:

```
var customer = new Object();
customer.firstName = 'John';
customer.lastName = 'Doe';
```

An equivalent way of creating a similar object is

```
var customer = { firstName: 'John', lastName: 'Doe' };
```

The right part of the assignment is an *object literal.* An object literal is a comma-separated list of name and value pairs enclosed in curly braces. Each pair represents a property of the object, and the two parts are separated by a colon. To create an array, you can create an instance of the Array object:

```
var somePrimes = new Array();
somePrimes.push(1, 2, 3, 5, 7);
```

But the preferred approach is to use an *array literal,* which is a comma-separated list of values enclosed in square braces:

```
var somePrimes = [ 1, 2, 3, 5, 7 ];
```

The previous examples demonstrate that object and array literals can contain other literals. Here is a more complex example:

```
var team = {
   name:'',
   members:[],
   count:function() { return members.length }
}
```

The object assigned to the team variable has three properties: name, members, and count. Note that '' represents the empty string, and [] is an empty array. Even the value of the count property is a literal—a *function literal:*

```
function() { return members.length }
```

A function literal is constructed with the function keyword followed by an optional name and the list of arguments. Then comes the body of the function, enclosed in curly braces.

Having covered literals, we can now introduce JavaScript Object Notation (JSON), a notation that's used to describe objects and arrays and that consists of a subset of JavaScript literals. JSON is becoming popular among Ajax developers because it can be used as a format for exchanging data, often in place of XML.

3.2 *Working with JSON*

JSON is a textual data-interchange format. Its purpose is to offer a representation of structured data that is independent of the language or platform used. This makes it possible to interchange data between applications written in different languages and run the applications on different machines. Compared to XML, which is probably the best-known data-interchange format, JSON has a compact syntax. This means that often, less bandwidth is required to transmit JSON data through a network.

JSON is based on a subset of the JavaScript language. As a consequence, encoding and parsing are nearly immediate. Because the majority of Ajax developers are also JavaScript developers, there's almost no learning curve.

3.2.1 *JSON structures*

JSON is built on two structures: a collection of name and value pairs, called an *object*; and an ordered list of *values*, called an *array*. In JSON, a *value* can be one of the following:

- An object
- An array
- A number
- A string
- `true`
- `false`
- `null`

An object is represented by a JavaScript object literal, and an array is represented by a JavaScript array literal. The remaining values are represented by the corresponding literals.

Because JSON is a *subset* of JavaScript literals, there are some restrictions on the syntax. In a JSON object, the name part of a name/value pair must be a string, and the value part must be one of the supported values. The following is the JSON representation of an object with two properties:

```
{ "firstName":"John", "lastName":"Doe" }
```

The names of the properties (firstName and lastName) must be strings and must be enclosed in double quotes. Compare the previous code with the following, which represents a similar object:

```
{ firstName: "John", lastName: "Doe" }
```

In JavaScript, both the objects have the same structure. However, the second object isn't a valid JSON representation, because the names of the properties aren't enclosed in double quotes.

Restrictions also apply to JSON arrays, where elements must be supported values. For example, a Date object isn't in the list of supported values and therefore can't be an element of a JSON array or a property of a JSON object. A String has the same representation as a JavaScript string literal, except that strings must always be enclosed in double quotes. Numbers are similar to JavaScript number literals, but octal and hexadecimal formats aren't supported. Here is an example of a JSON array:

```
[1, 2, 3, 5, 7]
```

The Boolean values true and false, as well as null, have the same representation as the corresponding JavaScript literals.

NOTE Methods can't be represented using JSON, because function literals aren't part of its syntax. Furthermore, the JavaScript new operator isn't part of the JSON syntax and can't be used in objects or arrays.

One of the advantages of JSON is that it's easy to parse. Many JSON parsers, written for numerous languages, have been developed to automate the process of generating and parsing JSON. (A list is available at the official JSON site, http://json.org.) In JavaScript, the parsing process is immediate: All you have to do is pass the JSON string to the JavaScript eval function. If you have a jsonString variable that contains the JSON data, the following code parses it and returns the corresponding JavaScript object:

```
var parsedJson = eval('(' + jsonString + ')');
```

Note that you should enclose the JSON data in parentheses before calling eval. By doing this, you force eval to consider the argument an expression, and an object literal {} won't be interpreted as a code block. But the eval function can execute arbitrary code, which can lead to security issues if the data come from an untrusted source. For this reason, it's always recommended that you validate the JSON data before calling the eval function.

NOTE The official JSON site, http://json.org, provides a regular expression for validating JSON data. You can find it in the JavaScript implementation downloadable from the website.

The Microsoft Ajax Library has its own JavaScriptSerializer object, contained in the `Sys.Serialization` namespace, which is responsible for encoding and decoding JSON data. Let's see how it works.

3.2.2 *JSON and the Microsoft Ajax Library*

The Microsoft Ajax Library provides the Sys.Serialization.JavaScriptSerializer object in order to encode and decode JSON. This object exposes two methods called `serialize` and `deserialize`. The `serialize` method accepts a JavaScript object as an argument and returns a string with the corresponding JSON representation:

```
var customer = {firstName: 'John', lastName: 'Doe'};
var serializer = Sys.Serialization.JavaScriptSerializer;
var json = serializer.serialize(customer);
```

The `json` variable in this code holds a string with the JSON representation of the object stored in the `customer` variable. The `deserialize` method performs the inverse job. It takes a JSON string and returns the corresponding JavaScript object:

```
var customer = serializer.deserialize(json);
```

When you're dealing with a JSON parser, be aware of how dates are represented. JavaScript doesn't support a date literal. And expressions like `new Date()` can't be embedded in a JSON object because the `new` keyword isn't part of the protocol syntax. As a consequence, parsers need to establish a convention about how dates and times are represented.

You can represent a date by using a string or a number. For example, you could use the ISO 8601 format for date strings and the UTC format to represent a date as a number. In the UTC format, you specify the number of milliseconds elapsed from midnight January 1, 1970 (UTC). In some situations, however, these conventions aren't enough to disambiguate between a date representation and a simple string or number. For example, how can you tell if 1169125740 should be interpreted as a simple number or as the representation of the date January 18, 2007, 13:09:00 AM?

The JavaScriptSerializer object provides a different, custom mechanism for parsing dates, which are represented using a string similar to the following:

```
\/Date(1169125740)\/
```

In this string, the number is the number of milliseconds since UTC. The `\/` characters at the beginning and the end of the string are two escaped forward-slashes. Because JSON supports the backslash (`\`) as the escape character, the string is equivalent to `/Date(62831853854)/`. However, when the JavaScriptSerializer object detects the escape backslash, it recognizes the string as a date representation and instantiates the corresponding Date object. If you wrote the same string without the backslashes, it would be interpreted as a simple string instead of a date. This makes JSON strings fully compatible with the specification and with any deserializer, while allowing you to reliably pass dates with serializers that know this convention.

You'll encounter JSON again in chapter 5, which is dedicated to the communication layer of the Microsoft Ajax Library. Now, it's time to discuss the use of object-oriented constructs like classes, interfaces, and enumerations in JavaScript. In the following sections, we'll explain how the Microsoft Ajax Library leverages the object model provided by JavaScript. The goal is to make it easy and straightforward to write object-oriented client code.

3.3   *Classes in JavaScript*

The Microsoft Ajax Library leverages the JavaScript type system to simulate object-oriented constructs not currently supported by JavaScript. Such constructs include classes, properties, interfaces, and enumerations. The idea is to use the dynamic capabilities of the language to extend the Function object and store additional information related to a particular type. Adding information to a function object makes it possible to treat constructors as classes and, as you'll see later, to easily implement interfaces and inheritance. This enhanced type system offers the possibility to perform *reflection* on client types.

3.3.1   *Client classes*

In this section, we'll discuss how the Microsoft Ajax Library upgrades a JavaScript constructor to a client class. Throughout the book, we'll use the term *client class* to refer to a class created in JavaScript with the Microsoft Ajax Library. From a developer's point of view, the process is straightforward: All you have to do is add a single statement after the declaration of the constructor. Listing 3.4 illustrates this concept by showing how to create a Pet class starting from a Pet constructor.

> **Listing 3.4   A `Pet` class defined with the Microsoft Ajax Library**

```
function Pet() {
    this._name;
    this._age;
}
Pet.prototype = {
    speak : function() {
        throw Error.notImplemented();
    }
}
Pet.registerClass('Pet');
```

90 | **CHAPTER 3**
JavaScript for Ajax developers

The last statement in listing 3.4 contains a call to the `registerClass` method. As we'll discuss shortly, this method is responsible for setting up the constructor to make it behave as a class.

To recap, defining a client class is a three-step process:

1 Declare the constructor, which declares the fields of the class.

2 Fill the prototype object, which defines methods of the class.

3 Add a call to `registerClass`, which upgrades the constructor to a client class.

The `registerClass` method alone has the power to transform a simple JavaScript function into a client class. For this reason, it deserves some more attention.

3.3.2 The registerClass method

As shown in listing 3.4, the call to `registerClass` is the only thing you have to add to a classic JavaScript function to make the Microsoft Ajax Library recognize it as a class. This method accomplishes three important tasks:

- Registers the type name in the constructor
- Lets you specify a base class and takes care of automatically resolving the inheritance relationship
- Accepts one or multiple interface types that the client class will implement

You store the type name in the constructor so you can access this information at runtime. As you'll see in a moment, you usually declare classes by assigning an anonymous function to a *namespaced* variable. By doing so, there's no way to programmatically know the name of the variable and thus know the fully qualified type name. This is why you need to *register* the type name by storing it as a string in the constructor.

Figure 3.2 shows how the `Sys._Application` class—whose single instance is the Application object—is registered in the MicrosoftAJAX.debug.js file.

Figure 3.2 How the `Sys._Application` class is registered using the `registerClass` method. The class-registration process also lets you specify a parent class and the interfaces implemented by the class.

The figure shows the complete syntax for the registerClass method, which is called as a static method of the function you'll register as a class. Because the class can belong to a client namespace, you must pass a string with the *fully qualified name* of the class. This is the name of the class prefixed by the name of the containing namespace. In figure 3.2, Sys is the namespace that contains the _Application class. We'll discuss client namespaces in section 3.3.4.

The second argument is a reference to the base class. In the Microsoft Ajax Library, a client class can have a single parent class. The advantage of specifying a base class in the call to registerClass is that you avoid writing the code needed to resolve the inheritance relationship. Instead, the library takes care of configuring instances of child classes automatically on your behalf.

The subsequent arguments specify the list of interfaces implemented by the class. In figure 3.2, the _Application class implements a single interface called Sys.IContainer. In general, a client class can implement multiple interfaces.

How does it work?

Because calls to registerClass are contained outside of any functions, they're executed by the client runtime when the code is parsed. As part of the registration process, various pieces of information are stored in the constructor. In debug mode, checks are performed to ensure that you're providing valid references to the base class and the interface types, and that you aren't registering the same class twice. Finally, the new type is tracked by adding it to an internal collection stored in the Sys object. This completes the registration process for a client class.

Once you create a class, you can take advantage of the other object-oriented constructs provided by the Microsoft Ajax Library. For example, you can expose the values of private fields through client properties.

3.3.3 *Properties*

In this section, we'll explain how to expose properties in JavaScript objects. In this case, the term *property* doesn't refer to the properties of objects, as discussed in previous sections. Instead, we'll talk about methods that let you read and write the values of class fields. In object-oriented languages, it's a good practice to expose the values of private members through methods that enable you to read or write them. A method used to read a value is called an *accessor*, and a method used to write a value is called *mutator*. A class can selectively expose the values of its members and prevent an external object from directly accessing them. Also, by using accessors and mutators, code can perform additional logic before returning or storing a value.

NOTE   In languages such as C# and VB.NET, this mechanism is available as a built-in construct called a *property*. A property is usually made with a *getter* (the block of logic used to read a value) and a *setter* (the block of logic used to write a value), but you can also have read-only and write-only properties.

In JavaScript, it's not possible to define a private scope for an object's fields. It may seem useless to rely on methods for reading and writing their values. But you can still use methods to perform additional logic, such as validation. The Microsoft Ajax Library defines a naming convention for declaring properties of a client class:

- A *getter* is a method whose name is prefixed by get_, as in get_name.
- A *setter* is a method whose name is prefixed by set_, as in set_name.

Following this convention, get_name and set_name are the methods used for reading and writing the value of the _name member.

TIP   The Microsoft Ajax Library relies on properties to perform many tasks such as configuring components and parsing XML Script code. We'll talk about the client component model in chapter 8 and about the XML Script declarative language in chapter 11. We recommend that you always use properties to expose the values of class fields.

Listing 3.5 shows how to expose the values of the _name and _age members through two properties called name and age in the Pet class. Note that the setters (set_name and set_age) accept the value to store as an argument. In the set_age method, you also check that the value passed is an integer and ensure that it's always greater than or equal to zero.

Listing 3.5   The Pet class with two properties

```
function Pet() {
    this._name = '';
    this._age = 0;
}
Pet.prototype = {
    speak : function() {
        throw Error.notImplemented();
    },


    get_name : function() {
        return this._name;          Getter
    },
```

```
    set_name : function(value) {
        this._name = value;                    Setter
    },

    get_age : function() {
        return this._age;
    },

    set_age : function(value) {
        if(isNaN(value) || value < 0) {
            throw Error.argument('age');
        }

        this._age = 0;
    }
}
Pet.registerClass('Pet');
```

So far, you know how to create client classes and how to expose client properties. In the .NET framework, namespaces are used as containers of classes in order to minimize name conflicts. JavaScript doesn't support namespaces, but you can simulate them using objects. Let's see how you can create namespaces in JavaScript using the Microsoft Ajax Library.

3.3.4 Namespaces

A *namespace* is a container of classes. Its main purpose is to let you group classes in a logical and functional manner and even create classes with the same name, as long as they're contained in different namespaces. This is useful when you're attempting to avoid function name collisions from multiple script files. For example, an Ajax application may take advantage of multiple Ajax frameworks, and this increases the risk of name collisions. Or an application may need to download script files from different locations on the Internet, each with its own naming conventions; thus, conflicts are more likely to arise. JavaScript doesn't support a namespace construct yet, but you can use objects to define a particular scope. For example, suppose you've defined an empty object named `Samples`. Let's expand the Samples object by adding a method to it:

```
var Samples = {};

Samples.Pet = function() {
    this._name = '';
    this._age = 0;
}
```

This code assigns a constructor to the `Pet` property of the Samples object. The Samples object defines a new scope and can be seen as the containing namespace for the `Pet` constructor. You've assigned the constructor to the *namespaced variable* `Samples.Pet`. By turning the constructor into a client class, the name of the namespaced variable that holds the constructor becomes the fully qualified name of the class.

The Microsoft Ajax Library leverages the same pattern to simulate namespaces. The only difference is that you can take advantage of the `Type.registerNamespace` method to create a namespace automatically:

```
Type.registerNamespace('Samples');
```

To create a child namespace, you have to append its name to the parent namespace. The library takes care of creating the corresponding child object and also the parents, if they don't already exist:

```
Type.registerNamespace('Samples.ChildSpace');
```

NOTE   The Microsoft Ajax Library defines Type as a simple alias for Function.

You create a class in a namespace by assigning the constructor to a namespaced variable and then registering the constructor with the `registerClass` method. This procedure is shown in listing 3.6, in which the `Pet` class is declared in the `Samples` namespace. The namespace registration must always precede the declaration of any child class.

Listing 3.6   Declaring a class in a namespace

```
Type.registerNamespace('Samples');

Samples.Pet = function() {
    // Class fields.
}
Samples.Pet.prototype = {
    // Class methods.
}
Samples.Pet.registerClass('Samples.Pet');
```

With classes, properties, and namespaces, writing object-oriented code in JavaScript is becoming similar to writing code in languages such as C# and VB.NET. Now, we're ready to explore one of the main features of object-oriented languages: inheritance.

3.4 Understanding inheritance

In object-oriented languages such as Java, C#, and VB.NET, inheritance is class-based. This means you can make a child class inherit all its public and protected members from a parent class. In JavaScript, things work differently because you don't have classes. Inheritance is *prototype-based*, because properties and methods are usually inherited from the prototype object. In the following sections, we'll do a quick overview of prototype-based inheritance. Then, we'll explain how you can easily implement inheritance in JavaScript using the Microsoft Ajax Library.

3.4.1 Prototype-based inheritance

In a prototype-based language like JavaScript, objects inherit all the properties defined in the prototype object. Let's return for a moment on the Cat constructor defined in listing 3.3. The Cat constructor is an object of type Function that, following the principle, inherits all the properties defined in the prototype object of the Function object. In turn, Function inherits all the properties defined in the prototype of Object, which is the root type of all the JavaScript objects. The final result is that every object created using the Cat constructor will inherit the properties defined in the Function and Object prototypes, as illustrated in figure 3.3. The mech-

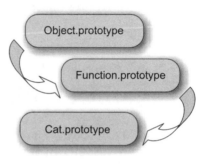

Figure 3.3   Inheritance in JavaScript is prototype-based. An object inherits all the properties defined in the prototype of the parent objects.

anism is similar to that of class-based inheritance; the main difference is that instead of having a chain of classes in parent-child relationship, you have a *prototype chain*.

In JavaScript, implementing inheritance is simple; but it's done differently than in class-based languages, where the parent class can be specified in the class declaration. For example, one approach is to assign the object returned by the parent constructor to the prototype object of the child constructor. Without going into too much detail, the code in listing 3.7 shows how you can define a Cat object that inherits all the properties from a Pet object using prototype-based inheritance.

Listing 3.7   An example of prototype-based inheritance in JavaScript

```
function Pet() {
    this._name;
    this._age;
}
Pet.prototype = {
```

```
    speak : function() {
        throw Error("This method should be
            ➥overridden by derived classes.");
    }
}

function Cat() {
                          Call base class's
    Pet.call(this);   ◁─┘ constructor
}
Cat.prototype = new Pet();   ◁─┐ Inherit properties
                               └ defined in prototype

Cat.prototype.speak = function() {   Override
    return "Meeeeooow!";             speak method
}
```

To create a Cat object that inherits from Pet, you perform three steps:

1 Inherit the properties defined in the Pet constructor by invoking the Pet constructor in the Cat constructor.

2 Inherit the properties defined in the prototype of Pet by assigning a new instance of Pet to the Cat prototype.

3 Override the inherited speak method by declaring a method with the same name in the Cat prototype. Note that this step isn't mandatory: It provides a meaningful implementation of the speak method in the Cat constructor.

You can run the following code to ensure that Cat has effectively inherited all the properties from Pet:

```
var cat = new Cat();
cat.speak();
```

If you use the Microsoft Ajax Library, you have to specify the name of the base class when calling the registerClass method on the child class. Listing 3.8 shows how to define a Cat class that derives from Pet, using the Microsoft Ajax Library.

Listing 3.8   Deriving from a base class with the Microsoft Ajax Library

```
Type.registerNamespace('Samples');

Samples.Cat = function() {
                                         Resolve inheritance and
    Samples.Cat.initializeBase(this);  ◁─┘ call base constructor
}
Samples.Cat.prototype = {
```

```
    speak : function() {                 Override
        alert('Meeeeooow!');             speak method
    }
}
Samples.Cat.registerClass('Samples.Cat', Samples.Pet);
```

The reference to the base class is passed as the second argument to the register-Class method. When you derive from a base class, you must remember to invoke the initializeBase method in the constructor of the child class. The initializeBase method is always called on the child class with the this keyword as an argument. As shown in figure 3.4, the initializeBase method is responsible for walking the inheritance chain until the child class has inherited all the properties from the parent class and its ancestors.

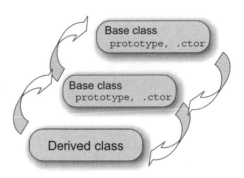

Figure 3.4   In the Microsoft Ajax Library, inheritance is resolved by making a child class inherit all the properties defined in the prototype object and in the constructor of the ancestor classes.

Typically, when dealing with inheritance, you need to perform common tasks such as passing arguments to the base class's constructor and overriding methods inherited by the base class. Let's see how to perform these tasks with the help of the Microsoft Ajax Library.

3.4.2   *Passing arguments to the base class*

To pass arguments to the constructor of the base class, you have to pass them to the initializeBase method. Let's rewrite the constructor of the Pet class to accept the values of the _name and _age members as arguments:

```
Samples.Pet = function(name, age) {
    this._name = name;
    this._age = age;
}
```

If you want to pass these arguments from the Cat class to the base Pet class, you add them to an array and pass it as the second argument to the initializeBase method. This process is illustrated in listing 3.9, where the constructor of the Cat class is rewritten to accept the same arguments as the Pet constructor.

Listing 3.9 How to pass arguments to the constructor of the base class

```
Samples.Cat = function(name, age) {                    Pass name and
                                                        age arguments
    Samples.Cat.initializeBase(this, [name, age]);   ◁─── to base class
}
Samples.Cat.registerClass('Samples.Cat', Samples.Pet);
```

At this point, an instance of the Cat class can be created as follows:

```
var cat = new Cat('Kitty', 1);
```

This statement creates an instance of the Cat class and sets the _name and _age members, inherited from the base Pet class, to Kitty and 1, respectively.

Object-oriented languages let you redefine the implementation of a method inherited from a parent class. When you redefine the implementation of an inherited method, you create an *override*. For example, in listing 3.7, you override, in the Cat class, the speak method inherited from the base class. In this case, invoking the speak method from an instance of the Cat class no longer throws a client exception, because the new function replaces the one inherited from the Pet class. Let's see how you can override a base method and call the base class's implementation using the Microsoft Ajax Library.

3.4.3 Overrides

In JavaScript, you can override a method by assigning a new function to the same property: You replace the previous function with the new one. This raises an interesting question: If you're deriving from a base class, how can you call the implementation of the base class if you're replacing it? The answer is that you should store a reference to the base method before replacing it in the child class. The good news is that this is done automatically when you implement inheritance using the Microsoft Ajax Library. Base methods can be invoked through a method named callBaseMethod. Listing 3.10 shows how you can invoke the Pet implementation of the speak method from the child Cat class.

Listing 3.10 Calling the implementation of a method defined in the base class

```
Samples.Cat.prototype = {
    speak : function() {
        Samples.Cat.callBaseMethod(this, 'speak');
    }
}
```

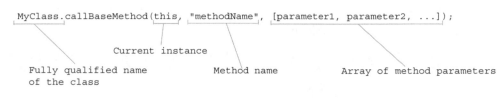

Figure 3.5   Syntax of the callBaseMethod method, which is used for invoking the base implementation of a method

The first argument accepted by `callBaseMethod` is always the current instance, pointed to by `this`. The second argument is a string with the name of the method to invoke on the base class. In this case, because the base implementation of the `speak` method was defined in listing 3.4 to throw a client exception, the overridden method will behave in the same manner as the base method and throw the same client exception. If the base method accepts parameters, you encapsulate them into an array and pass it as the third argument to `callBaseMethod`, as shown in figure 3.5.

We're almost at the end of our journey through the object-oriented constructs provided by the Microsoft Ajax Library. So far, you know how to create client classes and add them to namespaces, define client properties, and implement inheritance. The last two constructs we'll examine are interfaces and enumerations.

3.5   *Understanding interfaces and enumerations*

JavaScript doesn't support interfaces and enumerations, but the Microsoft Ajax Library simulates these constructs using functions as it does classes. The pattern is similar: You declare a function and then upgrade it to an interface or an enumeration using the `registerInterface` or `registerEnum` method, respectively. In the same manner as `registerClass`, these methods store in a function various pieces of information that allow them to be treated as interfaces or enumerations rather than as simple functions. Let's start by examining interfaces; enumerations will follow.

3.5.1   *Interfaces*

An *interface* allows an object to know *what* another object can do, without knowing *how*. An interface is said to define a *contract* between a class and the outside world. Interfaces are different from classes in the sense that they define a list of methods and properties that a class must expose, but it's the class's responsibility to provide an implementation. Listing 3.11 contains the declaration of an interface called

IComparable that exposes a single method, compareTo, which performs a generic comparison between objects.

Listing 3.11   Declaring the IComparable interface

```
Type.registerNamespace('Samples');

Samples.IComparable = function() {
    throw Error.notImplemented();
}
Samples.IComparable.prototype = {

    compareTo : function(comparand) {          Define single method
        throw Error.notImplemented();          called compareTo
    }
}
Samples.IComparable.registerInterface('Samples.IComparable');
```

To define the interface, you start by creating a JavaScript function. Because you're dealing with an interface type, you need to prevent the function from being used as a constructor. To do this, you throw a client exception of type notImplemented as soon as you try to call the function.

The same thing must be done for the methods defined by the interface. When a client class implements an interface, its methods are copied into the constructor's prototype. As a consequence, a client exception of type notImplemented will be thrown if you don't override the implementation of the method. This is how interfaces work in the Microsoft Ajax Library.

The final step is to register the interface by calling the registerInterface method on the interface type. The only argument accepted by the method is a string with the fully qualified name of the interface. The call to registerInterface ensures that the interface is properly recognized by the type system.

Now, you'll define a Temperature class that implements the IComparable interface. The compareTo method returns an integer based on the result of the comparison. The return value is 0 if the two temperature values are the same, -1 if the compared value is less than the value held by the object that performs the comparison, and +1 if it's greater. The code for the Temperature class appears in listing 3.12.

Listing 3.12 Implementing the `IComparable` interface

```
Samples.Temperature = function(value) {
    this._value = value;
}
Samples.Temperature.prototype = {
    compareTo : function(comparand) {                               Check
        if(Samples.Temperature.isInstanceOfType(comparand)) {   ◁──┘ types
            var thisValue = this.get_value();
            var comparandValue = comparand.get_value();

            if(thisValue == comparandValue)      Values are
                return 0;                    ◁──┘ equal

                                                            Values are
            return (thisValue > comparandValue) ? 1 : -1;  ◁──┘ different
        }
        else {
            throw Error.argumentType();   ◁──┐ Types are
        }                                     └ different
    },

    get_value : function() {
        return this._value;
    },

    set_value : function(value) {
        this._value = value;                    Implement
    }                                           IComparable  ❶
}
Samples.Temperature.registerClass('Samples.Temperature', null,
    Samples.IComparable);
```

As soon as you pass the `Samples.IComparable` interface to the `registerClass` ❶ method, all the methods defined in the interface are copied in the prototype object of the `Temperature` constructor. If you forget to specify the interface type, the runtime doesn't raise an error, but the interface isn't recognized as being implemented by the `Temperature` class.

Together with interfaces, enumerations are a feature supported by many object-oriented languages. Because JavaScript doesn't support them, let's see how you can fill this gap using the Microsoft Ajax Library.

3.5.2 *Enumerations*

Enumerations are a way to give names to numbers. The Microsoft Ajax Library lets you create enumerations to associate names with integer values. You can also specify values in hexadecimal format and create bit-field flags. Let's start with the pattern for creating a `Size` enumeration, shown in listing 3.13.

Listing 3.13   A `Size` enumeration

```
Type.registerNamespace('Samples');

Samples.Size = function() {
    throw Error.notImplemented();
}
Samples.Size.prototype = {
    Small: 1,
    Medium: 2,
    Large: 3
}
Samples.Size.registerEnum('Samples.Size');
```

As you did with interfaces, you define an enumeration by starting with a function. Because it makes no sense to instantiate an enumeration, you need to avoid the use of the `Samples.Size` function as a constructor. To do this, it's enough to raise a client exception of type `notImplemented` as soon as someone attempts to call the function.

The enumeration names are defined in the prototype object, and they must be integers. They can also be specified using the hexadecimal format. The name and value pairs in the prototype object are considered the names and values of the enumeration. In the example, you define three names (`Small`, `Medium`, and `Large`) associated with three integers (1, 2, 3). You call the `registerEnum` method, passing the fully qualified name of the enumeration as an argument.

Let's play a bit with enumerations to illustrate some of the methods available. Creating a variable of type Samples.Size is easy:

```
var size = Samples.Size.Medium;
```

At this point, the `size` variable holds the value 2. To display the name associated with a particular value, you call the `toString` method on the enumeration type, passing one of the enumeration values:

```
alert(Samples.Size.toString(size));
```

If you try to pass an invalid value, a client exception of type `ArgumentOutOfRange-Exception` is thrown. You can also parse a string as an enumeration value by calling the `parse` method on the enumeration type:

```
var smallSize = Samples.Size.parse('Small');
```

Keep in mind that the string passed to the `parse` method is case sensitive. If the enumeration type doesn't contain a matching name, a client exception of type `ArgumentException` is thrown.

You can also define enumerations to use *flags*. Flags are useful when you need to combine multiple values of an enumeration. Listing 3.14 shows an example that helps you understand the use of flags mode.

Listing 3.14 A `FileAccess` enumeration that uses flags

```
Type.registerNamespace('Samples');

Samples.FileAccess = function() {
    throw Error.notImplemented();
}
Samples.FileAccess.prototype = {
    Read : 1,
    Write : 2,
    Execute : 4
}
Samples.FileAccess.registerEnum('Samples.FileAccess', true);
```

In order for flags mode to work correctly, values must be powers of 2. To enable flags, you must pass `true` as the second argument to the `registerEnum` method. You can also combine flags by using the bitwise OR operator:

```
var readWritePermission = Samples.FileAccess.Read |
    ➥Samples.FileAccess.Write;
```

To remove a flag, you have to AND-NOT the combined flags with the one you want to remove, as in the following statement:

```
var readPermission = readWritePermission &
    ➥~Samples.FileAccess.Write;
```

Finally, if you call the `toString` method when in flags mode, you obtain a string that contains all the combined names, separated by commas. For example, the following statement displays a message box with the string `Read, Write`:

```
alert(Samples.FileAccess.toString(readWritePermission));
```

We've now covered all the object-oriented constructs provided by the Microsoft Ajax Library. In the next section, you'll see how this enhanced type system can be used to perform reflection on JavaScript objects.

3.6 *Using type reflection*

Reflection is the process of discovering information about objects at runtime. For example, you might be interested in knowing whether an object has defined a particular property, or if a property is a function rather than an array. Based on this information, you can either take different actions or raise errors.

The Microsoft Ajax Library provides a group of methods to reflect on types created with the enhanced type system. As you'll see, the goal is to be able to retrieve information about client objects while taking into account the enhanced type system and the object-oriented constructs provided by the library.

3.6.1 *Reflection methods*

The Microsoft Ajax Library provides an enhanced type system together with object-oriented constructs. You might need to know whether a constructor has been registered as either a class or an interface. Also, you might need to know whether two classes are in a parent-child relationship, or whether a certain class implements a particular interface. Table 3.1 lists a group of methods defined by the Microsoft Ajax Library that can be used to retrieve information on client objects at runtime.

Table 3.1 Methods defined by the Microsoft Ajax Library to perform reflection on client objects that take advantage of the enhanced type system

Method name	Parameters	Returns...
Type.isClass	Type	True if a function has been registered as a class
Type.isInterface	Type	True if a function has been registered as an interface
Type.isNamespace	Object	True if a function has been registered as a namespace
getName	-	The name of the current type as a string
getBaseType	-	A reference to the base class
getBaseMethod	Object, String	A reference to a method with the given name from an object
isInstanceOfType	Object	True if the given instance is of type Type
getInterfaces	-	A list with all the interfaces implemented by a class
implementsInterface	Type	True if an instance's class implements the given interface
isImplementedBy	Type	True if an interface is implemented by the given instance's class

The first set of methods, `Type.isClass`, `Type.isInterface`, and `Type.isName-space`, determine how a particular object has been registered in the context of the enhanced type system. As we explained in the previous sections, JavaScript functions are objects, and the Microsoft Ajax Library leverages them in order to simulate classes, interfaces, and enumerations. For example, the `Type.isInterface` method accepts a reference to a function and returns `true` if the function has been registered as an interface. In the same manner, the `Type.isClass` method returns `true` if the function passed as an argument has been registered as a class using the `registerClass` method. In the following code, the `petIsAClass` variable holds `true`:

```
var petIsAClass = Type.isClass(Samples.Pet);
```

In section 3.3.4, you saw that namespaces can be simulated by expanding generic objects. The `Type.isNamespace` method accepts an object and checks whether it has been registered as a namespace using the `Type.registerNamespace` method. As a consequence, the `isNamespace` variable in the following code holds `true`:

```
var isNamespace = Type.isNamespace(Samples);
```

Let's continue our exploration of the methods for reflecting on client objects by talking about the techniques that you can use to determine an object's type.

3.6.2 *Object typing*

In JavaScript, you can use the `typeof` operator to distinguish an object from another primitive type such as string, a number, or a Boolean value. However, the `typeof` operator doesn't distinguish between objects and other objects. If you create objects using different constructors, the `typeof` operator always returns `function`, which is the type of the constructor.

To distinguish between objects instantiated with different constructors, you could use JavaScript's `instanceof` operator. Due to the way inheritance is resolved, the `instanceof` operator doesn't work with classes created with the Microsoft Ajax Library. Instead, you have to use the `isInstanceOfType` method. This method is called on the type that you will test. It accepts an object as an argument and returns `true` if the object is an instance of that type. In the following code, the `test1` and `test2` variables hold `true` because both instances are of type `Pet`. The `test3` variable holds `false` because `tmpr1` isn't of type `Cat`:

```
var pet1 = new Pet();
var cat1 = new Cat();
var tmpr1 = new Temperature();

var test1 = Samples.Pet.isInstanceOfType(pet1);
var test2 = Samples.PetIsInstanceOfType(cat1);
var test3 = Samples.Cat.isInstanceOfType(tmpr1);
```

To retrieve information about the inheritance relationship between classes, you use the `inheritsFrom` method. This method is called on a child class and accepts the potential parent class as an argument. It returns `true` if the class passed as an argument is effectively the parent class. In the following code, the `catIsAPet` variable hold `true` because `Cat` inherits from `Pet`:

```
var catIsAPet = Samples.Cat.inheritsFrom(Samples.Pet);
```

When talking about client classes, we stated that the Microsoft Ajax Library stores information about the type name in constructors. If you want to know the name of a type as registered by the Microsoft Ajax Library, you can call the `getName` method and get back a string with the type name:

```
var customTypeName = Samples.Pet.getName();
var booleanTypeName = Boolean.getName();
```

The first statement calls `getName` on the `Pet` class defined in section 3.3.1. The variable `customTypeName` holds the string `Samples.Pet`. In the second statement, you can see that the method also works on JavaScript's built-in types, like Boolean. In this case, the variable `booleanTypeName` holds the string `Boolean`.

To complete our discussion of reflection in JavaScript, let's combine some of the methods illustrated in the previous section to build a more complex example. In the next section, you'll build a class browser for displaying the classes and interfaces defined in the root namespaces of the Microsoft Ajax Library.

3.6.3 *Building a simple class browser*

In this section, you want to combine some of the reflection methods presented in the previous section to obtain a class browser for exploring classes and interfaces defined in the root namespaces of the Microsoft Ajax Library. Figure 3.6 shows the example running in Internet Explorer.

The code in listing 3.15 creates a list with the namespaces defined in the library. When the user chooses one from the list, you use some of the reflection methods to display all the classes and interfaces defined in that namespace.

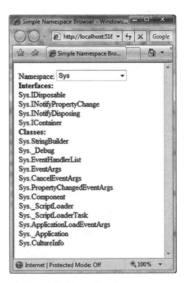

Figure 3.6   The Simple Namespace Browser running in Internet Explorer

Listing 3.15 Code for the namespace browser

```
<div>
    <span>Namespace:</span>
    <select id="ddNamespace">
        <option>Select a namespace</option>
        <option>Sys</option>
        <option>Sys.Net</option>
        <option>Sys.UI</option>
        <option>Sys.Services</option>
        <option>Sys.Serialization</option>
    </select>
    <div id="info"></div>
</div>

<script type="text/javascript">
<!--
    function pageLoad(sender, e) {
        var ddl = $get("ddNamespace");

        $addHandlers(ddl, {change:onNamespaceChange}, this);
    }

    function onNamespaceChange(evt) {
        var interfaces = [];
        var classes = [];
        var info = $get("info");
        var ddl = evt.target;

        if(ddl.selectedIndex == 0) {
            info.innerHTML = "";
            return;
        }

        var ns = eval(ddl.options[ddl.selectedIndex].text);      ◁──❶ Parse namespace

        for(var attr in ns) {
            var currMember = ns[attr];

            if(typeof(currMember) == "function") {               ❷ Look for class
                if(Type.isClass(currMember)) {       ◁──
                    Array.add(classes, currMember.getName());
                }                                                ❸ Look for interface
                else if(Type.isInterface(currMember)) {   ◁──
                    Array.add(interfaces, currMember.getName());
                }
            }
        }
                                                    ❹ Client StringBuilder instance
        var sb = new Sys.StringBuilder();     ◁──
```

```
        displayArray(interfaces, "Interfaces:", sb);          5  Format content
        displayArray(classes, "Classes:", sb);                   of arrays
        info.innerHTML = sb.toString();
    }

    function displayArray(arr, title, sb) {
        sb.append("<b>");
        sb.append(title);
        sb.append("</b><br />");

        sb.append(arr.join("<br/>") + "<br/>");
    }
//-->
</script>
```

The markup for the example defines a drop-down list with all the namespaces defined by the Microsoft Ajax Library. When a namespace is selected, the corresponding string is evaluated ❶ to obtain a reference to the namespace.

Then, you loop the selected namespace to search for classes and interfaces contained in it. To do this, you first check for functions (recall that classes and interfaces are simulated with functions by the Microsoft Ajax Library). You use the isClass and isInterface methods ❷❸ to determine whether you've found a class or an interface and then add it to the corresponding array.

Finally, you use a string builder instance ❹ to format the elements of the arrays ❺ and display the information about classes and interfaces in a label on screen. We discussed the Sys.StringBuilder class in chapter 2.

With this example, our discussion of the object-oriented constructs provided by the Microsoft Ajax Library is complete. JavaScript developers will benefit from the enhanced type system, and .NET developers will have a chance to become more comfortable with the JavaScript language.

In the following section, we'll introduce the event model provided by the Microsoft Ajax Library. With this model, you can expose and raise events in Java-Script objects.

3.7 *Working with events*

JavaScript developers are acquainted with the event model provided by the DOM. You can program against the DOM elements of a web page by hooking up their events and executing code in event handlers. For example, a button element can raise a click event when it's clicked by the user. The window object raises a load event when the page is loaded and an unload event when the user navigates away from the page.

Although DOM objects can raise events, this isn't true for generic JavaScript objects. The Microsoft Ajax Library provides an event model that lets you expose events in client objects, following a model that closely resembles the one used in the .NET framework. We'll divide this discussion into two parts. First, you'll see how to expose an event in a JavaScript object. Then, you'll learn how to subscribe to and handle an event.

3.7.1 Exposing an event

With the Microsoft Ajax Library, you can expose an event in a JavaScript object and subscribe to it with multiple handlers. This means that events are multicast, because you're able to handle them with multiple functions. Exposing an event is a three-step process:

1 Create a method that adds an event handler.
2 Create a method that removes an event handler.
3 Create a method that is responsible for raising the event.

The methods responsible for adding and removing the event handlers must follow a naming convention defined by the Microsoft Ajax Library:

- The name of the method responsible for adding an event handler must be add_*eventName*, where *eventName* is the name of the event.
- The name of the method responsible for removing an event handler must be remove_*eventName*, where *eventName* is the name of the event.

For example, if the object exposes an event called initialize, it has two methods called add_initialize and remove_initialize. These methods are responsible for adding and removing event handlers for the initialize event. The Application object, which we introduced in chapter 2, exposes some events, one of which is init. The Sys.Application object has two methods called add_init and remove_init.

> **NOTE** In the .NET framework, the process for exposing events is conceptually similar. There, you use a delegate to add and remove event handlers, and you fire the event by executing the delegate. You can read a good article about the .NET event model at http://msdn.microsoft.com/msdnmag/issues/03/02/BasicInstincts/.

Figure 3.7 illustrates the pattern used in the Microsoft Ajax Library to expose an event in a JavaScript object.

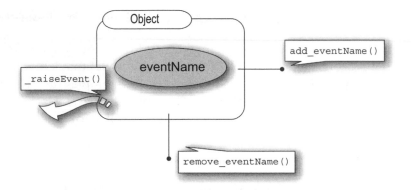

**Figure 3.7   With the Microsoft Ajax Library, objects can expose events. The `add_eventName`
and `remove_eventName` methods (where `eventName` is the name of the event) are used to
add and remove an event hander, respectively. Internally, a function called `_raiseEvent` can
be used to raise the event.**

In order to be able to manage multiple event handlers, the Microsoft Ajax Library
provides a class called `Sys.EventHandlerList`, which encapsulates an object used
to store multiple event handlers for multiple events. You access this through two
class methods: `addHandler` and `removeHandler`. Objects that want to expose
events usually create an instance of the class in the constructor and store it in a
private property:

```
this._events = new Sys.EventHandlerList();
```

At this point, the event methods interact with the event handlers list to manage
event handlers.

> **NOTE**   The base `Sys.Component` class, used for creating client components,
> comes with an instance of the `Sys.EventHandlerList` class and support
> for client events. Client components are discussed in chapter 8.

Listing 3.16 puts the theory into practice and shows how this is done in a `Collec-
tion` class that wraps an array. The class can raise an `itemAdded` event whenever a
new element is added to the array. For simplicity, we show only the code for the
add operation, but removing an element can be implemented with similar code.

Listing 3.16   A `Collection` class that wraps an array

```
Type.registerNamespace('Samples');

Samples.Collection = function() {
    this._innerList = [];
    this._events = null;          ❶  List of event
}                                      handlers
```

```
Samples.Collection.prototype = {
    add : function(member) {
        this._innerList.push(member);
        this._raiseEvent('itemAdded', Sys.EventArgs.Empty);
    },

    get_events : function() {
        if(!this._events) {
            this._events = new Sys.EventHandlerList();
        }

        return this._events;
    },

    add_itemAdded : function(handler) {                    Add handler to list ❷
        this.get_events().addHandler('itemAdded', handler);     ◁
    },

    remove_itemAdded : function(handler) {            Remove handler from list ❸
        this.get_events().removeHandler('itemAdded', handler);  ◁
    },

    _raiseEvent : function(eventName, eventArgs) {
        var handler = this.get_events().getHandler(eventName);  ◁
                                                  Get handler for event ❹
        if (handler) {
            if (!eventArgs) {
                eventArgs = Sys.EventArgs.Empty;
            }
            handler(this, eventArgs);    ◁    Fire
        }                                  ❺  event
    }
}
Samples.Collection.registerClass('Samples.Collection');
```

The add_itemAdded and remove_itemAdded methods are responsible for adding
and removing event handlers for the itemAdded event. They interact with the
event-handlers list by invoking its addHandler ❷ and removeHandler ❸ methods.
In the code, the list of event handlers is accessed through a method called
get_event, which returns the instance stored in the _events field ❶. Note that the
creation of the Sys.EventHandlerList instance is done (lazily) only the first time
the object tries to access the events property, so that constructing an instance
doesn't cost the creation of the event list if it's not going to be used. This is done to
remain consistent with the model used by client components, which encapsulate
an instance of the Sys.EventHandlerList class by default. More information is
given in chapter 8, which is entirely dedicated to client components.

Instead of writing a separate method to fire each event you're exposing, it's preferable to write a single _raiseEvent method and pass it a string with the event name and the event arguments. The _raiseEvent method calls getHandler on the event-handlers list to retrieve all the handlers for the given event. Stored in the handler variable ❹ is a function that, when called ❺, executes all the handlers for the event.

When the handlers are called ❺, each receives two arguments: a reference to the object that raised the event and an object that contains the event arguments. This paradigm should be familiar to .NET developers, because in the .NET framework, event handlers receive similar arguments. Note that if you don't specify any event arguments, the _raiseEvent method uses Sys.EventArgs.Empty, which is the static, singleton instance of the Sys.EventArgs class. This instance represents the absence of event arguments.

In the add method, you explicitly pass the Sys.EventArgs.Empty instance when calling _raiseEvent to fire the itemAdded event. A full implementation would probably derive a custom class from Sys.EventArgs that includes a reference to the item that was just added.

Now that you know how to expose an event, let's see how external objects can subscribe to and handle it.

3.7.2 Subscribing to and handling events

In the previous section, we discussed how to expose an event in a client object. Now to this question: How can you subscribe to and handle such an event? Subscribing to an event is simple: All you have to do is call the method responsible for adding an event handler.

For example, if you want to subscribe to the itemAdded event raised by the Collection class defined in listing 3.16, you pass a JavaScript function to the add_itemAdded method of the Collection instance. This function is an event handler for the itemAdded event. If you pass the same function to the remove_itemAdded method, you remove it from the list of event handlers. To add multiple handlers, you have to invoke the add_itemAdded method multiple times. Translated into code, event subscription is performed as follows:

```
var collection = new Samples.Collection();

collection.add_itemAdded(onItemAdded);
```

Now, you need to define the onItemAdded function, which is the event handler that you passed to the add_itemAdded method. You can do so this way:

```
function onItemAdded(sender, e) {
    alert('Added an item to the collection');
}
```

The event handler is a function that accepts two arguments. As we explained in the previous section, the event handler receives references to the object that raised the event and an object that represents the event arguments. We called these arguments `sender` and `e` to emphasize the similarity with the event model used in the .NET framework. Finally, you add an item to the collection to fire the `itemAdded` event. This can be done as follows:

```
collection.add('test string');
```

3.8 Summary

In this chapter, we reviewed the most important concepts of the JavaScript language and discussed how to leverage the Microsoft Ajax Library in order to become more productive with JavaScript.

We started by discussing the main data structures provided by JavaScript, such as objects and arrays. Then, we made an extensive overview of functions, which are objects you can use to define methods and create custom objects. After taking a peek at the various literals supported by JavaScript, we introduced JSON, a lightweight data format that lets Ajax applications exchange data; it's often preferred to XML, due to its compactness and ease of parsing.

The Microsoft Ajax Library leverages the object model provided by JavaScript and provides object-oriented constructs commonly found in class-based languages, such as classes, interfaces, and enumerations. With the library, you can also easily create namespaces, implement inheritance, and override methods. The enhanced type system provided by the Microsoft Ajax Library lets you perform reflection on objects. For example, you can discover whether a type is a class rather than an interface. You can also determine whether an instance is of a certain type or whether a class is in parent-child relationship with another class.

Finally, we discussed how you can expose multicast events in JavaScript objects using the event model provided by the Microsoft Ajax Library, which closely resembles the one used in the .NET framework.

Now, it's time to take a break from the Microsoft Ajax Library and focus on the server framework. In the next chapter, we'll introduce the ASP.NET AJAX server controls and explain how to upgrade an ASP.NET website to ASP.NET AJAX.

Exploring the
Ajax server extensions

4

What makes ASP.NET AJAX unique and separates it from other Ajax toolkits and frameworks is the fact that its architecture spans both the client and server. In addition to a rich set of JavaScript libraries, it provides a set of server controls to assist in Ajax development. In the previous two chapters, we revealed the basics of the Microsoft Ajax Library and its ambitions of simplifying Ajax and JavaScript for client-side development. Because most Ajax development originates from the client, these chapters are a pivotal part of the book and will serve as a valuable reference for many of the later chapters.

In this chapter, we continue our discussion of ASP.NET AJAX by delving into the server-side portion of the framework, called the *Ajax server extensions.* If you're familiar with the basics of the server extensions, you may wish to skim this chapter or jump ahead to chapters 6 and 7 to gain a deeper understanding of their inner workings. Nonetheless, the foundation we lay here is important and will be beneficial for even experienced Ajax developers.

As the name implies, Ajax server extensions offer Ajax support for server-side development. To help you understand why this is so valuable, we'll expose some of the issues and challenges of Ajax development from the client perspective.

4.1   Ajax for ASP.NET developers

An Ajax application runs in the browser and is written primarily in JavaScript. This process is initiated when a richer and more intuitive application is delivered from the server to the browser. This includes the logic for rendering and updating the UI, as well as communicating with a server for data needs. The end result is an application that runs more smoothly over time and provides a better user experience. This sounds great and is the recommended approach for Ajax development. However, with this approach comes a new set of issues to address.

For example, what about ASP.NET developers who are unfamiliar with JavaScript or prefer to keep the application logic on the server? What about the rare cases when the browser has JavaScript disabled? What about complex controls like the GridView—does it make sense to rewrite these controls for the client? What about security and exposing the application logic on the client?

These are just a few of the common concerns that surface with Ajax development. Thankfully, the ASP.NET AJAX framework offers an alternative.

4.1.1   What are the Ajax server extensions?

Built on top of ASP.NET 2.0, the Ajax server extensions include a new set of server controls and services that simulate Ajax behavior on the client. The extensions

don't adhere to the Ajax model in the traditional sense but respond in a manner that provides that illusion to the end user. In this
chapter, we'll focus on the server controls that
provide this functionality; the next chapter
will give you some insight into how ASP.NET
services such as authentication and profile are
also supported.

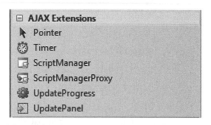

As a quick overview, let's look at the server
controls you have at your disposal. Figure 4.1
shows the new controls that are available to
the ASP.NET toolbox in Visual Studio. We'll
cover each of these controls in this chapter by
explaining *when* and *how* they should be used.

**Figure 4.1   The Ajax server extensions
are a new set of server controls that
complement the already powerful
controls in the ASP.NET toolbox.**

Since you're reading this book (and have come this far), chances are you've
previously done some ASP.NET development. If you're looking to take an application you wrote previously and add Ajax support to it, then the next few sections
should be right up your alley.

4.2   *Enhancing an existing ASP.NET site*

The goal for the next few sections is straightforward: to take a traditional web
application written in ASP.NET and enrich the user experience by adding the Ajax
server extensions. In addition to showing how the controls are used, this
approach will also demonstrate why and how they're applied in a normal situation. One of the reasons the server extensions are so enticing in this scenario is
that they allow you to rapidly integrate Ajax-like behavior into existing applications. It's important to note that without some care and thought, use of the server
extensions can be abused and in some cases can even degrade performance.

We'll assess each portion of the application as we reach it; but first, here are
some general guidelines to keep in mind:

- *Improve network latency*—Do your best to cut back on the amount of data
  passed between the browser and server. If you can eliminate unnecessary
  data, network latency and response time will improve.

- *Eliminate full-page refreshes*—Keep the interaction between the user and the
  application as fluid as possible, and avoid a full-page refresh whenever
  feasible.

- *Keep UI and application logic in code-behind files*—Keep any logic used to render or manipulate the UI in the server-side code. This gives you the luxury of supporting browsers that have JavaScript disabled as well as not exposing logic to savvy web users via the client script.

- *Use seamless, transparent integration*—Try to keep the existing application intact as much as possible so that future changes will be easy to integrate and few or no changes to the existing logic will be required.

- *Stick to a familiar paradigm*—Leverage the server controls so that a typical ASP.NET developer can continue to develop using an already familiar paradigm (server controls and ASP.NET postback mechanism).

If you can meet these goals, you'll have done something rather impressive. Let's begin our journey by examining the existing site you'll be working with for the remainder of the chapter.

4.2.1 A sample ASP.NET site

Figure 4.2 shows the home page for a fictitious and wealthy record company: *Song Unsung Records*. Although it's visually appealing, the application is in desperate need of help in the usability department.

For the sake of a realistic scenario, let's imagine that the site has grown in popularity and that you've been brought aboard as a highly paid consultant to (you hope) improve its usability and performance. After taking a quick look at the interface, you notice immediately that a few areas on the page encourage user interaction: the Artists search at the top, the list of recent feedback items at lower left, and the section for news about a music genre on the right. Unfortunately, interacting with some of the controls in these regions invokes a *postback,* which causes the page to refresh and takes away any interaction the end user has with the site.

We briefly touched on postbacks in chapter 1, but it's worth mentioning again that a postback is costly because of the amount of data sent back and forth to the server and the loss of interaction for the user. Understanding this behavior is important because it's an integral part of how ASP.NET behaves and what the Ajax server extensions are all about.

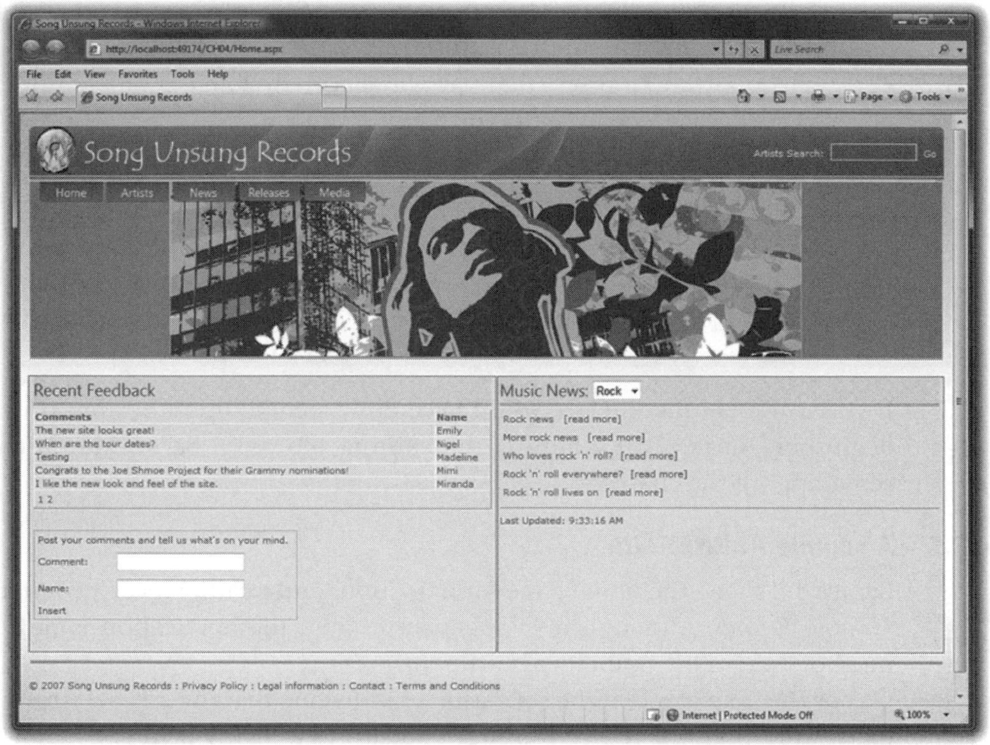

Figure 4.2 This application was written for a fictitious record company. Numerous areas on the page encourage user interaction. Each interaction, unfortunately, causes the page to refresh.

4.2.2 Configuring an existing ASP.NET site

Creating new sites that are Ajax-enabled is simple: You select the appropriate template from the New Site dialog (see chapter 1 and appendix A) in Visual Studio, and the configuration work is done for you. Taking an existing application and adding Ajax support requires a few more steps. The first involves adding a reference to the library.

NOTE   If you're planning to follow along at home, you can download the files from the book's website. If you don't currently have access to the code, the snippets and concepts covered in the following sections are fundamental enough that you can grasp the concepts. The existing sample also requires SQL Server Express—a free version of SQL Server that other samples in the book use as well.

> **Postbacks in a nutshell**
>
> In ASP.NET, an event—typically a user-driven one such as the clicking of a button—causes a page to send its contents back to the server for processing. This happens principally because pages are stateless, and in order for the server to retrieve the most recent status of a page, the page and all its contents are included in the request back to the server. This is made possible by a hidden field on the page called *ViewState*, which is responsible for storing information about the state of all the server controls in an encoded format. As you can imagine, passing this information back and forth on each postback can become costly over time, not just in terms of bandwidth for the server but also in terms of frustration for the user.
>
> One of the primary objectives of the Ajax server extensions is to find an alternative to some of this undesirable behavior. We'll go deeper into postbacks later in the chapter and with greater detail in the chapters that address the UpdatePanel control. You should understand now that postbacks cause a full-page refresh to occur, which is a behavior that Ajax applications seek to suppress or eliminate.

To add a reference to a library in a website or project, you can select the Add Reference option from the Website or Project menu in the menu bar. You can also right-click the site or project in the Solution Explorer tab of Visual Studio and choose the same option. A dialog similar to the one depicted in figure 4.3 is displayed.

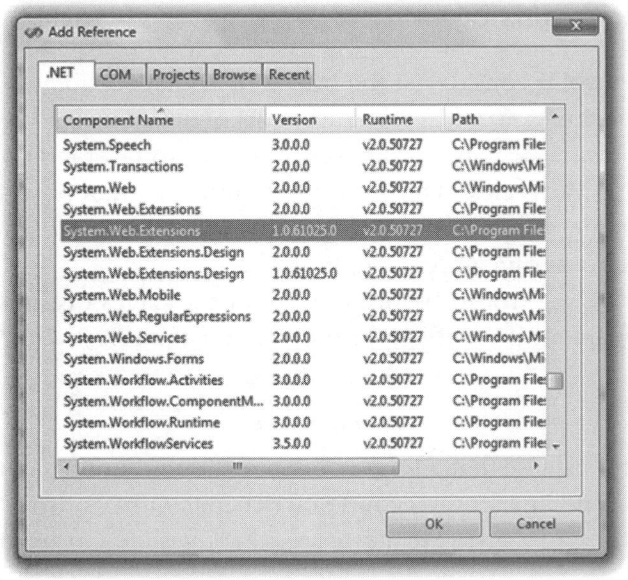

Figure 4.3
The System.Web.Extensions library is visible in the .NET tab of the Add Reference dialog. If this isn't visible but the framework has been installed, then you can select the 'Browse' tab to add the dll manually. If you don't see this, you might want to investigate your installation and confirm that the framework has been installed correctly.

From the dialog, select System.Web.Extensions to add a reference to ASP.NET AJAX—this should appear after you've successfully installed the framework. If this option isn't present in the list, take a moment to confirm that you've installed the framework correctly, and then select the Browse tab to navigate to the System.Web.Extensions.dll file on your local machine. Next up is the web.config file that defines some of the settings for the application.

The web.config file defines the configurations of ASP.NET applications. Items like handling error pages, permissions, and connections strings are placed there for reference and integration with other libraries and components. For ASP.NET AJAX, web.config is used to incorporate HTTP handlers, configuration settings, the generating of proxies, and a few other settings that a website needs to leverage the framework.

Most developers create a new Ajax-enabled site and merge the changes between the new web.config file and the one on their existing site. We'll leave this as exercise for you because it entails simple cut-and-paste steps that are too gratuitous to list here. For a detailed explanation of the web.config settings, see http://ajax.asp.net/docs/ConfiguringASPNETAJAX.aspx. A helpful video is also available on the ASP.NET AJAX homepage at http://www.asp.net/learn/videos/view.aspx?-tabid=63&id=81.

Assuming you've configured the site accordingly, it's time to add Ajax support by including the most important control in the framework: the ScriptManager.

4.3   ScriptManager: the brains of an Ajax page

The ScriptManager control is considered the brains of an Ajax-enabled page and is by far the most important control in the framework. As we move along in this chapter and throughout the book, we'll demonstrate how to leverage the Script-Manager and reveal its intricacies. The important thing to understand at this point is that, as the name suggests, this control is responsible for many of the operations that take place during an Ajax application.

Because you want this control to be present on all the pages of the site, you place it in the master page of the web application rather than in the home page (or content page):

```
<asp:ScriptManager ID="ScriptManager1" runat="server" />
```

You place it in the master page so that any content pages that inherit from it receive the same functionality. This is generally a good practice for similar controls that are used across multiple content pages. Furthermore, this invisible control must be

> **More on master pages**
>
> Master pages are used to define a consistent look and feel, as well as behavior, for a group of pages in an application. Each page that adopts the look and feel of a master page is called a *content page*. Whenever possible, it's best to place the ScriptManager in a master page so that each content page that inherits from it adopts the same behavior. For more information on master pages, visit http://msdn2.microsoft.com/en-us/library/wtxbf3hh.aspx.

declared *before* all other Ajax-enabled server controls in the page hierarchy to ensure that they're loaded and initialized accordingly.

Even though the ScriptManager control isn't declared in the content page, you can easily retrieve an instance of it by calling its static method `GetCurrent` and passing in the current `Page` instance:

```
ScriptManager scriptManager = ScriptManager.GetCurrent(this.Page);
```

With this instance, you can manage and configure the way the errors, scripts, and other settings on the page behave. We'll explore some of this in a moment; first, let's see what adding the ScriptManager to the page does to the application.

4.3.1 Understanding the ScriptManager

The primary responsibility of the ScriptManager is to deliver scripts to the browser. The scripts it deploys can originate from the ASP.NET AJAX library—embedded resources in the System.Web.Extensions.dll, local files on the server, or embedded resources in other assemblies. By default, adding the control to the page, declaratively or programmatically, delivers the required scripts you need for Ajax functionality on the page. To see the evidence, right-click the home page from the browser, and select the View Source option (or select View > Source in IE, or View > Page-Source in Firefox). In the viewed source window, search for an occurrence of Script-Resource.axd. You'll find something similar to (but not exactly like) listing 4.1.

> **Listing 4.1   An example of how a script is deployed with the ScriptManager**

```
<script src="/04/ScriptResource.axd?d=zQoixCVkx8JK9a1Az_4OOriP7
  iw9S-TvBA24ugyHeZ8NSIfT6_bRe7yPttg-
  sOhCr1ud1jBUWNQa9KSAugqepLY7DN4cuXzH5ybztCger
  rk1&amp;t=633141075498906250"
  type="text/javascript">
</script>
```

Let's decode what this tag means; this is at the core of how scripts are delivered to the client.

In ASP.NET 2.0, resources embedded in an assembly are accessed through the WebResource.axd HTTP handler. In the ASP.NET AJAX framework, a new HTTP handler called ScriptResource.axd replaces it with some additional functionality for localization and browser compression. Listing 4.1 shows a reference to a script assigned by the ScriptManager that is eventually downloaded by the new handler.

What about the cryptic text? How does the browser decipher it, and what does it mean? A closer look exposes two parameters: d and t. They assist the browser in identifying and caching the resource. The first is the encoded resource key, assigned to the d parameter. The second is the timestamp, t, that signifies the last modification made to the assembly (for example, t=632962425253593750). When the page is loaded a second time, the browser recognizes the parameters and spares the user the download by using what's in its cache to retrieve the resources.

NOTE Embedding resources in an assembly is a common technique for controls and libraries that require resources like images and scripts. This approach simplifies how controls are packaged and deployed.

Now that you understand how the scripts are downloaded, let's see how you can leverage the ScriptManager control to deploy additional scripts.

4.3.2 *Deploying JavaScript files*

Earlier, we examined how the ScriptManager control downloads resources to the browser by using a new HTTP handler: ScriptResource.axd. You also got a glimpse of this in chapter 2 when we discussed the Microsoft Ajax Library and how the core JavaScript files in the framework are delivered and manipulated with the ScriptManager. The next logical step is for you to learn how other scripts can be deployed.

The ScriptManager control has a property called Scripts that contains a collection of ScriptReference objects. A ScriptReference is nothing more than a way of registering a JavaScript file for use on a page. Listing 4.2 demonstrates how to include a few scripts on the page using the ScriptReference collection.

Listing 4.2   A ScriptReference, which registers files for deployment to a web page

```
<asp:ScriptManager ID="ScriptManager1" runat="server">
 <Scripts>
   <asp:ScriptReference Path="~/scripts/Script1.js" />
   <asp:ScriptReference Path="~/scripts/Script2.js" />
```

```
    <asp:ScriptReference Assembly="Demo"
      Name="Demo.SuperScript.js" />
  </Scripts>
</asp:ScriptManager>
Cueballs in code and text
```

In the first two entries, local JavaScript files are registered as references for the page. In the third entry, an embedded JavaScript file from an assembly is deployed to the site. Each reference added to the collection results in another ScriptResource.axd entry in the response's payload to the browser.

Now that you have a general grasp of how scripts are deployed, let's examine another functionality of the ScriptManager: registering service references.

4.3.3 Registering services

Working with JavaScript files is an important component of Ajax programming. However, accessing the server for data from JavaScript is what makes Ajax truly possible. In order to be granted this support with the ASP.NET AJAX framework, you must register a service reference for each local web service you wish to interact with.

The ScriptManager has a property called `Services` that contains a collection of `ServiceReference` objects. A ServiceReference object is a mechanism for registering services you can access from JavaScript. The end result is a JavaScript proxy that serves as the gateway to the service from the browser. Listing 4.3 demonstrates how to register local services with the ScriptManager.

> **Listing 4.3   A ServiceReference, which provides a gateway to the service from JavaScript**

```
<asp:ScriptManager ID="ScriptManager1" runat="server">
    <Services>
        <asp:ServiceReference Path="~/Services/MainService.asmx" />
        <asp:ServiceReference Path="~/Services/TestService.asmx" />
    </Services>
</asp:ScriptManager>
```

Chapter 5 will take you deeper into how to communicate with services. For now, you can see that the pattern for adding script references is also applied to service references.

Another important feature of the ScriptManager is the ability to support localization for languages and cultures. Let's quickly examine how this works before moving back to the existing ASP.NET application.

4.3.4 *Localization*

The process of supporting specific languages and cultures in an application is commonly referred to as *localization*. You can also consider localization the act of translating the interface. In ASP.NET, this is typically done by embedding localized resources into an organized structure of assemblies, also known as *satellite assemblies*. The ASP.NET AJAX framework supports both this model and a more client-centric model of using static JavaScript files on the server. Let's explore both of these occurrences to gain a general grasp of localization.

Localized script files

Localized JavaScript files are nothing more than files mapped to a specific culture. You create this mapping by including the name of the UI culture in the filename. For instance, a script file that is targeted for the Italian language could be named SomeScript.it-IT.js. The *it-IT* stands for the well-known culture identifier of the Italian language in Italy. Proceeding with this pattern, a French version of the file could appropriately be named SomeScript.fr-FR.js, and our comrades in the Ukraine could name their file SomeScript.uk-UA.js (you get the point).

Rather than implementing logic that gets the current culture on the user's machine and loads the correct file accordingly, you can (and should) use the ScriptManager control to do the work for you. The first step in configuring this is to enable script localization:

```
<asp:ScriptManager ID="ScriptManager1" runat="server"
        EnableScriptLocalization="true">
</asp:ScriptManager>
```

Setting the `EnableScriptLocalization` property of the ScriptManager to `true` forces the control to retrieve script files for the current culture, if they're available. By default, this property is set to `false`, which means it doesn't perform any localization lookup for you. Consequently, if you now include a script reference for SomeScript.js, intentionally omitting the culture name, the appropriate file is downloaded:

```
<asp:ScriptManager ID="ScriptManager1" runat="server"
    EnableScriptLocalization="true">
    <Scripts>
        <asp:ScriptReference Path="SomeScript.js" />
    </Scripts>
</asp:ScriptManager>
```

To reiterate, if the UI culture on your machine were set to Italian, then Some-Script.it-IT.js would be downloaded. Under the hood, the ScriptManager uses the naming convention you just exposed to look for a match against the current culture. You can also force a specific culture by setting the `ResourceUICultures` property in the `ScriptReference`:

```
<asp:ScriptReference Path="SomeScript.js"
  ResourceUICultures="it-IT" />
```

Pretty straightforward so far, but what about debug versions of your JavaScript files? In section 2.1.3, you were introduced to the `ScriptMode` property, which determines the version of a script file to load: release, debug, or auto (based on configuration settings on the page or site). Luckily, the same applies to localized scripts—if you had a debug version of the file called SomeScript.debug.it-IT.js, you could load it explicitly by setting the `ScriptMode` property:

```
<asp:ScriptReference Path="SomeScript.js" ResourceUICultures="it-IT"
  ScriptMode="Debug" />
```

The result is that the debug version of the Italian resource is loaded. That's all there is to localization on static JavaScript files. Next, let's see how loading script resources from an assembly works with ASP.NET AJAX.

Using assembly resources

Packaging scripts and resources as embedded assets into an assembly is a common technique that control developers use. This approach is popular primarily because it simplifies how resources are deployed with the control.

In order for a resource to be recognized by the ASP.NET AJAX framework, it must be decorated with the `WebResource` attribute:

```
[assembly: WebResource("ControlNamespace.Control.js",
  "text/javascript")]
```

In this example, `ControlNamespace` represents the default namespace used in the assembly. The remaining portion, Control.js, is the name of the resource.

It's highly recommended that the JavaScript file in the assembly not contain any hard-coded string literals. Instead, it should look up values from a resource file that follows the same naming conventions for the scripts. For example, you could use a .NET resource file named Messages.it-IT.resx (or Messages.en-IE for our Shillelagh-wielding friends in Ireland) to define strings for that culture. The ASP.NET AJAX script loader automatically converts the .NET string resources into a JavaScript object:

```
Messages={
"SayThankYou":"Grazie mille.",
"EnjoyMeal":"Buon appetito!"
};
```

The logic on the client can then be UI culture-independent and reference the string easily:

```
alert(Messages.SayThankYou);
```

This gives you a general understanding of how to use embedded scripts in a localization context. The topic of how to embed resources into assemblies is slightly out of the scope of this section; for more detailed information, see http://msdn2.microsoft.com/en-us/library/ms227427.aspx.

Most of the work of loading and managing localization is handled by the ScriptManager, thus saving you a load of code and time. Using the ScriptManager for localization also comes with additional benefits.

ScriptManager localization benefits

If your application supports multiple cultures, we strongly recommend loading and leveraging the ScriptManager for localization support. Some of the benefits of using the control include:

- *UI culture detection*—When the `EnableScriptLocalization` property is enabled, the ScriptManager detects and loads the appropriate script resource for you.

- *Custom UI culture support*—The `ResourceUICultures` property in the Script-Reference object lets you override and determine which UI cultures are supported for a particular script.

- *Avoidance of indefinite caching*—The ScriptManager employs a timestamp to ensure that embedded scripts aren't cached indefinitely by the browser.

- *Encrypted URLs to resources*—As a security measure, the key that directs the browser to the appropriate script is encrypted.

The ScriptManager makes localization very easy and includes an additional set of features that make it an attractive solution for managing localization.

You should now have a general idea of what the ScriptManager is capable of. More instances of how and when it should be used are covered throughout the book as we mentioned. Let's get back to the application and make use of another server control called the *ScriptManagerProxy.*

4.3.5 Using the ScriptManagerProxy

One and only one ScriptManager can exist on a page. Adding more than one causes an `InvalidOperationException` to be raised at runtime. But in some situations, a content page may require a reference to a service or script that isn't made by the ScriptManager in the parent or master page. The additional references may also be required for only a single page and not for others. In these situations, the ScriptManagerProxy control comes to the rescue.

Suppose the customer has requested that you include a certain script on the home page but not on any of the other pages on the site. Adding this script to the master page would deploy it everywhere, which is the undesired result. Instead, you can leverage the ScriptManagerProxy on the target page to ensure that it's included only there.

Listing 4.4   Using the ScriptManagerProxy control in a master-page scenario

```
<asp:ScriptManagerProxy ID="ScriptManagerProxy1" runat="server">
    <Scripts>
        <asp:ScriptReference Path="~/scripts/DummyScript.js" />
    </Scripts>
</asp:ScriptManagerProxy>
```

Just like its parent control, the ScriptManagerProxy has a collection of script and service references. Think of the ScriptManagerProxy as an extension of the ScriptManager control: The influence and settings of the ScriptManager control can be extended to content pages, user controls, and more. At runtime, the settings are merged for each page accordingly.

The key purpose of the ScriptManagerProxy is to add references that weren't included with the ScriptManager. This situation occurs most commonly when you're working with master pages.

We've been laying the groundwork by adding support for the Ajax framework and dropping in the ScriptManager control to deploy JavaScript files. Now we can address those dreaded postbacks and start enhancing the overall user experience. We'll return to the ScriptManager later in the chapter when we discuss error handling.

4.4   Partial-page updates

Earlier in the chapter, we listed the goals for the existing application and mentioned that eliminating complete page refreshes from occurring would greatly enhance the user experience. To reiterate, instead of updating the whole page all at once, as in traditional ASP.NET applications, you should strive to update only portions of the page—dynamically, without changing any of the application logic if possible.

In a conventional Ajax solution, when the UI and application logic reside on the browser, you're responsible for updating the UI with DHTML techniques and a strong grasp of JavaScript. With the UpdatePanel control, the burden of this type of development is abstracted away with all the heavy lifting done for you by the server extensions. The best way to fully understand this is to see it in action.

4.4.1 Introducing the UpdatePanel control

The UpdatePanel is an Ajax-enabled server control that works closely with the ScriptManager to apply partial-page updates to a page. Portions of the page declared by the UpdatePanel can now be updated incrementally rather than as a result of a page refresh. To demonstrate, let's add the UpdatePanel control to the existing application.

The right column on the home page displays news about a selected genre. Using a DropDownList control to display the available genres and a Repeater control to display news about the selected item, the controls work together to inform the user about the latest relevant news. When the user selects a new item in the drop-down list, a postback occurs, and the page is refreshed. Examining the markup for the DropDownList explains this behavior.

In listing 4.5, you can see that the `AutoPostback` property of the dropdown list is set to `True`. As you can probably guess, this setting invokes the postbacks on each selection change. During the postback, the server-side code processes the request by looking up the selected genre and retrieving its relevant news. Listing 4.6 demonstrates how the server code binds the Repeater control on the form with news about the selected genre.

> **Listing 4.5   Selecting an item from the music genre list generates a postback to the server.**

```
<asp:DropDownList ID="Genres" runat="server" AutoPostBack="True"
  OnSelectedIndexChanged="Genres_SelectedIndexChanged" >
  <asp:ListItem Text="Rock" Value="~/App_Data/RockFeed.xml"
    Selected="true" />
  <asp:ListItem Text="Jazz" Value="~/App_Data/JazzFeed.xml" />
  <asp:ListItem Text="Blues" Value="~/App_Data/BluesFeed.xml" />
</asp:DropDownList>
```

Listing 4.6 Selecting an item in the list updates the Repeater's data source.

```
protected void Genres_SelectedIndexChanged(object sender,
                                           EventArgs e)
{
    UpdateGenre();        ◁─────┐  Call method to
}                            ❶  update news

private void UpdateGenre()
{                                          ❷  Update data
    GenreSource.DataFile = Genres.SelectedValue;  ◁──┘  source

    GenreNews.DataBind();  ◁─────┐  Bind to latest
}                            ❸  data source
```

The `Genres_SelectedIndexChanged` method is invoked when the selected genre is changed. It then calls the ❶ private `UpdateGenre` method to ❷ configure the data source (in this case it's an XML file that represents an RSS feed) and ❸ rebind the Repeater.

Because each selection invokes a page refresh, the behavior in the browser isn't appealing to users. Technically, however, it makes a lot of sense. This pattern is common in ASP.NET applications. The postback mechanism is frequently used (and, unfortunately, often abused) to bridge the gap between what is displayed on the UI and the logic on the server.

If you add the UpdatePanel control, you can keep everything intact and change the way it behaves for the user. The next time you run the site and select a new genre, the news for a recently selected item is updated without a full-page refresh. For clarity, the relevant source on the page is included in listing 4.7.

Listing 4.7 Dynamically updating regions during asynchronous postbacks

```
<asp:UpdatePanel ID="GenrePanel" runat="server">
 <ContentTemplate>
   <div class="columnheader">Music News:
    <asp:DropDownList ID="Genres" runat="server"
    AutoPostBack="True"
    OnSelectedIndexChanged="Genres_SelectedIndexChanged" >
    <asp:ListItem Text="Rock" Value="~/App_Data/RockFeed.xml"
      Selected="true" />
    <asp:ListItem Text="Jazz" Value="~/App_Data/JazzFeed.xml" />
    <asp:ListItem Text="Blues" Value="~/App_Data/BluesFeed.xml" />
    </asp:DropDownList>
   </div>
```

```
  <asp:Repeater ID="GenreNews" runat="server"
   DataSourceID="GenreSource" >
   <ItemTemplate>
    <div class="newshead">
     <asp:HyperLink ID="HyperLink1" runat="server"
       NavigateUrl='<%#XPath("link") %>'
       Text='<%#XPath("title") %>' />
      
     <asp:HyperLink ID="HyperLink2" runat="server"
      NavigateUrl='<%#XPath("link") %>' Text="[read more]" />
    </div>
   </ItemTemplate>
  </asp:Repeater>
  <hr />
  Last Updated: <%= DateTime.Now.ToLongTimeString() %>

 <asp:XmlDataSource ID="GenreSource" runat="server"
    DataFile="~/App_Data/RockFeed.xml" XPath="/rss/channel/item">
 </asp:XmlDataSource>

 </ContentTemplate>
</asp:UpdatePanel>
```

The `ContentTemplate` property of the `UpdatePanel` class defines the regions of the page that are updated dynamically. This time, instead of a normal postback that refreshes the entire page, a new type of postback is introduced: an *asynchronous postback*. An asynchronous postback goes through the page lifecycle and operates like a normal postback, minus the page refresh. This refreshing (pun intended) news means the logic for the UI and application can remain intact.

To demonstrate, let's add code to detect when you're in an asynchronous postback by asking the ScriptManager control for more information; see listing 4.8.

Listing 4.8   During an asynchronous postback, the page goes through the normal page lifecycle.

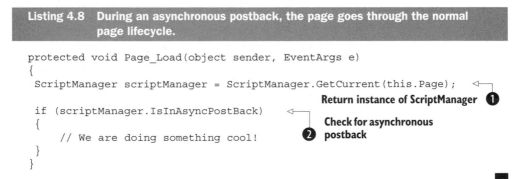

```
protected void Page_Load(object sender, EventArgs e)
{
  ScriptManager scriptManager = ScriptManager.GetCurrent(this.Page);   ◁─┐
                                                            Return instance of ScriptManager ❶

  if (scriptManager.IsInAsyncPostBack)   ◁─┐
  {                                         Check for asynchronous
      // We are doing something cool!    ❷  postback
  }
}
```

You first ❶ retrieve an instance of the ScriptManager on the page by calling the static method `GetCurrent` and passing in the parent page. Remember, you declared the ScriptManager on the master page, not the content page, so this is the best way to find and retrieve an instance of the ScriptManager when in a content page (or child control). An alternative would be to find the control in the `Controls` collection of the master page, but this approach is ostensibly much simpler—under the hood, it does the same thing.

Next, you query the ❷ `IsInAsyncPostBack` property of the ScriptManager to determine if you're in the process of handling a normal postback or an asynchronous one. This offers you the option of coding custom logic for each occasion.

> **WARNING** Adding an UpdatePanel to a page seems so effortless, and the rewards are so great, that many developers entertain the idea of placing the contents of an entire page in a single UpdatePanel. This practice is highly discouraged. Although the illusion of Ajax is present, the cost of each postback is significant, and the application's overall performance will suffer greatly over time. As a general rule, try to avoid such solutions, and instead look for portions of the page that can be updated instead of the entire page.

So far, so good—you've added a single UpdatePanel to the page and in the process stopped a page refresh from happening each time the user selects a different music genre. Let's now place the focus on the other interactive portion of the site: the feedback area.

4.4.2 More UpdatePanels

Adding multiple UpdatePanel controls to a page is not only supported but also encouraged. Doing so means that more regions of the page can be updated dynamically instead of each time a page refreshes. This approach also allows you to take more control of which portions of the page are updated and which ones aren't, thus helping conserve the amount of data passed between the client and server during each postback. To demonstrate, let's add another UpdatePanel to address the postbacks that come out of the page's Recent Feedback section.

Figure 4.4 captures Visual Studio's Design view of the related controls before adding the UpdatePanel. You see a GridView control that is used to display, sort, and page through feedback items. Below the GridView is a DetailsView control that is used to enter new feedback to the site.

Each time the user attempts to sort, navigate to the next page of results, or add feedback, a postback occurs. Because both controls invoke postbacks and are relatively close to each other in the page layout, you can place a single UpdatePanel

Figure 4.4
This snapshot is from the Design view in Visual Studio; it shows the state of the controls before adding Ajax support.

around both of them. After adding the UpdatePanel, the design view of the form resembles figure 4.5.

When you run the site once more, the page refreshes previously invoked from interaction with the news and feedback sections are gone. It's worth mentioning again that postbacks still occur, but now they take place asynchronously and, as a result, update the page incrementally, thus eliminating the flicker.

Unfortunately, you aren't done yet. As you hand over the site to the client for testing, they notice a behavior that they deem undesirable. When a new feedback item is entered, the contents of both UpdatePanel controls are updated instead of just the one for recent feedback. In other words, when a user enters in a new

Figure 4.5
Adding the UpdatePanel around the GridView and DetailsView controls replaces their traditional postbacks with asynchronous postbacks.

feedback item or sorts one of the columns, the recent news about a genre (on the right side of the page) also gets updated. You can confirm this by sorting a column like Name on the GridView and watching the Last Updated time in the right column change.

The content of both UpdatePanel controls is updated because by default, every time an asynchronous postback occurs on the page, regardless of which control on the page invoked the postback, an UpdatePanel updates its contents. To solve this, all you need to do is set the UpdateMode property on both panels to Conditional. Doing so tells the UpdatePanel to update its contents only if the postback originates from within itself (from one of its child controls).

> **TIP** The default value for the UpdateMode on UpdatePanel controls is Always. However, this setting is rarely needed. A best practice is to always set the mode to Conditional and let the Always condition present itself naturally in your application. Doing so cuts back on the amount of data passed between the server and client and ultimately increases the site's performance. There are limitations to both, which we'll cover in chapters 6 and 7, dedicated to the UpdatePanel control.

This time, when you run the site again, only the contents of the UpdatePanel relative to the user interaction are updated.

Let's take a moment to recap. So far in the chapter, you've eliminated full-page refreshes, you've cut back on the amount of data passed between the client and server, and you've kept all the application and UI logic on the server intact. You've also improved network latency and written no JavaScript code in the process! For extra credit, if the browser had JavaScript disabled, the existing application would continue to function, with normal postbacks and page refreshes—just as it did before you made any updates.

Because most of the initial goals have been met, and given that this is ultimately all about the user experience, perhaps you can find other things to add to the site that add more value and interactivity for the user.

4.4.3 *Insert feedback here*

Adding the UpdatePanel controls to the site radically improves the behavior and overall feel for users. They're spared a page refresh when they interact with the controls, which is a tremendous improvement from the intermittent nature you had before. But as a side effect of this achievement, the user isn't given any indication that something is being updated until it has happened.

Imagine (for the sake of this example) that the source used to retrieve information about a music genre comes from an external RSS feed. This scenario introduces the possibility of slow responses when retrieving a news feed, which means partial-page updates may not happen immediately—and may not happen for quite a while. Previously, the page refresh was an indication that something was happening and that eventually the page would be updated. With partial-page updates, the user is given no visual cue that their actions have been accepted and that work is being done on the other end.

Fortunately, in chapter 1, we introduced the UpdateProgress control as a solution for this problem. You'll use the control again here to notify the user that you're retrieving news about the selected genre. Listing 4.9 shows the insertion of the UpdateProgress control on the page, right before the Repeater control that displays the recent news.

Listing 4.9   Displaying the UpdateProgress control when the UpdatePanel's contents are being updated

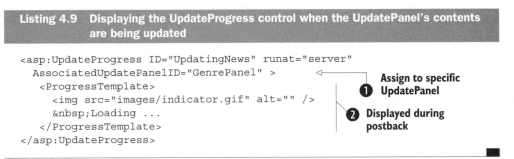

```
<asp:UpdateProgress ID="UpdatingNews" runat="server"
  AssociatedUpdatePanelID="GenrePanel" >                    ← ❶ Assign to specific UpdatePanel
    <ProgressTemplate>
      <img src="images/indicator.gif" alt="" />              ❷ Displayed during postback
       Loading ...
    </ProgressTemplate>
</asp:UpdateProgress>
```

First, you'd prefer to display the contents of the UpdateProgress control only when news about a genre is being retrieved, and not when other UpdatePanel controls are being updated. To accomplish this, you set the ❶ `AssociatedUpdatePanelID` property to the ID of the UpdatePanel associated with the music news. This lets you have multiple UpdateProgress controls on a single page and gives you added control over how the page is rendered during an asynchronous postback. The UpdateProgress control has a ❷ `ProgressTemplate` property that encapsulates what is to be displayed during an asynchronous postback. For this instance, you use an animated GIF image and some informative text.

Now, when you select a new item from the drop-down list, a subtle but informative message is presented while the data is retrieved. Figure 4.6 displays the UpdateProgress control in action.

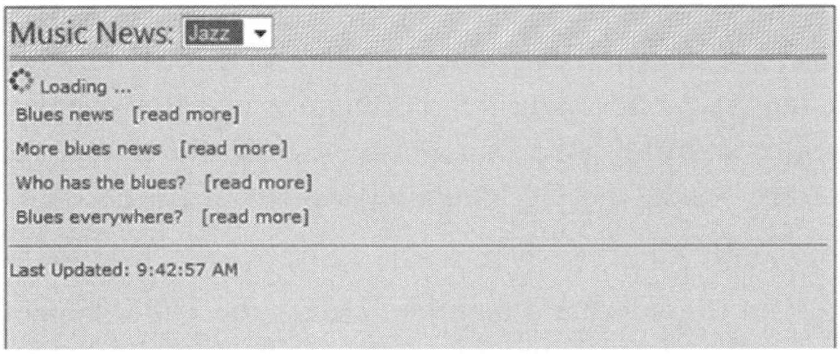

Figure 4.6   The UpdateProgress control offers a simple and useful tool for keeping the user informed about asynchronous updates on the page.

TIP   It's easy to get carried away with *Loading* messages. In general, you should try to inform the user with a subtle and informative message that is relevant to the portion of the page being updated. Unless the entire page is being updated, it's usually more considerate and less intrusive to use smaller, useful icons and text to relay messages to the user. Gratuitous messages can have a negative effect on the overall user experience and should generally be avoided.

You're almost finished with the server-extension controls. You've used every one of them except the Timer control, which, when used effectively, can complement the UpdatePanel control and give you the ability to apply partial-page updates at set intervals.

4.4.4   Working with a timer

Included in the Ajax server extensions is a control called the Timer. As its name implies, the control creates a timer on the client that invokes a postback at an interval you specify (in milliseconds). For the existing application, you'll use the Timer control in conjunction with the UpdatePanel to retrieve and display the latest news about the selected genre. Because news about a genre can change often, this subtle addition adds a little extra value to the site because it keeps the user's attention. Listing 4.10 shows how to declare the Timer control on the page.

Listing 4.10   The Timer runs in the client and invokes a postback at each interval.

```
<asp:Timer ID="NewsTimer" runat="server" Interval="10000"
  OnTick="UpdateNews" />
```

The declaration sets the interval to 10 seconds (or rather, its equivalent, 10000 milliseconds) and also assigns an UpdateNews handler to the OnTick event. Normally, this would be too frequent of an interval for news updates—we use it here for demonstration purposes only. Also, for reasons we're about to discuss, you place the Timer control *outside* the UpdatePanel instead of in the ContentTemplate declaration, as in previous examples.

> **TIP** It's important to understand that the ticks for the Timer happen on the browser, not the server. Using this control requires you to be mindful of the system resources on the end user's machine. In general, set the control's interval to the highest value possible. Setting the interval value to too short an amount may put too much strain on the system and cause unpredictable behavior.

To accompany the declarative code, the server-side code calls the same Update-Genre method used earlier to update the interface. Listing 4.11 shows the code-behind for the Tick event handler.

> **Listing 4.11   The Tick event, which calls the private UpdateGenre method**

```
protected void UpdateNews(object sender, EventArgs e)
{
    UpdateGenre();
}

private void UpdateGenre()
{
    GenreSource.DataFile = Genres.SelectedValue;
    GenreNews.DataBind();
}
```

Because the Timer control isn't encapsulated by the UpdatePanel, each interval that invokes a postback causes the page to refresh. This happens because the UpdatePanel hasn't been made aware that you'd like to use the Tick event of the Timer control to invoke an asynchronous postback. To resolve this, you register the Tick event with the UpdatePanel by adding the event to the control's Triggers collection. The next time you run the application, you'll notice that the Last Updated time is incremented at each interval.

Listing 4.12 shows the entire contents of the music genre section as well as the declaration of the Timer control at the end.

Listing 4.12 Registering the Timer control's `Tick` event to ensure asynchronous postbacks

```
<asp:UpdatePanel ID="GenrePanel" runat="server"
 UpdateMode="Conditional">
 <ContentTemplate>
  <div class="columnheader">Music News:
   <asp:DropDownList ID="Genres" runat="server"
    AutoPostBack="True"
    OnSelectedIndexChanged="Genres_SelectedIndexChanged" >
    <asp:ListItem Text="Rock" Value="~/App_Data/RockFeed.xml"
      Selected="true" />
    <asp:ListItem Text="Jazz" Value="~/App_Data/JazzFeed.xml" />
    <asp:ListItem Text="Blues" Value="~/App_Data/BluesFeed.xml" />
   </asp:DropDownList>
  </div>

  <asp:UpdateProgress ID="UpdatingNews" runat="server"
    AssociatedUpdatePanelID="GenrePanel" >
    <ProgressTemplate>
       <img src="images/indicator.gif" alt="" /> Loading ...
    </ProgressTemplate>
   </asp:UpdateProgress>

  <asp:Repeater ID="GenreNews" runat="server"
    DataSourceID="GenreSource" >
    <ItemTemplate>
      <div class="newshead">
       <asp:HyperLink ID="HyperLink1" runat="server"
         NavigateUrl='<%#XPath("link") %>'
         Text='<%#XPath("title") %>' />
          
       <asp:HyperLink ID="HyperLink2" runat="server"
         NavigateUrl='<%#XPath("link") %>' Text="[read more]" />
      </div>
    </ItemTemplate>
   </asp:Repeater>
   <hr />
   Last Updated: <%= DateTime.Now.ToLongTimeString() %>

 </ContentTemplate>
 <Triggers>
   <asp:AsyncPostBackTrigger ControlID="NewsTimer"
    EventName="Tick" />        ◁── Register async
 </Triggers>                         postback
</asp:UpdatePanel>
                                                    Postback
                                                    every 10
                                                    seconds
<asp:Timer ID="NewsTimer" runat="server" Interval="10000"  ◁──┘
   OnTick="UpdateNews" />
```

You've now used every control in the Ajax server extensions, and the result is an application that is far more engaging and responsive than when you started. Along the way, you picked up a collection of best practices for getting the most out of the extensions, and you also got a glimpse into how the ScriptManager works under the hood.

But you're not done yet. Even the best applications contain errors or raise exceptions.

4.4.5   *Error handling*

Things have been working smoothly so far, but in the real world, errors and exceptions occur. To wrap up this chapter, let's examine what you have at your disposal to make handling these occurrences more manageable. Listing 4.13 shows a snippet of code that purposely throws an exception after the user has selected a new music genre from the drop-down list.

Listing 4.13   Throwing an exception to see how the page handles it

```
protected void Genres_SelectedIndexChanged(object sender,
                                           EventArgs e)
{
    UpdateGenre();
    throw new Exception("Look out!");
}
```

Earlier, you set the `AutoPostBack` property of this control to `true` and also placed it in an UpdatePanel. This means the postback that originates from here is asynchronous, also known as an *Ajax postback*. Typically, depending on the settings of the web.config file, an error during a normal postback results in the stack trace and error information being shown on the screen. This time, the browser relays the exception information in a dialog box (see figure 4.7).

This result can be informative for developers, but displaying the same message from the exception back to the user isn't always the best idea. Fortunately, the

Figure 4.7   By default, exceptions that occur during asynchronous postbacks are displayed in alert dialogs.

ScriptManager control throws an event called `AsyncPostBackError` that provides you with an opportunity to update the text in the dialog box before it's presented to the user. Listing 4.14 demonstrates how a handler for the event is registered and the message updated before reaching the user.

Listing 4.14 Raising the `AsyncPostBackError` event before the dialog is displayed to the user

```
protected void Page_Load(object sender, EventArgs e)
{
  ScriptManager scriptManager = ScriptManager.GetCurrent(this.Page);
  scriptManager.AsyncPostBackError += new
    EventHandler<AsyncPostBackErrorEventArgs>(OnAsyncPostBackError);
}

void OnAsyncPostBackError(object sender,
                          AsyncPostBackErrorEventArgs e)
{
  ScriptManager.GetCurrent(this.Page).AsyncPostBackErrorMessage =
    "We're sorry, an unexpected error has occurred.";
}
```

Now, when you select another music genre from the list, you're presented with a message box that contains the custom message instead of the one coming from the exception.

Even with the custom error message, it's still considered a best practice to provide a default error page for a website rather than display an alert dialog or stack trace to the user. This way,

Figure 4.8 You can change the error message during the `AsyncPostBackError` event.

when an exception occurs, the user is redirected to a friendly page that is informative and useful. The mechanism for handling errors is configurable in the `customErrors` section of web.config:

```
<system.web>
 <customErrors mode="On|Off|RemoteOnly"
  defaultRedirect="ErrorPage.aspx">
 ...
 </customErrors>
```

The `mode` property of the `customErrors` section governs how error messages are to be handled. When this property is set to `On`, the user is redirected to the error page defined in the `defaultRedirect` property. The `Off` setting always shows the stack trace—or, in this case, the dialog box with the error message. The `RemoteOnly` value redirects the user to the error page only if they're on a remote machine; otherwise, the same behavior used for the `Off` setting is applied. Due to its flexibility, the RemoteOnly setting is the most appropriate for developers who wish to debug applications locally and view details about exceptions as they occur.

The ScriptManager control provides a property for overriding this mechanism. By default, the AllowCustomErrorsRedirect property is set to true. This setting honors the values set in the customErrors section. Setting this property to false forces the dialog to appear when exceptions occur (see listing 4.15).

Listing 4.15   The `AllowCustomErrorsRedirect` property overrides the web.config settings.

```
protected void Page_Load(object sender, EventArgs e)
{
    ScriptManager scriptManager = ScriptManager.GetCurrent(this.Page);
    ...
    scriptManager.AllowCustomErrorsRedirect = false;
}
```

The AllowCustomErrorsRedirect value must be set on or before the Load event in the ASP.NET page lifecycle. Doing so afterward has no affect on the settings configured in the customErrors section. Chapter 7 will show you how to handle errors more elegantly when we examine the events that occur on the client side during asynchronous postbacks.

For now, the lesson is this: always provide a general error page for users. If you have to show the user a dialog box during an exception, handle the AsyncPost-BackError event to display a friendly and user-centric message as opposed to the message from the exception itself.

4.5   Summary

We began this chapter by presenting an alternative to client-side Ajax development. Using the Ajax server extensions, ASP.NET developers can simulate Ajax behavior in the browser. Sometimes a client-centric Ajax solution isn't appropriate for a site. In these cases, you can still use a server-centric solution that leverages these new controls to improve the user experience. In many situations, using both approaches makes sense.

The next chapter will round out your understanding of the core ASP.NET AJAX framework by examining how asynchronous calls are made from the browser. It will also pick up where we left off with the server extensions by exposing how you can use the authentication and profile services in ASP.NET from client script.

Making asynchronous
network calls

5

At the heart of Ajax programming is the ability to make asynchronous calls from the browser to the server. Establishing this dialogue eliminates the need for the browser to reload as a result of each request or user interaction. Instead, relevant data can be exchanged in the background while updates to the page are applied incrementally from the browser. Web pages that leverage this technique remain responsive, and the user experience is greatly improved.

In chapter 1, you got a glimpse into how this type of programming works with ASP.NET AJAX—we called this approach the *client-centric development model*. This model grants you more control over the application by moving the logic from the server into the browser. This shift from traditional ASP.NET development means the server is primarily used for data rather than application logic and data together.

This chapter will explain how you can make asynchronous network calls from JavaScript using the ASP.NET AJAX framework. We'll explore the Microsoft Ajax Library classes that make asynchronous communication possible. In addition, we'll unveil how to make calls to ASP.NET Web Services, both local and external, from client-side script. Let's begin with what will be the most likely scenario you'll leverage when making asynchronous calls: working with ASP.NET Web Services.

5.1 *Working with ASP.NET Web Services*

A website is a perfect example of the client/server architecture. Each instance of a browser (the client) can send requests to a server for data and content. When the client initiates a request to a known remote server to execute a procedure or subroutine, it's often called a *remote procedure call (RPC)*. Working closely with ASP.NET Web Services, the ASP.NET AJAX framework significantly simplifies the effort it takes to execute RPC patterns from JavaScript. In simpler terms, the framework makes it easy for you to communicate with Web Services from JavaScript.

Before we dive into working with Web Services, let's take a few moments to explain how communicating with RPC services works and how these services differ from another style called Representation State Transfer (REST).

You communicate with an RPC service using commands defined through methods. This is similar to how you interact with a normal object from a library. For example, suppose an RPC application defines a method called `GetStoreSpecials`. A consumer of that service can then communicate with it like so:

```
storeService = new StoreService("aspnetajaxinaction.com:42");
storeService.GetStoreSpecials();
```

REST services expose their communication endpoints slightly differently. They expose objects as resources or *nouns*, which have more of an emphasis on diversity. For the same functionality, a REST service typically offers a resource this way:

http://ajaxinaction.com/specials/. A caller in this scenario then accesses the application in a fashion similar to this:

```
storeResource = new StoreResource("http://ajaxinaction/specials/");
storeResource.GetStoreSpecials();
```

We're giving you this overview of these two service models to provide the context in which communication works in ASP.NET AJAX. As we walk through the first set of examples, you'll notice how you declare and work with RPC-like services for applications. It's interesting to note that under the hood, the communication layer in the framework is implemented with REST-like patterns. More of this will make sense as we proceed.

NOTE   An entire book could be dedicated to topics such as REST and RPC services. We provide a brief introduction here, but it's in no way a thorough explanation. For more information about REST services, see http://rest.blueoxen.net/cgi-bin/wiki.pl?FrontPage. You can find a helpful resource about RPC here: http://www.cs.cf.ac.uk/Dave/C/node33.html.

Let's get into some code and begin working with the framework. We'll start with a simple web service that you can expose to the client-side script.

5.1.1   Configuring a web service

Let's start with a clean slate and create a new Ajax-enabled website from Visual Studio (see chapter 1 for an example). Selecting this option updates the web.config file with all the settings and references you need to get going. The next step is to add a local web service to the site. You can accomplish this by choosing the Web Service option in the Add New Item dialog (see figure 5.1).

To keep everything in one place and for clarity, deselect the Place Code in Separate File option. Building on the Starbucks example in chapter 1 (more on this soon), you'll name the service StarbucksService.asmx. You'll target this service from the client to retrieve relevant data in the examples.

Starbucks revisited

Earlier, we explained the nature of asynchronous operations by telling a story of ordering a beverage from a coffee shop. In brief, we associated placing an order at the shop with making a request to a service. We then likened the processing of that order to an asynchronous operation in which, due to its nature, we were informed of the operation's status and completion at another time. For the remainder of this section, we'll use this tale as the premise for the examples. If you aren't familiar with how an asynchronous operation behaves, please take a moment to visit the story in chapter 1 for a high-level explanation.

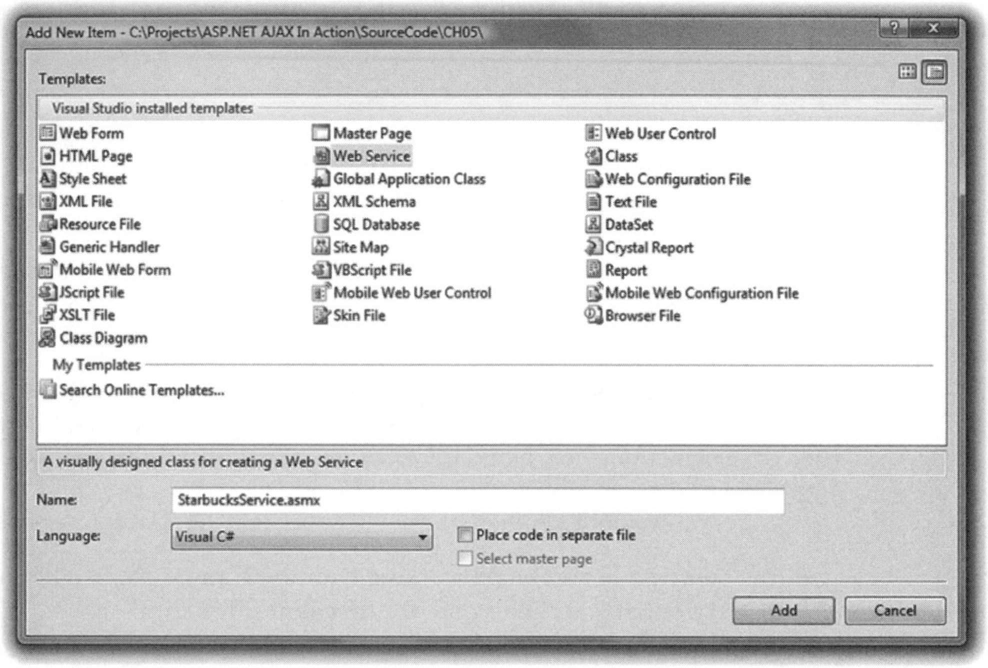

Figure 5.1 Use the Add New Item dialog to add a web service to the site.

Listing 5.1 shows the beginnings of this service and how it's exposed to the client-side script.

Listing 5.1 Configuring a web service for client-script interaction with a few attributes

```
<%@ WebService Language="C#"
  Class="AspNetAjaxInAction.StarbucksService" %>

using System;
using System.Web;
using System.Web.Services;
using System.Web.Services.Protocols;        ❶ Namespace for
using System.Web.Script.Services;              script services

namespace AspNetAjaxInAction      ❷ Ajax-enabled
{                                    service
  [ScriptService]
  [WebService(Namespace = "http://aspnetajaxinaction.com/")]
  [WebServiceBinding(ConformsTo = WsiProfiles.BasicProfile1_1)]
  public class StarbucksService : System.Web.Services.WebService
  {

    [WebMethod]
```

```
    public int GetLocationCount(int zipCode)
    {
      int locations = 0;
      switch (zipCode)
      {
        case 92618:
         locations = 148;
         break;

        case 90623:
         locations = 3;
         break;

        case 90017:
         locations = 29;
         break;

        default:
         break;
      }

      return locations;
    }

  }
}
```

**Exposed web
method** ❸

Exposing a web service to the client in ASP.NET AJAX is done with a few simple steps. The first step, which isn't required, is to include the ❶ namespace for the script services in the framework. This serves as a shortcut so you don't have to fully qualify each attribute and type used from the library. Next, you must decorate the class for the service with the ❷ ScriptService attribute, defined in the System.Web.Script.Services namespace. The service and its web methods are now ready for remote calls from the browser.

Currently, the service contains only one method: ❸ GetLocationCount, which returns the number of stores in a specified ZIP code. Because this is strictly demo code, we hard-coded a few examples and values in order to get results to experiment with.

NOTE The 1.0 release of the ASP.NET AJAX framework doesn't support integration with Windows Communication Foundation (WCF). In earlier Community Technology Previews (CTPs), when the project was known by the codename *Atlas*, WCF integration was supported experimentally. In the next version of the .NET Framework, currently codenamed *Orcas*, WCF support will return.

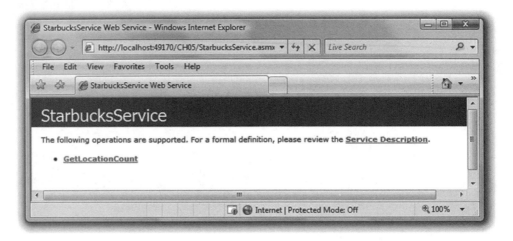

**Figure 5.2   The generated page for an ASP.NET web service gives a summary of its public methods
and a link to the service description.**

To validate your work so far, open a browser window and direct it to the service's
.asmx file. As expected, you see the generated summary page that you've become
accustomed to with normal ASP.NET Web Services. Figure 5.2 shows the summary
page and the single method it currently exposes.

Everything appears normal so far, but this isn't your typical web service. If you
append */js* to the end of the URL, such as http://www.samplewebsite.com/sam-
pleservice.asmx/js, then instead of seeing the friendly generated page for the service, you're presented with JavaScript content that represents the client-side proxy
for this service. (Firefox displays the script in the page, and Internet Explorer 7
prompts you to save the contents into a local file.) We'll dig deeper into how this
is made possible soon. The important thing to remember right now is that you get
a set of JavaScript functions that you can leverage to call the web methods from
the script. This JavaScript code, or proxy, is also known as a *web service proxy*.

The next logical step is to add a page to the site that interacts with this service.

5.1.2   *Invoking web service methods from JavaScript*

The first step in Ajax-enabling a page is to add the ScriptManager control.
Remember, the ScriptManager is the brains of an Ajax page because its responsibilities primarily include managing and deploying scripts to the browser. In this
case, you want to leverage the ScriptManager so the page can use the web service
proxy you just generated. Listing 5.2 shows how adding a reference to the local
Web Service makes this possible.

Listing 5.2   Adding a service reference to the ScriptManager control

```
<asp:ScriptManager ID="ScriptManager1" runat="server">
 <Services>
     <asp:ServiceReference Path="~/StarbucksService.asmx"
       InlineScript="true" />
 </Services>
</asp:ScriptManager>
```

The Services property of the ScriptManager contains a collection of ServiceReference objects. A ServiceReference is a reference to a local service on the site. Adding this reference informs the ScriptManager that you would like to include the web service proxy from the service on the page.

The Path for the service reference is set to the .asmx file on the site. By default, the InlineScript property of the reference is set to false. However, in this case it's set to true to demonstrate how the web service proxy will be downloaded, in the page, to the browser. When set to false, the JavaScript for the proxy is instead downloaded to the browser separately.

Using a debugging tool called Firebug (see appendix B for details) from the Firefox browser, you can see the client-side proxy generated for the page (see figure 5.3).

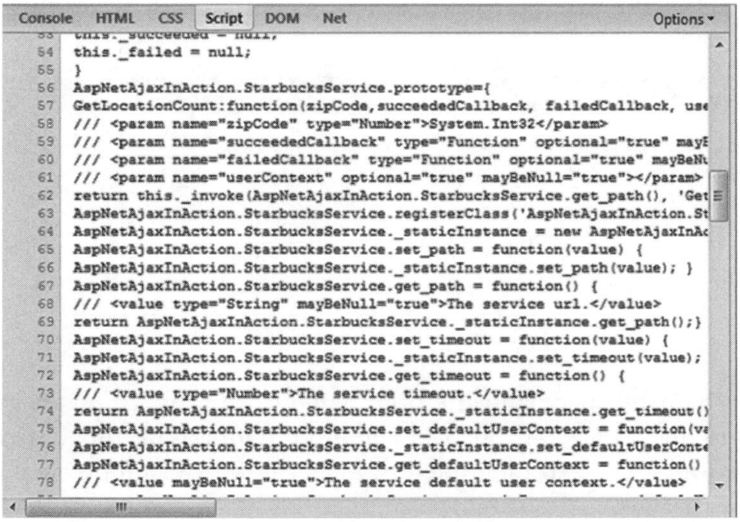

Figure 5.3   Firebug shows a glimpse of the client-side proxy that is included in the page for calling the web methods in the service.

Now that the infrastructure is in place, you can begin making calls to the service. To invoke the single method in the service, add a text box and button to the page to provide the user with an interface for passing in data. The markup portion for this example is presented in listing 5.3.

Listing 5.3   Text box and button to provide an interface for passing parameters to the service

```
<div>
  <input id="Location" type="text" />
  <input id="GetNumLocations" type="button" value="Get Count"
     onclick="getLocations()" />
  <div id="NumLocations"></div>
</div>
```

Notice how the `onclick` event for the button is assigned to the JavaScript function `getLocations`. In this function, you read the value from the text box and pass it along to the web method.

Calling a web method

Making a web method call from JavaScript is similar to calling a method from a library in .NET, except for a few differences that we're about to uncover. Listing 5.4 demonstrates how you make the call to the service for retrieving the number of locations in a ZIP code.

Listing 5.4   Calling a web method from JavaScript

```
function getLocations(){
   var zip = $get("Location").value;
   AspNetAjaxInAction.StarbucksService.GetLocationCount(zip,
                                      onGetLocationSuccess,
                                      onGetLocationFailure,
                                      "<%= DateTime.Now %>");
}
```

Prefixed with the namespace and then the name of the service, `StarbucksService`, a call to the `GetLocationCount` method defined in the .asmx file is invoked along with a few extra parameters. Let's carefully examine each of these extra parameters.

Web method parameters

Passed in to the first parameter is the value in the text box that you retrieved by calling `$get("Location").value` in the previous line. The second parameter is the name of the callback function, `onGetLocationSuccess`, which informs you when the method has successfully completed. Optionally, passed in to the third parameter is the name of another callback function that is invoked if anything goes wrong during the processing of the request. This can include a timeout on the request, loss of connectivity, and a number of other possibilities.

The last parameter provides a mechanism for passing along user context that can be retrieved from either of the callback functions. This example passes in the current time, but any JavaScript object will do. The Microsoft Ajax Library maintains this context for you on the client so that it's conveniently available later when the callbacks are invoked. After the call is made, you wait for either callback function to be invoked.

Callbacks

When the call successfully completes, the function you specified—`onGetLocationSuccess`—is called, and you can update the page with its return value:

```
function onGetLocationSuccess(result, context, methodName){
    $get("NumLocations").innerHTML = result + " location(s) found.";
}
```

Three parameters are passed in to the callback function. The first, often called the *result parameter*, returns the results of the web method. For this example, it's an integer that signifies the number of store locations in the ZIP code. The second parameter is the user context you optionally passed in when you called the method. The last parameter contains the name of the client-side method that initiated this callback. Because the same callback function can be used for different method calls (doing so is common), this parameter can be handy for determining where the call originated and applying additional custom logic.

Everything is straightforward so far, but what happens when an error occurs on the server or the call fails to return successfully due to network complications? In this scenario, the second callback function, `onGetLocationFailure`, is called:

```
function onGetLocationFailure(error, context, methodName){
  var errorMessage = error.get_message();
  $get("NumLocations").innerHTML = errorMessage;
}
```

Inspecting the parameters in the callback, notice that the second and third items are the same as in the successful callback routine earlier. The difference this time is the result parameter (the first parameter), which returns an error object. For this occasion, you can retrieve the error message by calling `error.get_message()` to update the UI accordingly.

The last thing we'll touch on to round off your basic understanding of making JavaScript calls to services is the issue of timeouts.

Timeouts

When you're calling a web service proxy from JavaScript, you sometimes have to take into consideration the amount of time it takes for a request to process. In some cases, you want the call to return immediately, so adjusting the timeout for a shorter interval is preferable. In other instances, a longer timeout that grants the server sufficient time to process the request is better suited. The client-side proxies in ASP.NET AJAX expose a property called `timeout`, which allows you to adjust the interval in milliseconds:

```
AspNetAjaxInAction.StarbucksService.set_timeout(1000);
```

If a response isn't received before the timeout elapses, an exception is generated on the client and the failure callback function is invoked. The error object passed to the callback contains the client-generated exception for a timeout. We'll discuss how to handle errors in a moment.

> **Timeout considerations**
>
> Determining the right timeout interval can be tricky. Ideally, you want to provide the user with feedback as soon as possible, which means short timeouts are preferred. You may want to consider reissuing the request if it initially fails. On the other hand, you want to give the Web Service adequate time to process the request. This time can vary between services and can depend on how busy the service is. Sometimes, it's beneficial to implement a more complex algorithm that issues a short timeout at first and then adjusts itself with a slightly longer timeout interval the next time. You may have to manage and refine the timeout interval for processing a request when you're working with complex scenarios.

So far, we've covered the basics of working with ASP.NET Web Services. We have a lot more to cover, especially relating to working with complex types.

5.1.3 Managing complex types

We've walked through the simplest scenario possible when working with ASP.NET Web Services: calling a method that returns an integer. But applications work with more complex, custom types that closely resemble entities in the real world. In this section, we'll work with these complex types and walk through a series of exercises to demonstrate how you can access them and instantiate them in the script.

You're hired!

With the help of a good book (wink), word around town is that you've become quite the Ajax developer. Management of a well-known coffee shop has asked you to update some of their Web Services so their developers can add more interaction to the company's home page. Your first task is to add a web method that returns the latest deals on the most popular beverages.

You begin by creating a server-side object called Beverage. Keeping things simple, the object has only a few properties: a name, a description, and a cost. Included in the class's implementation is an overloaded constructor that initializes the object with the passed-in properties. Listing 5.5 shows the implementation for this custom type.

Listing 5.5   Implementation of a custom `Beverage` class

```
using System;

namespace AspNetAjaxInAction
{
    public class Beverage
    {
        public Beverage()
        { }

        public Beverage(string name, string desc, double cost)
        {
            this.name = name;
            this.description = desc;
            this.cost = cost;
        }

        private string name;
        public string Name
        {
            get { return this name; }
            set { this.name = value; }
        }

        private string description;
        public string Description
        {
            get { return this description; }
            set { this.description = value; }
        }
```

```
        private double cost;
        public double Cost
        {
            get { return this.cost; }
            set { this.cost = value; }
        }


    }
}
```

Next, you add to the Web Service a method called `GetDeals`, which returns a collection of beverages (see listing 5.6).

Listing 5.6   Implementation for the `GetDeals` method

```
using System.Collections.Generic;
...
[WebMethod]
public List<Beverage> GetDeals()
{
  List<Beverage> beverages = new List<Beverage>();

  // Hard-coded for testing
  Beverage b1 = new Beverage("House Blend",
                  "Our most popular coffee",
                  2.49);

  Beverage b2 = new Beverage("French Roast",
                  "Dark, bold flavor",
                  2.99);

  beverages.Add(b1);
  beverages.Add(b2);
  return beverages;
}
```

Let's examine the newly added `GetDeals` method. Notice how you import the `System.Collection.Generic` namespace at the top. You do this because you'd like to use Generics (a .NET 2.0 feature that is similar to templates in C++) in the return type as opposed to a normal array. On the client side, this doesn't matter, because it's serialized into an array anyway. On the server side, however, Generics provides an easy way to manage typesafe lists.

NOTE Generics aren't required for this solution; you can just as easily set the method to return an array of the Beverage type (`Beverage[]`). But unless you're targeting both .NET 1.1 and .NET 2.0, you should take advantage of Generics when possible. If you aren't familiar with Generics, devoting some time to learning about its benefits would be a worthwhile investment. For C#, see http://msdn2.microsoft.com/en-us/library/ms379564(vs.80).aspx. For VB.NET, see http://msdn2.microsoft.com/en-us/library/ms379608(vs.80).aspx.

A close look at the implementation of the method reveals that a hard-coded list of beverages is created and returned to the caller. The question now is, how can the client-side script handle this new type?

By default, the ASP.NET Web Services used by the Ajax framework use the JSON (see chapter 3) data format for the transfer of data between the client and server. This means the value is first serialized with a JSON serializer before it's written in the response's payload. One of the key reasons JSON is used is because of its natural integration with JavaScript and its lightweight nature. (You can convert JSON into a JavaScript object by passing it into the `eval` method.)

When the result reaches the callback in the JavaScript code, you're given an object that you can manipulate and work with like a normal .NET object. To demonstrate, let's put this all together by calling the `GetDeals` method from JavaScript (see listing 5.7).

Listing 5.7 Calling and handling from JavaScript a web method that returns a complex type

```
<div>
  <input id="GetDeals" type="button" value="Get Deals"
     onclick="getDeals()" />
  <div id="Deals"></div>
</div>
...

function getDeals(){                                    Retrieve deals  ❶
 AspNetAjaxInAction.StarbucksService.GetDeals(onGetDealsSuccess,
                                     onGetDealsFailure);
}

function onGetDealsSuccess(result, context, methodName){  ❷ Instantiate
  var sb = new Sys.StringBuilder();                            StringBuilder
  for (var i = 0; i < result.length; i++){
    var bev = result[i];
    sb.append(bev.Name + " - ");
    sb.append(bev.Description + " - ");        ❸ Declare
    sb.append(bev.Cost + "<br />");               properties
  }
```

```
  $get("Deals").innerHTML = sb.toString();
}

function onGetDealsFailure(error, context, methodName){
  $get("Deals").innerHTML = error.get_message();
}
```

Listing 5.7 begins with the declaration of a button on the form that you use to kick off the request in a function called getDeals. From there, you call the ❶ GetDeals method on the server and assign callback functions for both success and failure scenarios.

If the call returns successfully, you instantiate an instance of the client ❷ StringBuilder object and format the result. Notice how the ❸ properties you declared in the server class (Name, Description, and Cost) are accessed from the script to format the message. All the work of serializing and deserializing the object is transparent to you, and you didn't have to do anything extra to introduce the new object into the proxies.

> **NOTE** As soon as the browser receives the response, the Microsoft Ajax runtime processes it and uses the client-side serializer (the Sys.Serialization.JavaScriptSerializer class) to deserialize the JSON sent by the server. The runtime then invokes the callback that you set to process the results. This lets you access and work with the result as an object, like the one defined on the server.

Let's look at the output. Figure 5.4 demonstrates the results of your efforts up to now.

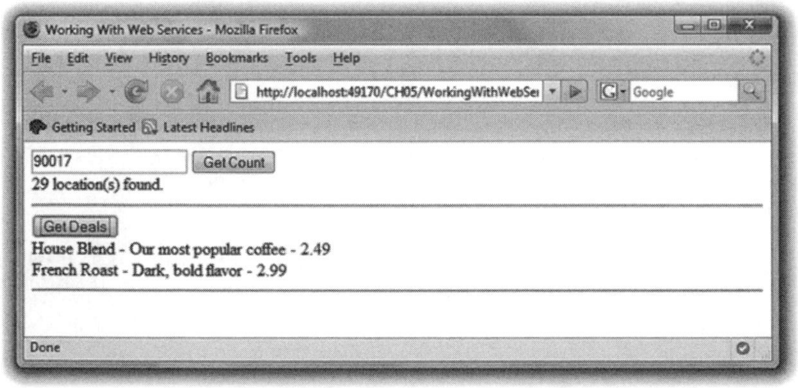

Figure 5.4 A snapshot of what you've built so far: calls to two Web Service methods, one that returns a simple type and another that returns a collection of a custom type

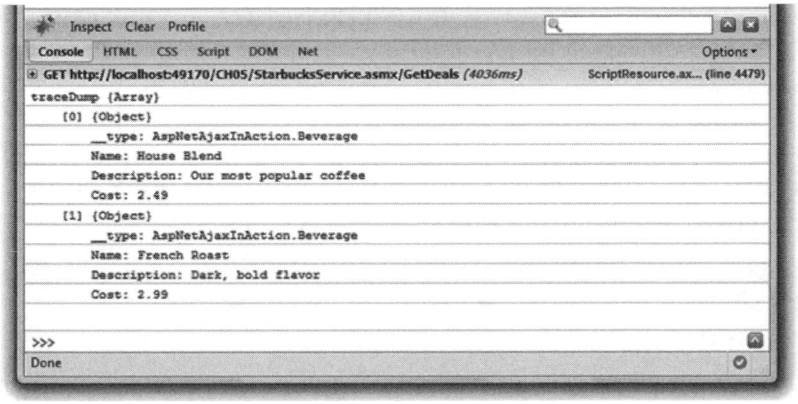

Figure 5.5   Using Firebug for Firefox, this snapshot shows the contents of what is being returned by the server.

If you insert a call to `Sys.Debug.traceDump(result)` from the callback function for the `GetDeals` method, you can use the Firebug tool to inspect what comes back from the server (see figure 5.5).

More details about debugging and using tools such as Firebug and Web Developer Helper are provided in appendix B. We encourage you to become familiar with these tools and leverage them when you're authoring rich-client applications.

Creating server types on the client

The client is thrilled with your work so far, particularly the way the object you defined on the server can be used seamlessly in the browser as well. This prompts them to ask if it's possible to instantiate an instance of a server-side class from the client.

Because the Beverage type is used in the service's `GetDeals` method, the client proxies already include a definition for it. This happens when the proxies are generated and the type is resolved by the Ajax runtime. Creating and initializing an instance of the Beverage type from JavaScript looks similar to how you would do this in .NET code:

```
var bev = new AspNetAjaxInAction.Beverage();
bev.Name = "Holiday Blend";
bev.Description = "A warm and spicy blend.";
bev.Cost = "2.55";
```

What about classes that aren't used in the Web Service? In some cases, the client would like to use the same class they defined on the server, in the browser as well. It seems redundant to have to define the same object in JavaScript because it isn't used by the service.

To demonstrate how you can resolve this situation, let's create another class on the server called `Employee`. For simplicity, this class also has three basic properties: first name, last name, and title. Listing 5.8 shows the implementation for the class.

> **Listing 5.8 The `Employee` class: another complex type defined on the server**

```
using System;

namespace AspNetAjaxInAction
{
    public class Employee
    {
        public Employee()
        {

        }

        private string first;
        public string First
        {
            get { return this.first; }
            set { this.first = value; }
        }

        private string last;
        public string Last
        {
            get { return this.last; }
            set { this.last = value; }
        }

        private string title;
        public string Title
        {
            get { return this.title; }
            set { this.title = value; }
        }
    }
}
```

The goal is to instantiate and update the object in JavaScript as you did with the Beverage object previously. Because the class hasn't been used in any method calls, the Web Service isn't aware that you'd like to include this class in the proxies. To enlighten the Web Service about your intentions, you can leverage the GenerateScriptType tag. If you apply this tag to the Web Service class, along with the type of class you'd like to include, it too will be supported in the web service proxy. Listing 5.9 shows how the Web Service class is updated with the script-type declaration of the Employee class.

Listing 5.9 Adding support for the Employee class on the client using GenerateScriptType

```
[ScriptService]
[GenerateScriptType(typeof(Employee))]
[WebService(Namespace = "http://aspnetajaxinaction.com/")]
[WebServiceBinding(ConformsTo = WsiProfiles.BasicProfile1_1)]
public class StarbucksService : System.Web.Services.WebService
{
  ...
```

This is all you need to do to provide support for instantiating a server-side object on the client. To prove that this class can be created and manipulated from Java-Script, add the following lines of markup and script to the page:

```
<hr />
<div>
<input id="CreateEmployee" type="button"
   value="Instantiate Employee" onclick="createEmployee()" />
</div>
...
function createEmployee(){
    var emp1 = new AspNetAjaxInAction.Employee();
    emp1.First = "Frank";
    emp1.Last = "Rizzo";
    emp1.Title = "Principal";
}
```

Without the GenerateScriptType annotation in the Web Service class, a runtime exception would occur when you try to instantiate the Employee object. Instead, you're able to create an instance and update its properties accordingly.

Making asynchronous requests from JavaScript to a Web Service is pretty easy. What isn't as easy is changing the way these request are submitted. Let's take a closer look at the types of requests we're talking about.

5.1.4   *Using HTTP GET*

So far, all the calls you've made to the Web Service have used the HTTP POST verb. As a security measure, which we'll delve into in a minute, ASP.NET AJAX accepts these types of requests only from the browser by default. To accommodate an HTTP GET request, you're forced to explicitly adorn a method with the `Script-Method` attribute as well as set its `UseHttpGet` property to `true`. This subtle but conscious declaration prevents you from inadvertently letting the browser invoke methods with the HTTP GET verb. Listing 5.10 demonstrates how to update one of the existing methods, `GetDeals`, with HTTP GET capabilities.

> **Listing 5.10   Enabling HTTP GET by updating the `ScriptMethod` attribute and `UseHttpGet` property**

```
[ScriptMethod(UseHttpGet=true)]
[WebMethod]
public List<Beverage> GetDeals()
{
    ...
```

What's all the fuss about?

Why is HTTP GET disabled by default? The primary reason is to avoid compromising security in Ajax applications. To help you understand the kind of security we're talking about, we'll describe how *JSON hijacking* works.

A common approach for JSON hijacking is to introduce into a page a malicious script that invokes an HTTP GET request, like so:

```
<script type="text/javascript" src="someReallyEvilScript.js">
</script>
```

Because the script is included on the page, it evades the origin policy that browsers enforce. This policy is put in place to limit objects like XMLHttpRequest from calling URLs in the same domain. This exploit leaves the JSON payload open for viewing and manipulation of the script. Thankfully, the ASP.NET AJAX framework provides more than one barrier for stopping this problem (a technique known as *security in depth*).

The first layer of security for this scenario forces you to explicitly enable HTTP GET on a method, as we just covered. Second, validation against the Content-Type header field of the request is applied to ensure that it's set to `application/json`. It's interesting to note that when browsers parse external scripts that are included on a page, the content type is never set to `application/json` when making the request. If any of these conditions aren't met (HTTP GET settings or the `application/json` content type), then the request is promptly rejected.

Before we wrap up this section on working with Web Services, we'll explore one more approach. It involves making JavaScript calls to methods on a page, instead of to a Web Service.

5.1.5 *Page methods*

An interesting feature in ASP.NET AJAX is the ability to call, from JavaScript, methods that are declared in the ASP.NET page itself. Because these methods are declared on a page, not from a Web Service, they're appropriately called *page methods*. To demonstrate how this works, let's add a simple static method called `HelloEmployee` to the page. This method takes as a parameter an instance of the `Employee` class you created earlier. The method returns to the caller a formatted greeting:

```
[WebMethod]
public static string HelloEmployee(AspNetAjaxInAction.Employee emp)
{
    return string.Format("Hello {0} {1}.", emp.First, emp.Last);
}
```

Notice how the method is decorated with the `WebMethod` attribute (defined in the `System.Web.Services` namespace), similar to public methods in a Web Service. This required attribute must be adorned on any methods you want to expose as a page method.

In the .aspx page, you enable support for these types of methods by setting the `EnablePageMethods` property of the ScriptManager to `True`. By default, this setting isn't enabled, and any static web methods on the page are omitted from the web service proxy:

```
<asp:ScriptManager ID="ScriptManager1" runat="server"
  EnablePageMethods="True">
  <Services>
    <asp:ServiceReference Path="StarbucksService.asmx"
      InlineScript="true" />
  </Services>
</asp:ScriptManager>
```

To complete this example, you need to call the method from JavaScript and process the response. You do so in much the same manner as the previous asynchronous requests, but this time the calls are prefixed with PageMethods as opposed to the name of the service class. To demonstrate, let's extend the `createEmployee` function you wrote earlier to pass in the `Employee` instance to the `HelloEmployee` method (see listing 5.11).

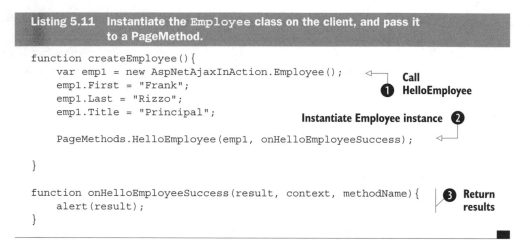

Listing 5.11 Instantiate the `Employee` class on the client, and pass it to a PageMethod.

```
function createEmployee(){
    var emp1 = new AspNetAjaxInAction.Employee();      ◄─────┐  Call
    emp1.First = "Frank";                                   ① HelloEmployee
    emp1.Last = "Rizzo";
    emp1.Title = "Principal";            Instantiate Employee instance ②

    PageMethods.HelloEmployee(emp1, onHelloEmployeeSuccess);    ◄─────┘

}

function onHelloEmployeeSuccess(result, context, methodName){    ③ Return
    alert(result);                                                  results
}
```

You call the ① static method `HelloEmployee` that is declared on the page. Passed into the method is an instance of the `Employee` class that you ② instantiated on the browser. When the code is executed and the ③ results are returned, an alert dialog is displayed to greet the employee (see figure 5.6).

Figure 5.6 The results of passing in a complex type to the server from JavaScript

Page methods offer an alternative to creating a local Web Service for a site. One of the caveats is that only the script from the current page can access the method, as opposed to offering it to other pages on the site. You can look at it as a private web method for that page.

You should now have a solid understanding of how to work with Web Services and JavaScript. The next section will bring you closer to what goes on behind the scenes with asynchronous network calls.

5.2 *The asynchronous communication layer*

In this section, we'll examine the network layer, also known as the *asynchronous communication layer*, in the Microsoft Ajax Library. Briefly, this layer of the Ajax stack provides a set of client classes that abstract away from the client any browser-specific discrepancies for network communication. This enables you to write consistent, solid code for sending asynchronous requests to a web server. Let's begin by examining a simple request and the components that glue it together.

5.2.1   *A simple WebRequest*

The process of sending an HTTP request with the Microsoft Ajax Library involves three objects:

- *Sys.Net.WebRequest*—The HTTP request client object
- *Executor*—Determines how requests are sent and provides status about the request
- *WebRequestManager*—A global object that issues the request by invoking the executor object

To grasp the role of these objects, let's put together a quick example that makes a simple request.

Suppose you have a file called message.txt on the site. To request the contents of this file from JavaScript, you can use code like that shown in listing 5.12.

Listing 5.12   A simple HTTP request for the contents of another file on the server

```
var request = new Sys.Net.WebRequest();
request.set_url("message.txt");
request.add_completed(onRequestComplete);
request.invoke();
```

The first step in putting together a request is to create an instance of the Sys.Net.WebRequest object. Then, you set the `url` property of the request to the file on the server. Next, you add an event handler for when the request completes by calling the `add_completed` function and passing in the name of the routine. The final statement in listing 5.12 is a call to the `invoke` method, which is responsible for issuing the asynchronous request.

NOTE   The `add_completed` function should be called before the `invoke` method on the `WebRequest` instance. If the browser has the message.txt file already in its cache, you don't need to issue an HTTP request to the server. In this case, the request completes synchronously, and the `onRequestComplete` handler is called before the `invoke` method returns.

Let's look now at the callback routine, `onRequestComplete`. Here, you receive the contents of the file requested from the server:

```
function onRequestComplete(executor, eventArgs) {
    alert(executor.get_responseData());
}
```

The `onRequestComplete` function is called with two parameters. The first, `executor`, is of type Sys.Net.WebRequestExecutor, and contains all the information about the status of the asynchronous request. The second, `eventArgs`, is always set to Sys.EventArgs.Empty—an object that represents the absence of event arguments.

> **NOTE** Sys.EventArgs.Empty plays the same role as the System.EventArgs.Empty object that is passed to event handlers in the .NET framework to indicate the absence of event arguments.

To retrieve the contents of the file, you can call the `get_responseData` method of the executor object. If the response completes successfully, the content of the message.txt file is returned. In section 5.2.4, we'll examine what happens when a request fails and how to handle it cleanly.

This executor object is important. Let's discuss its function in the process.

5.2.2 *The executor*

The executor object that you accessed in the earlier example is an instance of the `Sys.Net.XMLHttpExecutor` class. In turn, this class inherits from `Sys.Net.WebRequestExecutor`, which acts as an abstract class. By overriding the implementation of the `executeRequest` method, you can specify how an HTTP request is sent from script. For example, the default executor, `Sys.Net.XMLHttpExecutor`, sends a request using the XMLHttpRequest object. Other types of executors can be created to implement different techniques for sending asynchronous requests to the server.

> **NOTE** At the moment, the `XMLHttpExecutor` is the only executor provided by the Microsoft Ajax Library. Previous CTPs included other executors, such as the `IFrameExecutor`. However these executors were omitted from the final release for quality and security reasons.

The executor object provides all the information you need to know about the response sent by the web server. If you're expecting data in an XML format, use the `get_xml` method to retrieve the response in the form of an XML DOM object. Data returned in a JSON format can be retrieved with the `get_object` method. The executor also offers methods that you can use to examine the status code and text of each response:

```
var statusCode = executor.get_statusCode();
var statusText = executor.get_statusText();
```

Facilitating all this interaction is a single object on the client called the *WebRequestManager*. To help you understand how all the pieces fit together, we'll continue our exploration by briefly looking at how this object is used and where it fits.

5.2.3 WebRequestManager

The WebRequestManager is an instance of the `Sys.Net._WebRequestManager` class. When the Microsoft Ajax runtime is loaded, the instance is created and stored in a global JavaScript variable called `Sys.Net.WebRequestManager`.

When the `invoke` method is called on a WebRequest object, the request is passed to the WebRequestManager. Here, checks are made to determine the associated implementation of the executor object for the request. If an assigned executor isn't found, then the default `XMLHttpExecutor` is used. At this point, the WebRequestManager calls the `executeRequest` method on the executor object to launch the request.

This leads us to errors and how you should handle them correctly and efficiently. In the next section, you'll put together a useful error-handling mechanism that can be added to your toolbox for future Ajax development.

5.2.4 Handling errors

The `onRequestComplete` function that you used earlier has an obvious problem: It doesn't check for errors. It assumes that the request always succeeds and that the response always contains the expected data. Loss of network connectivity, an overloaded server, and runtime exceptions are a few of the reasons an error can occur. Too many things are not under your control and can have a negative impact on the outcome of a request. In such cases, you need to inform the user properly that an error occurred, or at least have logic in place to manage the error efficiently.

Errors fall into two categories: *server-returned HTTP errors* and *non-HTTP errors*. You can have a server-returned HTTP error when the request successfully reaches the server but fails to process it. A valid example is when an ASP.NET application throws an exception during the processing of the request, such as attempting to access an object with no reference. When this happens, you can obtain the exact error from the HTTP status code returned by the server. The response's payload also contains the error description. Table 5.1 summarizes the status codes you're interested in.

Table 5.1   HTTP status codes

Status code range	Meaning
100-199	Informational status codes. These status codes don't normally arise during ASP.NET AJAX development and can be ignored.
200-299	The request was received and successfully processed.

Table 5.1   HTTP status codes *(continued)*

Status code range	Meaning
300-399	The request needs to be redirected. The most common code in this range is 302, which is sent when `Response.Redirect` is called from ASP.NET code.
400-499	The request contains an error. A common error code is 404, which indicates that the resource (file) wasn't found on the server.
500-599	The request was valid, but the server failed to process the request. The most common error code in this range is 500, which is returned by ASP.NET when an exception occurs during request processing.

Based on your knowledge of the HTTP status codes, you can modify the `onRequestComplete` method as shown in listing 5.13.

Listing 5.13   Modified version of the `onRequestComplete` function to handle HTTP errors

```
function onRequestComplete(executor, args) {
 var statusCode = executor.get_statusCode();

 if (statusCode >= 200 && statusCode < 300) {          Check HTTP
  alert(executor.get_responseData());                  status code
 }
 else {
  var message = String.format('HTTP Error: {0}, Status Text: {1}',
                              executor.get_statusCode(),
                              executor.get_statusText());
  alert(message);
 }
}
```

This handles most exceptions, but what about making the code reusable? And what about timeouts and requests that are aborted? Perhaps it makes sense to make the error handling more granular. This way, more information is available in case additional logic is needed for specific types of errors.

Listing 5.14 demonstrates a snippet of code that extends the WebRequestExecutor object with a function called `checkError`.

> **Listing 5.14 A reusable error-checking routine that extends the WebRequestExecutor object**

```
Sys.Net.WebRequestExecutor.prototype.checkError = function() {
    var e = null;

    if (this.get_aborted()) {                          ❶ Check whether
        e = Error.create('Request Aborted.',              request was aborted
                    { name : 'RequestAbortedError' });
    }                                                  ❷ Check timedOut
    else if (this.get_timedOut()) {                       property
        e = Error.create('Request timed out.',
                    { name : 'RequestTimeoutError' } );
    }
    else {
        var statusCode;
        try {
            statusCode = this.get_statusCode();
        }
        catch(e) {
            statusCode = 0;                            Check
        }                                              status
                                                       code    ❸
        if (statusCode < 100 || statusCode >= 600) {
            e = Error.create('Connection Error.',
                        {name : 'ConnectionError' });
        }
        else if ((statusCode < 200) || (statusCode >= 300)) {
            e = Error.create('HTTP Error.',
                        { name : 'HTTPError',
                        "statusCode" : statusCode,
                        statusText : this.get_statusText() } );
        }
    }

    return e;
}
```

Let's walk through the code in the checkError routine to learn more about the other ways of investigating errors. First, the variable e is declared and initialized to null. If no error is found, the fact that this variable remains null signifies to the caller that the request succeeded. Next, you check to see if the request was ❶ aborted by checking the aborted property of the executor object. If this condition is true, then an Error object is created along with the status code and text from the WebRequestExecutor object.

If the request wasn't aborted, the next check queries the ❷ timedOut property to determine if the server took too long to process the request. The final check examines the ❸ status code. If the code's value doesn't fit between 200 and 300, then you create an Error object accordingly.

NOTE Connection failures are handled differently depending on the browser. Internet Explorer, for example, sometimes returns a status code that is greater than 600 with text that conveniently says *Unknown*. Firefox throws an exception when get_statusCode is called. Opera prefers to return a status code of zero and empty status text. As you can imagine, a reusable function can come in handy.

The checkError function can become part of your toolbox moving forward. Because it extends the WebRequestExecutor object through the prototype property (see chapter 3 for details), you can use it conveniently in future projects.

This concludes our general overview of how to communicate with local services from the client. In some cases, you want to reach out to external services—in the same domain or outside. In the next section, we'll address a few approaches that work with ASP.NET AJAX.

5.3 *Consuming external Web Services*

Today's modern browsers impose security restrictions on network connections that include calls to the XMLHttpRequest object. These restrictions prevent a script or application from connecting to a web server other than the one the page originally came from. These calls are referred to as *cross-domain* requests. Figure 5.7 illustrates this basic restriction.

The rationale is simple: If it's possible to make such a call, then it's possible for a rogue website to access sensitive data from other websites. For example, a web page in http://www.rogue-domain.com can use the XMLHttpRequest object and access all of the user's e-mails from http://mail.live.com. Fortunately, such an action isn't permitted by the XMLHttpRequest object in its default configuration.

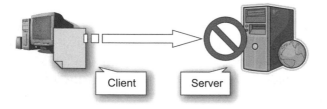

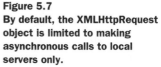

Figure 5.7
By default, the XMLHttpRequest object is limited to making asynchronous calls to local servers only.

NOTE Even though cross-domain calls aren't permitted by the XMLHttpRequest object in its default configuration, the user can change the browser settings to make certain cross-domain calls succeed. However, asking users to change their browser settings so they can access your website is generally a bad practice.

The following types of calls are considered cross-domain requests:

- *A change in the domain*—http://www.mywebsitesite.com can't access http://www.yourwebsite.com.

- *A change in the protocol*—http://www.mywebsite.com can't make a call to https://www.mywebsitesite.com. Note the *s* in https for the second URL.

- *A change in the port number*—http://www.mywebsite.com:8080 can't make a call to http://www.mywebsite.com:8088.

- *A change in the subdomain*—http://mail.mywebsite.com can't access http://calendar.mywebsite.com.

A few safe, recommended ways are available to access data across domains. In the following sections, we'll discuss a number of different approaches that bypass the cross-domain limitation.

5.3.1 *The script technique*

Even though the browser doesn't allow XMLHttpRequest calls across domains, it allows a website to load scripts hosted in a different domain. For instance, a web page in http://www.mywebsite.com can request a JavaScript file from http://www.yourwebsite.com using the following markup:

```
<script src="http://www.yourwebsite.com/somecoolscript.js"
  type="text/javascript"></script>
```

As usual, the src attribute of the script tag contains the URL of the script file to request. In some cases, parameters are passed in to the query string to retrieve more specific data. The handler for that URL on the server then usually parses the query string to generate JavaScript code based on the parameters passed in. The generated script sent from the server can even take actions on the client. If you wanted to make these calls asynchronous, you could create a dynamic script tag using JavaScript and the DOM instead of declaratively placing it on the page.

This method, widely used in Google Maps, Virtual Earth, and the Yahoo JSON APIs, is in many ways limited because the scripts are always requested with the HTTP GET verb. This confines the request to making queries for data with no support for altering the state of a local server (a possibility that a HTTP POST request offers). This comes in handy if you're providing such services, but it falls short of providing additional features for consumers.

You can resolve this situation by introducing something in the middle—a proxy, if you will—that facilitates communication between the local site and an external service. Let's explore this technique in the next section.

5.3.2 *Cross-domain calls through the server*

Let us recap what you know so far. First, you learned that including scripts in pages from other domains allows you to retrieve data from their services. But due to the way requests are delegated (via the HTTP GET verb), certain limitations restrict you from doing more than retrieving simple data. Second, you know that in the server-side code (in the code-behind files), you have full access to other domains through the rich APIs afforded to you in .NET. This leads to the second option for making cross-domain calls: calls through the server.

To better understand this scenario, let's revisit the first Web Service call you made at the beginning of the chapter. You called a `GetLocationCount` method to retrieve the number of stores in a ZIP code. Let's pretend that another Web Service on a different domain aggregates this total. You can't call that service directly from JavaScript, but you can instead leverage the local Web Service as a proxy to the outside service.

You can think of the local service as the middle-man in a transaction. As the client, you don't know much about the external service, nor should you. All you know is that you're interested in the data it provides. The local service handles all the plumbing and the complicated work of communicating with the remote server. Figure 5.8 illustrates the concept of using a local server as a proxy for calling the remote APIs of a remote server.

This is the recommended way of communicating with remote servers. Let's build an example that demonstrates how it works.

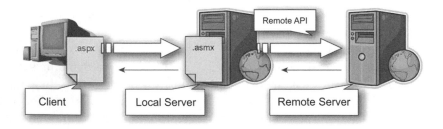

Figure 5.8 A local server can be used as a proxy to a remote server to get around cross-domain restrictions.

5.3.3 *Mash-it-up with ASP.NET AJAX*

In this section, you'll put together an application that retrieves and works with remote services like the Microsoft Virtual Earth map and the Yahoo! Geocoding APIs. This practice of pulling together content and data from other remote services into a single application is sometimes referred to as a *mashup*. Figure 5.9 shows the mashup application in action.

Origin of the term "mashup"

Mashup (or *mash it up*) is a Jamaican Creole term meaning "to destroy." In the context of reggae or ska music, it can take on a positive connotation and mean an exceptional performance or event. The term has also been used in hip-hop, especially in cities such as New York that have a large Jamaican population. In popular culture, a mashup can mean a musical genre of songs that consists entirely of parts of other songs, or a website or web application hybrid that combines content from more than one source into an integrated experience.

Figure 5.9   A simple geographical mashup

The first step in putting together this application is to create a local Web Service that you can use to communicate with other remote services. Because the Yahoo! APIs are on another domain, you'll use this service to facilitate any requests to the APIs for data. Listing 5.15 shows the contents of the local service called GeocodeService.

Listing 5.15 GeocodeService **that acts as the proxy to the Yahoo! Geocode APIs**

```csharp
<%@ WebService Language="C#"
  Class="AspNetAjaxInAction.GeocodeService" %>

using System;
using System.Web;
using System.Web.Services;
using System.Web.Services.Protocols;
using System.Web.Script.Services;

namespace AspNetAjaxInAction
{
    [ScriptService]
    [WebService(Namespace = "http://tempuri.org/")]
    [WebServiceBinding(ConformsTo = WsiProfiles.BasicProfile1_1)]
    public class GeocodeService : System.Web.Services.WebService
    {

      [WebMethod]
      public Location GetLocationData(string street,
                                      string zip,
                                      string city,
                                      string state,
                                      string country)
      {
        return YahooProvider.GetLocationData(street, zip,
                                      city, state, country);
      }
    }
}
```

The service has just one method: GetLocationData. The method returns an instance of the Location class that you also define in the project. This class provides a simple structure for defining the geographical coordinates of a location on a map. Because you decorated the GeocodeService class with the ScriptService attribute, the methods and types (such as Location; see listing 5.16) that it interacts with are generated in the client proxies.

Listing 5.16 `Location` **class for defining coordinates on a Virtual Earth map**

```
using System;

namespace AspNetAjaxInAction
{
    public class Location
    {
        private double latitude = 0.0;
        private double longitude = 0.0;

        public double Latitude
        {
            get { return this.latitude; }
            set { this.latitude = value; }
        }

        public double Longitude
        {
            get { return this.longitude; }
            set { this.longitude = value; }
        }

        public Location()
        { }
    }
}
```

The last server-side class, an implementation class called `YahooProvider`, is used to encapsulate all the details of communication with the Yahoo! service. Listing 5.17 contains the implementation for the provider class.

Listing 5.17 **Implementation details for communicating with the Yahoo! APIs**

```
using System;
using System.Web;
using System.Net;
using System.Xml;
using System.Globalization;

namespace AspNetAjaxInAction
{
 public class YahooProvider
 {
   private readonly static string apiKey = "YahooDemo";
   private readonly static string geocodeUriFormat =
      "http://api.local.yahoo.com/MapsService/V1/geocode?appid=
   {0}&street={1}&zip={2}&city={3}&state={4}";
```

```
public static Location GetLocationData(string street,
                                       string zip,
                                       string city,
                                       string state,
                                       string country)
{
  // Use an invariant culture for formatting numbers.
  NumberFormatInfo numberFormat = new NumberFormatInfo();
  Location loc = new Location();
  XmlTextReader xmlReader = null;

  try
  {
    HttpWebRequest webRequest = GetWebRequest(street, zip,
                                              city, state);
    HttpWebResponse response =
            ➥(HttpWebResponse)webRequest.GetResponse();

    using (xmlReader = new XmlTextReader(
               ➥response.GetResponseStream()))
    {
      while (xmlReader.Read())
      {
        if (xmlReader.NodeType == XmlNodeType.Element &&
            xmlReader.Name == "Result")
        {
          XmlReader resultReader = xmlReader.ReadSubtree();
          while (resultReader.Read())
          {
            if (xmlReader.NodeType == XmlNodeType.Element &&
                xmlReader.Name == "Latitude")
            {
              loc.Latitude = Convert.ToDouble(
                                 ➥xmlReader.ReadInnerXml(),
                                 numberFormat);
            }

            if (xmlReader.NodeType == XmlNodeType.Element &&
                xmlReader.Name == "Longitude")
            {
              loc.Longitude = Convert.ToDouble(
                                 ➥xmlReader.ReadInnerXml(),
                                 numberFormat);
              break;
            }
          }
        }
      }
    }
    finally
```

```
      {
        if (xmlReader != null)
          xmlReader.Close();
      }

      // Return the location data.
      return loc;
    }

    private static HttpWebRequest GetWebRequest(string street,
                                                string zip,
                                                string city,
                                                string state)
    {
      string formattedUri = String.Format(geocodeUriFormat,
                                           apiKey,
                                           street, zip,
                                           city, state);

      Uri serviceUri = new Uri(formattedUri, UriKind.Absolute);
      return
        ➥(HttpWebRequest)System.Net.WebRequest.Create(serviceUri);
    }
  }
}
```

We won't go over the details of the `YahooProvider` class because the purpose of this example is to demonstrate how cross-domain calls can be initiated from the client. However, we include all the code to ensure that you can follow along and successfully perform a cross-domain request just as you will here.

> **NOTE** We decided to keep the logic for making the remote call separate from the local web service definition because the `YahooProvider` class is representative of the server class used to create and send the request to the remote web service. Nothing prevents you from, for example, using the server class generated using the WSDL of a remote web service instead of manually coding a specific provider.

All the pieces are in place on the server side for reaching out to a remote service. Now, you need to put the pieces together on the client to make this a true mashup.

Client code

Now that all the needed server classes are in place, you can kick off the cross-domain call using JavaScript from the browser. Listing 5.18 shows the client-side code for the geographical mashup. Add this code in the `form` tag of a web page in the ASP.NET AJAX enabled website.

Listing 5.18   Client code for the geographical mashup

```
<asp:ScriptManager ID="ScriptManager1" runat="server">
 <Scripts>
   <asp:ScriptReference                          Virtual Earth script ❶
    Path=
        "http://dev.virtualearth.net/mapcontrol/v4/mapcontrol.js" />
 </Scripts>
 <Services>                                     Web Service reference ❷
   <asp:ServiceReference Path="~/GeocodeService.asmx" />
 </Services>
</asp:ScriptManager>

<div id="theMap"                                              ❸ Virtual
  style="position:relative; width:400px; height:400px;">         Earth map
</div>

<script type="text/javascript">
<!--
    function pageLoad() {                        ❹ Create
        var theMap = new VEMap('theMap');          map
        theMap.LoadMap();

        var city = 'Paris';
        var country = 'France';
        GeocodeService.GetLocationData('', '', city,
                            country, '',          ❺ Get geo
                            onLocationReceived);     location
                                                   Add
        function onLocationReceived(result) {    location ❻
          var latLong = new VELatLong(result.Latitude,  pin
                            result.Longitude);
          var pinText = String.format('{0} ({1}, {2})', city,
              result.Latitude, result.Longitude);
          var pin = new VEPushpin(1, latLong, null, pinText);

          theMap.AddPushpin(pin);
          theMap.SetCenter(latLong);
        }
    }
//-->
</script>
```

First, included in the ScriptManager is the ❶ external script reference for the Virtual Earth map. It downloads the functionality you need to display and update the map on the page. Next in the ScriptManager declaration is a reference to the ❷ local service. This is the entry point into the other domains that are otherwise inaccessible from the client.

In the markup portion of the page is a simple ❸ div element, which is set aside to host the Virtual Earth map. Finally, in the script, when the pageLoad event is fired by the Application object (see chapter 2), you ❹ create the Virtual Earth map. Then, you make a ❺ call to the local service that returns the geographical coordinates for a location on the map. In the callback routine, you ❻ update the map with a new pushpin for the location.

This mashup demonstrates how to make cross-domain calls in a safe manner. It also shows how you can import functionality from external scripts to add additional resources to a page. Although this approach seems like the most logical one for communicating with remote services, there is another option we've yet to cover: bridges.

5.3.4   *Bridges*

The ASP.NET Futures CTP offers another alternative for communicating with remote services. This approach, or technology, is suitably referred to as *bridges* or the *bridge technology*. Developers who leverage bridges can create gateways to remote services both programmatically and declaratively with just a few lines of code. Because the bridge code runs in the scope of the web application, the browser can communicate exclusively with the local server. On the server side, the bridge can create a dialogue with external services and subsequently return data to the browser.

> **NOTE**   The bridge technology was almost removed from the ASP.NET AJAX framework shortly before it was released. Due to customer demand, it made its way back into the Futures CTP. At the time of this writing, the bridge technology suffers from a number of symptoms that make it complex and challenging to implement.

Bridge configuration

As we mentioned, bridges require the ASP.NET Futures CTP, which means the Microsoft.Web.Preview.dll assembly must be added as a reference to the website. The final step in configuring bridges is to update the site's web.config file. Beginning with the build provider, you must add a new entry to the <compilation> section to ensure that a server-side class is generated for a bridge file:

```
<compilation debug="true">
 <assemblies>
    ...
 </assemblies>
 <buildProviders>
  <add extension=".asbx"
    type="Microsoft.Web.Preview.Services.BridgeBuildProvider" />
 </buildProviders>
</compilation>
```

Finally, you need to include an entry for the HTTP handler that will manage the requests to the .asbx files:

```
<httpHandlers>
 ...
 <add verb="GET,HEAD,POST" path="*.asbx"
   type="System.Web.Script.Services.ScriptHandlerFactory,
   System.Web.Extensions, Version=1.0.61025.0, Culture=neutral,
   PublicKeyToken=31bf3856ad364e35" validate="false"/>
</httpHandlers>
```

You're now ready to begin experimenting with the bridge technology. Let's put together an example that communicates with a well-known site, Flickr, to query and display photos from users around the globe.

Bridging to Flickr

Flickr offers a wealth of options for how you can format requests and consequently retrieve responses. Some of the request formats include REST, XML-RPC, and SOAP. Response formats consist of REST, PHP, JSON, SOAP, and others. You can find a summary of these services and formats, and a good starting point for learning about Flickr services, at http://www.flickr.com/services/api/.

For this example, you're interested in performing a search against the photos on the site. To keep things simple, you'll use the REST option, which is available at http://api.flickr.com/services/rest/. Remember, REST services typically provide a flexible interface that lets you append details about the request to the URL. For instance, a search for photos tagged with the keyword *ajax* might look like this:

```
http://api.flickr.com/services/rest/?method=
  ⮑flickr.photos.search&api_key=
  ⮑5cbeb1d1a24ac4698a51f0762ee28c0c&tags=ajax&extras=tags
```

Notice how parameters for the search criteria, such as *tags=ajax*, and other important elements are passed along in the URL of the request. On the provider's end, the parameters are parsed from the request and then used to perform the search, resulting in a collection of photos that are returned in an XML format (see figure 5.10).

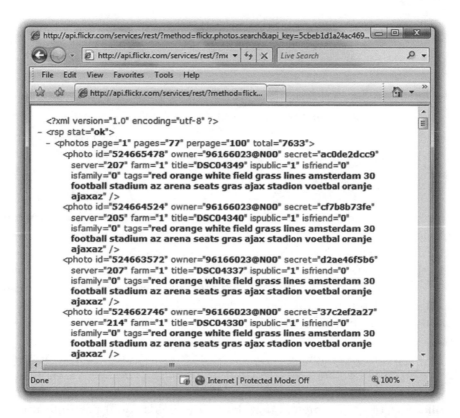

Figure 5.10   Search results from the Flickr REST service are returned in an XML format that you must parse.

We'll discuss how to decode this response shortly, but first let's put together the pieces that make the request by examining the bridge file that makes this possible.

The .asbx bridge file

Earlier, we mentioned a new file extension designated for bridges. This .asbx extension is basically an XML file that serves as a roadmap to an external service and its methods. Listing 5.19 provides an example of how a request to the Flickr REST service is mapped out.

Listing 5.19   The bridge file provides a roadmap or gateway to the remote service.

```
<?xml version="1.0" encoding="utf-8" ?>

<bridge namespace="AspNetAjaxInAction"        ❶ Bridge
     className="FlickrSearch">                     tag
<proxy type=
    "Microsoft.Web.Preview.Services.BridgeRestProxy"   ❷ Proxy
                                                          element
```

```
      serviceUrl="http://api.flickr.com/services/rest/" />       ◄───
      <method name="Search">                          REST service URL  ❸
        <input>
          <parameter name="method" value="flickr.photos.search" />
          <parameter name="api_key"
                     value="% appsettings: FlickrAppKey %" />
          <parameter name="tags" />
          <parameter name="content_type" value="1+" />
          <parameter name="extras" value="tags" />
        </input>                                        Input tag and  ❹
      </method>                                          parameters
    </bridge>
```

The roadmap begins with the ❶ bridge tag and the declaration of a namespace and class name for the service. You can relate this to the declaration of a local Web Service and how it's perceived by the client. In this tag are the proxy element and the declaration of the type of proxy you want to leverage: ❷ Microsoft.Web.Preview.Services.BridgeRestProxy. This type can also be a custom class from the App_Code folder of the website or one of a few other options. Also in the proxy tag is the URL to the ❸ REST service you'll be communicating with.

Subsequently, a collection of methods is exposed to the client. You can liken this to how web methods are declared in a service. The method tag declares the name of the method you can call from JavaScript. In this tag are the input tag and a collection of ❹ parameters that define the fields you'll pass into the request, ultimately forming the URL that is sent to the service.

The parameters were determined by examining the online documentation for the flickr.photos.search API (see http://www.flickr.com/services/api/flickr.photos.search.html). We chose a few of the optional ones to conserve space and maintain the focus on the bridge technology.

Communicating with the bridge

Now that you have the bridge file configured, you can move ahead with calling it from the JavaScript. In order for this to happen, you must first add a service reference to the ScriptManager on the page:

```
<asp:ScriptManager ID="ScriptManager1" runat="server">
    <Services>
        <asp:ServiceReference Path="flickr.asbx"
            InlineScript="true" />
    </Services>
</asp:ScriptManager>
```

Just like a reference to a local Web Service, this action provides you with a client-side proxy to the bridge file. The call to perform a search can now be executed as easily as a call to a local service:

```
AspNetAjaxInAction.FlickrSearch.Search({tags:"Microsoft"},
                                        onSearchComplete,
                                        onSearchFailed);
```

The first parameter of the call takes a collection of input parameters. In the .asbx file, you hard-coded all the parameters except one: tags. The next set of parameters follows the familiar pattern of making network calls—callback functions for success and failure, and the optional user-context parameter.

From the perspective of the client-side code, nothing has changed. But this time, the information returned isn't as friendly. This brings us to another feature of bridges: the ability to transform the data coming back into something more usable or presentable.

Transforming the bridge response

The bridge file supports the ability to transform or convert the response from the service before it reaches the caller. A few built-in transformers make this possible, including one that maps elements and tags in the response to an object. Listing 5.20 illustrates how adding a transformer to the bridge file can alter the response you get in the browser from XML to an object that's friendlier and easier to work with.

> **Listing 5.20** `XPathBridgeTransformer`, **which lets you query the response to an object**

```
<?xml version="1.0" encoding="utf-8" ?>
<bridge namespace="AspNetAjaxInAction" className="FlickrSearch">
   ...
  <transforms>
    <transform                                    XPathBridgeTransformer ❶
  type="Microsoft.Web.Preview.Services.XPathBridgeTransformer">
      <data>
        <attribute name="selector" value="/rsp/photos/photo" />
        <dictionary name="selectedNodes">           ❷ Map to
          <item name="ID" value="@id" />              photos
          <item name="Owner" value="@owner" />
          <item name="Secret" value="@secret" />
          <item name="ServerID" value="@server" />
          <item name="FarmID" value="@farm" />
          <item name="Title" value="@title" />     ❸ Map nodes
          <item name="Tags" value="@tags" />         to properties
        </dictionary>
```

```
    </data>
   </transform>
   </transforms>
  </method>
 </bridge>
```

You use the ❶ XPathBridgeTransformer to query the results and build a custom object. Another transformer that is available is the XsltBridgeTransformer, which lets you apply an XSLT style sheet to the response. Using ❷ XPath queries, you create a custom object by assigning the ❸ nodes in the response to a set of properties.

Now, from the newly formatted response, you can work with the array of objects returned to format the page with something more appealing to the user. Listing 5.21 shows the markup and client-side script used to provide the user with a visually meaningful set of results.

Listing 5.21 Contents of the Flickr bridge application

```
<div>
    <img src="/images/flickr_logo_gamma.gif.v1.5.7"
        width="98" height="26" />
    <input id="flickrSearch" type="text" />
    <input id="search" type="button" value="Search"
        onclick="doSearch();" />
    <span id="searching" style="display: none;">
         <img src="images/indicator.gif" /> Searching...
    </span>

    <div id="summary"></div><hr />
    <span id="photoList"></span>
</div>

<script type="text/javascript" language="javascript">

    function doSearch(){
        var keywords = $get("flickrSearch").value;
        $get("searching").style.display = "inline";
        AspNetAjaxInAction.FlickrSearch.Search( {tags:keywords},
            onSearchComplete, onSearchFailed);
    }
```

```
function onSearchComplete(results){
    $get("searching").style.display = "none";
    $get("summary").innerHTML = formatSummary(results,
                        $get("flickrSearch").value);

    var photos = new Sys.StringBuilder();
    photos.append("<table>");
    for (var i = 0; i < results.length; i++){
        var photo = results[i];
        photos.append("<tr>");
        photos.append(formatImage(photo));
        photos.append(formatDetails(photo));
        photos.append("<tr>");
    }
    photos.append("</table>");
    $get("photoList").innerHTML = photos.toString();
}

function onSearchFailed(error){
    $get("searching").style.display = "none";
    alert(error.get_message());
}

function formatSummary(photos, tags){
    var summary = new Sys.StringBuilder();
    summary.append(photos.length);
    summary.append(" results found for photos tagged with ");
    summary.append("<b>" + tags + "</b>" + ".");
    return summary.toString();
}

function formatDetails(photo){
    var details = new Sys.StringBuilder();
    details.append("<td>");
    details.append("<div>");
    details.append(photo.Title);
    details.append("</div>");
    details.append("<div>");
    details.append("Tags: " + photo.Tags);
    details.append("</div>");
    details.append("</td>");
    return details.toString();
}

function formatImage(photo){
    var link = new Sys.StringBuilder();
    link.append("<td>");
    link.append("<img src='http://farm");
    link.append(photo.FarmID);
    link.append(".static.flickr.com/");
    link.append(photo.ServerID);
```

```
        link.append("/" + photo.ID + "_");
        link.append(photo.Secret);
        link.append("_s.jpg'");
        link.append(" />");
        link.append("</td>");
        return link.toString();
    }
</script>
```

Now for the grand finale. When you execute the application and perform a search for *microsoft surface*, you get a result similar to that shown in figure 5.11.

Bridges offer another alternative for communicating with external services from JavaScript. You have to be aware of a few gotchas when working with them: They're hard to debug, they lack support in Visual Studio (no IntelliSense, debugging, or tracing), and they're still under development. For these reasons, we feel you should be cautious when working with bridges and give strong consideration to whether there is sufficient benefit to using them instead of calling a local Web Service.

Figure 5.11   The results of the Flickr search after transforming the data into a useful object and formatting the interface

In the next section, we'll dive into ASP.NET AJAX's support for some of the application services in ASP.NET—notably authentication, profile, and roles.

5.4 Using ASP.NET application services

ASP.NET 2.0 includes a rich set of application services. Their purpose is to serve as building blocks for common activities on a site. They significantly increase productivity and save time for developers who routinely perform these general actions (the ambitions of every framework). In this section, we'll examine how you can invoke these services from the client-side script.

5.4.1 Enabling ASP.NET application services

The first release of the ASP.NET AJAX framework supports two services: authentication and profile. The next version (which will ship with Orcas, the next version of Visual Studio) will include roles and perhaps a few more services as well. We'll begin this section by focusing on the services supported in the 1.0 version of the framework. Subsequently, we'll provide a preview of the roles service offered in Orcas.

Enabling these services requires a few updates to your web.config file. First, each service must be added to the `sectionGroup` section under the `configuration` group:

```
<sectionGroup name="webServices" ...
  <section name="profileService"
    type="System.Web.Configuration.ScriptingProfileServiceSection,
    System.Web.Extensions, Version=1.0.61025.0, Culture=neutral,
    PublicKeyToken=31bf3856ad364e35" requirePermission="false"
    allowDefinition="MachineToApplication"/>
  <section name="authenticationService"
      ➾type="System.Web.Configuration.
      ➾ScriptingAuthenticationServiceSection,
    System.Web.Extensions, Version=1.0.61025.0, Culture=neutral,
    PublicKeyToken=31bf3856ad364e35" requirePermission="false"
    allowDefinition="MachineToApplication"/>
```

Next, in the `webServices` collection of the `system.web.extensions` group, you must enable each service:

```
<system.web.extensions>
  <scripting>
    <webServices>
      <authenticationService enabled="true" requireSSL = "false"/>
      <profileService enabled="true" />
    </webServices>
  </scripting>
</system.web.extensions>
```

The last step is the configuration of the *data store*—the location where membership and profile information is stored. Out of the box, these application services use the SQL-Express provider. For this example and the others in the book, we'll stick with this option.

> **TIP**   If you'd like to use the full version of SQL 2000 or 2005, or you're interested in how to configure the database for application services, go here: http://msdn2.microsoft.com/en-us/library/aa479307.aspx.

With the configuration complete, you're ready to work with these services. Let's begin with the most common one: authentication.

5.4.2 Authentication service

Authentication is the means by which a user is identified with a set of credentials to validate. ASP.NET AJAX currently supports only forms authentication. This is a cookie-based authentication scheme where a user's credentials (username and password) are stored in a database or file. To configure this type of validation, you must update web.config as follows:

```
<authentication mode="Forms">
  <forms cookieless="UseCookies" loginUrl="~/Login.aspx" />
</authentication>
```

Notice how you include and initialize the `loginUrl` property. Users who attempt to view pages of the site that they aren't authorized to access will be redirected to this page. With this in mind, create a new folder for the site called Secure, and add to it its own web.config with the following settings:

```
<?xml version="1.0"?>
<configuration>
  <system.web>
    <authorization>
      <deny users="?"/>
      <allow users="*"/>
    </authorization>
  </system.web>
</configuration>
```

In this setup, you grant access to authenticated users and reject anonymous ones (for additional information about authorization support, see http://msdn2. microsoft.com/en-us/library/8d82143t(VS.71).aspx). In the secure folder, add another file called ContactInformation.aspx, which will ultimately allow authenticated users to update their home address information.

Now, if you attempt to reach the new page in the Secure folder, you're redirected to the login page as expected. Here, you provide the user with a form for entering in their credentials. Figure 5.12 shows the login page.

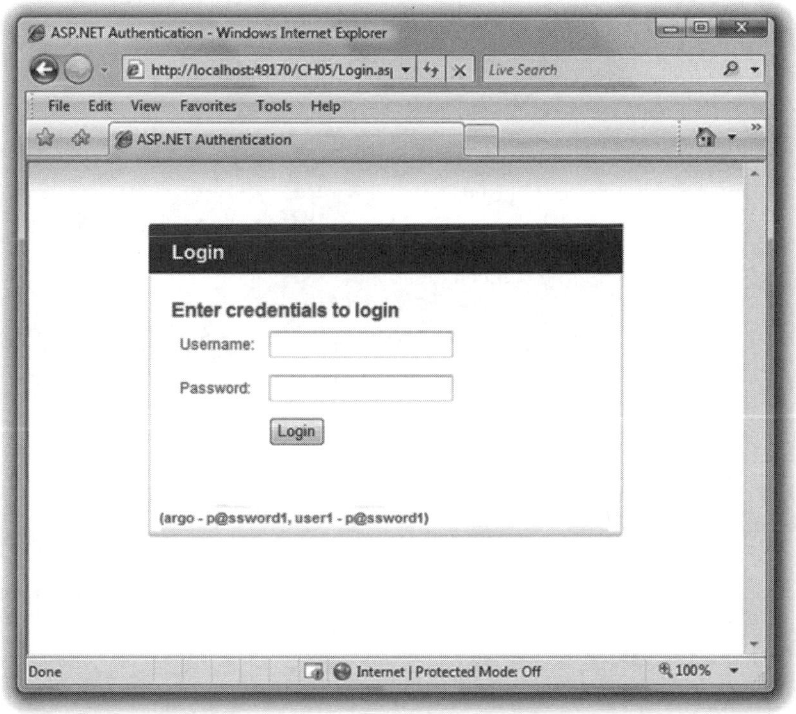

Figure 5.12 The login form used to authenticate users on the site

To authenticate the user, you have to read the values from the form and call the authentication service for validation. Listing 5.22 shows the client-side script that makes this possible.

Listing 5.22 Using the authentication service from JavaScript to validate a user's credentials

```
<script type="text/javascript" language="javascript">
<!--

function pageLoad(){
  with(Sys.Services.AuthenticationService){
    set_defaultLoginCompletedCallback(onLoginCompleted);
  }
  $get("username").focus();
}
```

❶ Default callback

```
function loginUser(){

  var username = $get('username');              Get
  var password = $get('password');              credentials          Validate
  Sys.Services.AuthenticationService.login(username.value,     ◄──┘   user
                        password.value,
                        false,
                        null,
                        "Secure/ContactInformation.aspx",
                        null,
                        onLoginFailed,
                         "User Context");
}
                                                    Validation
                                                    complete
function onLoginCompleted(validCredentials,   ◄──┘
                        userContext,
                        methodName){

    if (validCredentials == false){
        $get("loginStatus").innerHTML = "Login failed.";
    }
}
                                                    Validation
                                                    failed
function onLoginFailed(error, userContext, methodName){  ◄──┘
    alert(error.get_message());
}

//-->
</script>
```

When the page loads, you ❶ set the default callback function for the service's
login method. This isn't a requirement, and it can be overwritten when you call the
function—this is just another approach for setting the callback. Next, the login-
User function is called when the Login button on the form is clicked. You ❷
retrieve the user credentials and then call the ❸ login method to validate them. If
the call succeeds, regardless of whether the credentials are valid, the callback function ❹ onLoginCompleted is called. Passed into the function's first parameter is a
Boolean value that indicates if the credentials are valid. Because you specified a
URL in the fifth parameter, the user is redirected to that address if validation is successful. If something goes wrong during validation, such as an error on the server,
then the ❺ failed callback function is called.

   We briefly mentioned the login method used to validate the user credentials.
Listing 5.23 shows the structure of the method along with brief comments for
each parameter.

Where are the services?

You're calling the authentication service, but where exactly is it? The profile and authentication services are built into the framework. In the case of the authentication service, a class called Sys.Services._AuthenticationService contains the implementation for the service. The leading underscore indicates that the class is treated like a private member (there are no real private classes in JavaScript). You interact with this class through the Sys.Services.AuthenticationService variable. This abstraction between the object and the actual implementation class provides a singleton-like access point to the service.

Listing 5.23 Structure of the login method in the authentication service

```
public Object login(Object username,          // username to validate
                    Object password,          // password to validate
                    Object isPersistent,      // remember me?
                    Object customInfo,        // reserved for future
                    Object redirectUrl,       // redirect on auth
                    Object loginCompletedCallback,  // call on success
                    Object failedCallback,    // call on failure
                    Object userContext);      // user context
```

This gives you a brief introduction to how the authentication service can be called from JavaScript. Now that you're validating a user and redirecting them to a secure (authenticated users only) page, we can look at another service that adds interaction and personalization for users: profile.

5.4.3 *Profile*

In ASP.NET 2.0, the profile provider stores and retrieves information about a site's users, much like session. However, with profile, because the information is saved to a database, the data is persisted and can be retrieved and configured at any time. This differs from session, where information is erased once the user logs off the site or their session expires. Adding properties to a user profile is as easy as updating web.config with a few extra lines, as shown in listing 5.24.

Listing 5.24 Adding properties to the users profile

```
<profile enabled="true">
  <properties>
    <add name="Address1" />
    <add name="Address2" />
    <add name="City" />
    <add name="State" />
    <add name="Zip" />
  </properties>
</profile>
```

In this example, you add properties that relate to an individual's home address. By default, each property is of type `string`. The goal in this section will be to read from and update this profile information from the browser in a seamless and nonintrusive manner.

Contact information page

The contact page we discussed earlier is the perfect candidate for integrating with the profile service. Here, you'll provide a form for the user to update and read their information from their profile, all without the cost of a postback. Figure 5.13 shows the contact form when it's first loaded.

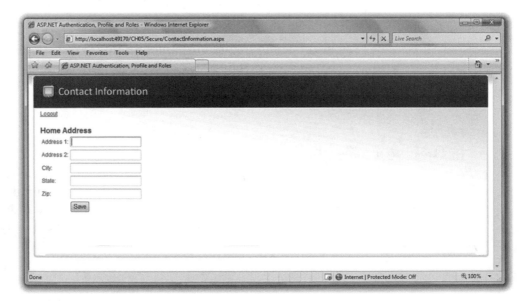

Figure 5.13 The contact information page gives the user a form for reading and updating their profile information.

At the top of the page is a link for logging out. When clicked, it logs out the authenticated user and directs them back to the login page:

```
function logoutUser(){
    Sys.Services.AuthenticationService.logout(null,
                                    onLogoutCompleted,
                                    onLogoutFailed,
                                    null);
}
```

The `logout` function of the authentication service is straightforward. The first parameter optionally takes in the URL for redirecting the user on success. If `null` is passed, the `loginUrl` specified in the web.config is used. The callback pattern for success and failure continues with the second and third parameters. The user context is available in the last parameter.

Reading from profile

To read from a user's profile, you call the service's `load` function and populate the elements on the page with the results; see listing 5.25.

Listing 5.25   Load method of the profile service, which retrieves a user's settings

```
function loadProfile(){
    Sys.Services.ProfileService.load(null, onLoadCompleted,      ❶ Pass null
                                onLoadFailed, null);                as first
}                                                                  parameter

function onLoadCompleted(numProperties, userContext, methodName){
    var profile = Sys.Services.ProfileService;
    $get("address1").value = profile.properties.Address1;
    $get("address2").value = profile.properties.Address2;
    $get("city").value = profile.properties.City;              ❷ Read
    $get("state").value = profile.properties.State;              properties
    $get("zip").value = profile.properties.Zip;
}

function onLoadFailed(error, userContext, methodName){
    alert(error.get_message());
}
```

Because you pass in ❶ null as the first parameter, you retrieve all the profile properties that you defined in web.config. Then, when the successful callback function is called, you can ❷ read the properties and populate the form accordingly.

Updating profile

Updating the user's profile properties is just as easy—all you have to do is initialize the values and then call the `save` function in the service. See listing 5.26.

Listing 5.26　Save function, which updates a user's profile information

```
function saveProfile(){
  var addr1 = $get("address1").value;
  var addr2 = $get("address2").value;
  var city = $get("city").value;
  var state = $get("state").value;
  var zip = $get("zip").value;

  Sys.Services.ProfileService.properties.Address1 = addr1;
  Sys.Services.ProfileService.properties.Address2 = addr2;
  Sys.Services.ProfileService.properties.City = city;
  Sys.Services.ProfileService.properties.State = state;
  Sys.Services.ProfileService.properties.Zip = zip;

  Sys.Services.ProfileService.save(null, onSaveCompleted,
                                    onSaveFailed, null);
}

function onSaveCompleted(numProperties, userContext, methodName){
    $get("updating").style.display = "none";
}

function onSaveFailed(error, useContext, methodName){
    alert(error.get_message());
}
```

Again, you follow the same pattern of calling the service, passing in the name of callback functions for success or failure, and updating the UI on return. Let's take this a step further by implementing a feature that automatically saves a user's profile as they edit their information.

AutoSave pattern

The simplicity and nature of this service provide you with a great opportunity: the ability to save user profile settings automatically. With the use of a timer, you can periodically save profile information. This added value will be appreciated by users who lose their Internet connection intermittently or forget to click the Save button on the form (it does happen).

To integrate this useful pattern, you kick off the timer after the profile settings are originally loaded. Then, when the interval for the timer elapses, you call the same saveProfile function you used earlier:

```
function onLoadCompleted(numProperties, userContext, methodName){
    ...
    window.setInterval(tryAutoSave, 10000);
}
```

```
function tryAutoSave(){
    saveProfile();
}
```

This is a nice feature that doesn't require a lot of coding. This leads us to the last service, roles, which grants you the ability to inquire about the roles a user has been assigned.

5.4.4 Roles: an Orcas preview

The next version of the ASP.NET AJAX framework will include another built-in application service: roles. The simplest way to demonstrate how to use the role service is to designate a portion of the page that only certain users in a role can view.

> **NOTE** The built-in roles service isn't part of the 1.0 release of ASP.NET AJAX. This section provides a sneak peek at what is to come in the next version. This version will be baked into the next release of Visual Studio, code-named Orcas. At the time of this writing, downloads for Orcas are available here: http://msdn2.microsoft.com/en-us/vstudio/aa700831.aspx.

Before we begin, update the web.config file for this service by adding another section for the service under the `sectionGroup` area:

```
<sectionGroup name="webServices"...
  ...
  <section name="roleService"
    type="System.Web.Configuration.ScriptingRoleServiceSection,
    System.Web.Extensions, Version=1.0.61025.0, Culture=neutral,
    PublicKeyToken=31bf3856ad364e35" requirePermission="false"
    allowDefinition="MachineToApplication"/>
```

Next, you need to enable the service along with the others:

```
<system.web.extensions>
  <scripting>
    <webServices>
      ...
      <roleService enabled="true" />
    </webServices>
  </scripting>
</system.web.extensions>
```

That's all you need for the configuration portion. For the UI, add a `div` element named `adminView` to the contact information page. By default, you hide this element by setting its `display` style to none:

```
<div id="adminView" style="display: none;">
    <b>Only admins can see this message!</b>
</div>
```

After the page loads, you can retrieve the current user's roles and make the admin-
View element visible if they're in the designated role:

```
function pageLoad(){
    $get("address1").focus();
    ...
    loadRoles();
}

function loadRoles(){                                              ❶ Call load
    Sys.Services.RoleService.load(onLoadRolesCompleted,   ◁──┘      function
                                  onLoadRolesFailed, null);
}

function onLoadRolesCompleted(result, userContext, methodName){
    if (Sys.Services.RoleService.isUserInRole("Admin")){   ◁──┐
        $get("adminView").style.display = "block";             │
    }                                                          │
}                                              Call isUserInRole │
                                                    function ❷ ─┘

function onLoadRolesFailed(error, userContext, methodName){
    alert(error.get_message());
}
```

The first task is to call the ❶ load function in the service. When it returns successfully, you check to see if the user is in the Admin role by calling the ❷ isUserIn-
Role function. An alternative would be to retrieve a comma-delimited list of roles
from the roles property:

```
Sys.Services.RoleService.get_roles();
```

This requires you to then split and parse the list—which for a different scenario
might be more efficient than calling isUserInRole repeatedly. Because you're
only comparing against a single role, the original approach makes more sense.

Working with the ASP.NET application services is simple. Because they're nothing more than built-in Web Services, the same patterns we covered earlier—callbacks, user context, timeout, and so on—apply here as well.

5.4.5 *Message board application*

We've created a sample message board application that combines all the topics discussed in this chapter, along with some content from chapter 9. The source code for
the message board application is available on the book's website at http://
www.manning.com/gallo. We mention it here as a reminder that you can download
the code from the site for additional examples. Figure 5.14 shows the application
in action.

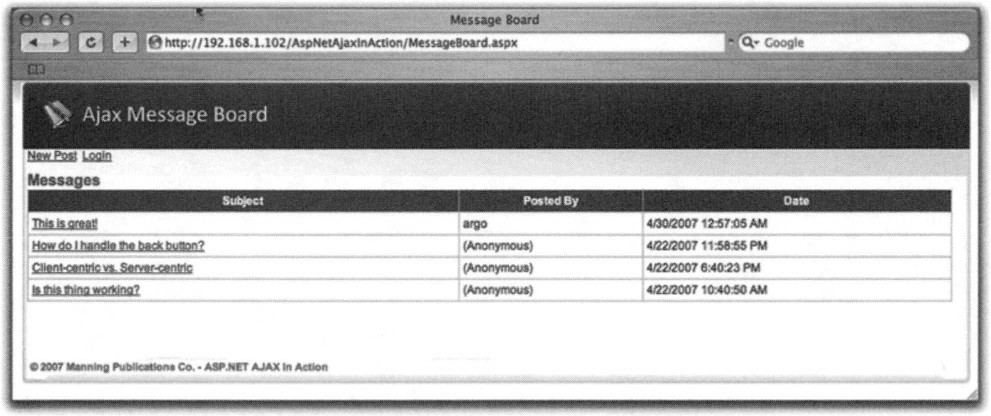

Figure 5.14   The message board application demonstrates a complex, real-world example of how to use some of the patterns discussed in this chapter.

5.5   *Summary*

In this essential chapter, we covered the most primitive and influential pattern used in Ajax programming: making asynchronous calls from the browser to the server. The plumbing work needed to accomplish this task, along with the abstraction of cross-browser discrepancies, are handled for you by the ASP.NET AJAX framework.

With the help of Web Service proxies generated by the framework, you can use local Web Services as a business layer to the applications that run on the browser. You can also use local Web Services to facilitate communication with other remote servers and services on the web. This chapter covered the most typical and recommended approach for building Ajax applications.

Although this chapter was dedicated solely to client-centric programming with ASP.NET AJAX, the next few chapters return to the server-side element of the framework. To become a solid ASP.NET AJAX developer, you must be comfortable with both realms of the architecture. In the next chapter, we'll revisit the UpdatePanel control and take a thorough walk through its features.

Partial-page rendering with UpdatePanels

6

In this chapter:

- Partial page updates
- Triggers and modes
- Nesting and repeating UpdatePanels
- Creating a live GridView filter

One of the most fascinating controls in the ASP.NET AJAX framework is the *UpdatePanel*. This new control replaces the need for a page to refresh during a postback. Only portions of a page, designated by the UpdatePanel, are updated. This technique is known as *partial-page rendering* and can be highly effective in improving the user experience.

At the end of chapter 1 and in segments of chapter 4, you got a glimpse into how the UpdatePanel works and how simple it is to apply to existing ASP.NET applications. In this chapter, the first of two dedicated solely to the UpdatePanel, we'll take you through a series of examples that demonstrate how to use the control effectively. In the process, you'll gain some insight into how it works together with the ScriptManager control to manage and orchestrate partial-page updates. By the end of this chapter, you'll have a solid understanding of how to apply the UpdatePanel correctly to enhance ASP.NET applications.

Just like any other powerful tool, the UpdatePanel requires care and knowledge to fully exploit its influence on a page's performance and behavior. We begin this chapter with some thoughts on its power and responsibilities.

6.1 With great power comes great responsibility

The most amazing thing about the UpdatePanel is how easy it is to use. With a few lines of code, and no client script, the behavior of a page is instantly transformed by its presence. If it isn't employed correctly, performance and the end-user experience can be diminished. Understanding how to use the UpdatePanel effectively, and how and why the control works the way it does, is a vital step toward creating superior and more engaging web pages.

After you become familiar with the UpdatePanel control, it will become one of those tools you can't live without. We liken it to a Tivo or digital video recorder (DVR)—before they came along, most of us didn't know what we were missing. Now that we own these appliances, we can't imagine life without them. To fully appreciate this, let's take a step back and see how the UpdatePanel came to be and why it was created.

6.1.1 Evolution of the UpdatePanel

For years, programming with the XMLHttpRequest object has been the most commonly used approach for communicating with the server from client-side script. The complexities involved in coding those types of applications scared away a lot of developers. To assist, the overall scripting model in ASP.NET 2.0 was significantly enhanced to introduce the idea of *script callbacks*—a way for server controls to communicate with client-side scripts between callbacks. This model was powerful because it offered access to the state of all the controls on the page during a callback. Unfortunately, many developers found the model difficult to work with, and numerous concerns were raised. The lack of support for passing complex types as parameters to the server (only strings were allowed) made the prototype too rigid and exposed its limitations. Developers began to look elsewhere for solutions.

In an effort to address these concerns, members of the ASP.NET team began work on a communication library built on top of the callbacks. The primary objective of the library was to simplify the use of callbacks and to provide a rich set of APIs for enabling the exchange of complex and simple types between the server and client. From this library came a control called the *RefreshPanel*. The purpose of the RefreshPanel was to offer a server control that refreshed the contents of a page without a page refresh. Out of this hard work, the UpdatePanel emerged, with deeper integration into the page lifecycle and a more transparent footprint on the page.

> **NOTE** A *callback* is a piece of code that is passed in as a parameter or argument to other code. The other piece of code can call the callback code (usually a function) at any time, even numerous times, in response to some processing.

With the history lesson out of the way, we can begin probing the UpdatePanel control by first looking at a simple example of its use. If you've used the control before or are familiar with its basics features, then skipping to section 6.2 will be the most logical step for you. If this is your first encounter with the UpdatePanel, read on to discover how you can use it to solve a common problem: the page refresh.

6.1.2 *A simple example*

Recently, a loyal and happy customer of yours requested that you develop an online poll feature for her company's website. The idea was that users could fill out the weekly poll on the site, and the company could then collect the information to learn more about their customers. You decided to implement the feature as a *user control*, and you placed it on the right column of the home page. Figure 6.1 shows the page in a state where the user has yet to complete the online poll.

When a user completes the online poll and clicks the Submit button, a postback occurs; the page refreshes while the user selection is recorded by the server

Figure 6.1 The online poll control in a state before any user interaction

and a new page is served to the browser. Figure 6.2 shows the online poll after the user has completed it.

As the site's traffic increases and weekly poll feature grows in popularity (man, you're good!), the site begins to slow down considerably. After some research, it becomes apparent that limited bandwidth and the stress of loading the entire page after each online poll is submitted are the main causes of the site's inadequate performance. This time, the company has approached you in search of suggestions for alleviating the stress recently placed on the site. They have made it clear that they would like to change the site as little as possible and are in search of a solution that is simple and easy to manage.

Your first thought is to use an IFRAME element. IFRAME stands for *inline frame;* this element is commonly used to include external objects such as HTML documents in a page. If you move the online poll feature to its own page and then host it in an IFRAME, only the contents in the frame will be posted back to the server. This solution lessens the strain put on the server, but it still causes that portion of the page

Figure 6.2 Feedback from the online poll after it has been completed

to reload and flicker in the process. For aesthetic reasons, this solution isn't acceptable to the customer.

With the IFRAME not returning pleasing results and the use of pop-up windows being out of the question, you decide to explore an Ajax solution by making a request to the server using the XMLHttpRequest object and then updating portions of the page dynamically from the client (with JavaScript). This approach requires you to abandon the user control and move most of the logic from the server to the client. It also introduces the effort of managing browsers that don't support the XMLHttp protocol and writing the online poll logic in two areas to compensate (once in JavaScript, again on the server).

So far, this seems like the most reliable solution, but it leaves you wondering if there is a better option.

At last, you decide to give ASP.NET AJAX a try. You start by purchasing a copy of *ASP.NET AJAX in Action* (a wise choice). You realize that the solution you're looking for is possible with the UpdatePanel control. Listing 6.1 shows a portion of the markup before adding the UpdatePanel to the page.

Listing 6.1   Markup for the home page before adding the UpdatePanel

```
<%@ Page Language="C#" AutoEventWireup="true"
    CodeFile="SimpleExample.aspx.cs"
    Inherits="SimpleExample" %>
<%@ Register Src="~/UserPoll.ascx" TagPrefix="demo"
    TagName="UserPoll" %>

...

 <div id="masthead">
   <a href="SimpleExample.aspx" >
    <img src="images/header.png" alt="Emily's Flowers"
     style="border: 0px;" />
   </a>
 </div>
 ...

 <div id="container">
   <div id="page_content">
     ...
   </div>
   <div id="right_col">
     <demo:UserPoll ID="FlowerPoll" runat="server" />        The online
   </div>                                                      poll control
 </div>
```

Listing 6.2 shows the same code with the addition of the ScriptManager and UpdatePanel controls. With these quick and minor updates, the next time the user fills out the online poll, the portion of the page encapsulated by the UpdatePanel is updated dynamically instead of a page refresh occurring.

Listing 6.2   Adding the ScriptManager and UpdatePanel to replace the page refresh with a partial-page update

```
<%@ Page Language="C#" AutoEventWireup="true"
    CodeFile="SimpleExample.aspx.cs"
    Inherits="SimpleExample" %>
<%@ Register Src="~/UserPoll.ascx" TagPrefix="demo"
    TagName="UserPoll" %>

                                                         Required
<asp:ScriptManager ID="ScriptManager1" runat="server" />  ScriptManager
```

```
...

<div id="masthead">
  <a href="SimpleExample.aspx" >
   <img src="images/header.png" alt="Emily's Flowers"
   style="border: 0px;" />
  </a>
</div>
...

<div id="container">
  <div id="page_content">
    ...
  </div>
  <div id="right_col">
     <asp:UpdatePanel ID="UpdatePanel1" runat="server">
       <ContentTemplate>
         <demo:UserPoll ID="FlowerPoll" runat="server" />
       </ContentTemplate>
     </asp:UpdatePanel>
  </div>
</div>
```

UpdatePanel enables partially updated region

Amazingly, that is all you needed to do to keep the page refresh from taking place. A postback still happens, but it takes place asynchronously (for more about asynchronous operations, see chapter 1). Best of all, the hard work needed to accomplish this was done for you.

> **TIP**   A common misconception about the UpdatePanel is that it enables a section of a page to be partially rendered without a postback. The truth is, a postback still occurs, and the price of going through the entire page lifecycle comes with it. Without a postback, none of this would be possible, and the application logic would have to change. Instead, an *asynchronous* postback occurs, and the only action that is replaced from the user's perspective is the full-page refresh. Throughout this book, we'll make a conscious effort to distinguish between a page refresh and a postback. Before the UpdatePanel, the two were incorrectly considered to be the same thing.

This simple example should give you a glimpse into what the UpdatePanel can accomplish. Now, we'll take a closer look at the control—its properties, methods, and limitations.

6.2   Getting to know the UpdatePanel

This section focuses on the basics of the UpdatePanel. Through a series of small and helpful examples, you'll gain an understanding of its core components. This section also covers how the UpdatePanel works with the ASP.NET page lifecycle to perform partial-page updates. In order for partial-page updates to occur, you need content, which brings us to the first step in using the UpdatePanel: specifying which content to update.

6.2.1   Content for the UpdatePanel

All content that is added to the UpdatePanel is a candidate for partial-page rendering. When content is added to the panel, either declaratively or programmatically, that content can be rendered (updated) when an asynchronous postback occurs. To demonstrate, let's walk through a few quick examples.

Listing 6.3 demonstrates how content is added declaratively to an UpdatePanel by placing it in a property called `ContentTemplate`.

> **Listing 6.3   Declaratively adding controls to the UpdatePanel**

```
<asp:ScriptManager ID="ScriptManager1" runat="server" />
<asp:UpdatePanel ID="UpdatePanel1" runat="server">
   <ContentTemplate>
      <div>                                              Current time
         Last Updated: <%= DateTime.Now.ToLongTimeString() %>    ◁──┘
      </div>
      <div>
         <asp:Button ID="Update" runat="server" Text="Update" />   ◁─┐
      </div>                                              Button to  │
   </ContentTemplate>                                  invoke postback
</asp:UpdatePanel>
```

In this example, inline code is used to display the current time. An ASP.NET Button control is declared to demonstrate what happens when a postback occurs. The Button control, by default, raises a postback when it's clicked. Because this control is placed in the `ContentTemplate` tag, it can be considered a *child* control of the UpdatePanel. When this example is executed and the button is clicked, the time displayed on the page is updated without a page refresh. Running the example produces the output shown in figure 6.3.

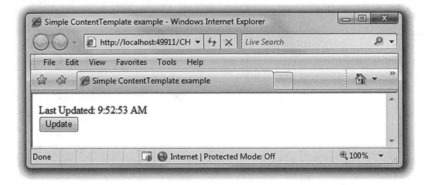

Figure 6.3   Simple ContentTemplate example

Subsequent clicks of the Button on the form continue to update the current time dynamically. This works by replacing the traditional postback with an *asynchronous* postback that the ScriptManager intercepts. During this type of postback, updates are applied to the page by injecting the necessary JavaScript that renders the contents in the UpdatePanel.

> **NOTE**   The UpdatePanel class has a private property called ChildControls, which is the type of a privately sealed class called SingleChildControl-Collection. When the page is loaded, the controls declared in the ContentTemplate tag are added to the collection of controls in the ChildControls property. Then, when an asynchronous postback occurs, the ScriptManager initializes the triggers on each UpdatePanel to invoke its rendering. Triggers will be covered later in the chapter.

As an alternative, you can add content added to an UpdatePanel programmatically. Listing 6.4 demonstrates how to programmatically add a control to the UpdatePanel.

Listing 6.4   Adding a control to the UpdatePanel programmatically

```
protected void Page_Load(object sender, EventArgs e)
{
  Button button1 = new Button();
  button1.ID = "Button1";
  button1.Text = "Update";

  Label label1 = new Label();
  label1.ID = "Label1";
```

```
    label1.Text = string.Format("Updated at: {0} ",
                        DateTime.Now.ToLongTimeString());

    UpdatePanel1.ContentTemplateContainer.Controls.Add(label1);      Add to
    UpdatePanel1.ContentTemplateContainer.Controls.Add(button1);     child
}                                                                    controls
```

A Button and a Label control are both programmatically added to the UpdatePanel by means of a property called `ContentTemplateContainer`. This approach is ideal for controls that are added during runtime, as opposed to controls added declaratively through markup. Because controls added this way aren't persisted, this is done on each `Page_Load` occurrence.

This should give you a grasp of how content is specified for partial updates with an UpdatePanel. Understanding this fundamental concept is extremely important. Once you've declared the content, you want some control over when it updates; so, you need to become familiar with the `UpdateMode` property.

6.2.2 *Update modes*

The `UpdateMode` property determines under what conditions the contents of an UpdatePanel are rendered. By default, this property is set to `Always`, which signifies that the contents are rendered on each and every postback, regardless of what control or UpdatePanel it originated from.

The preferred setting is `Conditional`, which indicates to the ScriptManager that the UpdatePanel should render its contents only if one of the following conditions are met:

- A child control of the UpdatePanel invokes a postback.
- A registered trigger, such as a button click outside the UpdatePanel, is invoked (we'll explain this in more detail when we talk about triggers).
- The `Update` method for the UpdatePanel is called.

To demonstrate how this setting works, let's extend the previous example by adding an additional UpdatePanel to the page with similar contents. In the second panel, you set the `UpdateMode` property to `Conditional`. The latest revision to the code is shown in listing 6.5.

Listing 6.5 Setting the `UpdateMode` property to `Conditional`

```
<asp:ScriptManager ID="ScriptManager1" runat="server" />
<asp:UpdatePanel ID="UpdatePanel1" runat="server">
    <ContentTemplate>
      <div>
          Last Updated: <%= DateTime.Now.ToLongTimeString() %>
      </div>
      <div>
          <asp:Button ID="Update" runat="server" Text="Update" />
      </div>
    </ContentTemplate>
</asp:UpdatePanel>
<hr />

<asp:UpdatePanel ID="UpdatePanel2" runat="server"          Conditional
    UpdateMode="Conditional">                              updates only
    <ContentTemplate>
      <div>
          Last Updated: <%= DateTime.Now.ToLongTimeString() %>
      </div>
      <div>
          <asp:Button ID="Update2" runat="server" Text="Update" />
      </div>
    </ContentTemplate>
</asp:UpdatePanel>
```

The results after clicking the button in the first UpdatePanel are shown in figure 6.4.

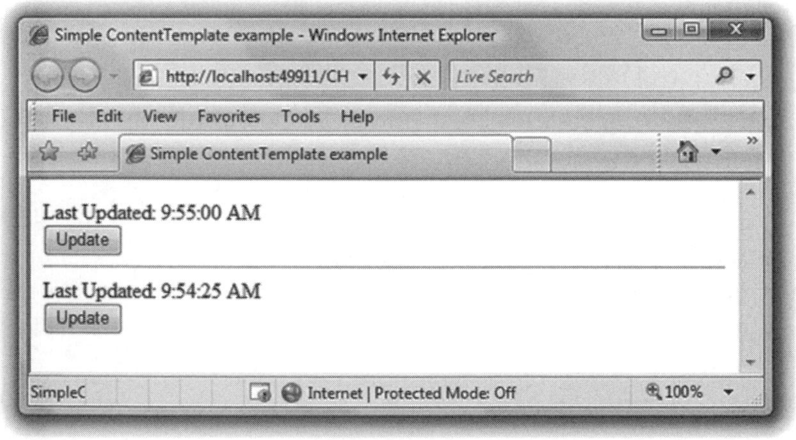

Figure 6.4 The results of an asynchronous postback invoked from the first
UpdatePanel. The second UpdatePanel isn't updated because its `UpdateMode`
is set to `Conditional` and none of its conditions have been met.

TIP   Setting the UpdateMode property to Always should be considered the last option for updating a region dynamically. The point of the UpdatePanel is to reduce the amount of data being passed down from the server by passing in only the contents that need to be updated. Instead of setting the property to Always, you should make it a habit to initially set it to Conditional and let a case for Always present itself when applicable. The UpdateMode property is set to Always by default to provide an out-of-the-box development experience for the creator.

The next time you run the application and click the button in the first panel (the one set to Always), notice that only the contents for that panel are updated. Because you've set the UpdateMode for the second panel to Conditional, it doesn't update because none of its conditions have been met.

If you click the button in the second panel (the one set to Conditional), notice that the contents of both panels are updated. This occurs because the postback was invoked by one of its child controls. Because the first panel's mode is set to Always, it updates for every postback. If possible, take the time to manipulate these settings and become familiar with how they work.

You're making good progress. Now that you're applying partial-page updates, it would be beneficial for you to understand how those updates are initially applied.

6.2.3 Render modes

When an UpdatePanel initially renders its contents, it places it in a <div> or <span> HTML tag. Subsequent postbacks look for the ID of the UpdatePanel to apply additional rendering from JavaScript. The RenderMode property determines which HTML tag is used when the initial rendering occurs. The default setting is Block, which correlates to the <div> tag. The other setting is Inline, which is associated with a <span> tag. Based on the layout of the page and the location of the UpdatePanel, one setting may be more ideal than the other. To illustrate their differences, consider the example in listing 6.6.

Listing 6.6   Rendering the UpdatePanel's contents as a <div> or <span> tag

```
<asp:ScriptManager ID="ScriptManager1" runat="server" />

<p>
  Last Updated:
  <asp:UpdatePanel ID="UpdatePanel1" runat="server"        Render as
    RenderMode="Inline">                                   <span>
    <ContentTemplate>
      <%= DateTime.Now.ToLongTimeString() %>
```

```
    </ContentTemplate>
  </asp:UpdatePanel>
</p>

<p>
  Last Updated:
  <asp:UpdatePanel ID="UpdatePanel2" runat="server"          Render as
    RenderMode="Block">                                      <div>
    <ContentTemplate>
      <%= DateTime.Now.ToLongTimeString() %>
    </ContentTemplate>
  </asp:UpdatePanel>
</p>
```

The contents of both UpdatePanel controls are nearly identical. They differ only in their settings of the RenderMode property. Figure 6.5 shows the difference between how each UpdatePanel renders its contents.

In the first panel, the <span> tag is used to render the contents of the panel inline. The second panel uses a <div> tag to define a division or section in a document, resulting in the UpdatePanel's contents being placed below the previous contents.

As you learn how the UpdatePanel is used, it's just as important to understand *how* it works. An essential piece of this puzzle is examining its relationship with the ASP.NET page lifecycle.

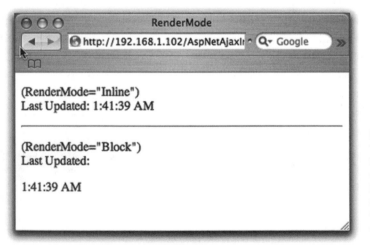

Figure 6.5
The results of two
UpdatePanel controls
with identical content
but different RenderMode
settings: the first set
to Inline, the second
to Block.

6.2.4 ASP.NET page lifecycle

In ASP.NET, when a request is made for a web page, an instance of the Page class is created. The class goes through a series of steps to process the request before it's destroyed. These steps include initialization, instantiating controls, rendering the UI. The process of going through these steps and firing events along the way, is known as the page lifecycle.

It's important for every ASP.NET developer to understand the events that occur in the page lifecycle. In the case of the UpdatePanel, being aware of when certain actions take place is critical to understanding how the control works. Table 6.1 shows the events in the page lifecycle that are closely tied to the UpdatePanel, and what measures the control takes to plug itself in to the page.

Table 6.1   Events in the ASP.NET page lifecycle that the UpdatePanel control interacts with

Page event	Description	UpdatePanel actions
Init	This is the first step in the lifecycle. It occurs when the page is initialized.	Each UpdatePanel on the page is registered with the ScriptManager control.
Load	After initialization is complete, this event is fired when the page is first loaded.	If the page is in an asynchronous postback, it initializes all the triggers for each UpdatePanel on the page.
PreRender	This occurs *before* the page is about to render.	Sanity checking is done here to ensure that all the settings for each UpdatePanel on the page are set correctly. For example, if the ChildrenAsTriggers property is set to True, the UpdateMode must be set to Conditional.
Unload	This event is fired after the page is removed from memory but hasn't yet been disposed.	Each UpdatePanel responsibly unregisters itself with the ScriptManager.

TIP   Custom control developers and page developers who wish to extend existing controls must be intimately familiar with the page lifecycle events in order to correctly initialize, maintain state, and execute control actions. For more information about the ASP.NET page lifecycle, see http://msdn2.microsoft.com/en-us/library/7949d756-1a79-464e-891f-904b1cfc7991.aspx.

You should have a general, high-level grasp of what goes on during the page lifecycle with the UpdatePanel. Examining the stages in the cycle should give you insight as to when certain actions are permitted. Speaking of events, you've built a solid foundation and will now learn about a important part of the UpdatePanel: triggers.

6.3 *Triggers*

A *trigger* is an event coming from a control that causes an UpdatePanel to refresh its contents. The following types of triggers can be associated with an UpdatePanel:

- AsyncPostBackTrigger—Invokes an asynchronous postback for the associated UpdatePanel and any other UpdatePanels on the form that have the UpdateMode property set to Always
- PostBackTrigger—Invokes a traditional postback to the page that causes the page to refresh

Similar to specifying content for an UpdatePanel, you can add triggers declaratively or programmatically. Let's start by examining the most common trigger you'll use: an asynchronous trigger.

6.3.1 *Asynchronous triggers*

Each child control of an UpdatePanel is by default an asynchronous trigger. This means postbacks resulting from interaction with these controls are replaced with asynchronous postbacks that invoke the UpdatePanel to render its contents. But what about controls that haven't been specified as content in an UpdatePanel? For example, say you want to refresh the contents of an UpdatePanel based on the click event of a button that isn't a child control.

This can be accomplished by registering the control as an asynchronous trigger. Listing 6.7 demonstrates how to achieve this programmatically when the UpdatePanel has its UpdateMode set to Conditional.

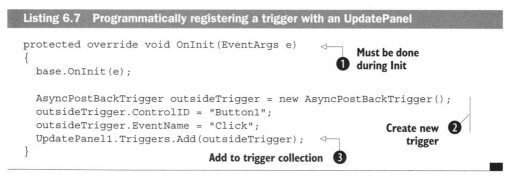

```
Listing 6.7   Programmatically registering a trigger with an UpdatePanel

protected override void OnInit(EventArgs e)          ◁──   Must be done
{                                                       ❶   during Init
  base.OnInit(e);

  AsyncPostBackTrigger outsideTrigger = new AsyncPostBackTrigger();
  outsideTrigger.ControlID = "Button1";
  outsideTrigger.EventName = "Click";                       Create new  ❷
  UpdatePanel1.Triggers.Add(outsideTrigger);     ◁──┐        trigger
}
                  Add to trigger collection  ❸
```

If you go back to the page lifecycle in the previous section, you'll notice that during the Load event, the ScriptManager initializes the triggers for each UpdatePanel on the page. This tells you that any triggers you want to add to an UpdatePanel must be added before the Load event is fired. Registering a trigger in the ❶ Init event seems like the most logical place. To do so, you need to create a new ❷ asynchronous trigger and add it to the triggers collection of that ❸ UpdatePanel.

An AsyncPostBackTrigger has two properties. The first is ControlID, which is the ID of the control that will raise the event. The second, optional, property is the EventName, which as you can guess, is the name of the event that the control raises for an asynchronous postback. If EventName isn't initialized, it defaults to the event that the control is most known for (for example, the click event for a button).

This approach is used primarily for adding triggers to a panel that has Update-Mode set to Conditional. It also works for panels that have UpdateMode set to Always, but another approach is available for those situations that makes more sense:

```
ScriptManager1.RegisterAsyncPostBackControl(this.FindControl
    ➥("Button1"));
```

Calling the RegisterAsyncPostBackControl method of the ScriptManager registers the postback for all the UpdatePanel controls on the form that have Update-Mode set to Always. Panels that have the property set to Conditional aren't rendered when this asynchronous postback occurs.

Adding triggers declaratively is even simpler; see listing 6.8.

Listing 6.8 Controls outside the UpdatePanel's declaration invoking asynchronous postbacks

```
<asp:UpdatePanel ID="UpdatePanel2" runat="server"
    UpdateMode="Conditional">
 <ContentTemplate>
     <div>
         Last Updated: <%= DateTime.Now.ToLongTimeString() %>
     </div>
     <div>
         <asp:Button ID="Update2" runat="server" Text="Update" />
     </div>
  </ContentTemplate>
  <Triggers>
   <asp:AsyncPostBackTrigger ControlID="Button1"      Add button click to
       EventName="Click" />                           trigger collection
  </Triggers>
</asp:UpdatePanel>
                                        Not a child control
<hr />
<asp:Button ID="Button1" runat="server" Text="Update" />   ⟵
```

Adding a trigger declaratively is as easy as adding it to the Triggers collection of the UpdatePanel.

This should be straightforward so far; we've introduced the asynchronous trigger and how to add it programmatically and declaratively. But what about controls for which you want a normal postback? For example, what if you want a button that is a child of an UpdatePanel to perform a normal postback, resulting in a page refresh when it's clicked? This brings us to the other type of trigger you can register with the panel: a postback trigger.

6.3.2 Postback triggers

Postback triggers work like traditional postbacks in ASP.NET. They cause the page to refresh and upload its contents to the server while a new page is eventually returned to the client. In some situations, you may want this behavior for controls that inherently become asynchronous triggers because of their association with an Update-Panel. For example, when a control is a child of the UpdatePanel, by default it becomes an asynchronous trigger and thus replaces any traditional postbacks that would have occurred.

Registering a postback trigger is as easy as an asynchronous trigger. Listing 6.9 demonstrates how to register a child control as a postback trigger programmatically.

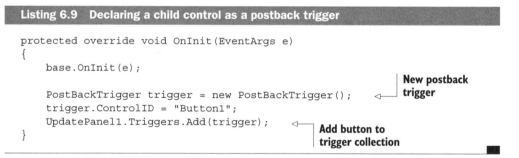

Listing 6.9   Declaring a child control as a postback trigger

```
protected override void OnInit(EventArgs e)
{
    base.OnInit(e);

    PostBackTrigger trigger = new PostBackTrigger();      New postback
    trigger.ControlID = "Button1";                        trigger
    UpdatePanel1.Triggers.Add(trigger);      Add button to
}                                            trigger collection
```

During the Init event, an instance of a PostBackTrigger is created and initialized to a child in the UpdatePanel by setting its ControlID property. Next, you add it to the collection of UpdatePanelTrigger items in the panel's trigger collection to inform the ScriptManager that this control performs traditional postbacks.

> **NOTE**   Each UpdatePanel has a collection of triggers of a type called UpdatePanelTriggerCollection. This collection contains items of an abstract class called UpdatePanelTrigger. Because the class is abstract, which means you can't create an instance of it, you can only add items that are of type PostBackTrigger or AsyncPostBackTrigger, because they both inherit from UpdatePanelTrigger.

Once more, adding the trigger declaratively is as easy as with an asynchronous trigger; see listing 6.10.

Listing 6.10 Registering a child control as a control that raises a normal postback

```
<asp:UpdatePanel ID="UpdatePanel1" runat="server" UpdateMode="Always">
    <ContentTemplate>
        <%= DateTime.Now.ToLongTimeString() %>
        <asp:Button ID="Button1" runat="server" Text="Update" />
    </ContentTemplate>
    <Triggers>
        <asp:PostBackTrigger ControlID="Button1" />         ←—┐ Reloads
    </Triggers>                                                │ entire page
</asp:UpdatePanel>
```

Excluding the `EventName` property, a `PostBackTrigger` is added programmatically and declaratively the same way as an `AsyncPostBackTrigger`. This covers how triggers are specified with an UpdatePanel.

What we have yet to cover is how to manually distinguish when triggers are fired. In some cases, you may not want the contents of an UpdatePanel to be rendered when an asynchronous postback occurs, even when one of its conditions has been met (see `Conditional UpdateMode`, earlier in the chapter). In addition, you may want to update the contents of another UpdatePanel on the page when a one panel is updated.

6.3.3 Manual triggers

The `ChildrenAsTriggers` property determines whether postbacks from a child control in an UpdatePanel result in its contents being refreshed. By default, this property is set to `True` and can be set to `False` only when the `UpdateMode` is set to `Conditional`. Attempting to do so without this condition results in an `InvalidOperationException` being thrown by the ScriptManager during the page's `PreRender` event.

Setting the property to `False` allows asynchronous postbacks to occur, but the ScriptManager bypasses any updates to the UpdatePanel that are associated with the postback. Listing 6.11 shows how `ChildrenAsTriggers` is used declaratively.

Listing 6.11 Setting `ChildrenAsTriggers` to `false` so as not to initialize triggers

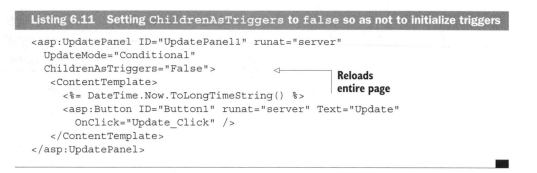

```
<asp:UpdatePanel ID="UpdatePanel1" runat="server"
  UpdateMode="Conditional"
  ChildrenAsTriggers="False">                    ◁─────── Reloads
   <ContentTemplate>                                       entire page
     <%= DateTime.Now.ToLongTimeString() %>
     <asp:Button ID="Button1" runat="server" Text="Update"
       OnClick="Update_Click" />
   </ContentTemplate>
</asp:UpdatePanel>
```

Programmatically, you can set this property after the `Init` event, giving you the luxury of waiting for other events in the page lifecycle to occur before determining if this property should be set:

```
UpdatePanel1.ChildrenAsTriggers = true;
```

> **NOTE** The ScriptManager is responsible for orchestrating the partial-page updates of each UpdatePanel on the page. When it comes time to update the page, it iteratively walks through the list of UpdatePanel controls on the page and invokes the triggers in each one to render its contents. In this case, the internal `Initialize` method that invokes a trigger isn't called, and the contents for the UpdatePanel remain the same.

The Update method

This brings us to the `Update` method of the UpdatePanel. With the `Update` method, you can force the contents of an UpdatePanel to render during an asynchronous postback. This includes other UpdatePanel controls on the page, as well, but these panels must have their `UpdateMode` property set to `Conditional` in order to successfully update. Listing 6.12 demonstrates an event raised from one UpdatePanel updating itself and other panels on the page.

Listing 6.12 Manually updating a page by calling its `Update` method

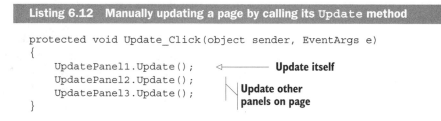

```
protected void Update_Click(object sender, EventArgs e)
{
    UpdatePanel1.Update();       ◁─────── Update itself
    UpdatePanel2.Update();
    UpdatePanel3.Update();            Update other
}                                     panels on page
```

The first `Update` method is called for the UpdatePanel that originated the asynchronous postback. Because the `ChildrenAsTriggers` property was set to `False`, the panel's contents can be updated only when its Update method is called. The next few lines call the Update method for other panels on the page to render their contents.

The previous sections will serve as a core reference to how the UpdatePanel is used, when you read later chapters. It's time to explore a few more advanced scenarios where you can apply the UpdatePanel.

6.4 Advanced techniques

So far, we've covered the basics of the UpdatePanel, including its properties, methods, and usage. Most of the time, using the UpdatePanel is as simple as applying some of the techniques demonstrated earlier. But sometimes, more complex situations arise where you can use the UpdatePanel in a more creative fashion.

6.4.1 Repeating UpdatePanels

When you're working with repeatable data structures, such as a Repeater, Data-List, or GridView, it's usually best to place the entire control in an UpdatePanel instead of each repeated item. However, in some cases you may want a panel around the repeatable item instead. Let's take, for example, a list of stocks in your portfolio. Next to each stock listing, you want a button that updates only that stock price. Listing 6.13 shows the markup listing of the portfolio application.

Listing 6.13 Repeating an UpdatePanel

```
<asp:ScriptManager ID="ScriptManager1" runat="server" />

<h1>My Portfolio</h1>

<asp:XmlDataSource ID="data" runat="server">      ❶ List of
<Data>                                                stocks
<stocks>
 <stock name="STOCK1" value="STOCK1" />
 <stock name="STOCK2" value="STOCK2" />
 <stock name="STOCK3" value="STOCK3" />
 <stock name="STOCK4" value="STOCK4" />
</stocks>
</Data>
</asp:XmlDataSource>

<div style="width: 200px; border: 1px solid gray; padding: 5px;">
<asp:Repeater ID="Stocks" runat="server" DataSourceID="data"
DataMember="stock">
```

```
<ItemTemplate>
 <asp:UpdatePanel ID="UpdatePanel1" runat="server"
    UpdateMode="Conditional">
  <ContentTemplate>
    <asp:Label runat="server" ID="StockName"
       Text='<%# Eval("name") %>' />
    <asp:Button runat="server" ID="UpdateStock" Text="Update"
      OnClick="UpdateStock_Click" />
    <asp:Label runat="server" ID="StockPrice" Text="" />
  </ContentTemplate>
 </asp:UpdatePanel>
</ItemTemplate>
<SeparatorTemplate>
 <hr style="border: 1px dashed gray;" />
</SeparatorTemplate>
</asp:Repeater>
</div>
```

❷ Repeating panels

In this example, an ❶ XmlDataSource stores a simple list of stocks in the portfolio. In the ItemTemplate of the Repeater is the ❷ UpdatePanel control. The panel contains a label for the stock name, a button to update the price, and another label to display the price. The server-side code that updates the price is shown in listing 6.14.

Listing 6.14 Updating the stock price

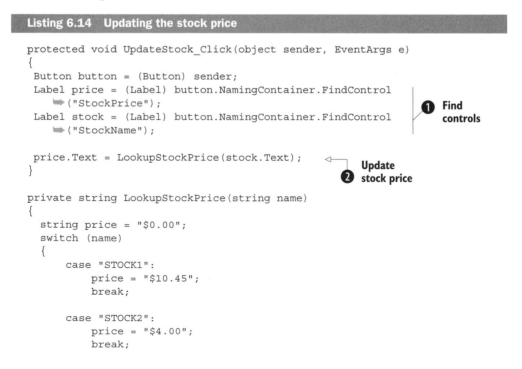

```
protected void UpdateStock_Click(object sender, EventArgs e)
{
 Button button = (Button) sender;
 Label price = (Label) button.NamingContainer.FindControl
    ⮩("StockPrice");
 Label stock = (Label) button.NamingContainer.FindControl
    ⮩("StockName");

 price.Text = LookupStockPrice(stock.Text);
}

private string LookupStockPrice(string name)
{
  string price = "$0.00";
  switch (name)
  {
      case "STOCK1":
          price = "$10.45";
          break;

      case "STOCK2":
          price = "$4.00";
          break;
```

❶ Find controls

❷ Update stock price

```
        case "STOCK3":
            price = "$5.58";
            break;

        default:
            break;
    }
    return price;
}
```

The server-side implementation ❶ finds the controls in the repeated item, then ❷ calls a private method to look up the stock price and update the label accordingly. For simplicity, you hard-code the values returned from the lookup method. When you run the application and select the first three stocks, you get the results shown in figure 6.6.

Again, normally it's best to place an UpdatePanel around a single repeatable control. In the cases where you want to place it around a repeated item, be conscious of the number of items that will be rendered: A strain on performance may occur after some time with a large number of items in a repeatable control. Section 7.3.1 provides more insight into why this happens.

Figure 6.6
Repeating UpdatePanel controls

6.4.2 *Nesting UpdatePanels*

In addition to being able to repeat UpdatePanel controls, you can also nest them. This makes sense only if the UpdateMode property of the outer panel is set to Conditional. For example, consider the nested panel implementation in listing 6.15.

Listing 6.15 Nesting UpdatePanel controls

```
<asp:ScriptManager ID="ScriptManager1" runat="server" />

<div style="border: 1px dashed gray;">
 <asp:UpdatePanel ID="upd1" runat="server"          Outer panel set to
  UpdateMode="Conditional">                          conditional update
  <ContentTemplate>
   <div>
     Last updated on: <%= DateTime.Now.ToLongTimeString() %>  
     <asp:Button ID="bntOuter" Text="Outer" runat="server" />
   </div>
   <div>
    <asp:UpdatePanel ID="upd2" runat="server"
     UpdateMode="Conditional">
     <ContentTemplate>
         
       Last Updated on: <%= DateTime.Now.ToLongTimeString() %>
        <asp:Button ID="btnInner" Text="Inner"
             runat="server" />
     </ContentTemplate>
    </asp:UpdatePanel>
   </div>
  </ContentTemplate>
 </asp:UpdatePanel>
</div>
```

In this example, the outer UpdatePanel is appropriately set to conditionally update. If the UpdateMode property were set to Always instead, there would be no need for the nested panel, because any updates to the inner panel would also invoke an update to the outer panel. Take a moment to run the sample and experiment with setting the outer panel UpdateMode property to Always and back to Conditional.

6.5 *Live GridView filter*

You should have an overall sense of how the UpdatePanel is used. The examples you've worked through so far demonstrated the simplest cases for each property and method the UpdatePanel offers. Now that you've established this foundation, let's have some fun by putting together something a little more useful: a GridView that you can sort, page, and *filter* without normal postbacks (page refreshes).

6.5.1 *Live GridView filter goals*

In ASP.NET 2.0, the GridView is the successor to the frequently used DataGrid control in ASP.NET 1.1. The GridView is powerful because it comes with built-in support for paging, sorting, and editing. But with this feature comes a cost—each of these functions performs a postback to the server. Every time the user sorts a column or pages through results, he loses his connection with the application as he's left waiting for it to be processed.

The first objective is obviously to stop the page from refreshing each time the user interacts with it. As you can guess, the solution is trivial with the UpdatePanel. But what makes this application unique is that it also allows the user to filter the results of a selected column. This brings us to the second goal. Currently, a user can filter a column in the GridView by entering text and clicking the Filter button on the form. Instead of requiring the user to click the Filter button, let's make the application more responsive by countering the user's keystrokes with *on-the-fly* filtering. In other words, you'll bring the GridView filtering to life by making it more intuitive and receptive to user actions instead of requiring them to click the Filter button.

Let's look at the application. Figure 6.7 shows the site in its initial state—before any filter has been applied.

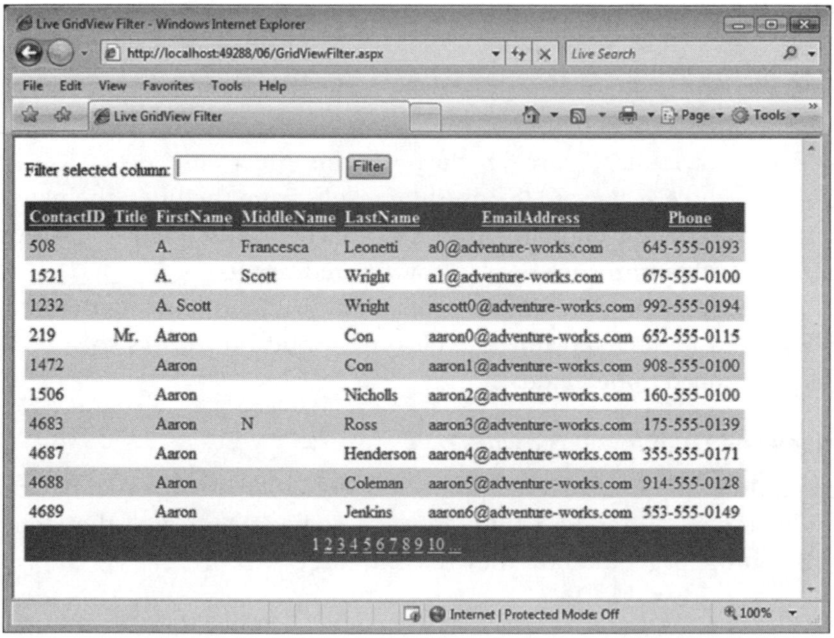

Figure 6.7   The GridView in its initial state shows the contents of the Contact table in the AdventureWorks database.

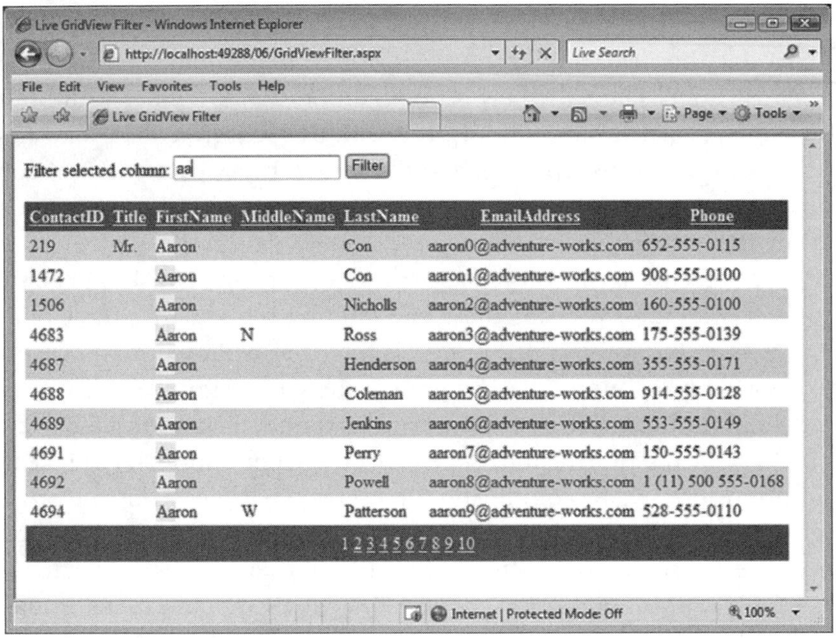

Figure 6.8 After the user enters text and clicks the Filter button, the contents of the selected column are filtered and updated.

If the user enters in some criteria and then clicks the button to invoke the filter, the column that is currently used for sorting (FirstName by default) is updated with the filtered results. Figure 6.8 illustrates this effect.

To effectively relay back to the user the results from the filter, the matched text found in the column is highlighted (a nice touch). Consequently, each update to the text box and button click display new filtered results.

Before you begin integrating the UpdatePanel and enhancing the filter behavior, you should understand how the current application works so you can assess what changes need to be made.

6.5.2 *How does the GridView filter work?*

Understanding how the current application works will assist you in deciding what steps to take next. A good starting point is to take inventory of the elements (or controls) on the page and how they're configured.

NOTE The data used to populate the GridView comes from the Adventure-Works database. AdventureWorks is a fictitious company created by Microsoft with the intention of simulating a real-world business. This example uses SQL Server Express (see appendix A for more information) but can also be configured for SQL Server 2000 or 2005.

Listing 6.16 contains the entire markup portion of the application *before* adding any enhancements.

Listing 6.16   The application contains a GridView and SqlDataSource configured to AdventureWorks.

```
<%@ Page Language="C#" AutoEventWireup="true"
   CodeFile="BeforeFilter.aspx.cs" Inherits="BeforeFilter" %>
<!DOCTYPE html PUBLIC "-//W3C//DTD XHTML 1.0 Transitional//EN"
   "http://www.w3.org/TR/xhtml1/DTD/xhtml1-transitional.dtd">

<html xmlns="http://www.w3.org/1999/xhtml" >
<head runat="server">
    <title>Live GridView Filter</title>
      <style type="text/css">
        .highlight{
          background-color: yellow;
        }
      </style>
</head>

<body>
 <form id="form1" runat="server">
  <div>
   <div>
    Filter selected column:
    <asp:TextBox ID="FilterText" runat="server" />        ❶ Filter
    <asp:Button ID="Filter" runat="server" Text="Filter"    criteria
       OnClick="Filter_Click" />                          ❷ Invoke filter
   </div>                                                    on server

   <p>                                                  ❸ Display
    <asp:GridView ID="GridView1" runat="server"            contacts
      AutoGenerateColumns="False"
      DataSourceID="SqlDataSource1"
      AllowPaging="True" AllowSorting="True"
      EmptyDataText="There are no data records to display." ❹ Built-in
      CellPadding="4" ForeColor="#333333" GridLines="None"    paging and
      OnRowDataBound="GridView1_RowDataBound"                 sorting
      OnPageIndexChanged="GridView1_PageIndexChanged"
      OnSorted="GridView1_Sorted">
```

```
<Columns>
 <asp:BoundField DataField="ContactID" HeaderText="ContactID"
    SortExpression="ContactID" />
 <asp:BoundField DataField="Title" HeaderText="Title"
    SortExpression="Title" />
 <asp:BoundField DataField="FirstName" HeaderText="FirstName"
    SortExpression="FirstName" />
 <asp:BoundField DataField="MiddleName"
    HeaderText="MiddleName"
    SortExpression="MiddleName" />
 <asp:BoundField DataField="LastName" HeaderText="LastName"
    SortExpression="LastName" />
 <asp:BoundField DataField="EmailAddress"
    HeaderText="EmailAddress"
    SortExpression="EmailAddress" />
 <asp:BoundField DataField="Phone" HeaderText="Phone"
    SortExpression="Phone" />
</Columns>
<FooterStyle BackColor="#1C5E55" Font-Bold="True"
    ForeColor="White" />
<RowStyle BackColor="#E3EAEB" />
<EditRowStyle BackColor="#7C6F57" />
<SelectedRowStyle BackColor="#C5BBAF" Font-Bold="True"
    ForeColor="#333333" />
<PagerStyle BackColor="#666666" ForeColor="White"
    HorizontalAlign="Center" />
<HeaderStyle BackColor="#1C5E55" Font-Bold="True"
    ForeColor="White" />
<AlternatingRowStyle BackColor="White" />
</asp:GridView>
```

Connection to AdventureWorks ❺

```
<asp:SqlDataSource ID="SqlDataSource1" runat="server"
 ConnectionString=
 "<%$ConnectionStrings:AdventureWorks_DataConnectionString1 %>"
 SelectCommand="SELECT [ContactID], [Title], [FirstName],
    [MiddleName], [LastName], [Suffix], [EmailAddress],
    [Phone] FROM [Person].[Contact]">
</asp:SqlDataSource>

  </p>
 </div>
 </form>
</body>
</html>
```

The page is simple so far. At the top are ❶ a TextBox and ❷ a Button that work together to pass in filter criteria to the server. The results are displayed in a ❸ GridView that has built-in ❹ paging and sorting enabled. The data source for the GridView is encapsulated in a ❺ SqlDataSource control that retrieves the connection string for the database from the web.config file.

This should give you an understanding of how things are displayed. To complete your understanding of how the application manages the filtering and updates on the form, listing 6.17 shows the entire code for the server-side logic.

Listing 6.17 Applying a filter expression to the data source and updating the results

```
using System;
using System.Web;
using System.Web.UI;
using System.Text;
using System.Web.UI.WebControls;

public partial class BeforeFilter : System.Web.UI.Page
{
    protected void Page_Load(object sender, EventArgs e)
    {
        if (!Page.IsPostBack)
            GridView1.Sort("FirstName", SortDirection.Ascending);
    }

    protected void GridView1_Sorted(object sender, EventArgs e)
    {
        UpdateFilter();
    }

    protected void GridView1_PageIndexChanged(object sender, EventArgs e)
    {
        UpdateFilter();
    }

    protected void Filter_Click(object sender, EventArgs e)
    {
        UpdateFilter();
    }

    protected void GridView1_RowDataBound(object sender,
                                          GridViewRowEventArgs e)
    {
        if (e.Row.RowType != DataControlRowType.DataRow)
            return;
```

```
        if (String.IsNullOrEmpty(SqlDataSource1.FilterExpression))
            return;

        int colIndex = GetColumnIndex(GridView1.SortExpression);
        TableCell cell = e.Row.Cells[colIndex];

        string cellText = cell.Text;
        int leftIndex = cellText.IndexOf(FilterText.Text,
                          StringComparison.OrdinalIgnoreCase);
        int rightIndex = leftIndex + FilterText.Text.Length;

        StringBuilder builder = new StringBuilder();               Highlight  ❶
        builder.Append(cellText, 0, leftIndex);                    matches
        builder.Append("<span class=\"highlight\">");
        builder.Append(cellText, leftIndex, rightIndex - leftIndex);
        builder.Append("</span>");
        builder.Append(cellText, rightIndex,
                       cellText.Length - rightIndex);

        cell.Text = builder.ToString();
    }
                                    ❷  Format and
    private void UpdateFilter()   ◄─┘   set filter
    {
        string filterExpression = null;
                                                         Format filter  ❸
        if (!String.IsNullOrEmpty(FilterText.Text))      expression
            filterExpression = string.Format("[{0}] LIKE '%{1}%'",  ◄─┐
            GridView1.SortExpression, FilterText.Text);                 

        SqlDataSource1.FilterExpression = filterExpression;
    }

    private int GetColumnIndex(string columnName)
    {
        for (int i = 0; i < GridView1.Columns.Count; i++)
        {
            BoundField field = GridView1.Columns[i] as BoundField;
            if (field != null && field.DataField == columnName)
                return i;
        }

        return -1;
    }
}
```

An interesting pattern is the way the event handlers for paging, sorting, and the filter button-click events each call a private method called ❷ UpdateFilter.

Because this logic is called from numerous places, it makes sense that it's encapsulated into a single function. In this function, the text that the user has entered is used to format an SQL statement to apply a ❸ filter expression to the data source. Then, when each row is bound in the GridView, a ❶ highlight is applied to the relative text in the table cell.

Now that you're up to speed about how the application operates, let's apply the enhancements that fulfill the goals of making it more responsive and engaging.

6.5.3 Adding Ajax to the GridView filter

Let's address the postbacks that originate from the GridView first. If you add the ScriptManager control to the page and wrap the GridView and SqlDataSource controls in an UpdatePanel (see listing 6.18), you get rid of the page refreshes related to the sort and paging events. Also, to coordinate the updates with the Filter button, you can add a trigger to the UpdatePanel that correlates to its click event.

Listing 6.18   Wrapping the GridView and SqlDataSource within an UpdatePanel

```
<asp:ScriptManager ID="ScriptManager1" runat="server" />
. . .

<asp:Button ID="Filter" runat="server" Text="Filter"
   OnClick="Filter_Click" />
. . .

<asp:UpdatePanel ID="UpdatePanel1" runat="server"          ⬅── Declare dynamic
    UpdateMode="Conditional">                                    content
   <ContentTemplate>
     <asp:GridView ID="GridView1" runat="server"
        AutoGenerateColumns="False"
        DataSourceID="SqlDataSource1"
        AllowPaging="True" AllowSorting="True"
        . . .
        </asp:GridView>
   </ContentTemplate>
   <Triggers>
     <asp:AsyncPostBackTrigger ControlID="Filter"
        EventName="Click" />         ⬅────── Associate button
   </Triggers>                                click with panel
</asp:UpdatePanel>
```

Notice how you set the `UpdateMode` of the UpdatePanel to `Conditional`. Again, this isn't the default setting—but it should be. By setting the mode to `Conditional`, you relay to the ScriptManager that the rendering of this fragment of the page needs to happen only if one of its conditions is met.

Running the application now shows that you've met the first goal of replacing page refreshes with partial-page updates. What's left is making the filtering more responsive to user actions, such as keystrokes in the TextBox.

6.5.4 It's alive!

Updating the application has drastically enhanced the user experience—but you can do more. Imagine if you could update the filtered columns as the user was typing. If you've ever captured keystrokes, you already know that this happens in the browser, not the server. This presents you with a departure: Until now, you've been adding Ajax-like behavior without a single line of JavaScript. As you develop more complex solutions, you need to write some client-side code to be more efficient and sometimes take control of the client-side application.

For this application, the first thing you can do is remove the Filter button—it won't be needed because you'll use the keystrokes entered by the user to stimulate the filtered data (see listing 6.19). On the server side, you need to add a handler for the `TextChanged` event of the TextBox, which also calls the `UpdateFilter` method.

Listing 6.19   Removing the Filter button and adding the event handler for the `TextChanged` event

```
<div>
  Filter selected column:
  <asp:TextBox ID="FilterText" runat="server"
    OnTextChanged="FilterText_TextChanged" />
</div>
  . . .

protected void FilterText_TextChanged(object sender, EventArgs e)
{
  UpdateFilter();
}
```

You may be wondering why you're adding server-side logic when we just mentioned that you'd be writing JavaScript code to make this happen. The reason is, the logic that performs the filtering still resides on the server. You need a way to invoke that logic from the client when the user is typing.

With the server-side logic in place, you need to bridge the gap between the capturing of the keystrokes on the client and the server-side code that updates the

GridView. Listing 6.20 shows the JavaScript to add at the bottom of the page to make this a reality. You hook into the TextBox's `keydown` event to launch a postback on the server; this calls the `UpdateFilter` method that refreshes the GridView.

Listing 6.20 Hooking into the `keydown` event to launch a postback on the server

```
<script type="text/javascript">

    Sys.Application.add_load(page_load);          ❶ Application
    Sys.Application.add_unload(page_unload);         events

  function page_load(){
    $addHandler($get('FilterText'), 'keydown', onFilterTextChanged);   ⟵
  }
                                                Register handler ❷
  function page_unload(){
    $removeHandler($get('FilterText'), 'keydown',    ❸ Release
              onFilterTextChanged);                      handler
  }

    var timeoutID = 0;

    function onFilterTextChanged(e){

        if (timeoutID){
            window.clearTimeout(timeoutID);
        }
        timeoutID = window.setTimeout(updateFilterText, 1000);
    }
                                    Invoke postback for ❹
    function updateFilterText(){    TextChanged event
        __doPostBack('FilterText', '');
    }

</script>
```

In chapter 2, you were introduced to the *application model* that the Microsoft Ajax Library provides for client-side development. This model gives you an opportunity to write event-driven code on the client, similar to the server-side page lifecycle and event-handling code that server-side developers have grown accustomed to.

In this example, you start by registering callback ❶ functions for the browser load and unload events. When the page loads, you register a handler for the ❷ keypress event. When the page unloads, you ❸ release that handler to avoid any leaks (yes, leaks happen in JavaScript too).

Now for the tricky stuff—when you register the handler for the `keypress` event, you assign it a callback function called `onFilterTextChanged`. When this function is called (each time a keypress occurs), ❹ you clear any delays you previously had with the timer and add another timer delay that ultimately invokes a postback to the server on behalf of the `FilterText` TextBox. You also give it a slight delay so the user can type in a few letters before the contents in the text box are submitted for the filter.

Because this is a postback and you want to handle it asynchronously (without a page refresh), you need to add it to the UpdatePanel's `Triggers` collection:

```
<Triggers>
 <asp:AsyncPostBackTrigger ControlID="FilterText"
      EventName="TextChanged" />
</Triggers>
```

This time, when you run the application, the contents of the GridView are updated shortly after each update is made to the text box—a cool achievement! The final results of your hard work are shown in figure 6.9.

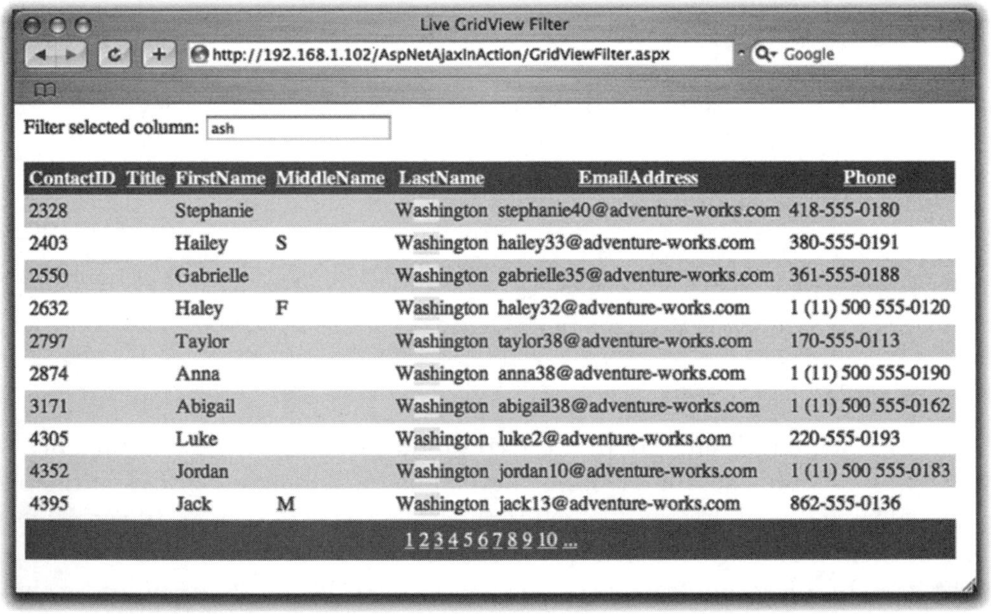
Live GridView Filter
http://192.168.1.102/AspNetAjaxInAction/GridViewFilter.aspx
Google
Filter selected column:
ash
ContactID Title FirstName MiddleName LastName EmailAddress Phone
2328 Stephanie Washington stephanie40@adventure-works.com 418-555-0180
2403 Hailey S Washington hailey33@adventure-works.com 380-555-0191
2550 Gabrielle Washington gabrielle35@adventure-works.com 361-555-0188
2632 Haley F Washington haley32@adventure-works.com 1 (11) 500 555-0120
2797 Taylor Washington taylor38@adventure-works.com 170-555-0113
2874 Anna Washington anna38@adventure-works.com 1 (11) 500 555-0190
3171 Abigail Washington abigail38@adventure-works.com 1 (11) 500 555-0162
4305 Luke Washington luke2@adventure-works.com 220-555-0193
4352 Jordan Washington jordan10@adventure-works.com 1 (11) 500 555-0183
4395 Jack M Washington jack13@adventure-works.com 862-555-0136
1 2 3 4 5 6 7 8 9 10 ...

Figure 6.9 The results of a filter applied to a GridView as a result of keystrokes entered by the user.

This example demonstrated how easy it is to take an existing ASP.NET application and improve the user's experience with partial-page updates in place of traditional postbacks. In addition, it showed some of the new types of behaviors you can introduce to existing applications that you couldn't do before—at least, not effectively.

6.6   *Summary*

In this chapter, we walked through basic examples that demonstrated how to use the UpdatePanel effectively. We also showed you a case where using JavaScript with the UpdatePanel can add interactivity and richness for the user. This chapter provides a solid foundation for understanding how the UpdatePanel works and should be used.

There remains a great deal more about the UpdatePanel. We didn't address its caveats and limitations, and we have yet to explore its client-side model and how it can be used with another object called the PageRequestManager. Finally, we only touched on advanced techniques and how you can use the UpdatePanel to solve complex situations. The next chapter is dedicated to these issues and continues our look at how things work under the hood.

Part 2

Advanced techniques

In the second part of the book, we'll go deep into the client-centric and server-centric development models introduced in part 1. Chapter 7 returns to the UpdatePanel control to examine the partial-rendering mechanism on the client side. Chapter 8 returns to the Microsoft Ajax Library to explore the client component model. Chapter 9 shows how to wire client components to ASP.NET server controls to obtain Ajax-enabled controls. Finally, chapter 10 introduces the Ajax Control Toolkit, the largest collection of Ajax-enabled controls available.

Under the hood
of the UpdatePanel

Using the UpdatePanel control can be a bit like using a Swiss Army knife. Most of the time, the primary utilities, such as the knife and scissors, are used to resolve issues. Other times, using additional functions and features of the tool make more sense when you're attempting to solve complex problems. For example, it's more feasible to use a screwdriver as opposed to the knife for a task such as tightening a screw. Knowing that these functions exist—and, just as important, how and when to use them—will make your use of the tool effective. The same notion is applied to the UpdatePanel: Understanding how to use its principal functions is only half the battle. Gaining a deeper knowledge of its capabilities and how it works will empower you to fully exploit its potential and take more control of your applications.

In previous chapters (specifically, chapters 4 and 6), you learned how to use the UpdatePanel control to effectively apply a partial-page rendering pattern to ASP.NET pages, thus greatly improving the user experience. If you've skipped to this chapter and haven't had any exposure to the UpdatePanel control, we encourage you to first read the earlier sections as prerequisites to the upcoming content. A basic familiarity with the UpdatePanel control will increase your aptitude and chances of successfully understanding the topics we're about to discuss.

This chapter will take you on a deep dive into the UpdatePanel and the partial-page rendering mechanism. It will reveal how partial-page updates work behind the scenes. In addition, it will demonstrate through a series of examples how to leverage this new-found knowledge to address a variety of scenarios, such as control development, performance enhancements, and client-side scripting support.

In the spirit of the Swiss Army knife, we'll begin our exploration by looking at a rarely mentioned but highly effective tool in the partial-page rendering mechanism: the *PageRequestManager*.

7.1   *The PageRequestManager: the unsung hero*

So far, the UpdatePanel has received much of the credit for partial-page rendering. With little effort, ASP.NET developers can leverage the control to declare regions of a page for partial updates. As a result, a normal postback is replaced with an *asynchronous* one that can update fragments of a page without causing the browser to refresh. You know that some of this behavior can't be done with a few server controls; essential to the solution is client-side scripting to at least update the UI. It should come as no surprise that the UpdatePanel server control looks to another resource on the client side to manage the updates and requests to the server.

The PageRequestManager is the client-side counterpart to the UpdatePanel control. When partial rendering is enabled, this JavaScript object manages the asynchronous postbacks and updates that take place in the browser. To help you comprehend how the UpdatePanel works, we'll shed light on where it all begins: with the PageRequestManager and its client-side event model.

7.1.1   *The client-side event model*

The PageRequestManager is a JavaScript object that becomes available when partial rendering is enabled on a page. Its primary responsibilities include managing the UpdatePanel controls on the page, performing asynchronous postbacks to the server, and processing the results to dynamically update the contents of the page. During this process, the PageRequestManager goes through a series of events, much like the ASP.NET page lifecycle, that presents an opportunity for you to take more control of what happens during an asynchronous postback.

Figure 7.1 illustrates the events that occur when an asynchronous postback is triggered from within an UpdatePanel.

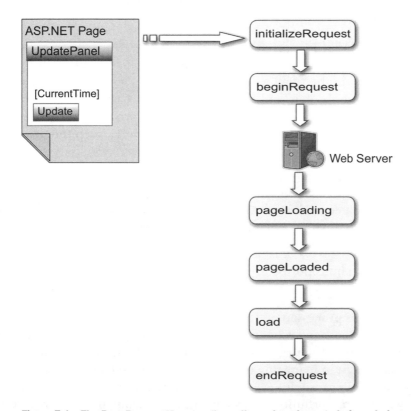

Figure 7.1   The PageRequestManager fires off a series of events before, during, and after an asynchronous postback. This allows the page and control developer to have more influence over how content is rendered during a postback.

Perhaps the best way to ease into explaining how you can use these events is to first outline the order in which they occur. A high-level understanding of the intentions of each event will give you more insight into the client-side event model. Once we've established this foundation, we can then take a more intrusive look into how the events work and how to leverage them. What follows is a brief explanation of each event in the model.

The initializeRequest event

When a trigger such as a button click or column sort on a GridView occurs, the asynchronous postback process is initiated. In response to this action, the Page-RequestManager fires a client-side event called `initializeRequest`. As its name suggests, the early stages of a request to the server begin to take shape here. Along with information about which DOM element caused this to occur, the event establishes an opportunity for you to cancel or give precedence to a particular asynchronous postback.

The beginRequest event

If the asynchronous postback hasn't been canceled or aborted in the previous event, the next step in the timeline is the `beginRequest` event. Raised just before the asynchronous postback is sent to the server, this occasion is typically used to relay to the user a visual cue that an asynchronous process is about to begin. When a process can end up being lengthy, it's important to keep the user in tune with the application by providing instant feedback.

> **TIP** The UpdateProgress control (discussed in chapters 1 and 4) leverages the `beginRequest` event to display its contents as a visual cue to the user during an asynchronous postback. It then uses the `endRequest` event to hide the visual cue—signifying an end to the request.

In addition, you can invoke custom scripts in response to the event. After this occurs, the asynchronous postback is sent to the server.

The pageLoading event

After the postback is processed on the server, its response is sent back down to the client, and the `pageLoading` event is raised. During this event, the updated HTML for declared regions of the page is sent down to the client. Additional scripts are also delivered to assist in managing the state of the UpdatePanel controls and subsequent postbacks. Because this event occurs before any updates are made, it presents you with an opportunity to inspect the data from the server and apply customizations, cleanup, or additional handling.

The pageLoaded event

The `pageLoaded` event signifies the completion of the partial updates to the page. During an asynchronous postback, this event is fired immediately after the `page-Loading` event. However, this event is also fired by the PageRequestManager when it's initially loaded on a page. What is important to remember right now is that the `pageLoaded` event (as its name states) is fired each time a page is loaded, regardless of what caused the page to load (or reload). Later, we'll demonstrate how to distinguish between normal and asynchronous requests during this event.

The load event

The next event fired is not a PageRequestManager event, but rather one that belongs to the Application object (introduced in chapter 2). To recap, the `load` event signifies that all scripts have been loaded and that all client-side objects in the application have been created and initialized. Because this event is significant to the event lifecycle that exists on the client, the PageRequestManager raises it during asynchronous postbacks, on behalf of the Application object.

> **NOTE** The PageRequestManager has a function called `pageLoaded`. When it's called, it's passed in a parameter that indicates whether this is the initial load for the page. If this is the initial load, the Application object naturally raises the `load` event during the client-side page lifecycle. If this isn't the initial load, a call is made to the `raiseLoad` function in the Application object, which, as its name suggests, raises the `load` event.

The endRequest event

Finally, if everything goes smoothly, the `endRequest` event is raised by the PageRequestManager after the `load` event. This event indicates that the processing for the request has completed. We chose our words carefully when we said "if everything goes smoothly"; this event is also raised when an error is thrown during the postback processing. If an error occurs, details about the error are passed along with the event arguments, allowing you to handle the error yourself or let it be dealt with elsewhere in the page. We'll spend more time on error handling later in the chapter. You can rely on the fact that the `endRequest` event will always be raised at the end of a partial postback.

You should now have a high-level understanding of the client-side event model offered by the PageRequestManager. If the previous overview wasn't thorough enough, have no fear—we've only just begun to explore how the model behaves. Soon, we'll provide more insight into what is happening behind the scenes and how to program against it effectively.

The next step is to understand how an asynchronous postback works. We'll walk through the process of how it originates from the client, how it's processed, and how it's sent back to the browser for partial updates to the UI.

7.1.2 *The anatomy of an asynchronous postback*

In this section, we'll walk through an asynchronous postback and uncover how it works behind the scenes. We'll examine how the pieces are initially put into place and how a request is formulated, sent to the server, and eventually parsed and updated in the UI. In the end, you'll have a deep appreciation of the partial-page rendering behavior that the ASP.NET AJAX framework provides.

Laying the foundation

While a page is loaded, a number of things are put into place that lay the groundwork for partial postbacks. The first significant event that occurs is the `OnInit` event for the ScriptManager. The ScriptManager calls the PageRequestManager server object to determine whether the page is in the process of handling an asynchronous postback. It then exposes this value through the read-only property `IsInAsyncPostBack`.

> **Did you say the PageRequestManager server object?**
>
> System.Web.Extensions.dll includes an internal sealed class called `PageRequestManager`. Guess which class the ScriptManager relies on to do most of its work? The `internal` modifier signifies that the class is made visible only in the current package: to other classes in the library, but not to you. A *sealed* class can't be inherited. This pattern is often applied to classes in a library that are meant to remain hidden or non-extendable. By doing this, the ASP.NET AJAX library can place the main engine of the partial-page rending mechanism in a single class and provide other extendible classes (ScriptManager, UpdatePanel) that are built on top of the core functionality.

At times, accessing this property can be helpful during the ASP.NET page lifecycle. For instance, you may wish to apply different or additional logic that depends on the type of postback. Listing 7.1 shows a simple example of how to access this useful information.

Listing 7.1 Using the `IsInAsyncPostBack` property to identify asynchronous postbacks

```
protected void Page_Load(object sender, EventArgs e)
{
  if (!Page.IsPostBack)
  {
    if (ScriptManager1.IsInAsyncPostBack)
    {
      // Perform some extra logic here....
    }
  }
}
```

After querying the asynchronous postback state, the `OnInit` event handler for the PageRequestManager is called. Here, the browser's capabilities are checked to determine whether partial rendering is even possible. Following a similar pattern, the ScriptManager exposes this value through the `SupportsPartialRendering` property. If this check passes and the ScriptManager has the `EnablePartialRendering` property set to `true` (its default value), then the prerequisites for partial rendering have been met and the PageRequestManager JavaScript object is made available in the browser.

Next up is the `Render` event of the ScriptManager control. As expected, it calls the `Render` method of the PageRequestManager (does this guy have to do everything?). Subsequently, it injects some JavaScript into the page that calls two internal methods, `_initialize` and `_updateControls`, for the JavaScript object. An example of how this is rendered by the browser appears in listing 7.2. Note that results vary based on what controls you declare on the page.

Listing 7.2 Configuring the page for partial updates with `_initialize` and `_updateControls`

```
Sys.WebForms.PageRequestManager._initialize('ScriptManager1',
                document.getElementById('form1'));

Sys.WebForms.PageRequestManager.getInstance().
  ➥_updateControls(['tUpdatePanel1'
                            ,'tUpdatePanel2']
                            , ['Update1']
                            , []
                            , 90);
```

> **TIP** We're almost there! If you've read this far into the asynchronous post-back process, you'll be relieved to know that you're close to establishing the foundation that will enable partial postbacks to occur. To complete your understanding of this first milestone, you need to traverse a few more steps: specifically, the recent calls to the PageRequestManager in the browser.

The first method, `_initialize`, calls another internal method, `_initialize-Internal`, which adds handlers for the following browser events: `submit`, `load`, `unload`, and `click` (handlers for these events are responsibly released during the `unload` event). It also creates a delegate for the window `__doPostback` function, so that normal postbacks raised by server controls and other elements can be intercepted. Registering for these events puts the PageRequestManager into a position where it can capture normal postbacks and replace them with asynchronous ones when applicable.

Last is the call to the PageRequestManager's internal `_updateControls` function. Passed into it is an array of UpdatePanel IDs on the page as well as the IDs of any controls that have been registered as asynchronous postback controls and normal postback controls (see chapter 6). The timeout value, in seconds, is the last parameter passed into the call.

Internally, this method builds and maintains a number of private arrays for the UpdatePanel IDs and relevant controls on the page. These arrays are used later during asynchronous postbacks to determine which element invoked the postback as well as how to determine which action to take (a normal postback versus asynchronous postback).

> **NOTE** The first parameter in the call takes an array of UpdatePanel IDs. Notice that they're prefixed with the character *t*. This relays to the PageRequest-Manager whether the panel has the `ChildrenAsTriggers` property (see chapter 6) enabled. If the property were set to `false`, the UpdatePanel ID would be prefixed with *f* instead.

With the foundation in place, the partial-rendering mechanism is ready to be invoked. Let's take the next step by examining what happens when a request is about to be made to the server.

Before the asynchronous postback

In ASP.NET, when a postback is about to happen, the first thing that is usually determined is which control invoked the process. Conveniently, the name of the control that invoked the postback is placed on the page in a hidden field called

__EVENTTARGET. From managed code, one of the many ways you can examine its value is through the Params collection of the Request object:

```
string controlName = this.Request.Params.Get("__EVENTTARGET");
```

This works for most controls, but it isn't supported for two common controls in the ASP.NET toolbox: Button and ImageButton. Instead of calling the __doPostBack JavaScript function that all other controls use, these button controls are rendered by the browser with simple input type='submit' tags. All these buttons do is cause the form to submit it to itself. When one of these buttons is clicked, you determine the control that invoked the postback by walking through the controls collection on the page and looking for the first and only button control. What about the other controls? Fortunately, this is the only input-type control added to the collection, so all you have to do is find the first (and only) button control in the collection.

Fortunately for you, the ID of the control that invoked the property is also exposed by the ScriptManager with the AsyncPostBackSourceElementID property. In addition, it's captured by the PageRequestManager in the browser (more on this soon).

What remains, is formatting the request to the server and sending it across the wire asynchronously. When one of the button controls is clicked, this process begins with an internal handler called _onFormElementClick. The _onFormElementClick handler is also the only way to track whether a submit button has been clicked, because the other controls invoke the __doPostBack function.

Here, it's determined whether the request should be sent asynchronously or as a normal postback. Alternatively, if the request originated from another control, other than the Button or ImageButton control, then the JavaScript __doPostBack function is called and intercepted by the PageRequestManager. Both approaches lead you to the _onFormSubmit function, where the following tasks are performed:

1 A sanity check is made to confirm that the submit event happened in an UpdatePanel or a registered asynchronous postback control.

2 The form body is formatted for the request to the server by iterating through the elements on the page.

3 A new Sys.Net.WebRequest object (introduced in chapter 5) is instantiated for the asynchronous request.

4 The initializeRequest event is raised, and its arguments are checked to catch any actions from the client to cancel the request.

5 Any previous postbacks are aborted—only one can happen at a time.

6 The `beginRequest` event is raised.

7 The Sys.Net.WebRequest object is populated with additional headers to indicate an asynchronous request.

8 The request is sent to the server with the `_onFormSubmitCompleted` function registered as the callback method to invoke when complete.

Determining an asynchronous postback

When the request is being formatted on the client, it adds a new `X-Microsoft-Ajax` header and sets its value to `Delta=true` to relay to the server that you don't want a typical response, but a delta response instead. You want to be returned only changes relevant to the regions you specified with the UpdatePanels, instead of changes for the whole page.

Another header called `Cache-Control` is initialized to `no-cache` to prevent caches from interfering with the request as well as preventing server-side page output cache. For more about the `Cache-Control` field, refer to the HTTP protocol at http://www.w3.org/Protocols/rfc2616/rfc2616-sec14.html.

As you continue to put together blocks of knowledge about how asynchronous postbacks work, you'll eventually have all the pieces to complete your understanding of a partial postback. You're more than halfway: All that remains is learning how the postback is processed and how the updates are applied.

During the asynchronous postback

When the request reaches the server, a new `Page` instance is created, and all the stages of the page lifecycle take place. These include events raised for other web controls on the page and routine events that occur during a typical postback. The server determines that the request is asynchronous by examining the headers in the request and finding the `X-MicrosoftAjax` field we mentioned earlier. Using a tool called *Web Developer Helper*, an IE browser plug-in developed by a member of the ASP.NET team, you can easily view the fields in the request made to the server. Figure 7.2 shows a screen shot of a captured request. This tool and others are discussed in appendix B.

As you can see by examining the Request Headers tab in the dialog, the `X-MicrosoftAjax` field is passed into the request along with the `Cache-Control` field we mentioned earlier.

Figure 7.2 also gives you insight into the response coming from the server. Typically, a response from the server during a normal postback includes the

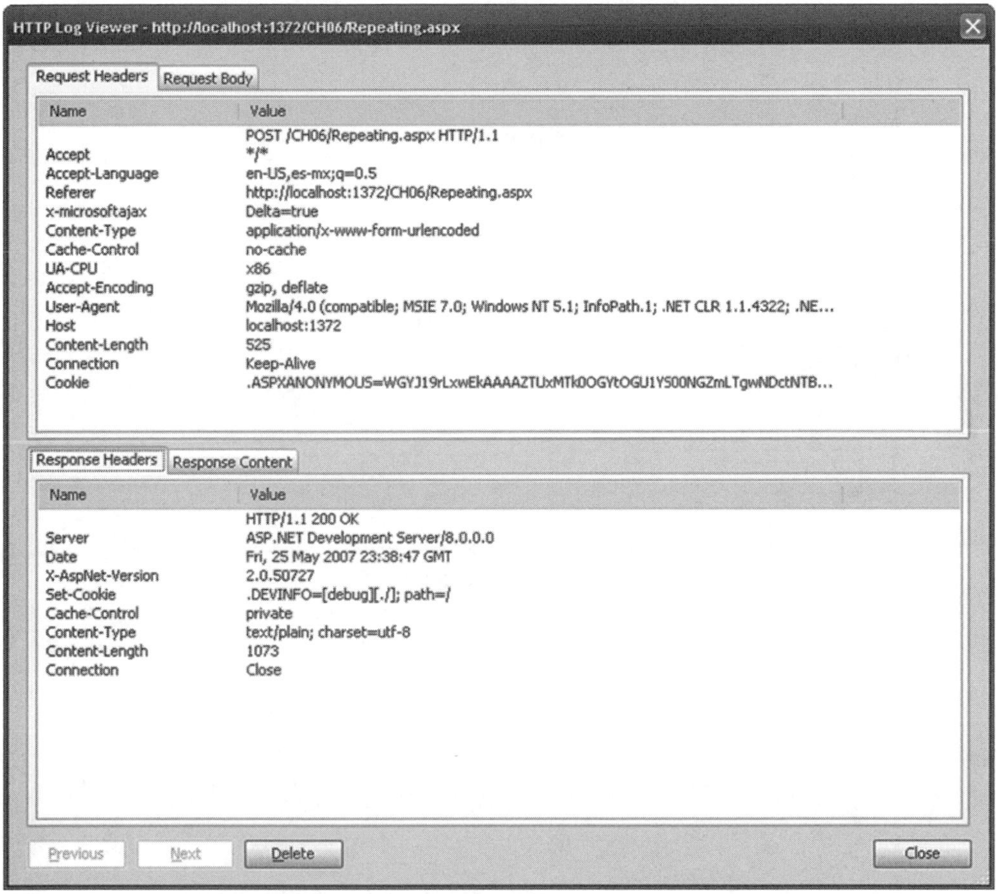

Figure 7.2   A capture of an asynchronous HTTP request confirms that the `X-MicrosoftAjax` fields is being added to the request.

HTML for the entire page to render in the browser. Also, the `Content-Type` is set to `text/html`. For partial postbacks, this type is set to `text/plain`; and instead of the entire HTML being sent from the browser, the payload instead includes the following:

- Only the HTML rendered for regions of the UpdatePanel controls on the page
- The updated ViewState for the page
- A set of script blocks, hidden fields, and data items for managing and applying updates to the page

Figure 7.3 gives you a glimpse into the payload sent from the server in response to an asynchronous request.

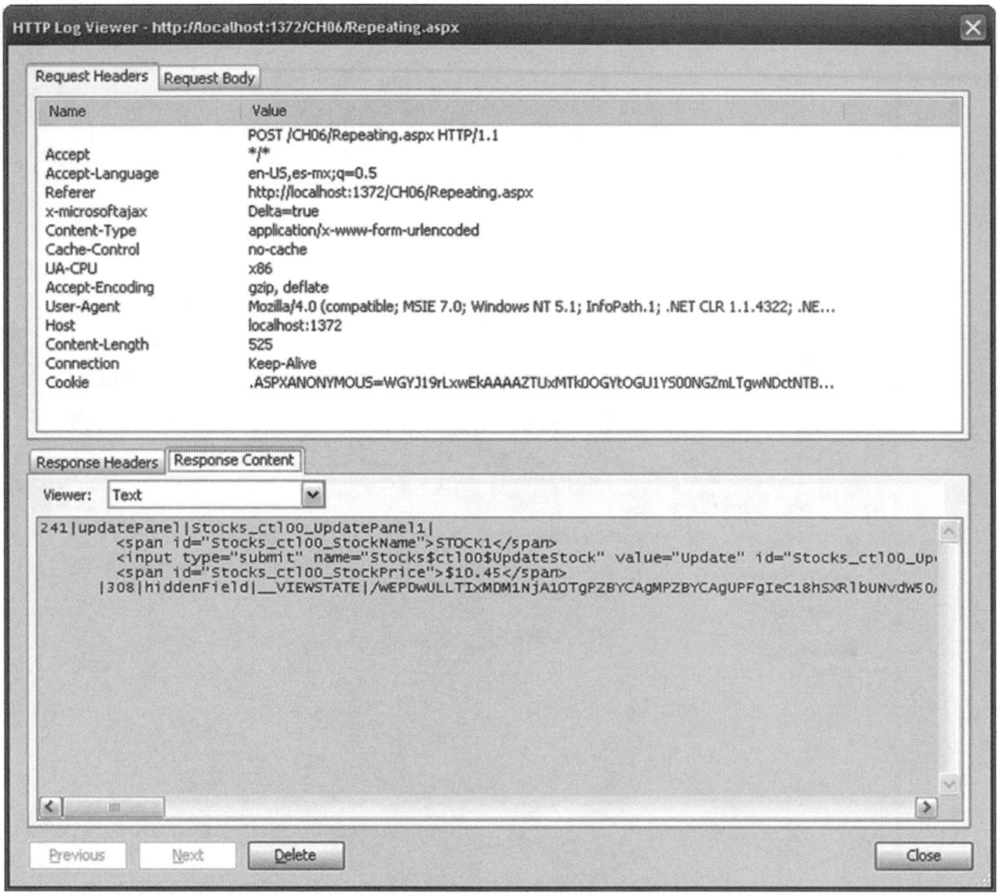

Figure 7.3 The response from the server during an asynchronous postback includes uniquely formatted text that is parsed by the PageRequestManager in the browser to apply the partial-page updates.

If you take a close look at the Response Content tab displayed in the bottom panel of figure 7.3, you'll see some strangely formatted content that is part HTML and part plain text. Prefixed with an integer that signifies the size of the payload, the character | is used as a delimiter for certain keys in the text (a format only a mother could love). It's important to note that this text shouldn't be tampered with and is parsed by the PageRequestManager to apply the updates to the page. Considering the warning, it doesn't mean you can't evaluate the content and add additional logic to your script based on the data. This brings you to the last and final step of the process: evaluating the data from the server and updating the interface.

After the asynchronous postback

Going back to when the request was made, you included a callback function called _onFormSubmitCompleted. This method is now invoked in the browser to signify that the server has completed its portion of the processing. If any errors occurred, they're also caught here in the browser and the endRequest event is raised prematurely in the client-side event model. Included in the endRequest event arguments is information about the error. If there are no errors, the page-Loading event is raised, and the PageRequestManager begins to parse the data from the response and apply the updates to the DOM. Additional scripts are also loaded at this time, and the scroll position, which was recorded before the request was sent, is restored at the end. Once complete, the pageLoaded, load, and endRequest events are raised in their respective order. At last, the partial-page rendering pattern comes to an end.

It's time to put this valuable knowledge to work and get back to coding. The best way to come full circle with all the information we've introduced is to apply it.

7.2 A client-side event viewer

Often, when .NET developers are learning about the page lifecycle, they throw together an application that displays the raised events on a page. This widespread technique helps them understand the order in which the events occur, the arguments that are passed along, and ultimately what can and can't be accomplished during each event. To reinforce your understanding of the client-side event model, you'll build a similar application that will let you observe what happens during partial-page updates. Figure 7.4 shows the application you'll build in this section: a client-side event viewer that hooks into the events of the PageRequest-Manager and Application objects.

Serving as a platform for comprehending the client-side events, this learning tool also lets you experiment with different scenarios that often occur during development. The application has a little style applied to it as well (this is all about the user experience, isn't it?). Rather than take up space displaying the stylesheet, we'll leave that up to you to download from the book's website if you want to produce the same look.

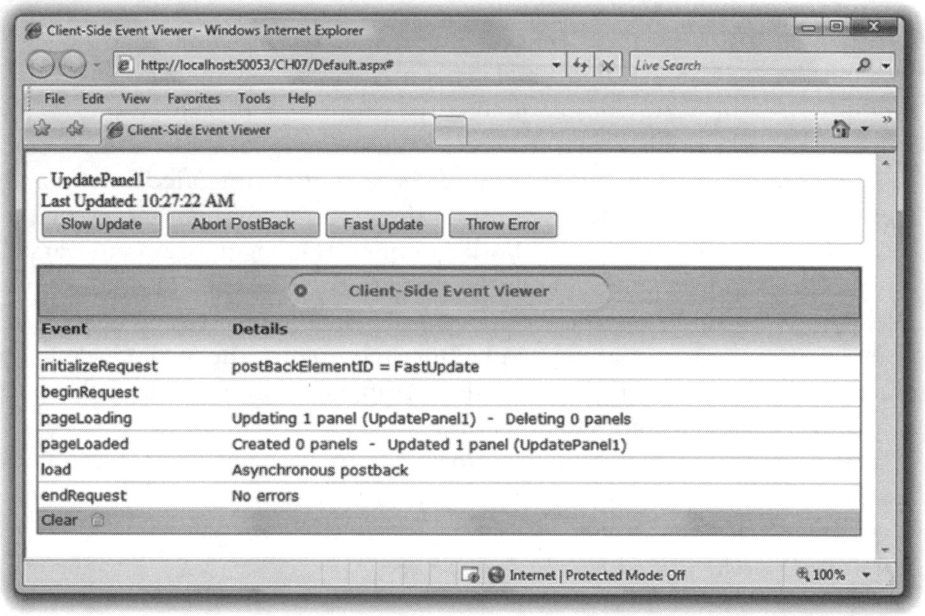

Figure 7.4   A client-side event viewer application will let you observe how the PageRequestManager and partial-page rendering mechanism works.

7.2.1   *Getting started*

The first step is to create a new Ajax-enabled site. Using the Visual Studio template provided by the installation package (see chapter 1 for more details), create the site and add the markup shown in listing 7.3.

Listing 7.3   The general layout for the client-side event viewer

```
<form id="form1" runat="server">
                                          Enable partial rendering  ❶
<asp:ScriptManager ID="ScriptManager1" runat="Server" />
<div>
  <table>
    <caption>Client-Side Event Viewer</caption>      Client-side
                                                  ❷ events

    <thead>
     <tr>
      <th scope="col">Event</th>
      <th scope="col">Details</th>
     </tr>
    </thead>
```

```
       <tfoot>
        <tr>
         <td align="left" colspan="2">
          <a href="#" onclick="clearEvents();">Clear         ←──❸ Footer
           <asp:Image ID="Clear" runat="server"
               ImageUrl="~/images/trashcan.gif"
               ImageAlign="AbsBottom" AlternateText=""/>
          </a>
         </td>
        </tr>
       </tfoot>
                                            ❹  Body for
                                                displaying events
       <tbody id="clientEvents">   ←──┘
       </tbody>

      </table>
     </div>

    </form>

    <script type="text/javascript">
                                            ❺  Clear
        function clearEvents(){               events
            var events = $get('clientEvents');   ←──┘
            while (events.firstChild) {
                events.removeChild(events.firstChild);
            }
        }

    </script>
```

Examining the code, the first thing to notice is the required ❶ ScriptManager control at the top. With its presence and the EnablePartialRendering property set to true (the default value), the page becomes Ajax-enabled and the PageRequestManager object is available. Next is the basic ❷ table structure you use to display the client-side events. Information about each event is populated in the ❹ body of the table and can be cleared from the ❸ footer by clicking the hyperlink that calls the ❺ clearEvents function. Pretty straightforward so far—you've put together the overall UI layout and can now start working with the events.

7.2.2 Handling client-side events

With the basic structure in place, you can begin by adding the first handlers for a few of the events raised by the Application object. Listing 7.4 demonstrates how to add the handlers and the way information about each of them is captured and displayed on the page.

Listing 7.4   Raising the `init` and `load` events with the Application object

```
<script type="text/JavaScript" language="javascript">
<!--
    // Application events
    Sys.Application.add_init(onInit);        ❶ Add event
    Sys.Application.add_load(onLoad);          handlers

    function onInit(sender, args){
      var row = createEventRow("init", "");   ❷ Show init
      $get('clientEvents').appendChild(row);     event
    }

    function onLoad(sender, args){
      var details;
      if (!args.get_isPartialLoad()){
        details = "Normal postback";
      }
      else{                                   ❸ Show load
        details = "Asynchronous postback";      event
      }

      var row = createEventRow("load", details);
      $get('clientEvents').appendChild(row);
    }

    function createEventRow(eventName, details){
      var row = document.createElement("tr");           Add row
      var eventCell = document.createElement("td");   ❹ to table
      var eventText = document.createTextNode(eventName);
      eventCell.setAttribute("width", "140px");
      eventCell.appendChild(eventText);
      row.appendChild(eventCell);

      var detailsCell = document.createElement("td");
      var detailsText = document.createTextNode(details);
      detailsCell.appendChild(detailsText);
      row.appendChild(detailsCell);

      return row;
    }

    ....

//-->
</script>
```

The events that you're interested in from the Application object are ❶ init and
load. The handler for the init event named ❷ onInit updates the event viewer
by adding a row to the table body. This is done by calling the local function ❹

createEventRow. This generic routine adds another row to the body of the table to display information about an event. You'll use this function throughout the section to add information about each event. For the init event, you pass in the name of the event and leave the second parameter, used to display additional details, as an empty string.

Next is the load event raised by the Application object and its corresponding ❸ onLoad handler. Here, you check to see if you're currently processing a normal postback or an asynchronous one by examining one of the properties passed in to the event arguments: isPartialLoad. Listing 7.5 reiterates how this is done to format more information about the event.

Listing 7.5 Querying the event arguments to determine whether the postback is asynchronous

```
var details;
if (!args.get_isPartialLoad()){
    details = "Normal postback";
}
else{
    details = "Asynchronous postback";
}
var row = createEventRow("load", details);      ⟵┘ Update event
                                                    viewer
```

The additional information is passed in to the second parameter of the createEventRow function. If you run the application now, you'll see that both events are populated in the event viewer, which shows that you're off to a good start and ready to handle more events.

Let's continue by addressing the events raised by the PageRequestManager. Listing 7.6 shows how to add handlers for each of those events as well as some simple code to update the event viewer.

Listing 7.6 Adding event handlers for events raised by the PageRequestManager

```
with(Sys.WebForms.PageRequestManager.getInstance()) {
  add_initializeRequest(onInitializeRequest);
  add_beginRequest(onBeginRequest);                  Add handlers for
  add_pageLoading(onPageLoading);                    PageRequestManager
  add_pageLoaded(onPageLoaded);                      events
  add_endRequest(onEndRequest );
}

function onInitializeRequest(sender, args){
    var row = createEventRow("initializeRequest", "");
    $get('clientEvents').appendChild(row);
}
```

```
function onBeginRequest(sender, args){
    var row = createEventRow("beginRequest", "");
    $get('clientEvents').appendChild(row);
}

function onPageLoading(sender, args){
    var row = createEventRow("pageLoading", "");
    $get('clientEvents').appendChild(row);
}

function onPageLoaded(sender, args){
    var row = createEventRow("pageLoaded", "");
    $get('clientEvents').appendChild(row);
}

function onEndRequest(sender, args){
    var row = createEventRow("endRequest",   "");
    $get('clientEvents').appendChild(row);
}
```

NOTE   There can be only one PageRequestManager on a page. In order to work with the object, you must retrieve an instance of it. You do so by calling the object's static getInstance method. To cut back on some typing, we used the JavaScript with statement to leverage the same instance for all the commands that add the handlers.

The handlers are in place; now you need events to initiate a partial-page update. To keep things simple, add an UpdatePanel to the page and assign it some child controls that invoke a postback when you interact with them (see listing 7.7).

Listing 7.7   Adding an UpdatePanel control and child controls to invoke asynchronous postbacks

```
<asp:Panel ID="Panel1" runat="server" GroupingText="UpdatePanel1">
 <asp:UpdatePanel ID="UpdatePanel1" runat="server"
         UpdateMode="Conditional">
   <ContentTemplate>
     Last Updated: <asp:Label ID="LastUpdated1" runat="server" />
     <div>
      <asp:Button ID="Update1" runat="server" Text="Update"
        OnClick="Update_Click" />
     </div>
   </ContentTemplate>
 </asp:UpdatePanel>
</asp:Panel>
```

You add a Label control and a Button control as the child controls for the UpdatePanel. When the button is clicked, the text in the label is updated with the current time (a pattern used throughout the book). When the time changes, this serves as the indication that a partial update has been applied:

```
protected void Update_Click(object sender, EventArgs e)
{
    LastUpdated1.Text = DateTime.Now.ToLongTimeString();
}
```

Because the button is declaratively placed in the ContentTemplate tag of the UpdatePanel, it performs a partial postback when you interact with it. This time, when you run the application and click the Update button, the events raised by the PageRequestManager and Application object are displayed in the event viewer application. Figure 7.5 proudly displays your progress. Notice how the distinction between the types of postbacks is made during the load event.

Let's evaluate where you are right now before going any further. You have an application that registers a handler for each of the events raised during a partial postback. We've started exploring some of the arguments passed in by initially adding more logic in the load event handler.

It makes sense to continue our investigation with the first event raised by the PageRequestManager: the initializeRequest event. This important occasion is when you can abort a request or determine which request has precedence over another. Let's continue to build out the application, resuming with how to abort a request.

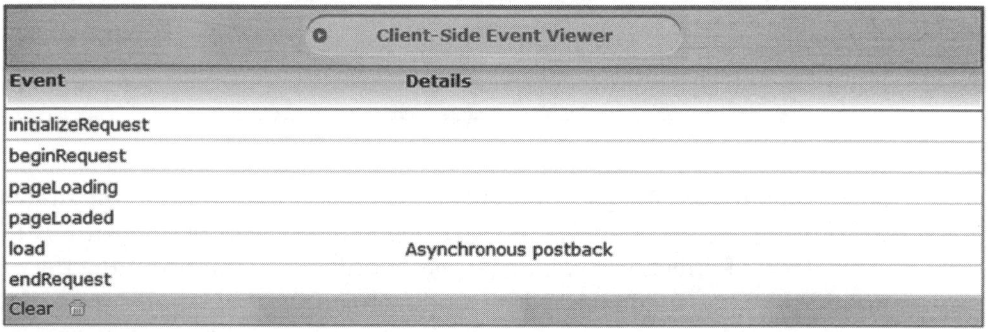

Client-Side Event Viewer	
Event	**Details**
initializeRequest	
beginRequest	
pageLoading	
pageLoaded	
load	Asynchronous postback
endRequest	
Clear	

Figure 7.5 Your progress thus far: capturing each event raised during an asynchronous postback

7.2.3   Aborting a postback

The `initializeRequest` event is raised to signify the early stages of an asynchronous request. The arguments passed along with the event are of the type `InitializeRequestEventArgs`. Here, you can retrieve the ID of the element that invoked the request by examining its `postBackElement` member. In addition, based on the ID, you may decide to abort a request by calling the PageRequest-Manager's `abortPostBack` method.

To see this in action, let's add another button to the UpdatePanel that will give you the opportunity to abort a request. In addition, you'll delay the logic on the server to increase the window of opportunity for aborting when the Update button is clicked. Both changes to the declarative markup and the code-behind are shown in listing 7.8.

Listing 7.8   Clicking the Abort button aborts the postback.

```
protected void Update_Click(object sender, EventArgs e)
{
  LastUpdated1.Text = DateTime.Now.ToLongTimeString();       ❶ Slow down
  System.Threading.Thread.Sleep(5000);          ◀              update
}


function onInitializeRequest(sender, args){
  var details = "postBackElementID = " +
        args.get_postBackElement().id;                      Abort
                                                          request ❷
  if (args.get_postBackElement().id == "Abort")
   Sys.WebForms.PageRequestManager.getInstance().abortPostBack();

  var row = createEventRow("initializeRequest", details);
  $get('clientEvents').appendChild(row);
}
```

First, you put a ❶ `Sleep` call into the code-behind to slow down the update, essentially giving you a 5-second window (5,000 milliseconds) of opportunity to test the abort logic. Remember, calling `Sleep` is only for demonstration purposes and should never be implemented in production code. Next, you compare the ID of the element that initiated the postback with that of the Abort button on the page; if they match, you call the ❷ `abortPostBack` function in the PageRequestManager. The result is a premature end to the request.

> **NOTE**   Because the `abortPostBack` function is like a static method of the PageRequestManager, you can also call it outside the `initializeRequest` handler. In some cases, you may wish to have a simple element on the form that can abort a request at any time.

The next time you run the application and click the Abort button during the asynchronous postback, you'll see that the request is aborted and the `endRequest` event is fired immediately. We encourage you to walk through this example to reinforce your understanding of how this works.

7.2.4 *Managing postback priority*

As we mentioned earlier, in addition to aborting a request, the `initializeRequest` event is also an opportunity for you to prioritize asynchronous postbacks. Because the framework handles only one request at a time, the latest one always gets sent—essentially canceling any previous request by default. At times, you may wish to take more control of this scenario by examining which element invoked the request and deciding whether it should take precedence over the current request. Or, you may wish to cancel all incoming requests until the current postback has been completed.

> ### Abort vs. cancel
>
> When the PageRequestManager's `abortPostBack` function is called, all asynchronous requests are stopped and the partial-page postback is terminated. This is different than setting the `cancel` property in the `InitializeRequestEventArgs` class. Because the framework handles only one asynchronous request at a time, it naturally gives precedence to the latest request. If one request is currently being processed, but another occurs in that time, the initial request is canceled and priority is given to the latest request. You can control this behavior by examining which element invoked the request and updating the `cancel` property accordingly.

The `InitializeRequestEventArgs` class has a property called `cancel`. Setting the `cancel` property to `true` cancels the latest request from being sent to the server. If an asynchronous request is currently being processed, then it proceeds without any interruptions. To demonstrate, let's add to the form another button called FastUpdate that does the same thing as the Update button, minus the `Sleep` call. This button demonstrates how you can assign priority to a specific request. Listing 7.9 shows the new button added to the page.

Listing 7.9   Adding a new button to assign precedence to a postback

```
<asp:Button ID="Update1" runat="server" Text="Update"
   OnClick="Update_Click" />
<asp:Button ID="Abort" runat="server" Text="Abort" />
<asp:Button ID="FastUpdate" runat="server" Text="Fast Update"
   OnClick="FastUpdate_Click" />
```

Now, when a request is made, you check to see if you're in the middle of an asynchronous postback. If so, then you cancel the latest request to give precedence (priority) to the previous postback. To accomplish this, make the updates to the `onInitializeRequest` handler shown in listing 7.10.

Listing 7.10   Aborting and canceling requests during partial updates

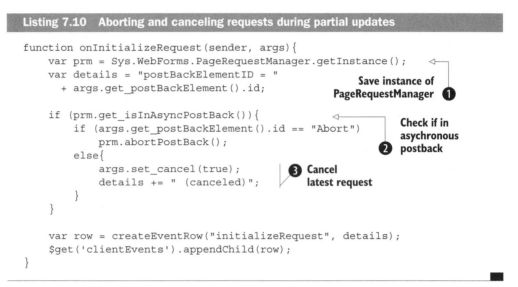

```
function onInitializeRequest(sender, args){
    var prm = Sys.WebForms.PageRequestManager.getInstance();        ◁─
    var details = "postBackElementID = "                        Save instance of
      + args.get_postBackElement().id;                          PageRequestManager ❶

    if (prm.get_isInAsyncPostBack()){                     ◁─
        if (args.get_postBackElement().id == "Abort")        Check if in
            prm.abortPostBack();                          ❷  asychronous
        else{                                                 postback
            args.set_cancel(true);            ❸ Cancel
            details += " (canceled)";            latest request
        }
    }

    var row = createEventRow("initializeRequest", details);
    $get('clientEvents').appendChild(row);
}
```

We may be lazy, but we pride ourselves on being proactively lazy. This example makes a copy of an instance of the ❶ PageRequestManager so you can use it later in the function without all the extra typing. Next, you check to see if you're currently in an asynchronous postback by getting the ❷ `isInAsyncPostBack` property from the PageRequestManager. This makes sense because you want to abort and cancel a request only if you're currently in the middle of one. Finally, if the Abort button wasn't the element that invoked the request, you set the ❸ `cancel` property to `true` to give priority to the previous request.

7.2.5   *Notifying the user*

Just before an asynchronous request is sent to the server, the PageRequestManager raises the `beginRequest` event. Similar to the previous example, the `BeginRequest-EventArgs` passed into this handler includes the `postBackElement` property. When raised, this occurrence gives you the opportunity to notify the user about the upcoming postback before it begins. For lengthy operations, what typically happens (and is recommended) is that the user is given a visual prompt signifying that work is in progress. The prompt is removed when the process is completed. Listing 7.11 demonstrates how you add this behavior to the existing application.

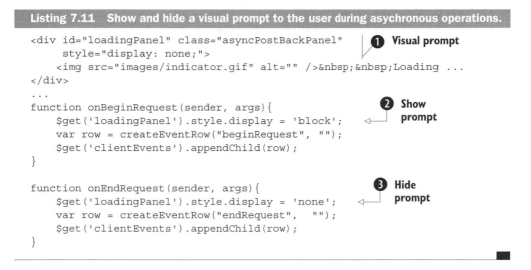

Listing 7.11 Show and hide a visual prompt to the user during asychronous operations.

```
<div id="loadingPanel" class="asyncPostBackPanel"          ❶ Visual prompt
    style="display: none;">
    <img src="images/indicator.gif" alt="" />  Loading ...
</div>
...
function onBeginRequest(sender, args){                      ❷ Show
    $get('loadingPanel').style.display = 'block';     ◁—┘      prompt
    var row = createEventRow("beginRequest", "");
    $get('clientEvents').appendChild(row);
}

function onEndRequest(sender, args){                        ❸ Hide
    $get('loadingPanel').style.display = 'none';      ◁—┘      prompt
    var row = createEventRow("endRequest",   "");
    $get('clientEvents').appendChild(row);
}
```

During the postback, the visual prompt you'd like to display to the user is declared in a div element called ❶ loadingPanel. When the onBeginRequest function is invoked, the element is displayed by ❷ changing its style. To complete the process, when the onEndRequest function is called, you hide the element by setting the ❸ style back to its original state. The next step is the server-side processing of the request.

7.2.6 Locked and loaded

Where are you in the process? Let's quickly recap. You've invoked the request and passed the stage where it could have been aborted or canceled gracefully. In addition, you're displaying to the user an indication that an update or request is being processed—there is no turning back now!

In between the beginRequest and endRequest events raised by the PageRequestManager are two additional events that notify you about the progress of the postback on the server. The first event, pageLoading, occurs when the most recent postback has been received but before any updates to the interface are applied. Passed in to the arguments is information about which UpdatePanel controls will be updated and deleted.

The second event, pageLoaded, is raised after the contents on the page have been rendered. This event also tells you which panels were created and updated. Listing 7.12 shows how you add this information to the event viewer application.

Listing 7.12 Determine which panels are being rendered as a result of a partial postback.

```
function onPageLoading(sender, args){
  var details = new Sys.StringBuilder();
  details.append(displayPanels("Updating",          ❶ Panels
    args.get_panelsUpdating()));                        updating
  details.append(" - ");
  details.append(displayPanels("Deleting",           ❷ Panels
    args.get_panelsDeleting()));                        deleting
  var row = createEventRow("pageLoading", details.toString());
  $get('clientEvents').appendChild(row);
}

function onPageLoaded(sender, args){
    var details = new Sys.StringBuilder();
    details.append(displayPanels("Created",          ❸ Panels
      args.get_panelsCreated()));                        created
    details.append(" - ");
    details.append(displayPanels("Updated",          ❹ Panels
      args.get_panelsUpdated()));                        updated
    var row = createEventRow("pageLoaded", details.toString());
    $get('clientEvents').appendChild(row);
}
                                                   ❺ Format
function displayPanels(action, panels){   ⬸┘        details
  var sb = new Sys.StringBuilder();
  sb.append(action + " " + panels.length + " panel");
  if (panels.length >= 0)
    sb.append("s");

  if (panels.length > 0){
    sb.append(" = ");
    for (var i = 0; i < panels.length; i++){
      if (i > 0)
        sb.append(", ");

      sb.append(panels[i].id);
    }
  }
  return sb.toString();
}
```

In the onPageLoading function, you retrieve the panels that are ❶ updating and ❷ deleting from the PageLoadingEventArgs object. To display information about each of them, you call a local utility function called ❺ displayPanels, which formats the details for the event viewer.

You follow a similar pattern in the `onPageLoaded` function by accessing the panels that are ❸ created and ❹ updated from the `PageLoadedEventArgs` object. The `displayPanels` function is leveraged again to update the viewer. After these occurrences, the `endRequest` event is raised by the PageRequestManager, thus completing a successful partial-page update.

But what if something doesn't go smoothly? What happens when an error occurs on the server during the postback processing? This question leads us to the last feature in the event viewer project: error handling.

7.2.7 *Client-side error handling*

Regardless of whether an error occurs during an asynchronous postback, the PageRequestManager always raises the `endRequest` event. Passed into the handler for this occasion is an instance of the EndRequestEventArgs object. If an error occurs, it can be retrieved with the `error` property. If you decide to handle the error, you can update the `errorHandled` member to prevent it from being thrown on the page, resulting in an unfriendly dialog box. To validate these statements, let's add a button to the page that throws an error when it's clicked; see listing 7.13.

Listing 7.13   Throw an unfortunate, but polite, error.

```
<asp:Button ID="ThrowError" runat="server" Text="Throw Error"
  OnClick="ThrowError_Click" />
...
protected void ThrowError_Click(object sender, EventArgs e)
{
    throw new InvalidOperationException("Nice throw!");
}
```

Now, let's capture the error and handle it in the event handler so it doesn't display that unfriendly dialog box we mentioned earlier. Listing 7.14 illustrates the updated handler for the `endRequest` event.

Listing 7.14   Handling an error from the client

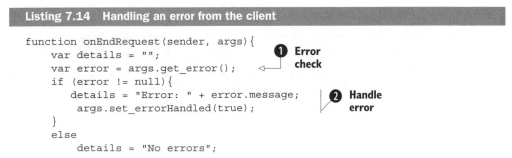

```
function onEndRequest(sender, args){
    var details = "";
    var error = args.get_error();           ❶ Error
    if (error != null){                         check
        details = "Error: " + error.message;  ❷ Handle
        args.set_errorHandled(true);             error
    }
    else
        details = "No errors";
```

```
        $get('loadingPanel').style.display = 'none';
        var row = createEventRow("endRequest",  details);
        $get('clientEvents').appendChild(row);
    }
```

The ❶ error property is retrieved from the arguments in the handler. If an error occurs, you update the client-side event details accordingly and set the ❷ errorHandled property to true.

This completes the event viewer application! You implemented a simple (but sharp looking) application that displays the client-side events that occur during a partial-page update. In the process, you picked up valuable knowledge about each of the events and how to exert more control over the application. Let's take this powerful knowledge a step further and begin to investigate more complex scenarios.

7.3 UpdatePanel cookbook

The beginning of this section marks an important milestone in the chapter. At this point, you should have a firm grasp of how the partial-page rendering mechanism works. You should have also picked up the tools necessary to take more control of the application during asynchronous postbacks. With this knowledge at your disposal, we can now tackle more intricate and challenging problems.

When we put together the content for this portion of the chapter, we decided to do something a bit different. First, we monitored the ASP.NET forums (see http://forums.asp.net/default.aspx?GroupID=34) for difficult problems developers were running into. We then put together a set of solutions to those problems that we could present here, after a strong foundation was established, to demonstrate both limitations and creative techniques. Sometimes, when technical books present this type of format, they call it a *cookbook*—hence the title for the section. What follows are the recipes for success.

7.3.1 Why is the UpdatePanel slow?

Sometimes, when the UpdatePanel contains many controls, a significant drop in performance occurs. As partial postbacks are invoked, the controls in the UpdatePanel begin to take a long time to render. This is most commonly observed when a GridView is used, particularly when many rows are displayed on the control.

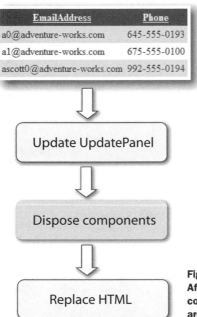

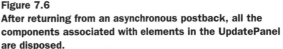

Figure 7.6
After returning from an asynchronous postback, all the components associated with elements in the UpdatePanel are disposed.

Figure 7.6 shows the steps that occur after the server-processing portion of an asynchronous postback is complete.

Just before the old markup is replaced with the updated HTML, all the DOM elements in the panel are examined for Microsoft Ajax behaviors or controls attached to them. To avoid memory leaks, the components associated with DOM elements are disposed, and then destroyed when the HTML is replaced. As the number of elements in the page region increases, this phase of the partial-page update can take a while.

Solution
The following solution works only if the elements in the UpdatePanel aren't associated with any Microsoft Ajax components or behaviors, including extenders. By disassociating the GridView from its parent node, the PageRequestManager bypasses the time-consuming step of checking for any leaks in the elements. Listing 7.15 demonstrates how this can be accomplished with a GridView control.

Listing 7.15   Removing the parent node to speed up the rendering process

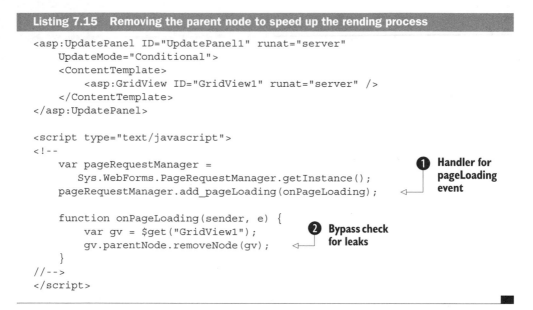

```
<asp:UpdatePanel ID="UpdatePanel1" runat="server"
    UpdateMode="Conditional">
    <ContentTemplate>
        <asp:GridView ID="GridView1" runat="server" />
    </ContentTemplate>
</asp:UpdatePanel>

<script type="text/javascript">
<!--
    var pageRequestManager =
        Sys.WebForms.PageRequestManager.getInstance();
    pageRequestManager.add_pageLoading(onPageLoading);

    function onPageLoading(sender, e) {
        var gv = $get("GridView1");
        gv.parentNode.removeNode(gv);
    }
//-->
</script>
```

❶ Handler for pageLoading event

❷ Bypass check for leaks

If you subscribe to the ❶ pageLoading event raised by the PageRequestManager, then you can get a reference to the GridView's container element and ❷ remove it. As a result, the PageRequestManager won't iterate through the elements in the GridView, and the new HTML will replace the old.

> **TIP** If you have multiple controls in an UpdatePanel that are also *not* associated with any behaviors or components, try placing them in a common container element, such as a div. Then, you can remove the parent node of the common container element instead of removing the container for each of the controls.

We hope that enhancement will come in handy one day. Next, let's talk about how to handle dynamic scripts.

7.3.2   *Inject JavaScript during a partial postback*

If you've ever inserted dynamic JavaScript into a page, then you're most likely familiar with the ClientScriptManager class. Accessible through the Client-Script property of the Page instance, this class exposes a number of useful methods. Among these methods are techniques for inserting JavaScript code and code blocks into a page:

- `RegisterClientScriptBlock`—Injects JavaScript code anywhere on the page, depending on *when* the method is called
- `RegisterStartupScript`—Injects JavaScript at the end of the page, ensuring that the script is parsed and loaded *after* the page has been rendered by the browser
- `RegisterClientScriptInclude`—Injects a `script` tag with an `src` attribute that specifies the location of a JavaScript file to load
- `RegisterClientScriptResource`—Similar to the previous call, except the `src` attribute specifies the location of a JavaScript file embedded in an assembly as a web resource

If you've called any of these methods during an asynchronous postback, you may have noticed that they no longer work reliably, and in most cases don't work at all. When an asynchronous postback occurs, the PageRequestManager anticipates that the data coming from the server is formatted in a special way. Earlier, in section 7.1.2, we mentioned this awkward format by examining what gets returned from the server as a response to an asynchronous request. Along with the new HTML for the page, the incoming payload includes the updated `View-State` of the page and other helpful information. Because these methods were around long before ASP.NET AJAX came into the picture, it makes sense that they no longer work in this context—they don't comply with the new format. What is the solution?

When you're working with UpdatePanel controls and partial postbacks, you must use a set of APIs provided by the ScriptManager that supplements the previously mentioned methods. Luckily, the methods are basically the same to the caller—taking in an additional parameter that defines what invoked the script (the `Page` or a `Control`). These methods are aware of the format the PageRequest-Manager expects and configure the injected script accordingly so the incoming data from the server can be interpreted in the browser.

Web controls in the UpdatePanel

If you've wrapped a web control in an UpdatePanel and would like to inject script into the page, you must use the methods provided by the ScriptManager to make it compatible. In addition, if you're using third-party controls that no longer work in an UpdatePanel, the reason is most likely that they call the traditional methods for injecting script into the page. For a resolution, download and install the latest patches or updates from the vendor to add support for ASP.NET AJAX.

Listing 7.16 demonstrates how to use one of the new APIs provided by the Script-Manager to inject JavaScript at the end of the page.

> **Listing 7.16   Registering script with the ScriptManager ensures that it's UpdatePanel-compatible.**

```
string msg = string.Format("alert(\"{0}\");",
                    "You've done this before, haven't you?");

ScriptManager.RegisterStartupScript(TestButton, typeof(Button),
                    "clickTest",
                    msg, true);
```

In this example, you format the message—a simple `alert` call—and then call the ScriptManager's static `RegisterStartupScript` method to dynamically place script at the end of the page. The only difference in the method call is the first parameter, which you use to pass in the instance of the Button control that invoked the insert.

Because we're on the topic of things that you must change in existing and previous code, let's look at those useful validator controls we've been so faithful to over the years.

7.3.3   Getting the validators to work

Just like the registered scripts in the previous section, you may also have noticed during your ASP.NET AJAX development that the ASP.NET 2.0 validator controls aren't compatible with the UpdatePanel. As a temporary fix, the ASP.NET team has released the source code for a set of compatible validator controls.

> **NOTE**   At the time of this writing, the controls are available as a download that you must apply. Future plans are to deploy the new validator controls through the Windows Update mechanism. If you've already installed this update, you can skip this section.

To replace the old controls with the new and improved ones, you must compile the source code and then reference the assemblies for your website (we also provide the assemblies in the source code for this chapter, on the book's website). You can do this by using the Add Reference dialog in Visual Studio. When you're developing a website (in contrast to a web application project) you can also copy the binaries into the bin folder and then refresh the folder.

After you add the references to the new controls, you have to make a few modifications to the site's web.config file to complete the transition. What's left is to use a technique called *tag mapping* to re-map the old controls to the new ones in an elegant fashion. This method allows you to preserve all the declarative code you've implemented with the existing validator controls. The other advantage of this approach is that when the new validator controls are eventually deployed from Windows Update, the only changes you'll have to make are removing the compiled binaries (DLL files) from the bin folder and the tag-mapping setting in web.config.

Listing 7.17 shows how to apply the tag mapping to the web.config file.

Listing 7.17 Exchange existing validators with the new set while preserving the tag.

```
<tagMapping>
    <add tagType="System.Web.UI.WebControls.CompareValidator"
      mappedTagType="Sample.Web.UI.Compatibility.CompareValidator,
          Validators,
      Version=1.0.0.0"/>
    <add tagType="System.Web.UI.WebControls.CustomValidator"
      mappedTagType="Sample.Web.UI.Compatibility.CustomValidator,
        Validators,
        Version=1.0.0.0"/>
    <add tagType="System.Web.UI.WebControls.RangeValidator"
      mappedTagType="Sample.Web.UI.Compatibility.RangeValidator,
        Validators,
        Version=1.0.0.0"/>
    <add tagType="System.Web.UI.WebControls.RegularExpressionValidator"
➥mappedTagType="Sample.Web.UI.Compatibility.
➥RegularExpressionValidator,
      Validators, Version=1.0.0.0"/>
    <add tagType="System.Web.UI.WebControls.RequiredFieldValidator"
➥mappedTagType="Sample.Web.UI.Compatibility.
➥RequiredFieldValidator,
      Validators, Version=1.0.0.0"/>
    <add tagType="System.Web.UI.WebControls.ValidationSummary"
      mappedTagType="Sample.Web.UI.Compatibility.ValidationSummary,
        Validators, Version=1.0.0.0"/>
</tagMapping>
```

Keeping up the pace of resolving complex issues, the next challenge is one you may have come across recently in your ASP.NET AJAX development. If not, you'll most likely be faced with it someday soon.

7.3.4 *Sys.WebForms.PageRequestManagerParseErrorException*

While working with the UpdatePanel control, you'll probably run into this long but descriptive exception. Although this message may sound more like a medical procedure than something you'd expect from the PageRequestManager, its expressive name is informative.

In earlier sections, we touched on the special format the PageRequestManager expects from a server response. A previous example showed you how to replace some of the register script calls from the `ClientScriptManager` class with the new and improved methods offered by the ScriptManager. This solution eliminated a lot of the headaches for working with dynamic scripts on the page. However, there are a few more cases where parsing errors are still prevalent. What follows is a list of the most common causes that throw this exception, as well as their respective solutions. Each of these scenarios involves the UpdatePanel control:

- *Calling* `Response.Write`—Normally, you use this as a debugging tool. If you're working locally, you may want to consider using the `Sys.Debug` class in the Microsoft Ajax Library or writing to a Label control on the form. Because `Response.Write` doesn't comply with the format that the Page-RequestManager expects, PageRequestManager fails to parse it.

- *Using* `Server.Transfer`—Because the client expects only fragments of the page in return, not a new page, it becomes confused and can't update the interface when it's presented with a new set of elements in the DOM. If you must call `Server.Transfer` from an UpdatePanel, register the control (either declaratively or programmatically) that invokes the call as a `Post-BackTrigger` (see chapter 6 for more details about triggers) or place it outside the UpdatePanel if possible.

- *Server trace is enabled*—Tracing uses `Response.Write`, which brings us back to the first noted issue. Searching for alternatives to tracing and debugging is your best approach.

To round off your understanding of the UpdatePanel and partial-page updates, let's look at some of the current limitations.

7.4 *Caveats and limitations*

As much as we love the partial-page rendering mechanism, it has its limitations. In this section, we'll point out some of the gotchas that you may come across during development. Although some limitations have possible workarounds, a client-centric approach (see chapter 1 for development scenarios) can sometimes alleviate a few of these restraints. Often, it's best to leverage both models (client- and server-centric development) to get the best out of each of them and at the same time let them complement each other.

7.4.1 *Asynchronous requests are sequential*

Normal postbacks occur sequentially because each postback, in effect, returns a new page. This model is applied to asynchronous postbacks as well, primarily because of the complexity involved in maintaining the page state during a postback. ViewState, for example, is commonly used to persist the state of items on a page. Now, imagine that several calls were handled asynchronously—it would become extremely challenging, and close to impossible, to merge the changes made to the page between requests. For stability, asynchronous requests from the browser are handled one at a time.

7.4.2 *Unsupported ASP.NET 2.0 controls*

In ASP.NET 2.0, a few server controls currently don't work with the UpdatePanel. The TreeView, Menu, and FileUpload server controls deliver unexpected results when they're registered as triggers for partial-page updates. In the next version of the .NET framework and Visual Studio (codename Orcas), most issues related to these controls will be resolved. For now, alternatives are to leverage third-party vendor controls or to not place them in the UpdatePanel.

7.5 *Summary*

You learned in this chapter that the partial-page rendering mechanism is more than a set of special server controls. We exposed a client-side counterpart to the server controls called the PageRequestManager, which does most of the work to make all this happen. Most importantly, you gained insight into how the UpdatePanel works under the hood. With this knowledge, you can now take more control of your applications and solve complex situations that you couldn't before. In addition, we explored limitations and issues of the ASP.NET AJAX framework, to keep you on your toes.

The next chapter takes you on a journey into how client-side components are authored with the Microsoft Ajax Library.

ASP.NET AJAX
client components

8

A widely used technique for developing applications uses components as building blocks. Components encapsulate the application's functionality and can be reused across different projects. A *component* is a special object that implements a well-defined set of interfaces. These *interfaces* define the base functionality that every component provides and specify how components interact with one another. Components that implement the same interfaces can be interchanged and can change their internal implementation without affecting other components that deal with their interfaces.

We gave a quick overview of client components in chapter 2, where we discussed the application model. In this chapter, we'll talk about the client component model provided by the Microsoft Ajax Library. This model lets you create components on the client side using JavaScript. We'll also explain the techniques used to create and access client components at runtime. To understand the material presented in this chapter, you need to know how to program in JavaScript using the object-oriented techniques presented in chapter 3.

8.1 *The client component model*

The Microsoft Ajax Library provides a client component model that closely resembles the one used in the .NET framework. As components on the server side derive from the `System.ComponentModel.Component` class, ASP.NET AJAX client components derive from the client `Sys.Component` class. In the MicrosoftAjax.js file, the `Sys.Component` class is registered as follows:

```
Sys.Component.registerClass('Sys.Component', null, Sys.IDisposable,
    Sys.INotifyPropertyChange, Sys.INotifyDisposing);
```

As we said, one of the main characteristics of components is that they implement a definite set of interfaces. Knowing which interfaces are implemented by the `Sys.Component` class is useful, so you're aware of the base features that components can leverage. It's also fundamental in order to understand how components can interact with one another.

A closer look at the `registerClass` statement shown in the previous code snippet tells you that the `Sys.Component` class implements the following interfaces:

- `IDisposable`—Defines a `dispose` method, whose purpose is to free the resources used by the component. Usually, components can initialize and dispose the resources they use; this mechanism is also available to client components created with the Microsoft Ajax Library.

- INotifyPropertyChange—Allows a component to raise an event when the value exposed by a property changes. As you'll see later, and then in chapter 11, you can take advantage of features like *bindings* to synchronize the values of two properties of the same or different components.

- INotifyDisposing—Makes a component able to raise a dispose event to notify external objects that it's releasing its resources. Client components can raise events; they follow the model illustrated in chapter 3 to expose and raise multicast events.

The set of interfaces supported by a client component is shown in figure 8.1. The diagram also shows a group of methods exposed by the Sys.Component class. These are the methods you'll most often use when dealing with client components.

Web developers use JavaScript mainly to program against the browser's DOM. For this reason, the client component model offers specialized components that can be *associated* with DOM elements in a web page. You can take advantage of the features provided by the client component model and, at the same time, create components that provide a UI.

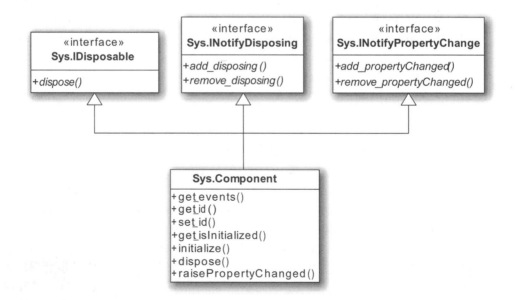

Figure 8.1   Every client component derives from the base Sys.Component class, which implements a well-defined set of interfaces.

We make a distinction between *visual* and *nonvisual* components. Although both the categories have access to the same base features, visual components are best suited when you need to work with the DOM.

> **NOTE** The `System.ComponentModel` namespace contains the component model classes used in the .NET framework. To learn more about component model namespaces, go to http://msdn2.microsoft.com/en-us/library/ ah4293af(VS.71).aspx.

8.1.1 *Visual and nonvisual components*

Client components are classified as *nonvisual* or *visual*. A nonvisual component doesn't provide a UI. For example, a Collection component that manages access to an array of objects is a nonvisual component. Another example of a nonvisual component is the Application object, stored in the global `Sys.Application` variable. A visual component provides a UI. In a web page, the UI is defined using HTML code. For this reason, a client visual component is typically associated with a portion of markup code. A menu is an example of a visual component: It manages a list of URLs and lets you navigate those URLs through hierarchical panels. Another example is a slider, which lets you select from a range of values by dragging a graphical handle.

In the .NET framework, visual components are called *controls*. On the client side, you can create either a control or a *behavior*. We'll discuss the differences between controls and behaviors shortly. Figure 8.2 shows the hierarchy of client components as defined in the client component model.

The base `Sys.Component` class is used to create nonvisual components. The `Sys.UI.Behavior` and `Sys.UI.Control` classes, which represent behaviors and

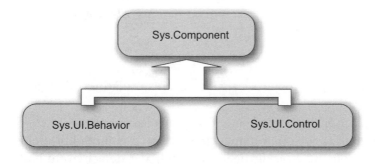

Figure 8.2   Hierarchy of components in the Microsoft Ajax Library. Nonvisual components provide generic component functionality and derive from `Sys.Component`. Visual components can be associated with DOM elements and can derive from `Sys.UI.Behavior` or `Sys.UI.Control`.

controls, respectively, are used to create visual components and are declared under the Sys.UI namespace.

8.1.2 Controls and behaviors

The differences between controls and behaviors are mostly semantic. Both are components associated with DOM elements in the page, and they offer a similar set of features. Behaviors enhance DOM elements without changing the base functionality they provide. If you associate a behavior with a text box element, the text field continues to accept the user's text input. But you can use the behavior to add client functionality to the text box and, for example, *upgrade* it to an auto-complete text box.

The chief purpose of client controls is creating *element wrappers*. For example, you can create a TextBox control that wraps an input element of type text. You can create a Label control that wraps a span element, and so on. This is similar to what happens with the ASP.NET TextBox and Label server controls. The difference is that they wrap DOM elements on the server side rather than on the client side. An element wrapper can be useful to enhance the way you program against a DOM element. For example, you can use controls as a way to program against DOM elements using declarative code. We'll discuss the XML Script declarative code in chapter 11.

A fundamental difference between behaviors and controls is that a DOM element can have multiple behaviors, but it can be associated with one and only one control. For this reason, behaviors are best suited to add client capabilities to a DOM element in an *incremental* way. On the other hand, a control is supposed to provide the whole client functionality to its associated element.

We'll go deep into controls and behaviors later in this chapter. Now, let's examine the general features offered by client components. The following section clarifies the concept of *component lifecycle*.

8.1.3 Component lifecycle

Components are complex objects capable of encapsulating other objects and child components.

For example, a nonvisual component may need to encapsulate child objects and even instantiate them programmatically. A visual component, being associated with a DOM element, typically needs to attach and detach event handlers, or may create dynamic elements. Having a centralized location for initializing and disposing an instance is critical.

The lifecycle of a component consists of two stages: *initialize* and *dispose*. The initialize stage begins when a component is created, and the dispose stage is reached before a component instance is removed from the memory. To accomplish the initialization routine, client components expose a method called `initialize`. The `dispose` method cleans up the current instance before it's garbage collected. Soon, you'll discover that participating in the lifecycle of a client component is about overriding the `initialize` and `dispose` methods of the `Sys.Component` class.

Before you start to work with components, you need to understand the relationship that exists between the lifecycle of a component and the client page lifecycle. As you'll see, components interact with the Application object during the whole page lifecycle. This is possible because the Application object hosts the components instantiated in the page.

8.1.4 Containers

A *container* is an object that holds a collection of child components and provides services to those components. Typically, a container exposes methods for adding, removing, and accessing the child components. The Microsoft Ajax Library defines the `Sys.IContainer` interface for implementing containers. The methods exposed by this interface are shown in figure 8.3.

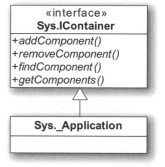

Figure 8.3 shows that the `Sys._Application` class, the single instance of which is the Application object, is a container. One of the goals of the Application object is to host and keep track of the client components instantiated in the page. As you'll discover in the following sections, hosting client components in a container has various advan-

Figure 8.3   Methods defined by the `Sys.IContainer` interface. The `Sys._Application` class is an example of a client class that is a container.

tages. For example, you can retrieve references to client components through the container, instead of storing them in global JavaScript variables. Another benefit of hosting components in the Application object is that they're automatically disposed by the container when the page is unloaded by the browser. This means you don't have to manually call the `dispose` method on each component instance. Client components become children of the Application object during their *creation process*, which is illustrated in section 8.2.1.

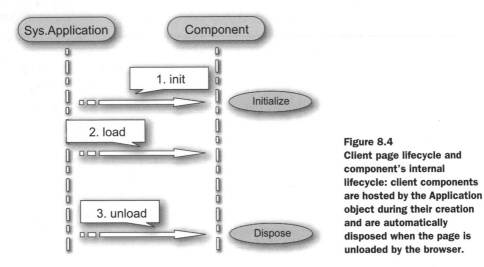

Figure 8.4
Client page lifecycle and component's internal lifecycle: client components are hosted by the Application object during their creation and are automatically disposed when the page is unloaded by the browser.

Figure 8.4 shows the interaction between the Application object and one of its child components. Client components are usually instantiated in the init stage of the client page lifecycle and initialized before the load stage is entered. This means that when the `load` event is raised, client components are already initialized and ready for use. Finally, components are disposed during the unload stage by the Application object.

> **NOTE** Interaction with client components shouldn't happen until the `load` event of the client page lifecycle is raised. Only when the `load` event is raised is everything hooked up and ready.

We discussed the client lifecycle of an ASP.NET AJAX page in chapter 2. Be sure you understood the material presented there before you proceed. After this overview of the client component model, you're ready to start working with client components; let's shift from theory to practice by creating your first trivial component.

8.2 Working with client components

The best thing for growing confidence in manipulating client components is creating a trivial component. All this component does is display a greet message on the screen and notify you each time a stage in its internal lifecycle is reached. Our goal is to show you how a component is created and how you can participate in its lifecycle. Look at the code shown in listing 8.1.

Listing 8.1 Code for the trivial component

```
Type.registerNamespace('Samples');

Samples.TrivialComponent = function() {
    Samples.TrivialComponent.initializeBase(this);
}
Samples.TrivialComponent.prototype = {
    initialize : function() {
        Samples.TrivialComponent.callBaseMethod(this, 'initialize');

        alert("I've been initialized!");
    },

    dispose : function() {
        alert("I'm being disposed!");

        Samples.TrivialComponent.callBaseMethod(this, 'dispose');
    },

    greet : function() {
        alert("Hello, I'm your first component!");
    }
}
Samples.TrivialComponent.registerClass('Samples.TrivialComponent',
    Sys.Component);
```

Looking at the call to `registerClass` in the previous listing, you see that the trivial component is a client class that derives from `Sys.Component`. To participate in the lifecycle of a component, you need to override the `initialize` and `dispose` methods in the constructor's prototype object. Method overriding was explained in chapter 3, when we talked about inheritance in the Microsoft Ajax Library. In the example, you override both methods to display a message box using the JavaScript `alert` function.

NOTE   Don't forget to call the base implementations of the `initialize` and `dispose` methods using the `callBaseMethod` method, as in listing 8.1. They perform important processing steps during the initialization and disposing phases of the component's lifecycle. Calling the base implementations ensures that a component is properly initialized and disposed.

The trivial component also defines a method called `greet`. This method displays a greeting message using the `alert` function. Its purpose is to demonstrate that you can declare methods in a component the same way as in a client class created with the Microsoft Ajax Library.

Let's see what it takes to create an instance of the trivial component. In chapter 3, you learned that you can create custom JavaScript objects by using a function—the constructor—in conjunction with the new operator. Unlike with custom JavaScript objects, using the new operator isn't enough to properly instantiate a client component. It's your responsibility to initialize the new instance and host it in the Application object. For this purpose, you must rely on a special method called $create, which is provided by the Microsoft Ajax Library. Listing 8.2 shows how that is done.

Listing 8.2 Code for testing the trivial component

```
Sys.Application.add_init(pageInit);

function pageInit() {
    $create(Samples.TrivialComponent, {'id':'trivialComponent'});
}

function pageLoad() {
    var trivialComponent = $find('trivialComponent');

    trivialComponent.greet();
}
```

This listing introduces the methods you'll most often use when dealing with client components. These methods create an instance of a client component and access it when needed.

$create is an alias or shortcut for the Sys.Component.create method. The advantage of this method is that it performs all the tasks related to the component-creation process. We'll look under the hood of the creation process in the next section; but note that $create is called in the init stage of the client page lifecycle. As you may recall from our discussion of the client component model, the init stage is the point at which client components are instantiated.

The other method introduced in listing 8.2 is $find. This method, an alias for the Sys.Application.findComponent method, accesses a child component of the Application object. This is possible because Sys.Application becomes the container of all the client components instantiated using $create. If you pass the ID of a component to $find, you get back the corresponding instance. We'll talk more about IDs and the $find method in section 8.2.2. In the meantime, look at figure 8.5 to see the component in action.

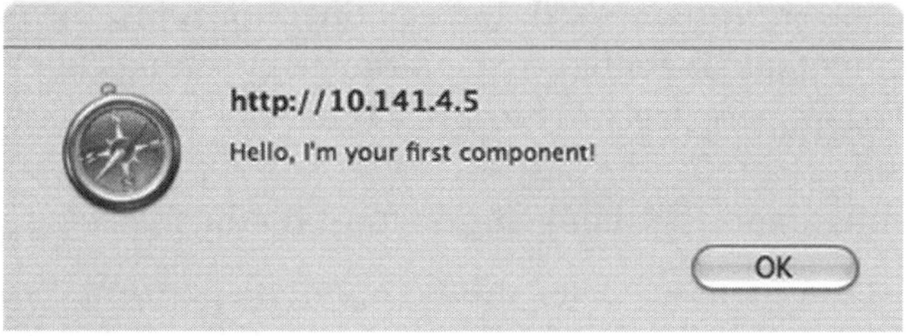

**Figure 8.5
The trivial component
greets you.**

Before we discuss in detail how client components are instantiated, let's review the aliases you'll use in the code that follows. Table 8.1 lists them along with the full method names and the tasks they accomplish.

Table 8.1   Some of the aliases defined by the Microsoft Ajax Library

Shortcut	Full method name	What it does
$get	Sys.UI.DomElement.getElementById	Returns a reference to a DOM element
$create	Sys.Application.create	Creates, configures, and initializes an instance of an ASP.NET AJAX client component
$find	Sys.Application.findComponent	Returns a reference to a component

Now, you need to become familiar with the process of instantiating client components. By understanding this procedure, you'll be able to use every kind of client components in web pages.

8.2.1   Creating components

At first glance, a component may appear to be a simple class that derives from Sys.Component. Why do you call $create rather than use the new operator to create an instance? The answer is that creating an instance isn't enough because a component needs to be initialized and added as a child component of the Application object. The following code shows how to create a new instance of the trivial component:

```
var trivialComponent = new Samples.TrivialComponent();
trivialComponent.set_id('trivialComponent');
trivialComponent.initialize();

Sys.Application.addComponent(trivialComponent);
```

Creating a `TrivialComponent` instance with the `new` operator is just the first step. The next (optional) thing to do is configure the instance by setting client properties. For example, the `id` property lets you retrieve a reference to the new instance using the `$find` method.

Once the initial configuration is complete, you must do the following:

1 Call the `initialize` method to let the component perform its internal setup.

2 Invoke the `addComponent` method of `Sys.Application` to add the new instance as a child component of the Application object.

Now you can safely say that the component is ready for use. The `$create` method is a lifesaver because it performs the entire procedure automatically. You can use `$create` to instantiate, configure, and initialize any client component in a single statement. You can also add event handlers and event references to child components.

`$create` is a powerful method that accepts various arguments. Figure 8.6 shows an example `$create` statement and points out the arguments passed to the method.

The first argument passed to `$create` is always the fully qualified name of the component to instantiate. The client component class must derive from `Sys.Component`; otherwise, a client exception will be thrown.

The last argument is the associated DOM element, which is mandatory for visual components (behaviors or controls). A nonvisual component like the trivial component doesn't need an associated element; a client error will occur if one is specified.

The remaining arguments are objects, passed as objects literals, used to configure the component after instantiation and before initialization. As an alternative

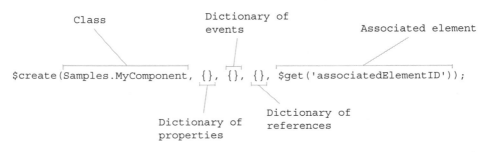

Figure 8.6   Syntax for the `$create` method. This method is responsible for creating, configuring, and initializing a client component instance.

to passing empty objects, as in figure 8.5, you can pass `null`. In the subsequent listings, we'll pass the empty object {} to evidentiate the type of the parameter. To explain the remaining arguments, let's return to the `$create` statement used in listing 8.1 to create an instance of the trivial component:

```
$create(Samples.TrivialComponent, {'id':'trivialComponent'});
```

In this statement, the second argument passed to `$create` is an object that assigns a value to the component's `id` property. To assign values to other properties, you must expand the object by adding a name/value pair. Each pair consists of a string with the name of the property to set and its value.

In a similar way, you can attach an event handler to one of the events exposed by a component. The following code shows you how:

```
$create(Samples.TrivialComponent, {'id':'trivialComponent'},
    {'disposing':onDisposing});
```

The third argument passed to `$create` is an object that maps the name of an event to its handler. The previous statement assumes that a JavaScript function called `onDisposing` is defined somewhere in the page or in a loaded script file. The name of the event, `disposing`, refers to the event defined in the `Sys.INotifyDisposing` interface. Whenever you pass the name of an event to `$create`, it calls the `add_eventName` method on the component instance—where `eventName` is the actual name of the event—passing the handler as an argument.

In figure 8.6, the fourth argument passed to `$create` is a dictionary of references. In this object, the name of a property exposed by the component is mapped to the ID of another component. At runtime, when the component is instantiated, the ID is used to retrieve a reference to the corresponding instance. Consequently, the reference is assigned to the specified property.

`$create` has its advantages and weaknesses. Here are some of them:

- `$create` offers a concise notation for performing the entire job related to component instantiation, configuration, and initialization. You avoid the risk of forgetting a call or making the steps in the wrong order.

- If you use `$create`, you pay a little overhead at runtime. A series of checks is performed to verify that you're trying to instantiate a component and that you aren't trying to set nonexistent or read-only properties. These checks are helpful in ensuring that a component is correctly instantiated and configured before initialization.

- `$create` is the method used by ASP.NET AJAX to wire client components to server controls. Chapter 9 is dedicated to Ajax-enabled controls.

The $create method works in conjunction with $find to help manage client components instantiated in a web page. In the following section, we'll provide more insight on the $find method.

8.2.2 Accessing components

Once a client component has been correctly instantiated and added to a container, you can access it by passing its ID to the $find method. Recall that every component exposes a property named id, which is defined in the base Sys.Component class, as shown in figure 8.1. The ID of a component can be passed to $find to retrieve a reference to the component itself, as shown in figure 8.7.

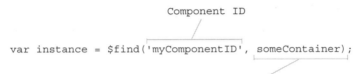

```
Component ID

var instance = $find('myComponentID', someContainer);

                                      IContainer instance
```

Figure 8.7 $find **lets you access a component created with the** $create **method by passing its ID and an instance of a class that implements the** Sys.IContainer **interface. If the second argument is omitted, the component is searched for in** Sys.Application.

$find works only if the component has been assigned an ID and if it's been added to a container. If you use $create, the component is automatically added as a child component of the Application object, and you only need to remember to set the value of the id property.

Note that $find can also accept a Sys.IContainer instance as the second argument. This lets you search for components in other containers while continuing to use the $find alias. If you omit the container, the component is searched for in Sys.Application by default.

The trivial example component was an ice-breaker and a pretext to illustrate the methods you'll use most when working with instances of client components. It's time to go deeper and continue our exploration of the client component model. In the next section, you'll see how client components can expose events, and we'll introduce the *property change notification* mechanism.

8.2.3 Events and property change notification

In chapter 3, we explained how to expose and raise events in JavaScript objects, using a model that closely resembles that used in the .NET framework. Before proceeding, let's recap the three steps necessary to expose an event in a client class created with the Microsoft Ajax Library:

1 Create a method that adds a handler for the event.

2 Create a method that removes a handler for the event.

3 Create a method that is responsible for raising the event.

The same process applies to client components that want to expose events. The only difference is that you don't need to store an instance of the Sys.EventHandlers-List class in the constructor, because every component inherits it from the base Sys.Component class. You also inherit the get_events method that you declared in listing 3.15 to access the Sys.EventHandlersList instance. Taking these differences into account, the entire process for exposing and handling events described in chapter 3 can be applied to client components without additional modifications.

Components reward you with a special mechanism for tracking changes in the values exposed by properties defined with the Microsoft Ajax Library. Client components expose an event called propertyChanged that can be raised whenever the value of a property changes. This mechanism is practical because you don't have to expose and raise a custom event for each value you want to monitor. Instead, you rely on the propertyChanged event—defined in the Sys.INotifyProperty-Change interface—that you can subscribe to, to know which property changes its value and when.

But why do you need to monitor property changes? In chapter 11, we'll introduce *bindings*, which are objects that leverage the property-change notification mechanism to keep the values of two properties synchronized. They do this by updating the value of one property as soon as the other is modified, without your having to manually write the logic to perform this task. Bindings reveal their power when used in declarative languages. (We'll discuss the XML Script declarative language in chapter 11.)

Using the property-change notification mechanism is straightforward. Whenever the value exposed by a property changes, all you have to do is call the raisePropertyChanged method. This method accepts a string with the name of the property whose value has changed. To detect the change, you usually perform a check in the setter of the property. As an example, listing 8.3 shows a simple Customer component that raises the propertyChanged event whenever the value of the fullName property is modified.

Listing 8.3   Property-change notification applied to a property of a client class

```
Type.registerNamespace('Samples');

Samples.Customer = function() {
    Samples.Customer.initializeBase(this);

    this._fullName;
}
Samples.Customer.prototype = {
    get_fullName : function() {
        return this._fullName;
    },

    set_fullName : function(value) {
        if(value != this._fullName) {
            this._fullName = value;

            this.raisePropertyChanged('fullName');
        }
    }
}
Samples.Customer.registerClass('Samples.Customer', Sys.Component);
```

Raise
propertyChanged
event

Note that in the set_fullName method—just before you call the raiseProperty-Changed method—you do a check to ensure that the new value is different from the one that was stored previously. At this point, an external object can subscribe to the propertyChanged event and retrieve a string with the name of the property. This is done through an instance of the Sys.PropertyChangedEventArgs class, which is passed as an argument to the event handler. The instance has a get_propertyName method that returns the name of the property whose value has changed. Listing 8.4 shows how event subscription works by testing the Customer component in a web page.

Listing 8.4   Subscribing to the propertyChanged event

```
<script type="text/javascript">
<!--
    function pageLoad(sender, e) {
        var customer = new Samples.Customer();

        customer.add_propertyChanged(onPropertyChanged);

        customer.set_fullName('John Doe');
    }
```

Add handler for
propertyChanged
event

Set fullName
property

```
    function onPropertyChanged(sender, e) {
        if(e.get_propertyName() == 'fullName') {          Retrieve
            alert('New value for the fullName property: ' +  property
                sender.get_fullName());                     name
        }
    }
//-->
</script>
```

Following the naming convention for client events established by the Microsoft Ajax Library, you can add an event handler for the `propertyChanged` event by passing the handler to the `add_propertyChanged` method. In the event handler, you test against the string returned by the `get_propertyName` method to determine which property has changed its value.

With the property-change notification mechanism, we've completed our discussion of the features that can be leveraged by nonvisual client components. Some topics remain, because you have a whole UI to take care of. The rest of the chapter is dedicated to the additional features provided by visual components. By understanding the nuts and bolts of behaviors and controls, you'll have a complete understanding of the client component model.

8.3   *Behaviors*

The name *behaviors* won't sound new to web developers experienced with programming in Internet Explorer. If you browse the documentation on the Microsoft Developer Network (MSDN) website, located at http://msdn.microsoft.com, you'll find the following definition: "Element behaviors are encapsulated components, so they can add new and interesting functionality to a Web page while improving the organization of content, functionality, and style."

Although the ASP.NET AJAX implementation is radically different—and cross-browser—the concept is much the same: You use behaviors to enhance the functionality of DOM elements. In this section, we'll introduce client behaviors and explain how to create them. By the end, you'll apply your new skills to create a behavior that uses CSS and the DOM to add client functionality to a text box element.

> **NOTE** You can find an introduction to DHTML behaviors in Internet Explorer at http://msdn.microsoft.com/library/default.asp?url=/workshop/author /behaviors/behaviors_node_entry.asp.

8.3.1 Sys.UI.Behavior

A *behavior* is a client class that derives from the base `Sys.UI.Behavior` class. In turn, `Sys.UI.Behavior` inherits from `Sys.Component`, as shown earlier in figure 8.1. As we stated during the overview of the client component model, behaviors are visual components because they're always associated with a DOM element. This element—the *associated element*—is passed to the constructor when you create a new instance of the behavior.

Being components, behaviors take advantage of all the features illustrated in the previous sections. These include the ability to raise events and use `$create` and `$find` to create instances and access them. The creation process is almost the same as that of nonvisual components. To better understand the few differences, let's start by creating the simplest behavior: an *empty* behavior. Listing 8.5 shows the code for the `EmptyBehavior` class.

Listing 8.5   The simplest behavior is an empty behavior.

```
Type.registerNamespace('Samples');

Samples.EmptyBehavior = function(element) {
    Samples.EmptyBehavior.initializeBase(this, [element]);
}
Samples.EmptyBehavior.prototype = {
    initialize : function() {
        Samples.EmptyBehavior.callBaseMethod(this, 'initialize');
    },

    dispose : function() {
        Samples.EmptyBehavior.callBaseMethod(this, 'dispose');
    }
}
Samples.EmptyBehavior.registerClass('Samples.EmptyBehavior',
    Sys.UI.Behavior);
```

The previous code acts as a *skeleton* class for client behaviors. The constructor of a behavior takes the associated DOM element as an argument. Then, it calls the `initializeBase` method to pass the element to the base class's constructor. Whenever you need to access the associated element from the class, you can retrieve it by calling the `get_element` method.

In the prototype object of the constructor, you typically override the `initialize` and `dispose` methods to participate in the component lifecycle. As explained in section 8.2, you must not forget to call the implementations of the base class, as you do in listing 8.5. Finally, the call to `registerClass` in the last statement turns the constructor into an ASP.NET AJAX client class that derives from `Sys.UI.Behavior`.

We need to talk about how to create and access instances of client behaviors. As you'll see, there are no major differences except an additional argument passed to the `$create` method and a special syntax used for accessing instances.

8.3.2 Creating behaviors

Behaviors are created the same way as nonvisual components: by calling the `$create` method during the init stage of the client page lifecycle. The only difference is that you must always pass the associated DOM element as the last argument to `$create`; otherwise, an error will be thrown. The following code shows how to create an instance of the `EmptyBehavior` behavior and set the value of its `name` property:

```
$create(Samples.EmptyBehavior, {'name':'myEmptyBehavior'}, {}, {},
    $get('elementID'));
```

Note that you set the value of the `name` property instead of setting the `id` property as you did with nonvisual components. Although there's no risk in assigning an ID, client behaviors expose the `name` property to easily access instances from the associated element, as the next section explains.

8.3.3 Accessing behaviors

You can access behavior instances by assigning them an ID—through the `id` property—and then passing it to the `$find` method, as with nonvisual components. By setting the `name` property of a client behavior, you can access it through its associated element. All you have to do is call `$find` with a string that contains the ID of the associated element concatenated to the value of the `name` property through a `$` character.

Figure 8.8 clarifies this syntax. In the diagram, you set the `name` property of an instance of the `EmptyBehavior` behavior to `myEmptyBehavior`—and the associated element has an ID of `someElement`.

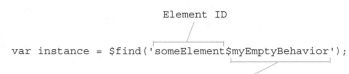

Figure 8.8 You can use the `$find` method to retrieve a reference to an instance of a client behavior by knowing the ID of the associated DOM element and the value of the behavior's `name` property.

If you set the name property, you can also access the behavior through a property added to the associated element. This property, added by the base class during the initialization of a new instance of the behavior, has the same "name" as the behavior. The following statement clarifies what we just said:

```
var emptyBehaviorInstance = $get('someElement').myEmptyBehavior;
```

Having covered the syntactic sugar, it's time to design a real and more complex behavior. The FormattingBehavior that you'll build in the next section will let you manage the style of a text box element in a programmatic way, based on the events raised by the DOM element. Once you have the behavior up and running, you'll learn how to use it in conjunction with CSS to simulate an effect called *in-place edit*.

8.3.4 *Enhancing a text box element*

We'll guide you step by step through the creation of a client behavior that is able to programmatically change the CSS class associated with a DOM element in response to its events. The following example focuses on a specific scenario: the emulation of the in-place edit functionality.

"Allow input wherever you have output" is one of the axioms of Alan Cooper, a famous advocate of UI design. Following his axiom, you'll implement a form where the input fields are styled as labels. When the user hovers over a text box, its style changes to visually suggest that a text field is present—and it effectively appears as soon as the user gives focus to the text box. When the user tabs away from the text box or clicks outside it, the text box will be styled to again look like a label. This kind of functionality is called *in-place editing*, and it can enhance the appearance and usability of a web form. If you're unsure about the final result, figure 8.9 shows the example up and running. Let's open Visual Studio and start writing some code.

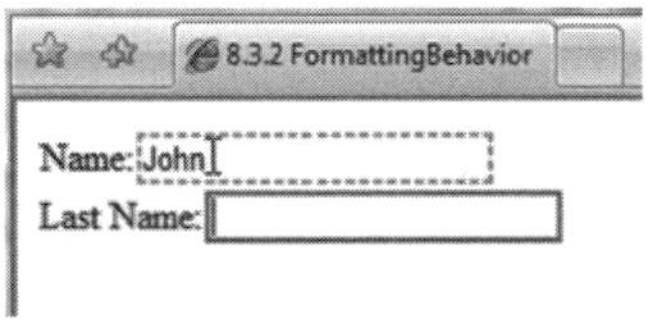

Based on what you've learned in the previous sections, your mission is to encapsulate the client logic into a behavior. In the class's prototype, you handle the behavior's lifecycle as well as the events raised by the associated DOM element. The complete code for the FormattingBehavior behavior is shown in listing 8.6.

Figure 8.9 The FormattingBehavior lets you implement the in-place-edit functionality in a web form. By using CSS, you can simulate a visual effect that turns a label into a text field.

Listing 8.6   Code for the `FormattingBehavior` class

```
Type.registerNamespace('Samples');

Samples.FormattingBehavior = function(element) {
    Samples.FormattingBehavior.initializeBase(this, [element]);

    this._hoverCssClass = null;
    this._focusCssClass = null;          ❶ Fields
    this._currentCssClass = null;
    this._mouseOver = null;
    this._focus = null;

}
Samples.FormattingBehavior.prototype = {
    initialize : function() {
        Samples.FormattingBehavior.callBaseMethod(this,
            'initialize');

            $addHandlers(this.get_element(),
                {
                    mouseout:this._onMouseout,
                    mouseover:this._onMouseover,          ❷ Behavior's
                    focus:this._onFocus,                     lifecycle
                    blur:this._onBlur
                }, this);
    },

    dispose : function() {
        $clearHandlers(this.get_element());

        Samples.FormattingBehavior.callBaseMethod(this,
            'dispose');
    },

    _onMouseover : function() {
            this._mouseOver = true;
            this._setCssClass();
    },

    _onMouseout : function() {
            this._mouseOver = false;          ❸ Event
            this._setCssClass();                 handlers
    },

    _onFocus : function() {
            this._focus = true;
```

```
                this._setCssClass();
        },

        _onBlur : function() {
                this._focus = false;
                this._setCssClass();
        },

        _setCssClass : function() {
                if (this._currentCssClass) {
                        Sys.UI.DomElement.removeCssClass(this._element,
                            this._currentCssClass);
                        this._currentCssClass = null;
                }

                if (this._error) {
                    this._currentCssClass = this._errorCssClass;
                }
                else if (this._focus) {
                    this._currentCssClass = this._focusCssClass;
                }
                else if (this._mouseOver) {
                    this._currentCssClass = this._hoverCssClass;
                }

                if (this._currentCssClass) {
                        Sys.UI.DomElement.addCssClass(this._element,
                            this._currentCssClass);
                }
        },

        get_hoverCssClass : function() {
            return this._hoverCssClass;
        },

        set_hoverCssClass : function(value) {
            this._hoverCssClass = value;
        },

        get_focusCssClass : function() {
            return this._focusCssClass;
        },

        set_focusCssClass : function(value) {
            this._focusCssClass = value;
        }
}
Samples.FormattingBehavior.registerClass(
        'Samples.FormattingBehavior', Sys.UI.Behavior);
```

3 Event handlers

4 Properties

The code in listing 8.6 shows how a client behavior is typically structured. In the constructor, you declare the class fields ❶. For example, _focusCssClass and _hoverCssClass store strings with the names of the CSS classes you want to assign when the associated element is hovered over or focused on. The other fields keep track of the current state of the associated element. For example, _focus and _mouseOver are Boolean values that tell whether you gave focus to the text box or you're hovering over it with the mouse.

In the prototype object, you find the overrides of the initialize and dispose methods ❷. FormattingBehavior uses the $addHandlers method to hook up the mouseover, mouseout, focus, and blur events of the associated DOM element. Then, the same handlers are detached in the dispose method, using the $clearHandlers shortcut. Both the $addHandlers and $clearHandlers shortcuts were discussed in section 2.3.

Next, you find the event handlers ❸, which you use to set the state of the element based on the event that it raised. Each event handler calls the _setCssClass method, which takes care of switching the element's CSS class based on the event raised. Finally, a relevant portion of the code is used to declare the client properties ❹, which are needed if you want to take advantage of the $create method to configure a new instance of the client behavior.

Let's take time to copy the code for the client behavior to a JavaScript file and then reference it in an ASP.NET page through the ScriptManager control. This should be the easiest part if you read the previous chapters of the book. Listing 8.7 shows the code for simulating the in-place-edit effect in a simple form; embed this code in the form tag of the ASP.NET page.

Listing 8.7   Simulating the in-place edit functionality with the FormattingBehavior

```
<div class="form">
    <div>
        <span>Name:</span>
        <asp:TextBox ID="Name" runat="server"></asp:TextBox>
    </div>
    <div>
        <span>Last Name:</span>
        <asp:TextBox ID="LastName" runat="server"></asp:TextBox>
    </div>
</div>

<script type="text/javascript">
<!--
    Sys.Application.add_init(pageInit);
```

```
    function pageInit(sender, e) {
        $create(Samples.FormattingBehavior,
          {
           'hoverCssClass':'field_hover',
           'focusCssClass':'field_focus'
          },
          {}, {}, $get('Name'));

        $create(Samples.FormattingBehavior,
          {
           'hoverCssClass':'field_hover',
           'focusCssClass':'field_focus'
          },
          {}, {}, $get('LastName'));
    }
 //-->
 </script>
```

The simple form declared in listing 8.7 consists of two text boxes. With a little imagination, you can think of it as a simplified version of a more complex form used for collecting user data. Note that the pageInit function—which handles the init event of the Application object—includes two $create statements. Each statement is used to create an instance of the FormattingBehavior behavior and wire it to the corresponding text box element. The values of the hoverCssClass and focusCssClass properties supplied in the $create statement are the names of the CSS classes used to obtain the in-place-edit effect. The CSS file used in the example is as follows; you should reference it in the ASP.NET page before running the example:

```
input {
    border: solid 2px #ffffff;
    margin: -2px;
}

.form div
{
    margin-bottom: 5px;
}

.field_hover {
    border: dashed 2px #ababab;
}

.field_focus {
    border: solid 2px Green;
}
```

Behaviors let you encapsulate a portion of client logic and plug it into a DOM element. Multiple behaviors can be associated with a single element, so a DOM element can acquire, at the same time, the client functionality provided by your behavior and, say, a third-party behavior. The client functionality of the element is the *sum* of the client capabilities provided by each behavior.

In the next section, we'll experiment with controls, the other category of visual components. We'll follow an approach similar to that used for behaviors. You'll start by creating a simple control, and then we'll explain how to create instances of controls and how to access them in the application code. Finally, you'll see how to create custom controls. This will give you full control over ASP.NET AJAX client components.

8.4   Controls

Just like behaviors, controls are visual components associated with DOM elements. Conceptually, a control differs from a behavior in the sense that instead of just providing client functionality, a control usually represents—or *wraps*—the element, to provide additional properties and methods that extend its programming interface. In ASP.NET, for example, a text box element is represented on the server side by the TextBox control. You can program against a TextBox object to specify how the element's markup is rendered in the page. In the same manner, you can have a TextBox control on the client side and program against it using JavaScript.

In the following sections, we'll explore client controls and focus on a couple of scenarios where they're useful. We'll show you how to create an element wrapper and how to use a control to program against a block of *structured markup code*, instead of a single DOM element. In chapter 11, we'll explain how you can use a control to program against a DOM element using the XML Script declarative language.

8.4.1   Sys.UI.Control

A control is a client class that derives from the base `Sys.UI.Control` class. In turn, `Sys.UI.Control` is a child class of `Sys.Component`. Controls have an associated DOM element that is passed to the constructor during instantiation and returned by the `get_element` method. In the same manner as with behaviors, let's start by looking at the simplest control—an *empty* control. The code for the `EmptyControl` class is shown in listing 8.8.

Listing 8.8 The simplest control is an empty control.

```
Type.registerNamespace('Samples');

Samples.EmptyControl = function(element) {
    Samples.EmptyControl.initializeBase(this, [element]);
}
Samples.EmptyControl.prototype = {
    initialize : function() {
        Samples.EmptyControl.callBaseMethod(this, 'initialize');
    },

    dispose : function() {
        Samples.EmptyControl.callBaseMethod(this, 'dispose');
    }
}
Samples.EmptyControl.registerClass('Samples.EmptyControl',
    Sys.UI.Control);
```

An empty control is identical to an empty behavior, except that you derive from the
Sys.UI.Control class. As usual, both the initialize and dispose methods are typically overridden to perform the initialization and cleanup of an instance.

The rules for creating and accessing controls, outlined in the next section, are
simple, and the differences from behaviors are minimal. Let's examine them
before you begin coding custom controls.

8.4.2 Creating controls

Being client components, controls are created with a $create statement during
the init stage of the client page lifecycle. A control must always be associated with
a DOM element; otherwise, an error will be thrown at runtime by the Microsoft
Ajax Library. The following code shows how to create an instance of the Empty-
Control control, which you coded in listing 8.8, using the $create method:

```
$create(Samples.EmptyControl, {}, {}, {}, $get('elementID'));
```

As usual, the last argument passed to $create is the associated DOM element,
retrieved with a call to the $get method. The argument passed to $get is the ID of
the DOM element. A control is instantiated in the same manner as a nonvisual
component, as we explained in section 8.2.1. Now, let's peek at how controls are
accessed in web pages.

8.4.3 *Accessing controls*

Because controls are client components, you can access them with the $find method, passing the ID of the control as an argument.

> **NOTE**   The ID of a control can't be set programmatically. It's automatically set by the Sys.UI.Control class to the same ID as the associated element. You can get a reference to the control by passing the ID of the associated DOM element to $find.

Another way to access a control is through the associated element. Because an element can have one and only one associated control, a property called control—which stores the reference to the control—is created on the DOM element when the control is initialized. Supposing that you have a DOM element stored in the someElement variable, the following statement accesses the associated control (if it exists, of course) and stores a reference in the controlInstance variable:

```
var controlInstance = someElement.control;
```

Next, we'll examine two examples of custom controls created with the Microsoft Ajax Library. The first example is relative to an element wrapper: a control called TextBox that wraps a text box element on the client side. The second example illustrates how to use client controls to work on a block of structured markup code.

8.4.4 *Creating an element wrapper: text box*

The first client control you'll create is an element wrapper: a control that represents a DOM element on the client side. Your mission is to wrap a text box element with a client TextBox control. The reasons for using an element wrapper are varied. In this case, you want to be able to prevent the web form from being submitted when the Enter key is pressed in the text field, as normally happens in a web page. The logic needed to accomplish this task is controlled through a public property called ignoreEnterKey, which is exposed by the control. If you set the property to true, a press of the Enter key in the text field is ignored. If the property is set to false, the form is submitted to the server. Listing 8.9 shows the code for the Samples.TextBox control.

Listing 8.9   Code for the Samples.TextBox control

```
Type.registerNamespace('Samples');

Samples.TextBox = function(element) {
    Samples.TextBox.initializeBase(this, [element]);

    this._ignoreEnterKey = false;
}
Samples.TextBox.prototype = {
    initialize : function() {
        Samples.TextBox.callBaseMethod(this, 'initialize');


        $addHandlers(this.get_element(),
            {keypress:this._onKeyPress}, this);
    },

    dispose : function() {

        $clearHandlers(this.get_element());

        Samples.TextBox.callBaseMethod(this, 'dispose');
    },


    _onKeyPress : function(evt) {
        if(this._ignoreEnterKey && evt.charCode == 13) {
            evt.preventDefault();
        }
    },

    get_ignoreEnterKey : function() {
        return this._ignoreEnterKey;
    },

    set_ignoreEnterKey : function(value) {
        this._ignoreEnterKey = value;
    }
}
Samples.TextBox.registerClass('Samples.TextBox', Sys.UI.Control);
```

❶ Control lifecycle

❷ Event handler

The structure of a control is similar to that of a behavior. As always, you see the overrides of the initialize and dispose methods ❶, where you attach and detach handlers for the events raised by the associated element. In this example, you're interested in handling the text box's keypress event, which notifies you of any key pressed by the user in the text field. The corresponding event handler ❷—

_onKeyPress—does a check to determine if the `ignoreEnterKey` property is set to `true` and if the user pressed the Enter key. If the check is positive, it calls the `preventDefault` method on the event object to prevent execution of the event's default action. This, in turn, prevents the form from being submitted to the server. This functionality can be enabled or disabled through the `ignoreEnterKey` property.

To test the control, create a new ASP.NET AJAX page, declare a text box element, and associate it with a new instance of the TextBox control, as shown in listing 8.10.

Listing 8.10 Code for testing the Samples.TextBox control

```
<input type="text" id="myTextBox" />

<script type="text/javascript">
Sys.Application.add_init(pageInit);

function pageInit() {
    $create(Samples.TextBox, {'ignoreEnterKey':true}, {}, {},
        $get('myTextBox'));
}
</script>
```

It's no surprise that you instantiate the component with a `$create` statement during the init stage of the page lifecycle. The `$create` method sets the value of the `ignoreEnterKey` property to `true`. This activates the custom functionality and executes its logic every time the user presses a key in the text field.

> **TIP** The ASP.NET Futures package contains more examples of element wrappers, such as Label, HyperLink, and Button controls. They're defined in the PreviewScript.js file; you'll use them in chapter 11, when we discuss the XML Script declarative language. Appendix A contains instructions for how to install the ASP.NET Futures package.

So far, you've seen examples of visual components (both behaviors and controls) that target a single DOM element. In many situations, you have to deal with complex UIs that consist of a hierarchy of DOM elements—a *DOM subtree*.

For example, the UI of a menu is composed by many different elements—labels, hyperlinks, panels—and the same is true for complex controls such as the ASP.NET GridView or the TreeView. Is it possible to associate a client control with the complex markup code rendered by a GridView or—in general—to a portion of structured markup code? Are you restricted to developing only simple element wrappers?

The good news is that you can develop client controls associated with complex markup code. The trick is easy: You embed the markup in a container element (for example, a `div` or a `span` element), and you use the container as the associated element of the client control. Then, you access the child elements in the control. To clarify this concept, the following section explains how you can create a client control that relies on multiple DOM elements to implement a photo gallery.

8.4.5 Creating a PhotoGallery control

The goal of the following example is to show you how to build a client control with a complex UI. By *complex*, we mean the UI can consist of as many elements as you need, although you'll use only a few in order to keep things simple. The result of the work will be a dynamic photo gallery control that you can use to browse a set of photos saved on the website. The URLs of the photos are stored in an array passed to the control. Figure 8.10 shows the result.

The block of static HTML that you use for the PhotoGallery control is contained in a `div` element. As you can see by looking at the code in listing 8.11, the UI is represented by two buttons—used for browsing the previous or next photo in

Figure 8.10 A simple photo gallery control realized by associating a client control to a portion of structured markup code.

the sequence—and an `img` element with an ID of `gal_image` that displays the current photo. A second `img` element—`gal_progress`—displays an indicator during the loading of the next photo.

Listing 8.11   HTML code for the UI of the PhotoGallery control

```
<div id="photoGallery">
  <div>
    <input type="button" id="gal_prevButton" value="Prev" />
    <input type="button" id="gal_nextButton" value="Next" />
    <img id="gal_progress" src="Images/progress.gif"
         alt="" style="visibility:hidden" />
  </div>
```

```
  <div>
    <img src="Images/placeholder.png" id="gal_image" alt="" />
  </div>
</div>
```

For simplicity, the HTML code doesn't take into account the control's style, which is available in the code you can download from the Manning website at http://www.manning.com/gallo.

Let's examine the code for the client control. Because you want to develop a custom client control, you create a class called `Samples.PhotoGallery` that inherits from the base `Sys.UI.Control` class. To help you better understand what's going on, we've split the code into two listings. The first contains the code for the constructor and the call to the `registerClass` method. The second shows the code for the prototype object of the `Samples.PhotoGallery` class. You must merge the two listings to obtain the complete code for the PhotoGallery control. Let's start by exploring the code in the constructor, shown in listing 8.12.

Listing 8.12 Code for the `PhotoGallery` class's constructor

```
Type.registerNamespace('Samples');

Samples.PhotoGallery = function(element) {
    Samples.PhotoGallery.initializeBase(this, [element]);

    this._imageElement = null;
    this._nextElement = null;
    this._prevElement = null;
    this._progressElement = null;
    this._images = [];
    this._index = -1;
    this._imgPreload = null;
}
Samples.ImageGallery.registerClass('Samples.PhotoGallery',
    Sys.UI.Control);
```

The constructor, as usual, contains the class fields. The first four fields, whose names end with the word `Element`, hold references to the child nodes of the associated DOM element. Although the containing `div` element becomes the associated element of the PhotoGallery control, the child elements that you need to access are stored in some of the control's fields.

The `_images` array holds the URLs of the photos to display, and the `_index` variable keeps track of the index of the URL in the array. Finally, `_imgPreload` holds a dynamic `img` element that is responsible for loading the next photo while the current one is still displayed. As you'll see in chapter 10, this lets you play cool transitions between photos in the sequence.

The prototype object of the PhotoGallery control contains all the logic needed to load and browse the photos; see listing 8.13.

Listing 8.13   Prototype of the PhotoGallery control

```
Samples.PhotoGallery.prototype = {
    initialize : function() {
        Samples.PhotoGallery.callBaseMethod(this, 'initialize');

        $addHandlers(this._nextElement,
            {click: this.viewNext}, this);
        $addHandlers(this._prevElement,
            {click: this.viewPrev}, this);                     ❶ Attach event
                                                                  handlers
        this._imgPreload = document.createElement('IMG');
        $addHandlers(this._imgPreload,
            {load: this._onimageElementLoaded}, this);

        if(this._index >= 0) {
            this._render();
        }
    },

    dispose : function() {
        $clearHandlers(this._prevElement);
        $clearHandlers(this._nextElement);        ❷ Detach event
        $clearHandlers(this._imgPreload);            handlers

        Samples.PhotoGallery.callBaseMethod(this, 'dispose');
    },

    viewPrev : function(evt) {
        if(this._index > 0) {
            this._index--;
            this._render();
        }
    },

    viewNext : function(evt) {
        if(this._index < this._images.length - 1) {
            this._index++;
            this._render();
        }
    },
```

```
_render : function() {
    this._prevElement.disabled = (this._index == 0);
    this._nextElement.disabled =
        (this._index == this._images.length - 1);

    this._progressElement.style.visibility = 'visible';

    this._imgPreload.src = this._images[this._index];
},

_onimageElementLoaded : function() {
    this._displayImage();
},

_displayImage : function() {
    this._progressElement.style.visibility = 'hidden';

    this._imageElement.src = this._images[this._index];
},

get_images : function() {
    return this._images;
},

set_images : function(value) {
    this._images = value;

    if(this._images.length > 0) {
        this._index = 0;

        if(this.get_isInitialized()) {
            this._render();
        }
    }
},

get_prevElement : function() {
    return this._prevElement;
},

set_prevElement : function(value) {
    this._prevElement = value;
},

get_nextElement : function() {
    return this._nextElement;
},

set_nextElement : function(value) {
    this._nextElement = value;
},
```

❸ Display next photo

Display loading indicator

Preload image

Hide indicator

Display image

```
    get_imageElement : function() {
        return this._imageElement;
    },

    set_imageElement : function(value) {
        this._imageElement = value;
    },

    get_progressElement : function() {
        return this._progressElement;
    },

    set_progressElement : function(value) {
        this._progressElement = value;
    }
}
```

As usual, the `initialize` method is used to set up the control and to wire the events of the encapsulated DOM elements ❶. In this case, you're interested in the `click` events of the two buttons. During the initialize phase, you also create the dynamic `img` element used to preload the next photo. In the `dispose` method ❷, you perform the inverse job: You detach the event handlers and dispose the dynamic `img` element.

All of the control's logic is encapsulated in the methods defined in the `proto-type`. As soon as one of the buttons is clicked, the corresponding handler—`view-Prev` or `viewNext`, respectively—is invoked. In turn, the handler calls the `_render` method, which is responsible for displaying the previous or next photo based on the button clicked. To display a photo, the `_render` method ❸ performs the following steps:

4 It determines if you've reached the beginning or the end of the collection. If so, it disables or enables the buttons accordingly to avoid going out of the bounds of the `_images` array.

5 It displays the (previously hidden) indicator to suggest that the next photo is being loaded.

6 It preloads the next photo by taking its URL from the `_images` array and assigning it to the `src` attribute of the dynamic `img` element, stored in the `_imgPreload` variable.

As soon as the next photo is loaded, the `load` event of the dynamic `img` element is fired, and the corresponding handler—`_onImageLoaded`—is invoked. The handler calls the _displayImage method, which displays the photo by assigning its URL to the static img element. If you want to use the PhotoGallery control, you need to configure a new instance by passing the references to the DOM elements that it needs to access in the $create statement. This is shown in listing 8.14.

Listing 8.14 Creating an instance of the PhotoGallery control

```
<script type="text/javascript">
<!--
    Sys.Application.add_init(pageInit);

    function pageInit(sender, e) {
        $create(Samples.PhotoGallery,
            {
              'imageElement': $get('gal_image'),
              'prevElement': $get('gal_prevButton'),
              'nextElement': $get('gal_nextButton'),
              'progressElement': $get('gal_progress'),
              'images': ['Album/photo1.jpg', 'Album/photo2.jpg',
                          'Album/photo3.jpg']
            },
            {},
            {},
            $get('photoGallery')
        );
    }
//-->
</script>
```

The configuration of the new instance through the $create method is possible thanks to the client properties exposed by the PhotoGallery control. The control exposes a property for each child element it wants to access, as you can verify by looking again at the code in listing 8.14 Note how, in the previous listing, the images property is set to a JavaScript array that contains the URLs of the photos to display.

With this example, our discussion of client controls and the client component model is complete. Now that you know how to create client components and access them at runtime, we'll concentrate on the server-side capabilities of ASP.NET. The next chapter—a fundamental one—will teach you how to wire client components to ASP.NET server controls by automating the generation of $create statements on the server side.

8.5 Summary

The Microsoft Ajax Library leverages a model for creating client components that closely resembles the one used to create server components with the .NET framework. In this chapter, we introduced the Sys.Component class and discussed the features provided by the client component model. Then, we talked about visual and nonvisual components—so called depending on whether they have a UI—and explained how instances of client components are created and accessed at runtime.

Visual components can be behaviors or controls, and they're always associated with a DOM element. Behaviors are components that add client capabilities to a DOM element without changing its basic functionality. Controls are used to represent DOM elements on the client side; they can also provide specific client functionality to a block of structured markup code.

Now that you possess the skills required to create client components, you're ready to learn how to wire them to ASP.NET server controls in order to create powerful Ajax-enabled controls.

Building
Ajax-enabled controls

9

The power of technologies like ASP.NET lies in the ability to work with server controls and, particularly, web controls. A *web control* is an object that abstracts and manages a particular portion of the web page, be it a single element (like a text box) or a table (like a grid). A web control covers the tasks from the rendering of the HTML to postback handling and communication with other server controls. All of the web control's logic is programmed, encapsulated, and executed on the server side as soon as you declare the web control on the page.

Having learned how to use the Microsoft Ajax Library to build client components, you'll find out in this chapter how to wire them programmatically to ASP.NET server controls to obtain Ajax-enabled controls. By the end of the chapter, you'll learn how to build ASP.NET server controls with Ajax capabilities.

9.1 Script descriptors

In chapter 8, you saw how to create instances of client components in the page. Because the instantiation of a client component is a process that involves numerous steps besides creating a new instance, the $create method is a valid ally for successfully accomplishing this task.

All the listings in the previous chapter assumed that the $create statements were manually injected in a JavaScript code block in the page and executed during the init stage of the client page lifecycle. Given the possibilities that the ASP.NET server model offers, here's an idea: If you can use $create to automate the process of instantiating a client component, why not also automate the process of injecting a $create statement into the page? If a server control can perform this job, it can instantiate the client components it needs. Then, you can proudly say that you've created an Ajax-enabled server control.

The first step toward this goal is mastering the concept of *script descriptors*. A script descriptor is an object that can be used on the server side to generate a $create statement programmatically. To understand how script descriptors work and the reasons behind their usage, let's introduce some classes provided by the ASP.NET AJAX server framework.

9.1.1 Script descriptor hierarchy

Script descriptors are classes contained in the System.Web.Extensions assembly. They're part of the System.Web.UI namespace and derive from a base abstract class called ScriptDescriptor. Figure 9.1 shows that the hierarchy of script descriptors reflects how classes are organized in the client component model. For example, the ScriptComponentDescriptor class represents the script descriptor associated with the client Sys.Component class. The same kind of mapping exists between the other classes, as the figure suggests.

Script descriptors behave in an interesting manner. For example, if you create an instance of the ScriptComponentDescriptor class, you can generate the $create statement needed for creating and configuring an instance of a nonvisual component. In a similar manner, you can use instances of the ScriptBehaviorDescriptor and ScriptControlDescriptor classes to generate—on the server side—the $create statements needed for instantiating and configuring a client behavior or a control, on the client side.

Programmatically generating a $create statement offers two main advantages. First, you don't need to hard-code any strings in the application logic. Instead, you can instruct the script descriptor to generate the $create statement based, for example, on the values of some server-side variables. Second, an external object can receive the script descriptor and use it to generate the $create statement at the right time. As we'll explain in section 9.2.1, the ScriptManager control can query a server control for a list of script descriptors. All the script descriptors are collected during the Render phase of the server page lifecycle and used to render all the $create statements in the markup code sent to the browser.

Before we go deeper into this process, you need more confidence with script descriptors, because you'll use them often when programming Ajax-enabled controls. In the following sections, we'll focus on the ScriptBehaviorDescriptor

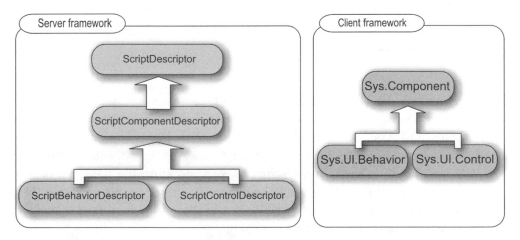

Figure 9.1   The hierarchy of script descriptors reflects, on the server side, the hierarchy of client components.

and `ScriptControlDescriptor` classes, which inherit almost all their functionality from the `ScriptComponentDescriptor` class. You'll gain a comprehensive knowledge of how script descriptors work.

9.1.2 Describing a behavior

Whenever you need to instantiate a client behavior, you can generate the corresponding `$create` statement on the server side by using an instance of the `ScriptBehaviorDescriptor` class. The relevant properties and methods exposed by this class are shown in figure 9.2.

To understand how it works, let's take a `$cre-ate` statement and see how you can generate the same statement using a script descriptor. The `$create` statement that you used in section 8.3.2 to create an instance of the `FormattingBehavior` behavior is perfect:

Figure 9.2   Public properties and methods exposed by the `ScriptBehaviorDescriptor` class

```
$create(Samples.FormattingBehavior,
    {'hoverCssClass':'field_hover', 'focusCssClass':'field_focus'},
    {}, {}, $get('Name'));
```

To generate the same statement on the server side, you can create an instance of the `ScriptBehaviorDescriptor` class. Then, you pass the client type and the client ID of the associated DOM element as strings to the class constructor:

```
ScriptBehaviorDescriptor desc =
    new ScriptBehaviorDescriptor("Samples.FormattingBehavior",
        "Name");
```

The client ID of the associated element, passed as the second argument to the class constructor, becomes the argument of the `$get` method when the `$create` statement is generated by the script descriptor. The string with the type of the client control becomes the first argument passed to the `$create` method.

The goal of the script descriptors is to configure the parameters accepted by the `$create` method. Figure 9.3 will help you understand which methods of the script descriptor classes are used to build the parameters passed to the `$create` statement generated on the server side.

The first and last arguments passed to `$create`—the client type and the associated element, respectively—are passed as arguments to the constructor of the script

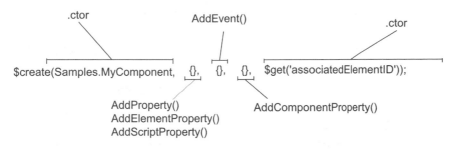

Figure 9.3 How the methods exposed by a script descriptor are used to generate a `$create` **statement**

descriptor. An exception is represented by the `ScriptComponentDescriptor` class, whose constructor accepts only a parameter with the client type (a nonvisual component doesn't have an associated DOM element).

As you know from chapter 8, the second argument accepted by `$create` is an object that maps properties of the client component to their values. To add a name/value pair to this object, call the `AddProperty` method of the script descriptor instance, passing the name of the client property and its value as arguments. Here's the code:

```
ScriptBehaviorDescriptor desc =
    new ScriptBehaviorDescriptor("Samples.FormattingBehavior",
        "Name");

desc.AddProperty("name", "myFormattingBehavior");
```

The previous code will generate the following `$create` statement:

```
$create(Samples.FormattingBehavior,
    {"name":"myFormattingBehavior"}, {}, {}, $get("Name"));
```

Note that the second argument passed to `AddProperty` is of type `object`. The script descriptor takes care of serializing the value using the JSON data format and embedding it in the `$create` statement. The `AddElementProperty` method behaves in a manner similar to `AddProperty`, but the value passed as an argument is the client ID of a DOM element and is passed to the `$get` method in the generated `$create` statement. The other methods exposed by the `ScriptBehaviorDescriptor` class—and by the other script descriptors—set the remaining parameters accepted by `$create`. They are as follows:

- `AddEvent`—Adds an event handler for a client event. The first argument passed to `AddEvent` is the name of the client event to subscribe. The second argument is the name of the JavaScript function (a global function or an instance method) that will handle it.

- `AddComponentProperty`—Maps an ID to a client component reference. The value passed to the method is a string with the ID of a client component. This ID is used in conjunction with `$find` to retrieve a reference to the component and assign it to the corresponding property.

- `AddScriptProperty`—Assigns some JavaScript code as the value for a given client property. Instead of being encoded as a JSON string, the value passed to this method is embedded as is and evaluated as JavaScript code at runtime.

These are all the methods you need to use to generate a `$create` statement. The same methods are found in the `ScriptControlDescriptor` class, which is the script descriptor associated with a client control. Examining the `ScriptControl-Descriptor` class, as we'll do in the next section, will help you become even more confident with script descriptors.

9.1.3 Describing a control

If you want to generate a `$create` statement to instantiate a client control, the `ScriptControlDescriptor` class is the right choice. Figure 9.4 shows the relevant properties and methods exposed by this class.

Except for the `Name` property (which is relevant only for behaviors), the `ScriptControlDescriptor` class exposes the same properties and methods found in the `ScriptBehaviorDescriptor` class. Again, let's take a `$create` statement and explain which methods you have to call to generate it with a script descriptor. What about the `$create` statement you used to build an instance of the PhotoGallery control in section 8.4.5? The code for this slightly more complex statement is shown in listing 9.1.

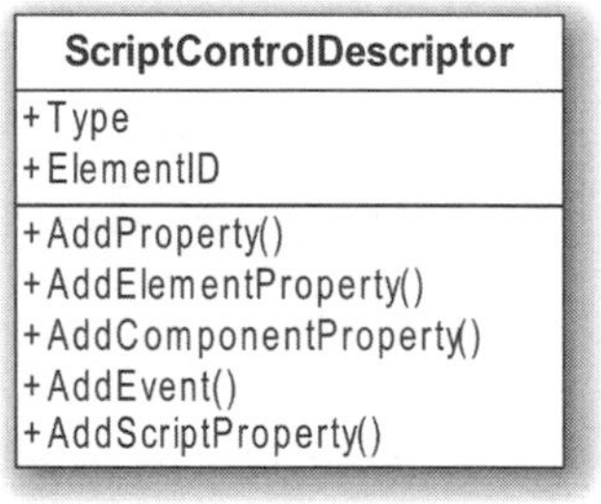

ScriptControlDescriptor
+Type
+ElementID
+AddProperty()
+AddElementProperty()
+AddComponentProperty()
+AddEvent()
+AddScriptProperty()

Figure 9.4   Public properties and methods exposed by the `ScriptControlDescriptor` class

Listing 9.1 Example `$create` statement used to create an instance of the PhotoGallery control

```
$create(Samples.PhotoGallery,
    {
        'imageElement': $get('gal_image'),
        'prevElement': $get('gal_prevButton'),
        'nextElement': $get('gal_nextButton'),
        'progressElement': $get('gal_progress'),
        'images': ['Album/photo1.jpg', 'Album/photo2.jpg',
                    'Album/photo3.jpg']
    },
    {},
    {},
    $get('photoGallery'));
```

How can you instruct a `ScriptControlDescriptor` object to generate a string with the same statement? The answer is shown in listing 9.2, where you use the `AddElementProperty` method to assign references to DOM elements to the properties of the client control. Note how the array of strings passed to `AddProperty` in the last statement is turned into a JSON array in the generated `$create` statement.

Listing 9.2 A script descriptor for configuring an instance of the PhotoGallery control

```
ScriptControlDescriptor desc =
    new ScriptControlDescriptor("Samples.PhotoGallery",
      "photoGallery");

desc.AddElementProperty("imageElement", "gal_image");
desc.AddElementProperty("prevElement", "gal_prevButton");
desc.AddElementProperty("nextElement", "gal_nextButton");
desc.AddElementProperty("progressElement", "gal_progress");
desc.AddProperty("images", new string[3] { "Album/photo1.jpg",
    "Album/photo2.jpg", "Album/photo3.jpg") });
```

Usually, client components are contained in external JavaScript files that must be loaded in the web page. In ASP.NET AJAX, you can do this by referencing the script files manually in the `Scripts` section of the ScriptManager control. For this reason, it's not enough for a server control to generate `$create` statements using script descriptors. You also need a way to automatically generate `script` tags with references to external JavaScript files. This is the purpose of the `ScriptReference` class, as we'll clarify in the following section.

9.1.4 *Script references*

In an ASP.NET AJAX page, you can use the mighty ScriptManager control to load all the JavaScript files needed by the page. To do this, you declare one or multiple ScriptReference elements in the Scripts section of the ScriptManager control. As you know from previous chapters, a ScriptReference object exposes all the properties needed for locating a script file, whether it's stored in one of the folders of the website or embedded in an assembly as a web resource.

If a server control wants to provide a list of script files to load in the web page, it can create instances of the ScriptReference class programmatically. For example, the following code uses an instance of the ScriptReference class to reference a script file called MyScriptFile.js, located in the website's ScriptLibrary folder:

```
ScriptReference scriptRef = new ScriptReference();
scriptRef.Path =
    Page.ResolveClientUrl("~/ScriptLibrary/MyScriptFile.js");
```

If the file is embedded as a web resource in a separate assembly, you have to specify values for the Assembly and Name properties. The Assembly property holds the name of the assembly that embeds the file. The Name property stores a string with the name of the registered web resource.

> **NOTE** Web resources are a feature of ASP.NET 2.0 that let you embed files, images, and documents in an assembly and load them in a web page through a HTTP handler. In section 4.3.1 we briefly discussed how to embed web resources in an assembly. To learn more about web resources, browse to http://support.microsoft.com/kb/910442/en-us.

Script descriptors and script references are the objects you need to build Ajax-enabled controls. Now that you have a foundation, let's examine how ASP.NET server controls can take advantage of these objects to become Ajax-enabled controls.

9.2 *Introduction to Ajax-enabled controls*

An ASP.NET AJAX-enabled control (or an *Ajax-enabled control*, as we'll call it) is an ASP.NET server control. It's associated with one or more client components that add client functionality to the markup code it renders. Usually, an Ajax-enabled control renders, in the page, some HTML code and one or more $create statements, depending on the client components it wants to instantiate. The Ajax-enabled control also takes care of loading the necessary script files in the page.

The problem of how to programmatically generate a $create statement without relying on hard-coded strings has been solved with the introduction of script descriptors. The ScriptReference object lets you programmatically reference a script file. You need to understand how and when these objects are used to render the various pieces of information in the page—in the right place, at the right time. The ScriptManager is the control elected to accomplish this delicate task. In this section, we'll shed some light on the mechanisms that let a server control become an Ajax-enabled control.

9.2.1 How Ajax-enabled controls work

When a server control wants to take advantage of client components, it must do two things. First, it must implement an interface that specifies which kind of Ajax-enabled control it's going to be. We'll introduce the two kinds of Ajax-enabled controls in the next section, but it's important to point out that by implementing one of these interfaces, a server control declares that it can provide a list of script references and script descriptors.

Second, it must *register* itself with the ScriptManager during the PreRender and Render phases of the server page lifecycle. When this happens, the ScriptManager knows that a server control wishes to instantiate client components. The ScriptManager queries the server control for a list of script descriptors and script references. The returned objects are used to render the $create statements and the script tags in the web page. Figure 9.5 uses an activity diagram to show the sequence of events involved in this rather elaborate process.

The diagram shows that the registration procedure begins during the PreRender stage of the server page lifecycle, where the Ajax-enabled control registers

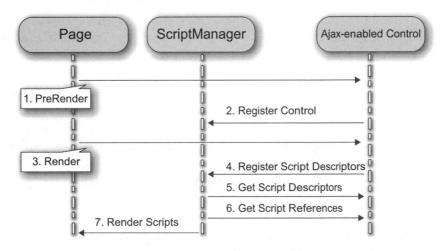

Figure 9.5   An Ajax-enabled control must register itself with the ScriptManager control. The registration procedure starts during the PreRender stage and is completed in the Render stage.

itself with the ScriptManager (event 2). During this step, the ScriptManager gets a list of script references from the server control. The second step happens during the Render phase, when the Ajax-enabled control provides the ScriptManager with a list of script descriptors (event 4). Finally, the ScriptManager renders in the page both the `script` tags with the references to the script files and the `$create` statements generated by the script descriptors.

If you're worried by the complexity of this procedure, have no fear. To make things simpler, ASP.NET AJAX provides base classes for creating Ajax-enabled controls. The advantage of deriving from these classes is that they take care of performing the entire registration procedure automatically. Creating an Ajax-enabled control is a matter of implementing the methods that return the list of script descriptors and script references. These methods are defined in the interfaces implemented by the base classes. As a consequence, you have to override them to get the job done.

In some situations, it's not possible to derive from a base class, and you need to implement the procedure manually. Later in the chapter, we'll go under the hood of the registration procedure. Now, it's time to introduce the base classes and interfaces that you'll use to create Ajax-enabled controls.

9.2.2 *Extenders and script controls*

In the previous section, we mentioned that you can choose between two kinds of Ajax-enabled controls: You can create either an *extender* or a *script control*. The difference between these two types of controls is mainly conceptual, because the goal of both is to provide a list of script descriptors and script references.

You can think of extenders as *providers* of client functionality. The goal of an extender is to attach client components to an existing server control at any time, without the need to derive a new class. To understand why you have to bother with extenders, suppose you've created a client component that adds auto-complete functionality—like the one provided by Google Suggest—to a text box element. To wire the client component to the text box, you could create an `AutoComplete-TextBox` class that derives from the `TextBox` class and provides the necessary script references and script descriptors.

Another approach keeps the `TextBox` class and lets an external object do the work of wiring a client component to the TextBox control. In this scenario, the external object is the extender, and the TextBox becomes the *extended control* or *target control*. An extender can upgrade or *extend* existing server controls to Ajax-enabled controls without the need to replace them with custom server controls. This concept is represented in figure 9.6.

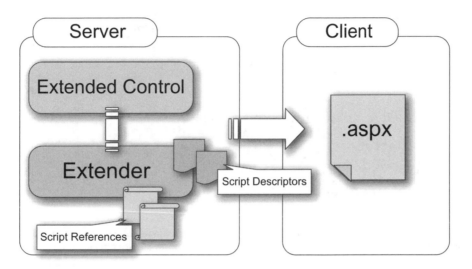

Figure 9.6 In the extender model, a server control receives the client functionality from the Extender control, which provides the script references and script descriptors needed to wire a client component to the extended control.

An ASP.NET AJAX extender is conceptually similar to an extender provider in Windows Forms. It keeps a portion of functionality separated from a server control, and it provides additional properties to the extended control. These properties are used, in turn, to configure the properties of the client component that are associated with the extended control.

NOTE To learn more about extender providers in Windows Forms, browse to http://msdn2.microsoft.com/en-us/library/ms171835.aspx.

If you decide that both the server and the client capabilities should be specified in the same place, you need a script control. It's a server control that is created as an Ajax-enabled control and can provide script references and script descriptors without the need for an external object. Returning to the example of an auto-complete text box, the `AutoCompleteTextBox` class that derives from `TextBox` is a good candidate for becoming a script control. This model is illustrated in figure 9.7.

Deciding whether to build an extender or a script control is a design choice you should make based on the requirements of the web application. Typically, an extender is the right choice when you want to plug client functionality into an existing server control, without the need to create a new control. A script control is the right choice if you want complete control over its capabilities both on the server and on the client side.

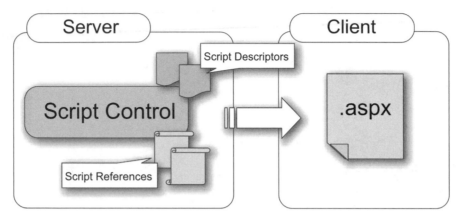

Figure 9.7 A script control is a server control that can both render markup code and provide the script references and script descriptors needed to instantiate client components.

From a slightly different point of view, the choice between an extender and a script control can be determined by the kind of client component you want to wire to the server control. Creating an extender is typically the right choice if you want to wire a client behavior to a DOM element. Because an element can have multiple behaviors, it makes sense to wire—on the server side—multiple extenders to a server control. Each extender contributes to the client capabilities of the extended control by providing a different client behavior. On the other hand, because a DOM element can be associated with one and only one client control, it makes more sense to associate the client control with a script control and have all the properties needed for configuring the client component embedded in the server control.

We discussed client components and the client component model in great detail in chapter 8. Figure 9.8 shows the base interfaces and classes you can use to create extenders and script controls.

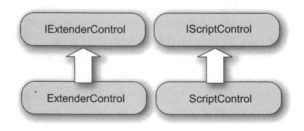

**Figure 9.8
Base interface and classes provided by ASP.NET AJAX to create Ajax-enabled controls**

There are two base classes: `ExtenderControl` and `ScriptControl`. The `Extender-Control` class creates extenders and implements the `IExtenderControl` interface. The `ScriptControl` class creates script controls and implements the `IScriptControl` interface.

The following sections will dive into the details of extenders and script controls. You'll study the base interfaces and classes and learn how to use them to create Ajax-enabled controls. Let's start the discussion by introducing extenders.

9.3   *Extenders*

You already know that an extender's goal is to wire a client component to an existing server control. You need to know how the client functionality is attached to the extended control.

The easiest way to build an extender is to declare a class that inherits from the base `ExtenderControl` class. This class implements an interface called `IExtenderControl` and takes care of registering the extender with the ScriptManager control. A derived class should override the methods defined in the `IExtenderControl` interface. Let's look at this interface before you develop your first extender.

9.3.1   *The IExtenderControl interface*

The `IExtenderControl` interface defines the contract to which a class adheres to become an extender. Figure 9.9 shows the methods implemented by the interface, which have the following responsibilities:

- `GetScriptDescriptors`—Returns the list of script descriptors. The method receives a `targetControl` parameter that contains a reference to the extended control.

- `GetScriptReferences`—Returns the list of ScriptReference objects. Each instance represents a script file that will be loaded in the page.

Figure 9.9   Methods defined in the `IExtenderControl` interface

Interestingly, both methods defined in the interface return an IEnumerable type. When you implement the method or override it in a derived class, you can return an array or a list or (if you're using C# 2.0) implement an iterator to return the lists of script descriptors and script references.

NOTE Iterators are a feature introduced in C# 2.0 to support foreach iteration in a class or a struct without the need to implement the entire IEnumerable interface. If you want to know more about C# iterators, browse to http://msdn2.microsoft.com/en-us/library/65zzykke.aspx.

Even if your main job is to override the methods defined in the IExtenderControl interface, it's important to know how the registration procedure is particularized for an extender. In the following section, we'll look at how an extender is registered with the ScriptManager control.

9.3.2 Extender registration

The process of registering with the ScriptManager lets the extender be recognized as an Ajax-enabled control. It's a two-step process:

1. During the PreRender stage, you call RegisterExtenderControl method, passing the extender instance and the extended control as arguments.
2. During the Render stage, you call the RegisterScriptDescriptors method to register the script descriptors.

As shown in figure 9.10, the first part of the registration procedure involves calling the RegisterExtenderControl method on the ScriptManager control (event 2). This method receives the current extender instance and the extended control as arguments. The registration procedure is completed during the Render phase, where you call the RegisterScriptDescriptors method on the ScriptManager, passing the current extender instance as an argument (event 4).

Luckily, the ExtenderControl class takes care of performing the registration procedure automatically on your behalf. Because you always create a new extender by deriving from the ExtenderControl class, you don't need to worry about the implementation details. However, when we discuss script controls, you'll discover that in some situations you need to manually register the Ajax-enabled control with the ScriptManager. For this reason, we'll postpone a deeper examination of the registration procedure until section 9.4.

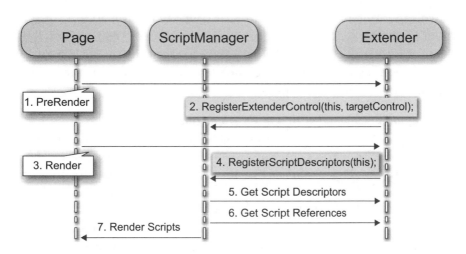

Figure 9.10 An extender must be registered with the ScriptManager control during the PreRender and Render phases of the server page lifecycle.

In general, the design of an extender follows three phases:

1   Build a client component—either a behavior or a control—that encapsulates the client functionality you intend to provide to a server control.

2   The real development of the extender starts. Determine which properties of the client component you want to configure on the server side. You can map them to a group of server properties and perform the configuration of the client component through the extender.

3   Build the extender class, which provides the lists of script references and script descriptors to the ScriptManager control.

Let's apply this design strategy to a concrete example. In the following section, you'll create an extender for the FormattingBehavior behavior you built in chapter 8. This will let you wire the behavior to an ASP.NET TextBox and configure it on the server side.

9.3.3   *An extender for FormattingBehavior*

In chapter 8, we demonstrated how to enrich a text box element by simulating in-place edit functionality with the help of a client behavior. Now that you've implemented this client component, it would be great if you could wire it to TextBox controls in different web applications. If your intention is to not write one more line of JavaScript code or change any web controls declared in a form, building an extender is the right path. If you have the code for the `FormattingBehavior` class stored in a JavaScript file you've completed the first phase of the design strategy and can move to the second phase.

Mapping client properties to server properties

Once the client functionality is encapsulated in a client component, you need to filter the client properties you want to configure on the server side. The goal is to create corresponding properties in the extender class and use them to set the value of the client properties. How is this possible? By using a script descriptor.

Recall from chapter 8 that the `FormattingBehavior` class exposes two properties called `hoverCssClass` and `focusCssClass`. They hold the names of the CSS classes used by the client behavior. To set their values from the server side, you need to expose corresponding properties in the extender. In preparation, it's useful to draw a table that shows the mapping between properties of the client component and properties of the extender; see table 9.1.

Table 9.1 Mappings between client properties and extender properties

Client property	Extender property
hoverCssClass	HoverCssClass
focusCssClass	FocusCssClass

Once you've drawn the table, you're ready to move to the third and final, where you'll create the extender class and implement the server-side logic.

Creating the extender

An extender is a class that inherits from the base `System.Web.UI.ExtenderControl` class. Usually, an extender includes a group of server properties and the overrides of the methods defined in the `IExtenderControl` interface. Other than these, an extender shouldn't perform any tasks. Because the purpose of an extender is to provide script descriptors and script references, all the other logic added to the extender should relate to the configuration of the associated client component.

Let's return to the example. The extender class is called `FormattingExtender`, and its code is shown in listing 9.3.

Listing 9.3   Code for the `FormattingExtender` class

```csharp
using System;
using System.Collections.Generic;
using System.Web;
using System.Web.UI;
using System.Web.UI.WebControls;

[TargetControlType(typeof(TextBox))]
public class FormattingExtender : ExtenderControl
{
    public string HoverCssClass
    {
        get { return (string)ViewState["HoverCssClass"]; }
        set { ViewState["HoverCssClass"] = value; }
    }

    public string FocusCssClass
    {
        get { return (string)ViewState["FocusCssClass"]; }
        set { ViewState["FocusCssClass"] = value; }
    }

    public string ScriptPath
    {
        get { return (string)ViewState["ScriptPath"]; }
        set { ViewState["ScriptPath"] = value; }
    }

    protected override IEnumerable<ScriptDescriptor>
        GetScriptDescriptors(Control targetControl)
    {
        ScriptBehaviorDescriptor desc = new
            ScriptBehaviorDescriptor("Samples.FormattingBehavior",
            targetControl.ClientID);

        desc.AddProperty("hoverCssClass", this.HoverCssClass);
        desc.AddProperty("focusCssClass", this.FocusCssClass);

        yield return desc;
    }

    protected override IEnumerable<ScriptReference>
        GetScriptReferences()
    {
        yield return new
            ScriptReference(Page.ResolveClientUrl(this.ScriptPath));
    }
}
```

❶ Properties

**IExtenderControl ❷
methods**

Above the class declaration is a `TargetControlType` attribute. Its goal is to put a constraint on the types of server controls that the extender can extend. Because you pass `typeof(TextBox)` as an argument to the attribute, only TextBox controls can be extended by the `FormattingExtender`. Associating the extender with a web control other than a TextBox will cause a server exception to be thrown by ASP.NET. If you pass `typeof(Control)`, all the controls can be extended, although it doesn't make much sense given the kind of client functionality that, in this example, you'll add to the target control.

The `FormattingExtender` class exposes a `ScriptPath` property ❶ that isn't listed in table 9.1. This property specifies the location of the JavaScript file that contains the code of the `FormattingBehavior` behavior. The property isn't listed in the table because it's not exposed by the client component. You'll need it when you create the `ScriptReference` instance that you return to the `ScriptManager`, so it makes sense to have it in the extender control.

The other two properties are those shown in table 9.1. The `HoverCssClass` property stores the value assigned to the `hoverCssClass` property of the client behavior. The same is true for the `FocusCssClass` property. Note that you store and retrieve all the values from the `ViewState` of the extender control.

For the first time, you can see how the methods ❷ defined in the `IExtenderControl` interface are overridden in the extender control. As expected, the `GetScriptDescriptors` method returns a script descriptor for the `FormattingBehavior` behavior. In the override, the script descriptor uses the values of the server `HoverCssClass` and `FocusCssClass` properties to build a `$create` statement that contains values for the client `hoverCssClass` and `focusCssClass` properties. Finally, the `GetScriptReferences` method returns a `ScriptReference` instance with the information needed to load the right JavaScript file in the page. The location of the file is configured through the `ScriptPath` property.

> **NOTE** Listing 9.3 uses the `yield return` construct in both the `GetScriptReferences` and `GetScriptDescriptors` methods. You use the `yield` keyword when implementing a C# iterator, to signal the end of an iteration.

Without much effort, you've built your first extender. But we've left some things unsaid: For example, how do you wire an extender to an ASP.NET control? The next section will teach you how to declare and configure extenders.

9.3.4 *Using an extender*

An extender is nothing more than a custom ASP.NET server control. The `ExtenderControl` class derives from the base `Control` class; an extender is registered and declared in an ASP.NET page like any other server control. Figure 9.11 shows how the files are organized in the sample ASP.NET AJAX-enabled website that you can download at http://www.manning.com/gallo.

As you can see, the extender class is contained in the App_Code directory. The file with the code for the client behavior, FormattingBehavior.js, is located in the ScriptLibrary folder. Another possible configuration

Figure 9.11   The extender class and the JavaScript file with the code for the client component can be hosted in an ASP.NET AJAX-enabled website.

has both the server class and the JavaScript file stored in a separate assembly; we'll cover this scenario in section 9.4, but the same rules apply to extenders.

To use the extender in an ASP.NET page, all you have to do is register the namespace that contains the `FormattingExtender` class in the page that will use it:

```
<%@ Register Namespace="Samples" TagPrefix="samples" %>
```

Now, you have to wire the extender to its target control. The code in listing 9.4 shows a simple ASP.NET TextBox with an associated FormattingExtender control.

Listing 9.4   How to extend an ASP.NET web control declaratively

```
<%-- Extended Control --%>
<asp:TextBox ID="txtName" runat="server"></asp:TextBox>

<%-- Extender --%>
<samples:FormattingExtender ID="FormattingExtender1" runat="server"
    TargetControlID="txtName"
    HoverCssClass="hover"
    FocusCssClass="focus"
    ScriptPath="~/ScriptLibrary/FormattingBehavior.js" />
```

All the magic of extenders happens when you set the extender control's `Target-ControlID` property to the ID of the target control. In listing 9.4, you extend the TextBox by assigning its ID to the `TargetControlID` property of the FormattingExtender control. The remaining properties of the extender are used to configure the CSS classes used by the client behavior. The `ScriptPath` property contains the path to the FormattingBehavior.js file.

NOTE   The `TargetControlID` property is the main property exposed by an extender. You always set this property, because it identifies the server control that's wired to the extender.

An extender can also be instantiated programmatically, as shown in listing 9.5. The extender must be always added to the same container as the target control; if the target control is declared in an UpdatePanel, the extender must be declared in the panel. If the target control is declared in the form tag, then the extender must be added to the Page.Form.Controls collection.

Listing 9.5   Extending an ASP.NET web control programmatically

```
FormattingExtender ext = new FormattingExtender();
ext.ID = "FormattingExtender1";
ext.TargetControlID = txtName.ID;
ext.HoverCssClass = "hover";
ext.FocusCssClass = "focus";
ext.ScriptPath = "~/ScriptLibrary/FormattingBehavior.js";

Page.Form.Controls.Add(ext);
```

To complete our discussion, let's run the ASP.NET page and look at the source code sent to the browser. After a bit of scrolling, you can find the script file required by the FormattingExtender control:

```
<script src="FormattingBehavior.js" type="text/javascript"></script>
```

After more scrolling, you see the $create statement generated by the script descriptor that the FormattingExtender returned to the ScriptManager control:

```
Sys.Application.add_init(function() {
    $create(Samples.FormattingBehavior,
        {"focusCssClass":"focus","hoverCssClass":"hover"},
        null,
        null,
        $get("txtLastName"));
});
```

Note how the $create statement is correctly injected into a JavaScript function that handles the init event raised by Sys.Application. So far, so good; everything went as expected.

Keep in mind that an extender is used to wire a client component to an existing server control. The extender provides the necessary script references and script descriptors to the ScriptManager control. It does so by overriding the methods defined in the IScriptControl interface. An extender control can also expose properties to enable the configuration of the properties exposed by the client component. Now, we're ready to explore the second category of Ajax-enabled controls: script controls.

9.4   *Script controls*

Extenders are great for providing client functionality to existing server controls in an incremental way. In many cases, though, you don't want or don't need an external control to wire client components to a server control. To describe both the server-side and the client-side functionalities in a single place, the server control is a good candidate for becoming a script control. Script controls are server controls that can provide script references and script descriptors without relying on an external object.

Building a script control can be slightly more difficult than building an extender. If you're writing the control from scratch, you can safely derive from the base ScriptControl class, which takes care of registering the script control with the ScriptManager under the hood. Coding the control is similar to coding an extender. The only difference is that the properties used to configure the client component and the overrides of the methods defined in the IScriptControl interface are embedded in the control rather than in a different object.

In some situations, you'll want to turn an existing control into a script control. In such a case, you have to derive a class from the existing server control and manually implement the IScriptControl interface. The following sections will introduce the IScriptControl interface and provide some insights as to how you implement the registration procedure.

9.4.1   *The IScriptControl interface*

The IScriptControl interface must be implemented by every script control. It's similar to the IExtenderControl interface, as shown in figure 9.12. A script control doesn't have a target control; this is why the RegisterScriptDescriptors method doesn't receive a reference to the extended control as happened with extenders. The methods defined by the IScriptControl interface have the following responsibilities:

- GetScriptDescriptors—Returns the list of script descriptors
- GetScriptReferences—Returns the list of ScriptReference instances

Figure 9.12
Methods defined in the
IScriptControl **interface**

```
              «interface»
             IScriptControl
+GetScriptDescriptors() : IEnumerable<ScriptDescriptor>
+GetScriptReferences() : IEnumerable<ScriptReference>
```

Sometimes you can't derive from the base `ScriptControl` class. Therefore, it's important to be familiar with what happens behind the scenes during the registration of a script control.

9.4.2 *Script control registration*

Registration with the ScriptManager is necessary in order to recognize a script control as an Ajax-enabled control. It's a two-step process similar to that used for extenders:

- During the PreRender stage, you call the `RegisterScriptControl` method, passing the script control instance as an argument.
- During the Render stage, you call the `RegisterScriptDescriptors` method to register the script descriptors.

As shown in figure 9.13, the first part of the registration procedure involves calling the `RegisterScriptControl` method on the ScriptManager control (event 2). This method receives the current script control instance as an argument. The registration procedure is completed during the Render phase, where you call the `RegisterScriptDescriptors` method, passing the current script control instance as an argument (event 4).

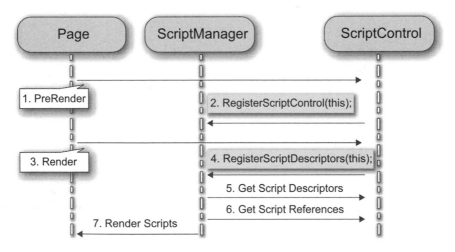

Figure 9.13 A script control registers with the ScriptManager control during the PreRender and Render phases of the server page lifecycle.

As promised, let's dive into the implementation details of the registration procedure. Typically, a script control that will register itself with the ScriptManager overrides the `OnPreRender` and `OnRender` methods. In the `OnPreRender` method, you first check that a ScriptManager control is present on the page before calling the `RegisterScriptControl` method. Listing 9.6 shows a possible override of the `OnPreRender` method.

Listing 9.6 Overriding the `OnPreRender` method to register the script control

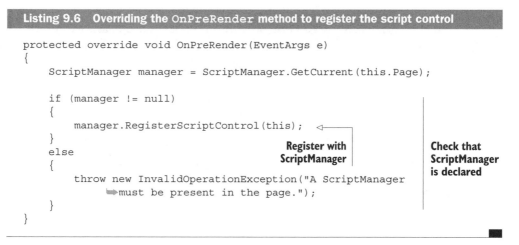

```
protected override void OnPreRender(EventArgs e)
{
    ScriptManager manager = ScriptManager.GetCurrent(this.Page);

    if (manager != null)
    {
        manager.RegisterScriptControl(this);       <—    Register with
    }                                                    ScriptManager
    else                                                                Check that
    {                                                                   ScriptManager
        throw new InvalidOperationException("A ScriptManager            is declared
            must be present in the page.");
    }
}
```

The registration procedure is completed in the `Render` method, where the script control registers its script descriptors by calling the `RegisterScriptDescriptors` method on the ScriptManager instance; see listing 9.7.

Listing 9.7 Overriding the `Render` method to register the script descriptors

```
protected override void Render(HtmlTextWriter writer)
{
    base.Render(writer);

    ScriptManager.GetCurrent(this.Page)                    Register script
                .RegisterScriptDescriptors(this);          descriptors
}
```

In the `OnRender` override, you don't perform the check on the ScriptManager because you already did it during the `OnPreRender` stage. This registration procedure should be implemented whenever you can't derive from the base `Script-Control` class. But when does it happen? The following section provides some design guidelines for creating script controls.

9.4.3 *Design strategies*

With ASP.NET, there are many ways to create a server control. For example, you can extend an existing server control by deriving from its class. As an alternative, you can inherit from one of the base classes contained in the `System.Web.UI` namespace. You can also build a control by compositing existing web controls. In this case, `CompositeControl` is the base class. If you need data-binding capabilities, the `DataBoundControl` class lets you easily build such controls. In addition, you can create a custom control with an associated declarative template. This is called a *web user control;* you've probably created many in your web applications. It consists of a .ascx file that contains the declarative markup code and a code-behind file that encapsulates the control's logic.

All these custom server controls can acquire Ajax capabilities and become script controls. Table 9.2 shows the categories of ASP.NET server controls and the suggested strategy for turning them into Ajax-enabled controls.

Table 9.2 How to Ajax-enable different kinds of ASP.NET server controls

I want to...	How to Ajax-enable it
Extend an existing web control.	Create an extender, or implement the `IScriptControl` interface.
Derive from `System.Web.UI.WebControl`, create a composite control, or create a data-bound control.	Implement the `IScriptControl` interface.
Start with an Ajax-enabled control.	Derive from `System.Web.UI.ScriptControl`.
Create a web user control.	Implement the `IScriptControl` interface.

Now that you have all the tools you need to start developing script controls, let's build one. You'll start by adding Ajax capabilities to the Login control, a server control shipped with ASP.NET 2.0 that, unfortunately, isn't compatible with the UpdatePanel at the moment. A quick look at table 9.2 reveals that in order to upgrade the Login control to a script control, you should derive from the `Login` class and implement the `IScriptControl` interface. That's what you'll do in the next section.

9.4.4 *Adding Ajax to the ASP.NET Login control*

Trying to put the ASP.NET Login control in an UpdatePanel reveals a sad truth: The control suddenly stops working, and your dreams of performing user authentication in the background vanish miserably. But you don't have to wait until the next update of the ASP.NET framework to make your dreams come true. With the help of a script control and a client control that leverages the ASP.NET authentication service, you can perform the desired task.

As we explained in chapter 4, the Microsoft Ajax Library provides a way to access the authentication service asynchronously on the client side. Given this premise, you'll create a client control that accesses the markup code rendered by the Login control and performs the authentication using an Ajax request. Finally, you'll create a script control that extends the existing Login control and instantiates the client control in the page.

Let's start by setting up the project for the new AjaxLogin control. Earlier, we explained how to embed the code files in an ASP.NET AJAX-enabled website. This time, we'll explain how to embed the files in a separate assembly referenced by the website.

Setting up the project

In Visual Studio 2005, let's create a new class-library project called `ScriptControls`. The Visual Studio template creates a file called Class1.cs, which you can safely delete. Add a new JavaScript file called AjaxLogin.js. Select it and, in the Properties panel, set the Build Action property to Embedded Resource. This instructs the compiler to embed the file as an assembly resource that can be loaded in a web page. The AjaxLogin.js file—empty at the moment—will contain the client AjaxLogin control that adds Ajax capabilities to the server Login control. To complete the project layout, add a new class file called AjaxLogin.cs to obtain the structure shown in figure 9.14.

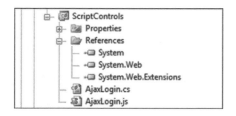

Figure 9.14 Structure of the `ScriptControls` **project**

Creating the AjaxLogin client control

The client AjaxLogin control leverages the authentication service proxy to authenticate a user on the client side using an asynchronous HTTP request. We discussed the authentication service and the other application services provided by ASP.NET AJAX in chapter 5. Once the user types her username and password and clicks the login button, you invoke the `Sys.Services.AuthenticationService.login` method, which performs the authentication procedure asynchronously. Listing 9.8 shows the code for the AjaxLogin client control; add it to the AjaxLogin.js file created in the project.

Listing 9.8   Code for the `AjaxLogin` client class

```
Type.registerNamespace("Samples");

Samples.AjaxLogin = function(element) {
    Samples.AjaxLogin.initializeBase(this, [element]);

    this._userName = null;
    this._password = null;
    this._rememberMe = null;
    this._loginButton = null;
}

Samples.AjaxLogin.prototype = {
    initialize : function() {
        Samples.AjaxLogin.callBaseMethod(this, 'initialize');

        $addHandlers(this._loginButton,
            {'click':this._onLoginButtonClicked}, this);
    },

    dispose : function() {
        $clearHandlers(this._loginButton);
        Samples.AjaxLogin.callBaseMethod(this, 'dispose');
    },

    _onLoginButtonClicked : function(e) {
      var validationResult =
        typeof(Page_ClientValidate) == 'function'
        && Page_ClientValidate(this._validationGroup) ?
            true : false;

        if (validationResult) {
            Sys.Services.AuthenticationService.login(
                this._userName.value,
                this._password.value,
                this._rememberMe && this._rememberMe.checked,
                null,
                null,
                Function.createDelegate(this,
                    this._onLoginComplete),
                Function.createDelegate(this,
                    this._onLoginFailed)
            );
        }
        e.preventDefault();
    },
```

❶ Fields

❷ Authentication logic

```
_onLoginComplete : function(result) {
    if (result) {
        alert("Login Succeeded");
    }
    else {
        alert("Login failed");
    }
},

_onLoginFailed : function(err) {
    alert(err.get_message());
},

set_UserName : function(value) {
    this._userName = value;
},

set_Password : function(value) {
    this._password = value;
},

set_RememberMe : function(value) {
    this._rememberMe = value;
},

set_LoginButton : function(value) {
    this._loginButton = value;
},

get_UserName : function() {
    return this._userName ;
},

get_Password : function() {
    return this._password ;
},

get_RememberMe : function() {
    return this._rememberMe ;
},

get_LoginButton : function() {
    return this._loginButton ;
}

};
Samples.AjaxLogin.registerClass('Samples.AjaxLogin',
    Sys.UI.Control);
```

3 Display login status

4 Display error message

The objective is to associate the client control with the DOM element that contains the markup code rendered by the Login control. You use some fields ❶ to store references to the child DOM elements. For example, the _userName and _password variables hold references to the text boxes rendered by the Login control.

In the prototype object, the initialize and dispose methods are overridden to participate in the client control's lifecycle. You use the $addHandlers method to attach a handler for the click event of the login button. The event handler ❷, _onLoginButtonClicked, takes into account the ASP.NET validators and invokes the login method of the authentication service proxy.

The last two parameters passed to the login method are callbacks. The first, _onLoginComplete, is invoked if the authentication procedure succeeds (whether the user has supplied right or wrong credentials); it ❸ displays the login status in a message box. The second callback, ❹ _onLoginFailed, is called if something goes wrong during the call to the authentication service proxy.

Building the AjaxLogin script control

The script control you'll build derives from the Login class and implements the IScriptControl interface. You need to override the methods of the IScriptControl interface as well as implement the registration procedure. You do so in the code for the AjaxLogin class, shown in listing 9.9.

Listing 9.9 Code for the `AjaxLogin` server class

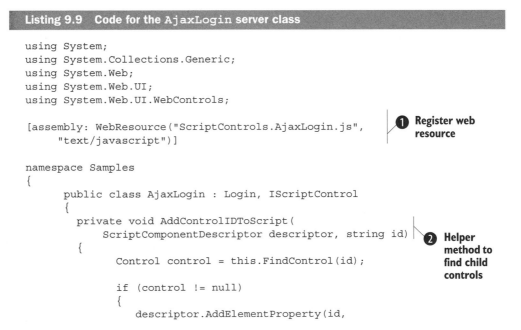

```
using System;
using System.Collections.Generic;
using System.Web;
using System.Web.UI;
using System.Web.UI.WebControls;

[assembly: WebResource("ScriptControls.AjaxLogin.js",
    "text/javascript")]

namespace Samples
{
    public class AjaxLogin : Login, IScriptControl
    {
        private void AddControlIDToScript(
            ScriptComponentDescriptor descriptor, string id)
        {
            Control control = this.FindControl(id);

            if (control != null)
            {
                descriptor.AddElementProperty(id,
```

❶ Register web resource

❷ Helper method to find child controls

```
                            control.ClientID);
        }
        else
        {
           throw new NullReferenceException(
              ➥"Unable to find a control with the
              ➥given ID");
        }
}

protected override void OnPreRender(EventArgs e)
{
    base.OnPreRender(e);

    ScriptManager manager;
    manager = ScriptManager.GetCurrent(this.Page);

    if (manager == null)
    {
        throw new InvalidOperationException("A ScriptManager
            is required on the page.");
    }

    manager.RegisterScriptControl(this);
}

protected override void Render(HtmlTextWriter writer)
{
    base.Render(writer);

    ScriptManager.GetCurrent(this.Page)
        .RegisterScriptDescriptors(this);
}

public IEnumerable<ScriptDescriptor> GetScriptDescriptors()
{
    ScriptControlDescriptor descriptor = new
    ScriptControlDescriptor("Samples.AjaxLogin",
      this.ClientID);                    Script descriptor ❸

    AddControlIDToScript(descriptor, "UserName");
    AddControlIDToScript(descriptor, "Password");
    AddControlIDToScript(descriptor, "RememberMe");
    AddControlIDToScript(descriptor, "LoginButton");

    yield return descriptor;
}
```

```
        public IEnumerable<ScriptReference> GetScriptReferences()
        {
            yield return new ScriptReference(
          Page.ClientScript.GetWebResourceUrl(typeof(AjaxLogin),
              "ScriptControls.AjaxLogin.js"));
        }                                              Reference ❹
    }                                               web resource
}
```

The `WebResource` attribute ❶ that decorates the `AjaxLogin` class is used to register the AjaxLogin.js file as a web resource. This is necessary in order to be able to reference the script file in a web page.

The first method declared in the `AjaxLogin` class ❷ is a helper method that can find child controls declared in the base Login control. It's also responsible for assigning references to the child elements to properties of the client control. As you saw in section 9.1.2, script descriptors ❸ expose a method called `AddElementProperty` that passes the client ID of an element to the `$get` method in the generated `$create` statement.

The subsequent two methods are the overrides of the `OnPreRender` and `Render` methods. You implement the registration procedure in the same way outlined in section 9.4.2. The last two methods are the overrides of the methods defined in the `IScriptControl` interface. As expected, the `GetScriptDescriptors` method returns a script descriptor for creating an instance of the AjaxLogin client control. In the `GetScriptReferences` method, you use the `GetWebResourceUrl` ❹ method to load the AjaxLogin.js file (embedded as a web resource) in the web page.

The first script control is complete, and you can safely build the project. As with extenders, we need to address a final point before we end our discussion of Ajax-enabled controls.

9.4.5 Using a script control

To use a script control, follow the usual steps required for using an ASP.NET server control. Steps include registering the custom control in the page using a `@Register` directive, like so:

```
<%@ Register Assembly="ScriptControls" Namespace="Samples"
TagPrefix="samples" %>
```

This code takes into account the fact that the script control is located in a separate assembly. You need to specify the values for the `Assembly` and the `Namespace` attributes.

Once the control is registered in the page, you can declare it as in the following example:

```
<samples:AjaxLogin ID="AjaxLogin1" runat="server" />
```

Because the AjaxLogin control plays with the authentication service, you need to enable the service in the web.config file through the `authenticationService` element:

```
<system.web.extensions>
  <scripting>
    <webServices>
        <authenticationService enabled="true" />
    </webService>
  </scripting>
</system.web.extensions>
```

You must also enable forms authentication to take advantage of the AjaxLogin control.

NOTE   You can learn about forms authentication by browsing to the following URL: http://msdn2.microsoft.com/en-us/library/aa480476.aspx.

The final touch is seeing what is rendered in a page that hosts the AjaxLogin control; see figure 9.15. The following code was extracted from such a web page:

```
[...]

<script src="/AspNetAjaxInAction_09/WebResource.axd?d=eoxf8D
   ➥IaviQBVsfEu1YjPF6KBBzaOSU3pQeO_UcQIK309neS2pzazIDzdhCZT9d0&amp;
   ➥t=633122647281397436" type="text/javascript"></script>

[...]

Sys.Application.add_init(function() {
    $create(Samples.AjaxLogin,
      {"LoginButton":$get("AjaxLogin1_LoginButton"),
      "Password":$get("AjaxLogin1_Password"),
      "RememberMe":$get("AjaxLogin1_RememberMe"),
      "UserName":$get("AjaxLogin1_UserName")},
      null, null, $get("AjaxLogin1"));
});
```

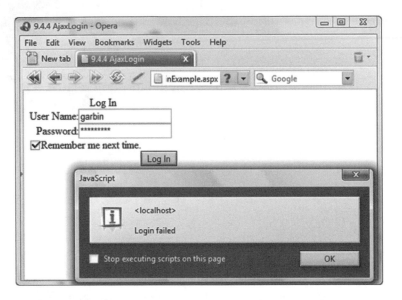

Figure 9.15   The AjaxLogin control running in the Opera browser

As expected, the `script` tag contains the URL of the AjaxLogin.js file embedded as a web resource in the `ScriptControls` assembly. The tag was generated thanks to the `ScriptReference` instance returned by the `GetScriptReferences` method overridden in the AjaxLogin control. The script descriptor returned by the Ajax-Login control generated the `$create` statement contained in the anonymous function passed as an argument to the `add_init` method.

9.5   *Summary*

In this chapter, we discussed how to wire client components to server controls to obtain Ajax-enabled controls. First, we introduced script descriptors and script references, which are the main objects used by server controls to instantiate client components and load script files in a web page.

Script descriptors can generate the `$create` statement used to instantiate a client component in the page. Script references let you specify the location of a script file to reference in a static `script` tag.

An Ajax-enabled control can return a list of script descriptors and script references to the ScriptManager, which in turn injects the generated `$create` statements and the `script` tags into the ASP.NET page sent to the browser. Extenders and script controls are the two kinds of Ajax-enabled controls you can create.

Extenders can provide a list of script descriptors and script references to an existing server control, which becomes the extended control. Script controls are server controls that don't need external objects in order to instantiate the client components they need.

In the next chapter, we'll take a lap around the Ajax Control Toolkit, which is the biggest collection of Ajax-enabled controls available at the moment.

Developing with the Ajax Control Toolkit

10

In this chapter:

- The auto-complete extender
- Additional properties of extenders
- The Ajax Control Toolkit API
- The animation framework

The Ajax Control Toolkit is an open source project that Microsoft started in the early days of ASP.NET AJAX. It's a collection of extenders, script controls, and client components written with the Microsoft Ajax Library. The Toolkit provides a server API for developing Ajax-enabled controls, a client API for testing client components, and a framework for creating visual effects and animations.

The project is located at the CodePlex hosting website (http://www.code-plex.com) and is owned by Microsoft's Agility Team. Rather than *agile programming* (and all that implies), the name *Agility* refers to *execution agility* (meaning the team is very flexible). Agility Team launched the Toolkit project in late January 2006 to facilitate the adoption of ASP.NET AJAX extensions among web developers. The project was soon opened to contributions from the community and now includes many controls developed by non-Microsoft programmers. A new release of the project is available nearly every month and ships with the source code for controls, a sample website that demonstrates their usage, and a suite of tests written with a JavaScript framework for testing. With a bug-tracker hosted at CodePlex and a dedicated forum on the ASP.NET website, the Toolkit is one of the biggest repositories of Ajax-enabled controls and one of the best resources for learning ASP.NET AJAX.

In this chapter, we'll explain how the Ajax Control Toolkit leverages the base framework provided by ASP.NET AJAX extensions. We'll introduce the properties added to extenders and show you how to develop Ajax-enabled controls using the Toolkit's API. The last part of the chapter is dedicated to the animation framework, a collection of client components for creating visual effects and animations. Let's start by introducing the auto-complete extender, one of the numerous controls provided by the Ajax Control Toolkit.

10.1 *A world of extenders*

The major role in the Ajax Control Toolkit is played by extenders. As we discussed in chapter 9, *extenders* are server controls that wire client components to existing ASP.NET server controls. Once an extender is associated with a server control, the extended control inherits a new set of properties for configuring the client-side functionality. Interestingly, all the extenders shipped with the Toolkit are built on top of a custom API that leverages the one provided by ASP.NET AJAX to build Ajax-enabled controls. Before we go deep into the Toolkit API, let's see how to configure and use one of the many extenders shipped with the Toolkit. To build the next example, you'll use the auto-complete extender, which upgrades a simple ASP.NET TextBox to a text box with auto-completion capabilities. In order to run the examples presented in this chapter, you must reference the Toolkit assembly in your website. Appendix A contains instructions on how to download, install, and configure the Ajax Control Toolkit.

10.1.1 *The auto-complete extender*

One of the first and best examples to demonstrate Ajax capabilities was to embed an auto-complete text box in a web page. This kind of text box, usually a feature of desktop applications, can display a list of suggested words in a pop-up panel below the text field. The list of suggestions is obtained by completing the portion of text typed by the user, as soon as the user types in the text field. As shown in figure 10.1, the auto-complete text box is a good example of how to enhance a simple text box with client capabilities.

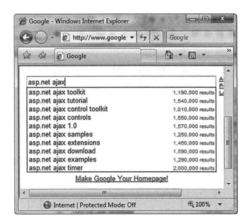

Figure 10.1   Google Suggest (http://labs.google.com/suggest) features an auto-complete text box that presents a list of suggested words with additional information about their numerical occurrences.

Making an Ajax request in the background lets you retrieve the list of suggestions from a database with millions of records. Without Ajax, you would have to send all the possible suggestions to the browser, embedded in the web page, and filter them using JavaScript. Millions of records can lead to a page size measured in megabytes. With Ajax, the filtering is performed on the server, and the list of suggestions is updated in real time while the user is typing.

The auto-complete functionality provided by the auto-complete extender is implemented in JavaScript. The logic is encapsulated in a client component—a behavior—called `AutoCompleteBehavior`. You can wire this component to an ASP.NET TextBox through the auto-complete extender without writing a single line of JavaScript code. (Behaviors and other kinds of client components were covered in detail in chapter 8.)

The following example will guide you in setting up a web page with an auto-complete text box similar to the one shown in figure 10.2. This web page should be part of an ASP.NET AJAX enabled website, which is a website configured for ASP.NET AJAX. Appendix A contains a tutorial on how to create such a website using the Visual Studio template shipped with the ASP.NET AJAX extensions

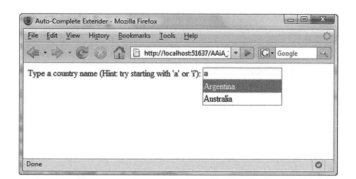

Figure 10.2
A web page with an
auto-complete text box, built
with an ASP.NET TextBox and
the auto-complete extender

installer. You must also reference the AjaxControlToolkit.dll assembly or manually add it to the website's bin folder.

The first step is to create a new page called AutoCompleteExample.aspx. In Visual Studio 2005, switch to Design mode and drag a TextBox control from the Toolbox to the page area. Give the TextBox the ID Country. If you have the Toolkit controls listed in your Toolbox, drag the AutoCompleteExtender control and drop it near the TextBox. If you don't have the Toolkit controls in the Toolbox, check appendix A for a walkthrough of how to add them. Dragging one of the Toolkit's extenders in the page adds the following @Register directive at the top of the page:

```
<%@ Register Assembly="AjaxControlToolkit"
             Namespace="AjaxControlToolkit"
             TagPrefix="ajaxToolkit" %>
```

In the previous code snippet, we replaced the default tag prefix (cc1) with ajax-Toolkit. If you aren't using the Visual Studio Designer, you should manually add the @Register directive at the top of the ASP.NET page. In the Designer, click the auto-complete extender, and open the Properties panel. The panel shows all the properties exposed by the extender. Table 10.1 lists each property and the value assigned to it in the example.

Table 10.1 Values assigned to the properties of the AutoCompleteExtender in the example

Property	Description	Value
ID	ID of the extender control	CountryAutoComplete
TargetControlID	ID of the target TextBox	Country
ServiceURL	URL of the web service used to retrieve the list of suggestions	CountryService.asmx

Table 10.1   Values assigned to the properties of the AutoCompleteExtender in the example *(continued)*

Property	Description	Value
ServiceMethod	Name of the web method that returns the list of suggestions	GetCountries
MinimumPrefixLength	Minimum number of characters needed to activate the auto-complete functionality	1

If you switch to Source mode, you should see that the code in listing 10.1 has been generated in the page's form tag. The TargetControlID property of the Auto-CompleteExtender control is set to the ID of the TextBox. In this way, the TextBox becomes an extended control and gains the auto-complete capabilities.

Listing 10.1   Code for the ASP.NET TextBox with an associated AutoCompleteExtender control

```
<asp:TextBox ID="Country" runat="server"></asp:TextBox>

<asp:AutoCompleteExtender ID="CountryAutoComplete" runat="server"
                          TargetControlID="Country"
                          ServicePath="~/CountryService.asmx"
                          ServiceMethod="GetCountries"
                          MinimumPrefixLength="1" />
```

You can use the AutoCompleteExtender control to configure the client component that will be associated with the text box element rendered by the extended TextBox control. For example, you need to specify the URL of a local ASP.NET web service and the name of a web method that returns the list of suggestions to display. The ServicePath property contains the path to the web service, which you'll add to the website in a moment. The ServiceMethod property specifies the name of the web method that will be called to get the list of suggestions. The last property, MinimumPrefixLength, determines the number of characters the user must type before the call to the web service is made.

Web service setup

The web service used in this example is located in the CountryService.asmx file in the root directory of the website. It exposes a web method named GetCountries, which returns a list of country names based on the text typed by the user in the text field. The code for the CountryService web service is shown in listing 10.2.

Listing 10.2 Code for the `CountryService` web service

```
<%@ WebService Language="C#" Class="CountryService" %>

using System;
using System.IO;
using System.Xml;
using System.Web;
using System.Web.Services;
using System.Web.Services.Protocols;
using System.Collections.Generic;
using System.Web.Script.Services;

[WebService(Namespace = "http://tempuri.org/")]
[WebServiceBinding(ConformsTo = WsiProfiles.BasicProfile1_1)]
[ScriptService]
public class CountryService : System.Web.Services.WebService
{
    [WebMethod]
    public string[] GetCountries(string prefixText, int count)
    {
        return GetCountriesFromXml(prefixText, count);
    }
}
```

The `GetCountries` method accepts two parameters: `prefixTest` and `count`. These two parameters must always be present in the web method signature and must be spelled exactly as in listing 10.2 (case matters); otherwise, the extender won't work.

The `GetCountries` method calls a private method named `GetCountries-FromXml`. This method accesses the data store and returns all the countries whose name starts with the value of the `prefixText` parameter. The `count` parameter specifies the maximum number of countries to return. In the example, you store the list of countries in an XML file called Countries.xml, located in the website's App_Data folder. Listing 10.3 shows a reduced version of the file, which contains six country names.

Listing 10.3 XML file containing the list of countries

```
<?xml version="1.0" encoding="utf-8" ?>
<Countries>
  <Country>Argentina</Country>
  <Country>Australia</Country>
  <Country>Germany</Country>
  <Country>India</Country>
```

```
    <Country>Italy</Country>
    <Country>United States of America</Country>
</Countries>
```

The XML file contains a root `Countries` element. The child elements are `Country` tags that hold the names of the countries. The `GetCountriesFromXml` method parses the XML file and filters the countries based on the values of the `prefix-Text` and `count` parameters, as shown in listing 10.4.

Listing 10.4 Code for the `GetCountriesFromXml` method

```
private string[] GetCountriesFromXml(string prefixText, int count)
{
    List<string> suggestions = new List<string>();

    using(XmlTextReader reader = new                            ❶ Open
        XmlTextReader(HttpContext.Current.Server                 XML file
                            .MapPath("~/Countries.xml")))
    {
        while (reader.Read())
        {
            if (reader.NodeType == XmlNodeType.Element &&
                    reader.Name == "Country")
            {
                string stateName = reader.ReadInnerXml();

                if (stateName.StartsWith(prefixText,            ❷ Suggestion
                    StringComparison.InvariantCultureIgnoreCase))    found
                {
                    suggestions.Add(stateName);                 Add
                                                                suggestion
                    if (suggestions.Count == count) break;    ❸ to list
                }
            }                          Break if count
        }                                    reached ❹
    }

    return suggestions.ToArray();
}
```

When a `Country` element is found in the XML file ❶, its value is compared with the `prefixText` parameter. If `prefixText` contains a prefix for the current country ❷, the name of the country is added to the suggestion list ❸. If you reach the maximum number of suggestions allowed, you break out of the loop ❹. When the method returns, the array with the country names is serialized in JSON format and sent back to the browser. On the client side, the instance of the `AutoCompleteBehavior` behavior configured and instantiated through the extender is responsible for displaying the returned strings in a pop-up panel under the extended text field.

The auto-complete text box is ready to be tested: Build the website, and run the AutoCompleteExample.aspx page. When the page is loaded, type some characters in the text field (hint: start with *A* or *I*). As soon as you type a character, the `CountryService` web service is invoked in the background to retrieve and display the list of matching suggestions. Figure 10.3 shows the asynchronous requests sent to the web service as soon as you type in the text field. To debug the HTTP traffic, we used Firebug, an add-on for the Firefox browser. Appendix B contains an overview of Firebug as well as the instructions to download and install it.

All of the Ajax Control Toolkit's extenders are used similarly to the auto-complete extender. A great advantage of extenders is that, most of the time, all you have to do to enhance existing ASP.NET controls with rich client capabilities is declare an extender in the page and wire it to an ASP.NET server control. As you saw in the previous example, you do this by setting the extender's `TargetControlID` property to the ID of the extended control. Due to the nature of Extenders, it's easy to take an existing page and enhance it by adding extenders to server controls that are already there. In other words, it's easy to start with what already works and then enhance it bit by bit by adding Toolkit controls.

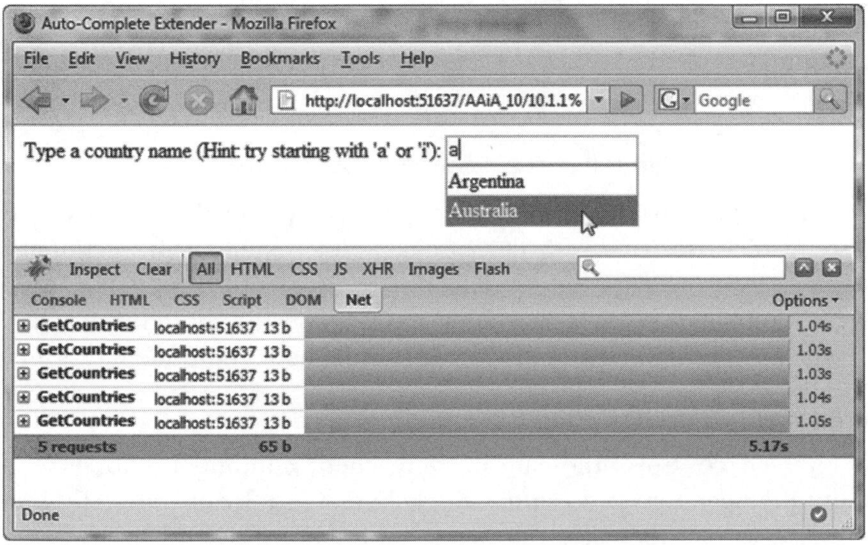

Figure 10.3 The Firebug console in Firefox shows the asynchronous requests made to the web service to retrieve the list of suggestions for the auto-complete text box.

The Toolkit's extenders expose additional properties to configure the client component that provides the Ajax functionality. These properties are exposed by the custom `ExtenderControlBase` class, which is the class from which all Toolkit extenders derive. This class is part of the Toolkit API for building Ajax-enabled controls, which we'll discuss in section 10.2. Now, let's examine the additional properties available in the Ajax Control Toolkit's extenders.

10.1.2 *The ScriptPath property*

Ajax-enabled controls usually reference a JavaScript file that is loaded in the page at runtime. This script file contains the code for the client component the Ajax-enabled control needs to instantiate in the web page. For example, the auto-complete extender needs to create an instance of the `AutoCompleteBehavior` client class, as we explained in the previous section. Usually, script files are either located in folders of the website or embedded as web resources in a separate assembly. In the case of the Ajax Control Toolkit, all the script files are embedded as web resources in the AjaxControlToolkit.dll assembly.

To load a script file from the file system rather than from the Toolkit's assembly, you can use the `ScriptPath` property. This property is exposed by all the Toolkit's controls and lets you specify the path to the script file associated with a Toolkit control. At runtime, this is the script file loaded in the page, instead of the one embedded in the Toolkit assembly.

For example, suppose you want to test or debug a modified version of the AutoCompleteBehavior component. Instead of recompiling the Toolkit project every time, you can reference the modified script file from the website as follows:

```
<ajaxToolkit:AutoCompleteExtender ID="AutoComplete1" runat="server"
        TargetControlID="TextBox1"
        ScriptPath="~/ScriptLibrary/AutoComplete.js" />
```

When the page is loaded, the AutoComplete.js file is loaded in place of the original script file associated with the auto-complete extender. In section 10.2, we'll discuss how to leverage the Toolkit API to associate a script file with an Ajax-enabled control. Now, let's look at another property exposed by Toolkit extenders, which is useful when you want to deal with client components at runtime.

10.1.3 *The BehaviorID property*

Ajax-enabled controls automatically wire client components to server controls without the need for you to write a single line of JavaScript code. This is an advantage because you don't need to be an experienced JavaScript developer to add

Figure 10.4   Example of a slider extender running in Safari

rich client capabilities to server controls in your web applications. Most of the time, wiring a Toolkit extender to the extended control is all you have to do to get the desired client functionality. Other times, you may need to interact with the client components that extenders or script controls instantiate in the page. Such components often expose methods and events that you can hook up on the client side as part of the client application's logic. For example, the slider extender—one of the Ajax-enabled controls shipped with the Toolkit—can upgrade an ASP.NET TextBox to a graphical slider, as shown in figure 10.4.

On the client side, the slider extender creates an instance of the `SliderBehavior` behavior. This client component exposes a `valueChanged` event that is raised whenever the value of the slider changes. (We explained how to expose and handle events raised by client components in section 8.2.3.) To hook up the `valueChanged` event on the client side, you need to first access the `SliderBehavior` instance. To simplify this task, every extender in the Ajax Control Toolkit exposes a property called `BehaviorID`, which you can use to assign an ID to the client component instantiated by the extender. Listing 10.5 shows how to use the `BehaviorID` property with the slider extender to subscribe to the `valueChanged` event on the client side.

Listing 10.5   Using the `BehaviorID` property with the slider extender

```
<asp:TextBox ID="TextBox1" runat="server" />

<ajaxToolkit:SliderExtender ID="SliderExtender1" runat="server"
                            TargetControlID="TextBox1"
                            BehaviorID="theSlider" />

<span>You can use the slider to change the font size.</span>
```

```
<script type="text/javascript">
<!--
    function pageLoad() {
        var slider = $find('theSlider');

        slider.add_valueChanged(onValueChanged);
    }

    function onValueChanged(sender, e) {
        var slider = sender;
        document.body.style.fontSize = slider.get_Value() + 'px';
    }
//-->
</script>
```

The value of the `BehaviorID` property becomes the value of the `name` property of the `SliderBehavior` instance. If you want to access the behavior on the client side, you have to pass the value of the `BehaviorID` property to the `$find` method, as you did in the `pageLoad` function.

NOTE   In templated controls such as the Repeater or the GridView, the `BehaviorID` property must be manually set to a unique ID for each item rendered by the server control. You must do this because two client behaviors can't have the same value for the `name` property. Also note that `BehaviorID` is an optional property. If it isn't set, the behavior still has an ID—but it's based on the client name of the target control.

Once you get a reference to the slider on the client side, you can invoke the `add_valueChanged` method to subscribe to the `valueChanged` event. In the event handler, `onValueChanged`, you use the slider's `get_Value` method to retrieve its value and change the font size of the page, as shown in figure 10.4.

TIP   The slider extender isn't the only Ajax-enabled control to expose methods, properties, and events that can be accessed on the client side. For a description of all the Ajax Control Toolkit controls, browse the Toolkit sample website, located at http://ajax.asp.net/ajaxtoolkit/. The sample website is also available as part of the source code that you can download from the CodePlex website, as explained in appendix B.

In the previous sections, we've mentioned that the Toolkit Ajax-enabled controls are built on top of a custom API that enhances the base functionality provided by ASP.NET AJAX. In the next section, we'll explain how to use the Ajax Control Toolkit as a platform for building extenders and script controls. Let's see what's under the hood of the Ajax Control Toolkit API.

10.2 The Ajax Control Toolkit API

As you learned in chapter 9, the ASP.NET AJAX framework provides base classes and interfaces for creating Ajax-enabled controls. These classes and interfaces are contained in the `System.Web.UI` namespace. To create an extender, you can derive from the `ExtenderControl` class and override the methods defined in the `IExtenderControl` interface. Similarly, to create a script control, you can inherit from the `ScriptControl` class and override the methods of the `IScript-Control` interface.

A big advantage of these classes is that they take care of doing most of the work related to configuring and registering the extender with the ScriptManager control. The Ajax Control Toolkit API provides new base classes for creating extenders and script controls. They extend the base functionality provided by ASP.NET AJAX and simplify the process of creating Ajax-enabled controls.

> **NOTE** If you've downloaded the source code for the Ajax Control Toolkit, you'll find the API classes in the AjaxControlToolkit project, in the Extender-Base folder. Appendix A provides instructions on how to download and install the Ajax Control Toolkit.

In the following sections, we'll tour the main features provided by the Toolkit API. Let's start by introducing the Toolkit's base classes.

10.2.1 The Toolkit's base classes

On the server side, the Ajax Control Toolkit defines two base classes: `Extender-ControlBase` and `ScriptControlBase`. The `ExtenderControlBase` class derives from the `ExtenderControl` class and is used to create extenders. The `ScriptControlBase` class inherits from the `ScriptControl` class and is used to create script controls. Figure 10.5 shows the base classes defined in the Toolkit API. All the classes defined by the API are contained in the `AjaxControlToolkit` namespace.

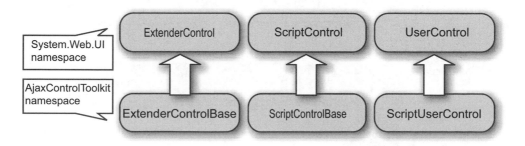

Figure 10.5 The Toolkit API provides enhanced base classes for creating extenders and script controls.

Figure 10.5 shows an additional pair of classes: The Toolkit API defines the `Script-UserControl` class as the base class for creating script user controls. These controls are nothing more than web user controls—custom controls with an HTML template defined in a .ascx file—turned into script controls.

On the client side, the Microsoft Ajax Library provides the `Sys.UI.Behavior` and `Sys.UI.Control` classes for creating visual components. In turn, the Toolkit API provides base classes that encapsulate additional functionality for creating behaviors and controls. These classes are called `BehaviorBase` and `ControlBase`, and they're shown in figure 10.6.

For the same reasons outlined in chapter 9, behaviors are usually associated with extenders. Similarly, client controls are usually associated with script controls. The same reasoning applies to the controls shipped with the Ajax Control Toolkit. Extenders usually instantiate a client class that derives from the `Behavior-Base` class. In the same way, script controls are usually associated with classes that inherit from the `ControlBase` class.

The main characteristic of the Toolkit API is that it can be considered a metadata-driven API. A whole group of metadata attributes are available to decorate classes, properties, and methods of Ajax-enabled controls.

NOTE *Attributes* are a declarative way of defining some functionality associated with a method, a class, a field, or a property. For further reading, please browse to http://msdn2.microsoft.com/en-us/library/5x6cd29c.aspx.

As we'll explain in the next section, the purpose of these attributes is to avoid the explicit override of the methods that return the list of script descriptors and script references to the `ScriptManager` control. Script descriptors and script references are generated by the base classes based on the attributes that decorate the class members. Sounds attractive, right? Let's discuss these attributes in more detail.

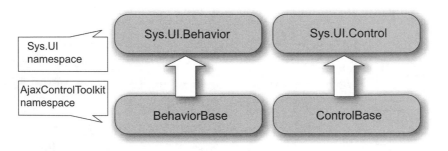

Figure 10.6   The Toolkit API also extends the base functionality on the client side, where new base classes for creating behaviors and controls are provided.

10.2.2 *A metadata-driven API*

As we mentioned in the previous section, the Toolkit API can build script descriptors and script reference instances by inspecting attributes that decorate class members. Attributes provide extra information—about a class, a field, a method, or a property—that you can query using the reflection capabilities offered by the .NET framework.

For example, the Toolkit API defines an attribute called `ExtenderControl-Property`, which you can use to decorate a property of an Ajax-enabled control. When the base class filters the properties that are decorated with this attribute, it knows that those properties are mapped to properties of the client component associated with the server control. The base class can use the value of the property when, say, generating a script descriptor. In this way, you can collect all the information you need without building script descriptors manually in a child class. Table 10.2 lists the attributes defined by the Toolkit API, along with a brief explanation of what they accomplish.

Table 10.2 Attributes defined in the Ajax Control Toolkit API

Attribute name	Entity decorated	Description
`Designer`	Class	Specifies the type of the designer class associated with an Ajax-enabled control.
`ExtenderControlProperty`	Property	Maps a server property to a property of the client component.
`ClientPropertyName`	Property	Specifies the exact name of the client property mapped to a server property.
`ExtenderControlEvent`	Property	The decorated property returns the name of a JavaScript function that will handle the event specified in the attribute.
`ExtenderControlMethod`	Method	The decorated method can be invoked from the client side using ASP.NET 2.0 callbacks support.
`ClientScriptResource`	Class	Specifies the name of a script resource that contains the JavaScript code for the client component.
`ClientCssResource`	Class	Specifies the name of a web resource that contains a CSS file to load in the page.
`RequiredScript`	Class	Specifies the name of a script resource to load in the page, or a type associated with multiple script resources. The `loadOrder` parameter is an integer used to define the loading order of script resources in case multiple `RequiredScript` attributes are used.

Table 10.2   Attributes defined in the Ajax Control Toolkit API *(continued)*

Attribute name	Entity decorated	Description
RequiredProperty	Property	The decorated property must be assigned a value.
ElementReference	Property	The decorated property returns the client ID of a DOM element in the page.
ComponentReference	Property	The decorated property returns the ID of a client component in the page.

The Toolkit's base classes can generate a single script descriptor and multiple script references based on the attributes listed in table 10.2. Most of these attributes are used to build the script descriptor, which is responsible for generating the $create statement that instantiates and configures the associated client component in the page.

The $create method, which we introduced in chapter 8, is a powerful method that performs all the work related to component instantiation and configuration. This task is accomplished based on the arguments you pass to $create. The attributes defined by the Toolkit API can be seen as a way to build the parameters passed to the $create method. Figure 10.7 helps to clarify this concept by showing how some attributes can influence the generation of a $create statement.

It's time to switch from theory to practice and see some of these attributes in action. You'll leverage the Toolkit API to build a new extender. The TextChanged-Extender will let you raise an event whenever the user stops typing in a text field for a certain amount of time. In the next section, you'll see why you would need such a control and how to wrap it in a Toolkit extender.

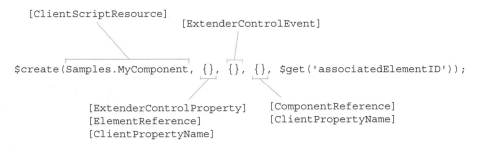

Figure 10.7   Some of the attributes of the Toolkit API determine how a script descriptor generates a $create statement.

10.2.3 Building Toolkit extenders: the TextChanged extender

The idea behind a control like the AutoCompleteExtender, which we discussed in section 10.1.1, is to provide the user with real-time feedback. As the user enters text in a text box, data is retrieved from the server and presented to them in a pop-up displayed under the text file. Ajax makes it possible to implement this pattern by sending asynchronous requests to the web server in the background.

Many variations on the auto-complete pattern are possible. For example, you can filter the content of a GridView in real time based on the filter expression the user is typing. You can also perform a live search on the web page and highlight the matching words as soon as the user types them. We presented an example of such functionality in section 6.5, where you built the Live GridView Filter. Figure 10.8 shows this control.

These controls need to capture the user input in real time and send an asynchronous HTTP request to the server. If you don't pay attention to how the

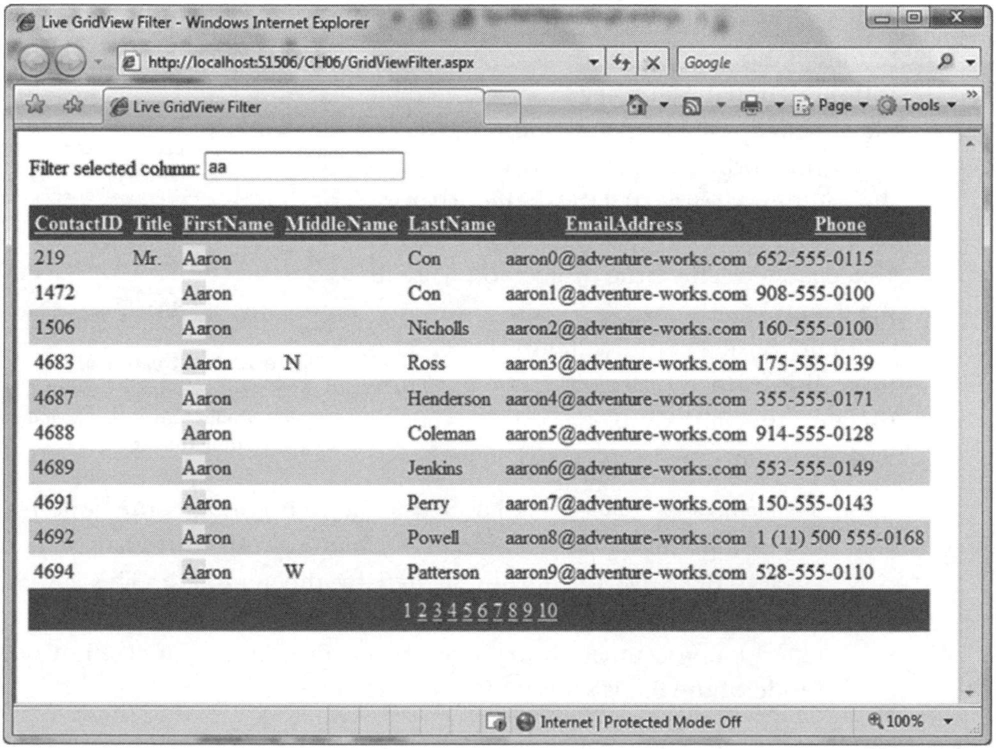

Figure 10.8 The Live GridView Filter that you built in chapter 6 is an example of a control that processes user input in real time.

mechanism is implemented, you may experience a huge performance drop. Imagine an Ajax request being sent to the web server each time you type a character in a text box. Now, multiply by the number of users that might be using the real-time filtering functionality at the same time. If the website generates a high volume of traffic, the web server will be flooded with requests.

> **NOTE** The auto-complete functionality provided by the Toolkit already uses this mechanism, together with an internal cache, to limit the number of asynchronous requests sent to the server.

To mitigate this issue, you'll write a client component that programmatically fires the change event of a text box element only after the user has stopped typing for a certain—and configurable—amount of time. Chances are, the user then wants the input to be processed, and you can safely issue the asynchronous request. Let's start by opening Visual Studio and creating a new Toolkit extender project.

Creating the extender project

The Ajax Control Toolkit ships with a Visual Studio template for creating an extender with the Toolkit API. You can select the template, called ASP.NET AJAX Control Project, when you add a new project to a Visual Studio solution. Figure 10.9 shows the structure of a new extender control project called TextChanged. This is the project you'll use in the example.

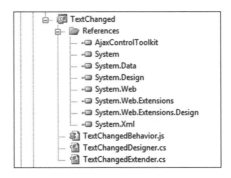

The Visual Studio template creates three files with the project name as a prefix and the suffixes Behavior, Designer, and Extender:

Figure 10.9 Structure of the TextChanged project created by the Visual Studio template shipped with the Ajax Control Toolkit

- *TextChangedBehavior.js*—A JavaScript file that contains the code for the client component. The commented skeleton code for a client behavior is already declared in the file created by the template. This JavaScript file must be compiled as a web resource; otherwise, it can't be referenced by the extender. You must ensure that, in the Properties panel, the Compilation mode of the file is set to Embedded Resource.

- *TextChangedExtender.cs*—Contains the extender class, which derives from the `ExtenderControlBase` class.

- *TextChangedDesigner.cs*—Contains a class that can be used to enhance the design-time experience in the Visual Studio designer. This class derives from the base `ExtenderControlBaseDesigner` class. More information on this class is provided in section 10.2.5.

Because part of the code is automatically generated by the template, and we want to focus on the Toolkit API, we'll illustrate only the relevant portions. The entire example, with commented code, is available for download at http://www.manning.com/gallo, as part of the code for chapter 10.

The TextChangedBehavior Class

The `TextChangedBehavior` class is the client behavior that enhances the text box element. The class inherits from the `AjaxControlToolkit.BehaviorBase` class and encapsulates all the JavaScript code needed to monitor the text typed in the text field. The client behavior is responsible for raising the DOM `change` event of the text box when a configurable timeout elapses. It also fires a `textChanged` component event, which can be subscribed to on the client side using the techniques introduced in section 3.7. Listing 10.6 shows the members of the class, as declared in the `TextChanged.TextChangedBehavior` constructor.

Listing 10.6   Constructor of the `TextChangedBehavior` class

```
TextChanged.TextChangedBehavior = function(element) {
    TextChanged.TextChangedBehavior.initializeBase(this, [element]);

    // TODO : (Step 1) Add your property variables here
    //
    this._text = '';
    this._timeout = 500;
    this._timer = null;
}
```

The first field, `_text`, holds the text typed by the user. The second field, `_timeout`, stores the time interval to wait before firing the `change` and `textChanged` events. The value of the `_timeout` field is exposed in a public property called `timeout`. The last field, `_timer`, holds the *opaque ID* returned by the JavaScript's `setTimeout` function. You'll use the `setTimeout` function to simulate a timer.

The client component handles the keypress event—raised by the text box whenever the user types a character—to start the timer. As soon as the user presses a key, the timer is reset and restarted. This prevents the events from being raised. If the timeout interval elapses before the user types another character, you raise the change and textChanged events.

The code in listing 10.7 shows how the timer is implemented using the setTimeout and clearTimeout functions provided by JavaScript. The _startTimer and _stopTimer methods are embedded in the TextChangedBehavior's prototype.

Listing 10.7 Implementing a simple timer in JavaScript

```
_startTimer : function() {
    this._timer = window.setTimeout(Function.createDelegate(this,
        this._onTimerTick), this._timeout);
},

_stopTimer : function() {
    if(this._timer != null) {
        window.clearTimeout(this._timer);
    }
    this._timer = null;
}
```

The setTimeout function invokes the _onTimerTick method as soon as the interval specified in the _timeout variable elapses. The setTimeout function returns an opaque ID that is stored in the _timer variable. If you pass the opaque ID to the clearTimeout function, the timer is stopped.

If the timeout value elapses before the timer is reset, the user has stopped typing for the desired amount of time. At this point, you can programmatically fire the DOM change event on the text box element.

NOTE   A DOM event fired programmatically is called a *synthetic event.*

Listing 10.8 shows the code needed to fire a DOM event programmatically with JavaScript. In this case, you're interested in raising the change event on the text box element. Because the text box is the associated element of the client behavior, you can retrieve a reference by calling the get_element method. Note that the else branch in the if statement contains code specific for the Internet Explorer browser.

Listing 10.8 Firing a DOM event programmatically

```
_fireTextBoxChange : function() {
    if (document.createEvent) {
        var onchangeEvent = document.createEvent('HTMLEvents');
        onchangeEvent.initEvent('change', true, false);

        this.get_element().dispatchEvent(onchangeEvent);
    }
    else if(document.createEventObject) {
        this.get_element().fireEvent('onchange');
    }
}
```

The client logic encapsulated in the behavior is simple, but it's helpful in case you want to reduce the HTTP traffic generated by a control that processes the user input in real time. The next step is to create an extender to wire this client functionality to an ASP.NET TextBox control.

The TextChangedExtender class

The `TextChangedExtender` class is located in the TextChangedExtender.cs file generated by the Visual Studio template. This class inherits from the `Extender-ControlBase` class and is supposed to wire the client functionality provided by the `TextChangedBehavior` component to an ASP.NET TextBox control. If you open the TextChangedExtender.cs file, you'll find the following statement just before the class declaration:

```
[assembly: System.Web.UI.WebResource(
    ➥ "TextChanged.TextChangedBehavior.js", "text/javascript")]
```

The `WebResource` attribute is used to register a file as a web resource embedded in an assembly. A URL can be generated to reference the embedded resource in an ASP.NET page. Through this URL, you can instruct ASP.NET to load the resource in a web page through a HTTP handler.

NOTE To learn more about web resources, browse to the following URL: http://support.microsoft.com/kb/910442/en-us.

The first argument passed to the `WebResource` attribute is the name of the web resource. The second argument is the MIME type (the Internet Media Type) of the web resource. In the example, you register the TextChangedBehavior.js file as a JavaScript resource. The corresponding MIME type is `text/javascript`.

Let's pass to the attributes that decorate the class. The `TextChangedExtender` class is decorated with the following attributes:

```
[TargetControlType(typeof(Control))]
[Designer(typeof(TextChangedDesigner))]
[ClientScriptResource("TextChanged.TextChangedBehavior",
    "TextChanged.TextChangedBehavior.js")]
```

The first attribute, `TargetControlType`, restricts the use of the extender to a particular type of web control. We introduced this attribute in chapter 9, when we discussed the base framework for creating extenders. Here, you want to extend ASP.NET TextBox controls. Therefore, you change the attribute as follows:

```
[TargetControlType(typeof(TextBox))]
```

Trying to extend a control other than a TextBox will result in an exception being raised by ASP.NET. The subsequent attributes have been all introduced by the Toolkit API. A quick look at table 10.2 reveals that the `Designer` attribute specifies the class you use to enhance the design-time experience of the `TextChanged` extender. In the example, this class is called `TextChangedDesigner`, and it's defined in the TextChangedDesigner.cs file generated by the Visual Studio template.

The `ClientScriptResource` attribute specifies which script file is loaded in the page by the extender. The first argument passed to the attribute is the fully qualified name of the client component. This information is needed by the `ExtenderControlBase` class to build the script descriptor for the client component used by the extender. The second argument is the name of the web resource associated with the JavaScript file. This is the same string you passed to the `WebResource` attribute.

Extender properties

As you know from chapter 9, an extender usually exposes properties that let you configure the client component from the server side. These properties are mapped to the corresponding properties of the client component, as shown in table 10.3.

Table 10.3 **Mappings between the properties of the `TextChangedExtender` class and the `TextChangedBehavior` class**

Client property	Extender property
timeout	Timeout
textChanged (event)	OnTextChanged

The first property, Timeout, lets you specify on the server side the value of the timeout property exposed by the client behavior. The second property, OnText-Changed, specifies a JavaScript function that handles the textChanged event. Listing 10.9 shows how these properties are declared in the TextChangedExtender class.

Listing 10.9 Complete code for the `TextChangedExtender` class

```
[Designer(typeof(TextChangedDesigner))]
[ClientScriptResource("TextChanged.TextChangedBehavior",
    "TextChanged.TextChangedBehavior.js")]
[TargetControlType(typeof(Control))]
public class TextChangedExtender : ExtenderControlBase
{
    [ExtenderControlProperty]
    [DefaultValue(500)]
    [ClientPropertyName("timeout")]
    [RequiredProperty]
    public int Timeout
    {
        get { return GetPropertyValue<int>("Timeout", 500); }
        set { SetPropertyValue<int>("Timeout", value); }
    }

    [ExtenderControlEvent(true)]
    [DefaultValue("")]
    [ClientPropertyName("textChanged")]
    public string OnTextChanged
    {
        get { return GetPropertyValue<string>("OnTextChanged",
                        String.Empty); }
        set { SetPropertyValue<string>("OnTextChanged", value); }
    }
}
```

The ExtenderControlProperty attribute tells the base class that the value of the decorated property maps to a corresponding client property. The exact name of the client property is specified in the ClientPropertyName attribute (note that you remove the get_ prefix from the name of the client getter). If you omit the ClientPropertyName attribute, the base class uses the name of the server property.

The GetPropertyValue<> and SetPropertyValue<> methods are generic methods for automatically storing and retrieving the value of a property from the control's ViewState. The first argument passed is the name of the ViewState field in which the value is stored. The second argument is the value that is returned if the ViewState's field is set to null.

NOTE   At the moment, the `GetPropertyValue<>` and `SetPropertyValue<>` methods are available only in the `ExtenderControlBase` class.

The `ExtenderControlEvent` attribute tells the base class that you want to specify a handler for an event raised by the client component. The name of the client event is specified in the `ClientPropertyName` attribute. The name of the JavaScript function that handles the event is contained in the string returned by the property.

Testing the TextChanged extender

Once the `TextChanged` project is compiled, you can use the TextChangedExtender like any other extender. Usually, an `@Register` directive is added at the top of an ASP.NET page to specify the assembly and the namespace in which the extender is contained, like so:

```
<%@Register Assembly="TextChanged" Namespace="TextChanged"
    TagPrefix="samples" %>
```

Listing 10.10 uses the TextChangedExtender control to refresh an UpdatePanel control each time the user stops typing in the text field for one second.

Listing 10.10   Example usage of the TextChangedExtender

```
<asp:UpdatePanel ID="UpdatePanel1" runat="server">
    <ContentTemplate>
        <div>Updated at: <%= DateTime.Now %></div>

        <asp:TextBox ID="TextBox1" runat="server"
                    AutoPostBack="true" />

        <samples:TextChangedExtender ID="TextChangedExtender1"
                                    runat="server"
            TargetControlID="TextBox1"
            Timeout="1000"
            OnTextChanged="onTextChanged"
            />
    </ContentTemplate>

</asp:UpdatePanel>

<script type="text/javascript">
<!--
    function onTextChanged(sender, e) {
        Sys.Debug.trace('textChanged event handled');
    }
//-->
</script>
```

Figure 10.10
The TextChangedExtender example running in Firefox. The current date is updated every time the `change` event of the text box is fired.

As usual, the extender is wired to the extended TextBox by specifying the ID of the extended control in the `TargetControlID` property. Note how you can use the `Timeout` and the `OnTextChanged` properties to configure the timeout value and the event handler for the `textChanged` event. The timeout property of the client behavior instance is set to one second. The event handler for the `textChanged` event is the `onTextChanged` function declared in the page. This function logs a message in the browser's console using the `Sys.Debug.trace` method, as shown in figure 10.10.

> **LIVE GRIDVIEW FILTER** — In the code downloadable at http://www.manning.com/gallo, you'll find a modified version of the LiveGridViewFilter example, rewritten to take advantage of the TextChangedExtender control.

To complete our tour of the Toolkit API, we'll do a quick overview of how the Toolkit enhances your design-time experience thanks to its support for the Visual Studio Designer.

10.2.4 Support for Visual Studio Designer

All the Toolkit controls can have an associated class to enhance the design-time experience provided by the Visual Studio Designer. The associated class must derive from the `ExtenderControlBaseDesigner` class contained in the `AjaxControlToolkit.Design` namespace. The associated designer class is specified in the `Designer` attribute, which decorates an extender or script control class. The argument passed to the `Designer` attribute is the type of the designer class, as in the following code:

```
[Designer(typeof(myDesignerClass))]
```

We need to discuss how the design-time experience can be enhanced for Ajax-enabled controls. The majority of Ajax-enabled controls rely heavily on JavaScript for rendering the control layout at runtime. An example is the Calendar-Extender control, which renders the calendar entirely on the client side using dynamic DOM elements. It's difficult to get a design-time experience similar to that of the ASP.NET Calendar control, which renders static HTML and can be displayed in the Visual Studio Designer. Using JavaScript lets you use the CalenderExtender control to render a full-featured calendar with support for animated transitions, similar to the one used in Windows Forms applications. Figure 10.11 shows a page that contains the CalendarExtender control.

Figure 10.11   The CalendarExtender control provides a calendar rendered using Dynamic HTML on the client side.

At the moment, the Toolkit offers basic design-time support that targets the configuration of the extender's properties. Figure 10.12 shows a portion of the Properties panel in the Visual Studio Designer. In the panel, you can see the properties of an ASP.NET Panel control. Interestingly, you can also edit the properties of all the extenders associated with the Panel control. This is reasonable because an extender, as the name implies, is supposed to provide additional properties to the extended control. In figure 10.12, the Panel has been extended with a CollapsiblePanel extender, which lets you dynamically show and hide the panel with an animation effect. A new Extenders category is added in the Properties panel. Inside is the list of properties added by each extender associated with the control.

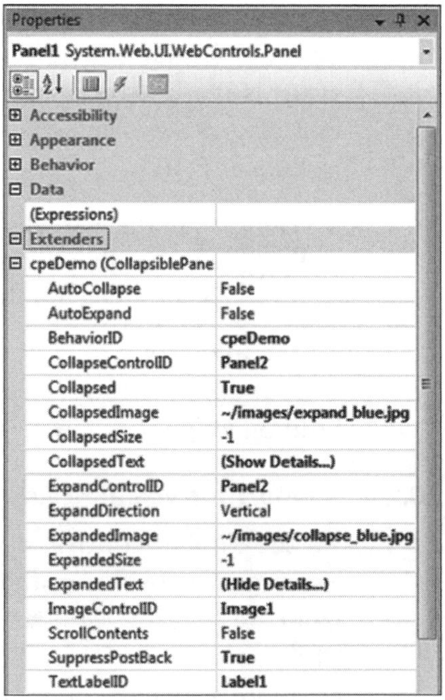

To provide additional design-time capabilities, you have to work with the associated designer class. A discussion of the Visual Studio Designer API is beyond the scope of

Figure 10.12   Example of design-time support offered by Toolkit extenders

this book. You can find a good introduction to Visual Studio design-time capabilities at http://msdn2.microsoft.com/en-us/library/37899azc.aspx.

Our overview of the Ajax Control Toolkit API is complete. This API makes it easier to create Ajax-enabled controls using an attribute-based programming model. It also provides the possibility to enhance the features provided by the base ASP.NET AJAX framework. As part of an open-source project, you can modify or expand the API based on your needs.

The Ajax Control Toolkit provides much more than the biggest available collection of Ajax-enabled controls and an API for creating them. You can leverage its powerful framework to add animations and visual effects to a web page's DOM elements.

10.3 Animations

The transition from static pages to Dynamic HTML pages opened the possibility of creating more appealing UIs. Static links, images, and panels turned into floating menus, slideshows, scrollers, and fading panels. Now, clever use of CSS and the DOM is required to obtain a modern web UI that enhances the user experience. Animations and visual effects are the key concepts you need to master. In the following sections, we'll examine the framework for creating animations and visual effects provided by the Ajax Control Toolkit.

10.3.1 Toolkit animation framework

The Toolkit animation framework consists of a group of client classes, each of which describes a particular type of animation. These classes derive, directly or indirectly, from a base class called `Animation`. Table 10.4 lists all the available animations along with their descriptions. As you can see, the list of animations is exhaustive—it includes fading effects, and you can move, resize, and scale elements; animate colors; and manage multiple animations.

Table 10.4 Classes of the Toolkit's animation framework

Name	Description
FadeInAnimation	Fade-in effect
FadeOutAnimation	Fade-out effect
PulseAnimation	Sequence of fade-in and fade-out effects
ColorAnimation	Animated transition between two colors
LengthAnimation	Animates the height or width style attributes of an element

Table 10.4   Classes of the Toolkit's animation framework *(continued)*

Name	Description
MoveAnimation	Animates the top and left style attributes of an element
ResizeAnimation	Changes the size of an element
ScaleAnimation	Scales an element, given a scale factor
SequenceAnimation	Plays a group of animations sequentially
ParallelAnimation	Plays a group of animations simultaneously
ConditionAnimation	Plays one of two child animations based on a condition
CaseAnimation	Plays one of the child animations based on a selection script

Animation classes are organized into families. Each family consists of a base class from which the animation classes derive. Figure 10.13 shows the families that make up the animation framework.

In the Toolkit animation framework, you can create animations three different ways:

- *Using the classic imperative syntax*—You create an instance of the class with the new operator and configure its properties as with any other client class.
- *Using JSON*—You describe a group of animations using JSON objects.
- *Using XML*—You define animations using XML syntax. This is the technique used by the `AnimationExtender`, which is an extender you can use to create animations in a web page. We'll discuss the `AnimationExtender` in section 10.3.3.

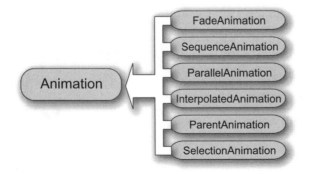

Figure 10.13
Base classes for the animations defined in the Toolkit animation framework

Using the imperative syntax is the fastest technique in terms of performance. JSON and XML descriptions are translated into imperative code to instantiate the corresponding animation classes. On the other hand, JSON and XML lead to compact and high readable code; this becomes relevant especially when you have to deal with many complex animations. The overhead introduced by JSON and XML description becomes substantive only in the most complex scenarios.

Because you know how to use the imperative syntax (assuming you're familiar with the JavaScript language), we'll focus mainly on the XML and JSON syntax. Before introducing them, let's do an overview of the common properties and methods exposed by the animation classes.

10.3.2 *Animation basics*

All the animations in the animation framework derive from a base client class called `Animation`. This class is contained in the `AjaxControlToolkit.Animation` namespace. It acts as an abstract class that provides the basic functionality needed by every animation. Whenever you create an instance of an animation class, you should set the following properties on it:

- `target`—The client ID of the DOM element that will be animated.
- `duration`—The overall duration of the animation, in seconds. The default value is 1 second.
- `fps`—The number of frames per seconds at which the animation is played. The higher is the value, the smoother the animation. The default value is 25 frames per seconds.

Every animation class exposes methods for controlling the animation status. The main methods are the following:

- `play`—Starts an animation, and resumes a paused animation.
- `pause`—Pauses an animation. If the `play` method is invoked after `pause`, the animation continues to play from the point where it was paused.
- `stop`—Stops an animation. If the `play` method is invoked after `stop`, the animation is played from the beginning.

You can detect when an animation is played or stopped by handling one of the events exposed by the base `Animation` class. These events can be handled with the techniques explained in section 3.7. At present, the `Animation` class exposes the following events:

- started—Raised as soon as the play method is invoked on the animation instance
- ended—Raised when the stop method is invoked on the animation instance

This is all you need to know to start working with the animation framework. The next step is to experiment with some of the animation classes provided by the framework. To do this, we'll introduce the animation extender, which is a Toolkit extender that lets you define animations using a declarative XML syntax.

10.3.3 *Using the AnimationExtender*

The animation extender is a Toolkit extender that defines animations in a web page based on an XML description. Being an extender, the AnimationExtender must extend a server control declared in the page. The extended control—set, as usual, through the TargetControlID property—is a control that triggers one or multiple animations. For example, if you wire the AnimationExtender to a Button control, you can play single or multiple animations based on the events raised by the button element. Listing 10.11 shows the skeleton structure for the Animation-Extender control.

Listing 10.11   Skeleton of the animation extender

```
<ajaxToolkit:AnimationExtender ID="AnimationExtender1" runat="server"
                     TargetControlID="Button1">
  <Animations>
    <OnLoad></OnLoad>
    <OnClick></OnClick>
    <OnMouseOver></OnMouseOver>
    <OnMouseOut></OnMouseOut>
    <OnHoverOver></OnHoverOver>
    <OnHoverOut></OnHoverOut>
  </Animations>
</ajaxToolkit:AnimationExtender>
```

The child Animations element contains XML elements mapped to events raised by the DOM element rendered by the extended control. Listing 10.11 assumes the extender is wired to a Button control with the ID of Button1. The elements under the Animations node represent events raised by the DOM button element. In the elements, you specify which animations you want to play in response to the event. For example, animations declared under the OnClick element are played as soon as the element is clicked. The only exception is represented by the OnLoad element:

Animations defined under this element are played as soon as the browser has finished loading the web page.

Let's see how to define animations using XML syntax. Listing 10.12 shows how you can fade out a div element by clicking a button. Note that the fade effect starts when you click the button, which is the element rendered by the extended Button control. The fade effect is applied to a different element, a div; this means you can trigger the animations based on the button events, but the animations can target any elements in the web page.

Listing 10.12   Animating a `div` element with the AnimationExtender control

```
<div id="thePanel" style="background-color:#aaa">
    <h2>Click the button to dismiss me.</h2>
</div>

<asp:Button ID="Button1" runat="server" Text="Click Me"
            OnClientClick="return false"
            UseSubmitBehavior="false" />

<ajaxToolkit:AnimationExtender ID="AnimationExtender1"
                    runat="server"
                    TargetControlID="Button1">
  <Animations>
    <OnLoad>
        <Scale ScaleFactor="2" />
    </OnLoad>
    <OnClick>
        <Sequence>
            <EnableAction Enabled="false" />
            <FadeOut AnimationTarget="thePanel"
                    MinimumOpacity="0"
                    MaximumOpacity="1"
                    Duration="0.5"
                    />
        </Sequence>
    </OnClick>
  </Animations>
</ajaxToolkit:AnimationExtender>
```

In the `OnLoad` element is a `Scale` tag, which is parsed as an instance of the `Scale-Animation` class. In general, you obtain the name of the tag to use in the XML description by removing the suffix `Animation` from the class name. As usual, attributes represent properties of the class. Because the value of the `ScaleFactor` attribute is set to 2, the button doubles its default dimensions. Note that because you haven't specified a duration, the button reaches its new dimensions in one second, which is the default value.

The `OnClick` element includes a sequence of animations to play as soon as the button is clicked. To play multiple animations in response to an event, you must encapsulate them into a `Sequence` or `Parallel` element. Otherwise, you can play only a single animation. The `Sequence` element defines an animation of type `SequenceAnimation`. This animation encapsulates a group of child animations that are played sequentially, one after another, as shown in figure 10.14.

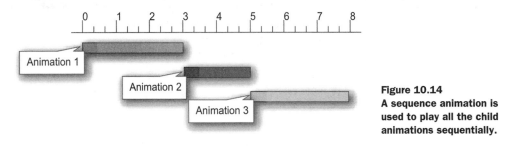

Figure 10.14
A sequence animation is used to play all the child animations sequentially.

When the previous animation is completed, the next one is played. The `start`, `pause`, and `stop` methods affect the entire sequence of animations. The `Sequence-Animation` class also exposes an `iterations` property, which can be set to an integer value. This value specifies the number of times the sequence is looped.

As an alternative, you can play a group of animations simultaneously, without waiting for the previous animation to complete before starting the next. In this case, you must declare the child animations in a `Parallel` element, which represents an animation of type `ParallelAnimation`. Note that the `duration` and `fps` properties affect the overall duration and smoothness of all the child animations. If one of the child animations sets different values for these properties, they're ignored if the animation is played in parallel. The concept of parallel animation is shown in figure 10.15.

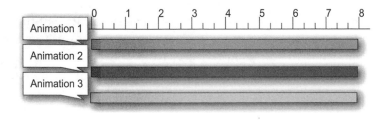

Figure 10.15
A parallel animation is used to play all the child animations simultaneously.

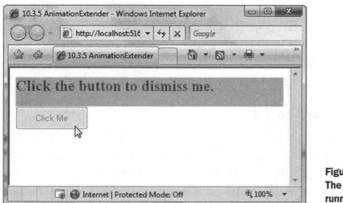

Figure 10.16
The AnimationExtender example
running in Internet Explorer

In listing 10.12, the second animation in the `Sequence` element is a `FadeOutAnimation`, represented by the `FadeOut` tag. This kind of animation can fade out the element whose client ID is set in the `AnimationTarget` attribute. In the example, you fade out a panel represented by the `div` element with the ID `thePanel`. The `MinimumOpacity` and `MaximumOpacity` attributes control the initial and final opacity for the fade-out effect. In this case, you pass from a value of 1 to 0, so the element is faded out until it disappears. The `FadeIn` element has the same attributes and can be used to play a fade-in effect. Figure 10.16 shows the example in listing 10.12 running in Internet Explorer.

The first animation in the `Sequence` element is neither a visual effect nor a real animation. You can consider it an *action*. Actions are atomic animations. They don't need a duration and don't need to be played at a certain frame-rate, because they perform tasks such as disabling an element or hiding it. But defining actions as animations means you can use them in sequence or parallel animations to perform atomic actions on DOM elements. Table 10.5 lists all the actions available in the animation framework, together with the description of what they accomplish.

Table 10.5 Actions available in the animation framework

Name	Description
EnableAction	Enables or disables a DOM element
HideAction	Hides an element or makes it visible
StyleAction	Sets the value of a CSS attribute of an element
OpacityAction	Changes the transparency of an element
ScriptAction	Evaluates a portion of JavaScript code

The Ajax Control Toolkit provides another extender to manage animations in a web page. The UpdatePanelAnimation extender works in a manner similar to the AnimationExtender, but it targets the UpdatePanel control and lets you play animations before and after a partial postback. Let's see how you can use this extender to implement a visual pattern known as the *yellow spotlight*.

10.3.4 *The UpdatePanelAnimation extender*

The UpdatePanelAnimation extender plays animations before and after a partial update. This extender must target an UpdatePanel control declared in the page. Animations are declared under the `Animations` node, in two elements called `OnUpdating` and `OnUpdated`. The `OnUpdating` tag contains all the animations to play before the partial postback begins, and the `OnUpdated` tag contains the animations to play after the content of the `UpdatePanel` has been refreshed.

Listing 10.13 shows how to use this extender to implement a visual pattern called the *yellow spotlight*. This effect notifies the user that a region of the page has been updated by animating the background color of the panel from a yellow color—or your preferred color—back to its original background color, in a short time. The purpose of the short color burst is to capture the user's attention on a refreshed portion of the page.

> **Listing 10.13   The yellow spotlight pattern applied to an UpdatePanel**

```
<asp:UpdatePanel ID="UpdatePanel1" runat="server">
    <Triggers>
        <asp:AsyncPostBackTrigger ControlID="Calendar1"
            EventName="SelectionChanged" />
    </Triggers>
    <ContentTemplate>
        <h3><%= Calendar1.SelectedDate.ToLongDateString() %></h3>
    </ContentTemplate>
</asp:UpdatePanel>
<asp:UpdatePanel ID="UpdatePanel2" runat="server">
    <ContentTemplate>
        <asp:Calendar ID="Calendar1" runat="server"></asp:Calendar>
    </ContentTemplate>
</asp:UpdatePanel>
  <ajaxToolkit:UpdatePanelAnimationExtender
                ID="UpdatPanelAnimationExtender1"
                runat="server"
                TargetControlID="UpdatePanel1">
    <Animations>
        <OnUpdated>
          <Color
              StartValue="#FFFF55"
              EndValue="#FFFFFF"
```

```
            Property="style"
            PropertyKey="backgroundColor"
            Duration="1" />
        </OnUpdated>
    </Animations>
</ajaxToolkit:UpdatePanelAnimationExtender>
```

The first UpdatePanel control is the one associated with the UpdatePanelAnimation extender. When the user selects a date in the Calendar declared in the UpdatePanel2 control, the first UpdatePanel is refreshed and the yellow spotlight animation is played. The animation is defined in the extender's OnUpdated element, in the Animations element. The effect is implemented with a ColorAnimation instance. The StartValue and EndValue attributes specify the start and end color, expressed in hexadecimal notation. The Property and PropertyKey attributes reach the property that the animation affects. In this case, you're interested in animating the background color of the panel. You must animate the backgroundColor property of the style object encapsulated by the div element rendered by the UpdatePanel control. Figure 10.17 shows the example running in the Opera browser.

Figure 10.17   You can use the UpdatePanelAnimation extender to implement the yellow spotlight visual pattern.

The extenders provided by the Ajax Control Toolkit, in conjunction with the elegant XML syntax used to describe animations, make it easy to create complex effects and to implement visual patterns like the yellow spotlight. In the next section, we'll look at another technique that uses JSON to instantiate animations. You'll use this technique to enhance the PhotoGallery control that you coded in section 8.4.5.

10.3.5   *JSON and animations: adding transitions to the PhotoGallery control*

When you use the AnimationExtender or the UpdatePanelAnimationExtender, the XML that defines the animations is parsed on the server side. The result is a JSON-serialized object that is sent on the client side and used to create instances of the animation classes. The following example will give you the opportunity to experiment directly with the JSON syntax for creating animations.

In this section, we'll return on the PhotoGallery control built in section 8.4.5. So far, you've created a client control to browse a set of images stored in the website. Your next goal is to enhance the control by adding an animated transition between the images. The transition you'll build isn't complex, but it's effective, as shown in figure 10.18. While the next image is being loaded, you partially fade-out the current image; then, you resize it until it reaches the width and height of the next image to display. Finally, the new image fades in and replaces the old image.

Let's start by opening the PhotoGallery.js file that contains the code for the PhotoGallery control. You have to modify the code so that when the next image is loaded, a new method named _playTransition is called. This method is responsible for playing the animated transition and then calling the _displayImage method as soon as the transition is completed. First, you must rewrite the _onImage-ElementLoaded method, declared in the PhotoGallery's prototype, as follows:

```
_onImageElementLoaded : function() {
    this._playTransition();
}
```

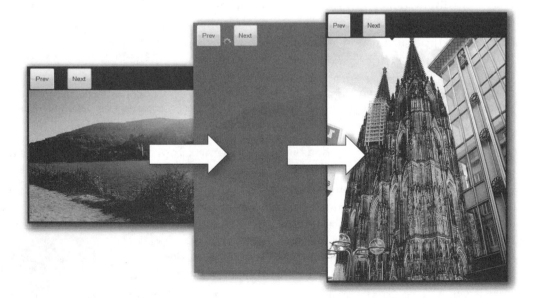

Figure 10.18   Example of an animated transition applied to the PhotoGallery control. The animations that make up the transition are defined through JSON objects.

Then, you must add a method called _playTransition to the constructor's prototype. The code for the _playTransition method is shown in listing 10.14.

Listing 10.14   Code for the `_playTransition` method

```
_playTransition : function() {
    var currentImageSize = {height: this._imageElement.height,
        width: this._imageElement.width};
    var nextImageSize = {height: this._imgPreload.height, width:
        this._imgPreload.width};

    var fadeIn = AjaxControlToolkit.Animation.createAnimation(          ◁┐  Fade-in
        {                                                                ❶  animation
            "AnimationName": "FadeIn",
            "AnimationTarget": this._imageElement.id,
            "Duration": 0.3,
            "MinimumOpacity": 0.2,
            "MaximumOpacity": 1
        }
    );
                                                     Sequence animation  ❷
    var sequence = AjaxControlToolkit.Animation.createAnimation(     ◁┘
        {
            "AnimationName": "Sequence",
            "AnimationTarget": this._imageElement.id,
            "AnimationChildren":
            [
                {
                    "AnimationName": "FadeOut",
                    "Duration": 0.3,
                    "MaximumOpacity": 1,
                    "MinimumOpacity": 0.2
                },

                {
                    "AnimationName": "Resize",
                    "Height": nextImageSize.height,
                    "Width": currentImageSize.width
                },

                {
                    "AnimationName": "Resize",
                    "Height": nextImageSize.height,
                    "Width": nextImageSize.width
                }
            ]
        }
    );
```

```
sequence.add_ended(Function.createDelegate(this,          Subscribe to
    onSequenceEnded));                                    ended event
                                                 Play
sequence.play();         ←─────┐ transition

function onSequenceEnded() {
    this._displayImage();                        Handle
    fadeIn.play();                               ended event
}
}
```

The first thing you do in the body of the method is save the height and width of the currently displayed image and the next one in the list. You need these dimensions in order to set up the animation that resizes the current image to the size of the next one.

The first animation you create is a fade-in ❶, stored in the fadeIn variable. The animation is created with a call to the AjaxControlToolkit.Animation.create-Animation method. This method accepts an object literal (a JSON object) and instantiates the animations defined in the object. In the JSON object, the value of the AnimationName attribute is the FadeIn string, which corresponds to a fade-in animation. You follow the same rule used in the XML description. The name of an animation is obtained by removing the Animation suffix from the name of the class.

The second attribute, AnimationTarget, specifies which element to animate. In this case, it's the img element that displays the current image. The third attribute, Duration, is the duration of the animation; the last two attributes define the values of the maximum and minimum opacity. The fade-in effect is obtained by animating the opacity value from 0.2 to 1.

You use the same technique to create the sequence animation ❷ that completes the transition. In this case, the AnimationChildren attribute holds an array with the child animations. When the _playTransition method is called, the transition is played in two parts. First, the sequence animation is played. To detect its end, you subscribe to its ended event. The event is handled by a function called onSequenceEnded, declared in the _playTransition method. When the sequence animation ends, the _displayImage method is called to replace the old photo with the new one. Finally, the fade-in animation is played to complete the transition between the two images.

The JSON description is compact and leads to highly readable code. The only drawback of this approach is that it's slower than the imperative syntax because an additional step is required to translate the JSON description into an instance of the `FadeInAnimation` class. For this reason, the imperative syntax is preferable when you need maximum performance. In most cases, though, you'll be able to use the shortest and most readable code.

10.4 Summary

In this chapter, we've explored the Ajax Control Toolkit, an open-source project started by Microsoft in the early days of ASP.NET AJAX. The Toolkit, which is open to contributions from the community, aims at becoming the biggest free collection of Ajax-enabled controls available.

The Toolkit controls are built on top of a custom API that enhances the base functionality provided by the ASP.NET AJAX extensions. The Toolkit API is a metadata-driven API: Ajax-enabled controls can be authored using attribute-based programming. All controls created with the Toolkit API provide support for the ASP.NET 2.0 callbacks framework and the Visual Studio Designer.

The Ajax Control Toolkit offers also a powerful framework for creating visual effects and animations. We explored the animation classes and explained how to create them in a web page using the AnimationExtender control. You can create animations using XML or JSON syntax, as we demonstrated by adding transition effects to the PhotoGallery control developed in chapter 8.

In the next chapter, we'll look at the XML Script declarative language, which is used to instantiate client components in a page using a declarative syntax.

Part 3

ASP.NET AJAX Futures

It's been almost a year since the first official release of ASP.NET AJAX, and plans for the next release are well under way. Currently, features for the next release are available in a separate package called the ASP.NET Futures. In this part of the book, we'll cover some of these features. Chapter 11 is dedicated to XML Script: a declarative language similar to the ASP.NET markup, which is used to instantiate client components in the page. Chapter 12 covers the drag-and-drop engine, which you can use to drag and drop DOM elements in the page. By the end of these chapters, you'll be ready to use the main features that will be included in future releases of ASP.NET AJAX.

11

XML Script

XML Script is a declarative language for creating instances of JavaScript objects at runtime, setting their properties, and specifying their behavior, using an XML-like syntax similar to the ASP.NET markup code.

In an HTML page, you can separate content (the markup code) from style by embedding the style information in a CSS file. Similarly, in an ASP.NET page, you usually define the page layout using declarative markup code in an ASPX page. Then, you can use a separate code-behind file to specify the behavior of server controls and how they're wired together, using the classic imperative syntax. XML Script lets you achieve this kind of separation and instantiate JavaScript components using a declarative script language embedded in a web page.

XML Script, like declarative languages, has a number of advantages over the imperative syntax. Building designers for markup is easier than building them for code. Great visual tools, like the Visual Studio Designer, take care of generating markup code for you. If a client can parse declarative markup, you can make server controls render the markup more easily than rendering imperative code. In addition, declarative markup carries semantics. For example, an application that parses a TextBox tag knows that it has to instantiate a text field, but it's up to the application to decide to instantiate a simple text field rather than a more complex auto-complete text box—for example, based on browser capabilities. Finally, declarative code can be more expressive and less verbose than imperative code. Features like *bindings* help keep the values exposed by object properties synchronized, without the need to deal with multiple event handlers.

This chapter illustrates these aspects of XML Script, beginning with the basics of the language and moving to advanced features like actions, bindings, and transformers. Keep in mind that because they're part of the ASP.NET Futures package, the features illustrated in this chapter aren't currently documented or supported by Microsoft.

11.1 XML Script basics

Your first goal is learning how to write XML Script code and understanding how it's turned into instances of client objects at runtime. As we'll explain in a moment, writing XML Script code is similar to writing ASP.NET declarative code. The main difference is that whereas you use ASP.NET markup to create instances of server-side classes, you use XML Script code to create JavaScript objects.

Before you begin using XML Script, you need to enable it in a web page. This turns out to be an easy job, because you have to reference the PreviewScript.js file in the ScriptManager control, as shown in listing 11.1. This file is embedded as a web resource in the Microsoft.Web.Preview assembly, which is shipped with the ASP.NET Futures package. You can find more information on how to install this package in appendix A.

Listing 11.1   Enabling XML Script in an ASP.NET page

```
<asp:ScriptManager ID="TheScriptManager" runat="server">
    <Scripts>
        <asp:ScriptReference Assembly="Microsoft.Web.Preview"
            Name="PreviewScript.js" />
    </Scripts>
</asp:ScriptManager>
```

XML Script code is embedded in `script` tags with the `type` attribute set to `text/xml-script`. This custom type was defined to distinguish blocks of XML Script code from other script code such as JavaScript. This is what the typical container of an XML Script code block looks like:

```
<script type="text/xml-script">
    <!-- Insert xml-script here -->
</script>
```

As you can see, XML Script comments have the same syntax as XML comments. You can have multiple blocks of XML Script code in the same page, and they can appear in any order and position. Unlike JavaScript code, though, at the moment XML Script can only appear inline in the page and can't be saved to separate files.

As with any programming language, a "Hello, World!" example is the ideal ice-breaker for introducing basic XML Script features. It's also a good starting point for learning how XML Script code is structured and to give you confidence with its syntax.

11.1.1 *Hello XML Script!*

This example shows how a block of XML Script code is structured and how you can deal with client objects using declarative code. You'll see how to handle an event raised by a client component using XML Script code. Normally, you'd accomplish this task by retrieving a reference to the component and writing the necessary JavaScript code to add an event handler. Listing 11.2 shows how to declaratively hook up the `init` event raised by `Sys.Application`, the Application object introduced in chapter 2. As promised, the event handler is a JavaScript function that displays a "Hello XML Script!" message onscreen.

Listing 11.2   Code for the "Hello XML Script!" example

```
<%@ Page %>

<!DOCTYPE html PUBLIC "-//W3C//DTD XHTML 1.0 Transitional//EN"
 "http://www.w3.org/TR/xhtml1/DTD/xhtml1-transitional.dtd">

<html xmlns="http://www.w3.org/1999/xhtml" >
<head runat="server">
    <title>Hello XML-script</title>
</head>
<body>
    <form id="form1" runat="server">
    <asp:ScriptManager ID="TheScriptManager" runat="server">
        <Scripts>
            <asp:ScriptReference Assembly="Microsoft.Web.Preview"
                    Name="PreviewScript.js" />
        </Scripts>
    </asp:ScriptManager>

    <script type="text/xml-script">
        <page xmlns="http://schemas.microsoft.com/xml-script/2005">
          <components>
            <application init="pageInit" />
          </components>
        </page>
    </script>

    <script type="text/javascript">
    <!--
        function pageInit() {
            alert("Hello XML Script!");
        }
    //-->
    </script>
    </form>
</body>
</html>
```

Block of XML ❶
Script code

Let's have a closer look at the block of XML Script code ❶ contained in the page. It has a root element called page and a single child element called components. The page element defines a global XML namespace associated with the following Uniform Resource Identifier (URI):

```
http://schemas.microsoft.com/xml-script/2005
```

The page/components structure is the basic form of an XML Script code block. All the blocks of XML Script code in the page must have this structure in order to be parsed correctly. In section 11.1.5 we'll return to the use of XML namespaces with XML Script.

NOTE An *XML namespace* is a collection of names, identified by a URI reference, used in XML documents as element types and attribute names. For more information on XML namespaces, check http://www.w3schools .com/ xml/xml_namespaces.asp.

The `components` tag always contains the list of client objects declared in the page. These objects are represented by XML elements and are instances of classes created with the Microsoft Ajax Library. In this chapter, we'll focus on client components, which are classes that derive from `Sys.Component`. The reason is that the XML Script engine already knows how to properly parse and instantiate such classes. If you recall, the creation process for a client component is rather elaborate, as we discussed in chapter 8.

In listing 11.2, `application` is the unique child node of `components`. In XML Script—as in the ASP.NET markup, for example—a tag is mapped to a class, and the element represents an instance of that class. The `application` tag is always mapped to the Application object, stored in the global `Sys.Application` variable. When the XML Script parser processes the `application` tag, it retrieves a reference to the Application object. Then, it recognizes the `init` attribute as the name of an event raised by the Application object. As a consequence, its value—`pageInit`—is treated as the name of the event handler.

The `pageInit` function declared in the JavaScript code block at the bottom of the page is invoked when the Application object raises the `init` event. This causes the greeting message to be displayed in a message box onscreen, as shown in figure 11.1.

Figure 11.1
The message displayed by a JavaScript function that handles the `init` event raised by `Sys.Application`. The `init` event is hooked up declaratively using XML Script code.

The page still includes some JavaScript code, but you were able to perform the logic for attaching the event handler using only declarative code. Later, you'll see how to make the JavaScript code disappear.

So far, you know how to access the Application object using XML Script. Usually, a rich web application hosts multiple components and even controls associated with DOM elements. Can you access them in declarative code and hook up their events? The answer is that all the kinds of client components can be instantiated and accessed using XML Script.

> **NOTE**   As you may have noticed while typing the first listing in Visual Studio, code completion isn't available at the moment for XML Script. In addition, no support is provided for debugging XML Script code and for the Visual Studio Designer. As we said in the introduction, XML Script is part of the ASP.NET Futures package and is still under development.

11.1.2 *Controls and XML Script*

In chapter 8, we introduced client controls and promised that they would be useful when dealing with XML Script. Client controls, when created as *element wrappers*, are the way to reach DOM elements using XML Script. An element wrapper is a control associated with a DOM element. As a wrapper, the client control exposes properties, methods, and events to deal with the associated element and enhance its functionality. As a client component, a control can be used in XML Script with little effort. The Microsoft Ajax Library ships with a collection of ready-to-use controls associated with the most-used DOM elements, such as labels and input elements.

Listing 11.3 is a slight variation on listing 11.2. It uses a button and a label to display the greeting message, instead of accessing the Application object.

Listing 11.3   Using the Label and Button controls in XML Script

```
<div>
    <input type="button" id="greetButton" value="Click Me" />      ❶  Button element
</div>
<div>                                                    ❷  Label element
    <h1><span id="msgLabel"></span></h1>
</div>
                                                         ❸  Label component
<script type="text/xml-script">
    <page xmlns="http://schemas.microsoft.com/xml-script/2005">
      <components>
        <label id="msgLabel" />
        <button id="greetButton" click="onGreetButtonClick" />
      </components>                                       ❹  Button component
    </page>
</script>
```

```
<script type="text/javascript">
<!--
    function onGreetButtonClick(sender, e) {
        $find('msgLabel').set_text('Hello XML-script!');
    }
//-->
</script>
```

The page's HTML contains an input ❶ and a span ❷ element. The goal is to display a message in the label when the button is clicked. To accomplish this task, you don't access the DOM elements directly. Instead, you deal with the corresponding controls, represented by the label ❸ and button ❹ elements in the XML Script code. Note that the value of their id attributes is set to the IDs of the DOM elements; this way, you associate the DOM elements with the client controls. We say that the DOM elements have been *upgraded* to client controls.

At runtime, the XML Script engine creates an instance of the Sys.Preview.UI.Label control and passes the span element as the associated element. Similarly, it creates an instance of the Sys.Preview.UI.Button control and passes the input element as the associated element. The value of the id attribute becomes the value of the id property exposed by the controls. This allows them to be referenced in XML Script code.

The click attribute of the button tag ❹ is mapped to the click event raised by the Button control. Its value is the name of the JavaScript function that handles the event. The function onGreetButtonClick uses the $find method to access the Label control and set the text of the associated span element through the set_text method.

Table 11.1 lists the element wrappers defined in the Sys.Preview.UI namespace. Note that you obtain the name of the associated tag—which is case insensitive—by removing the namespace prefix from the class name.

Table 11.1   Element wrappers defined in the Sys.Preview.UI namespace

Class name	Description	Tag name
Sys.Preview.UI.Button	Wraps an input element of type button	button
Sys.Preview.UI.Label	Wraps a span element	label
Sys.Preview.UI.CheckBox	Wraps an input element of type checkbox	checkbox
Sys.Preview.UI.HyperLink	Wraps an anchor element	hyperlink

Table 11.1   Element wrappers defined in the `Sys.Preview.UI` namespace *(continued)*

Class name	Description	Tag name
`Sys.Preview.UI.Image`	Wraps an `img` element	`image`
`Sys.Preview.UI.Selector`	Wraps a `select` element	`selector`
`Sys.Preview.UI.TextBox`	Wraps an input element of type `text`	`textbox`

What if you need to target an element like `div`, which doesn't have an associated wrapper control? You have to write an XML Script-enabled custom control that wraps it. But if you only need to wrap an element and access the base functionality provided by the `Sys.UI.Control` class, the easiest way is to use a `control` element. The `control` tag wraps a DOM element with a given `id`, with an instance of the `Sys.UI.Control` class, like so:

```
<control id="elementID" />
```

In XML Script, the markup code is always mapped to the properties of controls, not to the properties of the associated DOM elements. You need client components to interact with DOM elements using declarative code.

So far, we've talked about the components shipped with the Microsoft Ajax Library. You'll probably want to use custom components in XML Script. In the following section, you'll see how XML namespaces help the XML Script engine locate custom client classes.

XML namespaces

An XML *namespace* declaration tells XML Script where to find the client class corresponding to an element declared in the markup code. In XML Script, you usually declare a global namespace in the `page` element, with the following code:

```
<page xmlns="http://schemas.microsoft.com/xml-script/2005" />
```

When you declare the global namespace, the XML Script parser tries to map a tag name to a client class contained in one of the following namespaces:

- `Sys`
- `Sys.Net`
- `Sys.Preview.UI`
- `Sys.Preview.Data`
- `Sys.Preview.Services.Components`
- `Sys.UI`

- `Sys.Preview`
- `Sys.Preview.Net`
- `Sys.Preview.UI.Data`
- `Sys.Preview.UI.Effects`

If you want to use, in XML Script, a component defined in a different namespace, you have to declare an XML namespace that tells where to find it.

In general, you declare an XML namespace by associating a URI with a prefix. The URI identifies the location of a certain resource, which isn't necessarily associated with a browsable address: It acts as a unique identifier. The prefix is used as a shortcut that refers to the URI. For example, suppose you have a custom component declared as `SomeSpace.SomeComponent`. Because `SomeSpace` is a custom namespace, you have to declare an XML namespace if you want to use the component in XML Script. To do that, you have to act on the `page` element as follows:

```
<page xmlns="http://schemas.microsoft.com/xml-script/2005"
    xmlns:cc="javascript:SomeSpace" />
```

You declare an XML namespace with an `xmlns` attribute followed by a colon and the prefix that you'll use in the XML Script code. The value of the `xmlns` attribute is the URI (javascript:SomeSpace in the example). The string *javascript:* at the beginning of the URI is called the *scheme,* which is required in order to obtain a valid URI. In this case, the scheme suggests that what follows is a list of one or more client namespaces, separated by commas. You can associate multiple client namespaces with a single prefix, like so:

```
<page xmlns="http://schemas.microsoft.com/xml-script/2005"
    xmlns:cc="javascript:SomeSpace, SomeSpace.ChildSpace">
```

This code tells the XML Script parser which namespaces to search for the class corresponding to an element declared with the `cc` prefix. The prefix should be a short and, if possible, meaningful string. In this case, cc stands for *custom control.* Assuming it exposes a proper type descriptor, you can use the custom component in XML Script as follows:

```
<cc:SomeComponent />
```

As explained in the previous section, the type descriptor maps an element's attributes to properties of the component. The rules for writing XML Script code apply to custom components.

You may have noticed that the global namespace doesn't have a prefix. Elements without a prefix belong to the global namespace. Under the hood, the global XML namespace is associated with the script prefix; so, this prefix refers to the namespaces listed earlier.

Before you learn how to use the custom classes in XML Script, you should understand how XML Script code is parsed and turned into JavaScript code. This will give you some insight into how things work under the hood of the XML Script engine. Then, you'll be ready to explore some of the powerful features of the declarative language.

11.1.3 *From XML Script to JavaScript*

The process of converting the XML Script declarative code into JavaScript imperative code starts when a web page is loaded in the browser. If XML Script is enabled in the page, the Microsoft Ajax runtime instructs the XML Script parser to filter all the script tags with the type attribute set to text/xml-script. The XML Script parser is a JavaScript object stored in the Sys.Preview.MarkupParser variable. It exposes a group of methods for extracting and processing the XML Script code.

As the XML Script blocks are extracted, they're collected in an array and processed sequentially. For each block, a sanity check is performed on its structure, to ensure that a root element called page exists. Also, the page element must have a child node called components. The parser ignores all the other tags in the page element.

> **NOTE** The parser performs an additional check to see if a references element is declared in the page node. The references element was used in previous CTPs to provide a list of paths to script files to load in the page, but it's not supported in the latest CTP. If a references tag is found, the XML Script parser throws an error.

As the current XML Script block is processed, all the child elements of the components tag are extracted and stored in an array. These are all the client objects that need to be instantiated. The instantiation process is performed by the parseNode method, which is called by the parser on each tag to parse the markup code and create an instance of the object.

First, the parseNode method needs to determine the fully qualified name of the class to instantiate. To locate the class, it extracts the tag name and the namespace prefix from the markup code. The tag name is the case-insensitive name of the class; it's turned to uppercase. The information on the namespace is retrieved from the XML namespace prefix used in the tag. Finally, the fully qualified name of the class is obtained by appending the class name to its containing namespace.

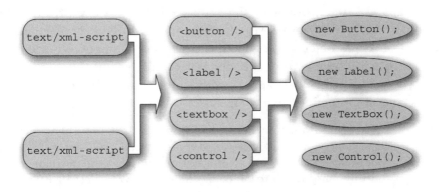

Figure 11.2   The XML Script parser extracts component declarations from XML Script code blocks. Then, it parses the declarative code and creates instances of the corresponding JavaScript objects.

If the class exists, the parser checks whether it exposes a static method called `parseFromMarkup`. This method must be defined in a class in order to be used in XML Script. It receives the markup code and is responsible for parsing it and creating a new instance of the class. This process is repeated for each XML Script block and for each tag extracted from the components node. When all the markup has been processed, all the client objects have been instantiated and can be safely accessed in the application code. This process is illustrated in figure 11.2.

Luckily, you can avoid writing the logic needed to parse the markup code and create an instance of a client class. The `Sys.Component` class exposes and implements the `parseFromMarkup` method; it's a good choice to derive the custom classes from the base `Sys.Component` class. This way, you can take advantage of the features offered by the client component model and also use the custom class in XML Script with little effort. The only requirement is that every component must expose a type descriptor in order to be used in XML Script.

11.1.4 *Type descriptors*

A *type descriptor* is an object that provides information about a particular type. In the .NET framework, you can perform *reflection* on objects to learn about their structure. For example, you can extract every sort of information about the fields, properties, methods, and events exposed by a class. On the server side, type descriptors can be used to provide additional reflection capabilities. On the client side, type descriptors have been introduced to achieve the same goal.

In chapter 3, we introduced the enhanced type system provided by the Microsoft Ajax Library, together with the methods used to reflect on client classes. Reflection on client objects is less powerful because many object-oriented constructs are *simulated* by extending function objects. You can use client type descriptors to partially fill this gap and provide information about the properties, methods, and events defined in a client class.

> **NOTE**   In the .NET framework, type descriptors are used to enhance reflection capabilities, especially for components that take advantage of the Visual Studio Designer. For more information on .NET type descriptors, browse to http://msdn2.microsoft.com/en-us/library/ms171819.aspx.

A client class can expose a type descriptor by storing it in a static `descriptor` property added directly to the constructor. For example, you would store and retrieve the type descriptor of a class called `SomeSpace.SomeClass` with the following statements:

```
SomeSpace.SomeClass.descriptor = {};

var descriptor = SomeSpace.SomeClass.descriptor;
```

Another way to expose a type descriptor is by implementing the `Sys.Preview.ITypeDescriptorProvider` interface. This interface defines a single method called `getDescriptor`, which must be implemented as an instance method of the client class. The implementation of the method should return the type descriptor associated with the client class, as in the following code:

```
SomeSpace.SomeClass.prototype.getDescriptor = function() {
    return {};
}
```

Client type descriptors aren't strictly tied to XML Script and can be leveraged by every client class. But the XML Script engine needs a type descriptor in order to parse the markup code into an instance of a client component, so only client components that provide a type descriptor can be used in XML Script code.

Structure of a type descriptor

In the previous code snippets, you returned {}—an empty object—as the type descriptor. The information should be packaged following specific rules that we'll explain in a moment. In general, a client type descriptor is a JavaScript object that can provide custom information about the client type. The XML Script engine recognizes the following properties:

- properties—Holds an array of property descriptors
- methods—Holds an array of method descriptors
- events—Holds an array of event descriptors

Each array, in turn, holds objects, each of which describes a property, a method, or an event exposed by the client class. To help you understand what a type descriptor looks like, listing 11.4 shows the one exposed by the Sys.Preview.UI.Button class.

Listing 11.4 Type descriptor exposed by the Sys.Preview.UI.Button class

```
Sys.Preview.UI.Button.descriptor = {
    properties: [ { name: 'command', type: String },
                  { name: 'argument', type: String } ],
    events: [ { name: 'click' } ]
}
```

The type descriptor of the Button class exposes two property descriptors and one event descriptor. The first property is called command, and the corresponding property descriptor is an object with two properties: name and type. The name property returns a string with the name of the property you're describing. The type property returns the type of the value exposed by the property. Here's the property descriptor extracted from the type descriptor:

```
{ name: 'command', type: String }
```

Similarly, the second property descriptor tells you that the Button class exposes a property called argument, of type String. We're talking about client properties as defined by the Microsoft Ajax Library, which we discussed in chapter 3. The unique event descriptor in listing 11.4 is relative to a click event. It's an object with a name property that returns a string with the name of the event:

```
{ name: 'click' }
```

The Button class doesn't provide any method descriptors. Describing a method requires additional work because you also have to describe its parameters. Figure 11.3 shows a method descriptor extracted from the type descriptor exposed by the Sys.Preview.InvokeMethodAction class. The method is called invoke, and it accepts a single parameter called userContext, of type Object. You'll encounter this method again when we talk about *actions* in section 11.2.

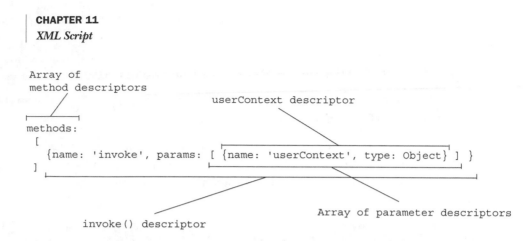

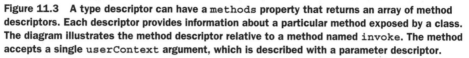

Figure 11.3 A type descriptor can have a `methods` property that returns an array of method descriptors. Each descriptor provides information about a particular method exposed by a class. The diagram illustrates the method descriptor relative to a method named `invoke`. The method accepts a single `userContext` argument, which is described with a parameter descriptor.

In general, a *method descriptor* is an object with two properties, `name` and `params`. The `name` property returns a string with the name of the method. The `params` property returns an array of parameter descriptors. A list of the properties that can be used in a parameter descriptor can be found in chapter 13, where we explain the parameter-validation mechanism. Method parameters are described in the same way in type descriptors and in validation routines.

Thanks to type descriptors, the XML Script engine can discover which members are exposed by a client class and map them to attributes declared in the markup code. For example, by querying the type descriptor of the `Button` class, the XML Script parser knows that the value of the `click` attribute of a `button` tag should be treated as an event handler for the `click` event exposed by the class. By iterating the same processing to all the elements, the XML Script code can easily be converted into JavaScript code.

So far, we have presented the syntax and the main rules to write XML Script code. You also possess the skills to enable XML Script usage in the custom components. This is the right moment to examine the main features of the language. You must understand concepts like actions, bindings, and transformers to run complex client code without writing a single line of JavaScript.

11.2 Actions

In the previous examples, you saw how to hook up an event raised by a client component using XML Script code. Things went smoothly, and you didn't have to write any client code to attach the handler to the event. But you did have to declare the function that handles the event, so some JavaScript code is still present in the page. Our main goal was to demonstrate that XML Script can effectively replace JavaScript code in many situations. Now we're ready to introduce *actions*, which are classes that encapsulate portions of JavaScript code. This code can be executed in response to events raised by client components. Actions are perfectly suited for handling events declaratively.

As usual, examples will help to clarify this concept. Let's start with an overview of the built-in actions in the Microsoft Ajax Library. Later, you'll create custom actions and use them in XML Script.

11.2.1 *SetPropertyAction*

A typical task performed when handling an event is to set one or more properties of an object. For example, you can intercept the `click` event of a button object and display some text in a label. To do the same thing using declarative code, you need the help of the `SetProperty` action. The `SetPropertyAction` class encapsulates the client code needed to set the value of a property exposed by a client object. Like all actions, this class can be used in XML Script. The code in listing 11.5 handles the `click` event of a button with the `SetProperty` action, in order to display a greeting message in a label.

Listing 11.5   Using the `SetProperty` action to handle an event

```
<div><input type="button" id="greetButton" value="Click Me" /></div>
<div><h1><span id="msgLabel"></span></h1></div>

<script type="text/xml-script">
    <page xmlns="http://schemas.microsoft.com/xml-script/2005">
      <components>
        <label id="msgLabel" />
        <button id="greetButton">
          <click>
            <setPropertyAction target="msgLabel"
                               property="text"
                               value="Hello XML-script!"
                               />

          </click>
        </button>
      </components>
    </page>
</script>
```

To handle an event with XML Script, you have to do two things: First you turn the name of the event into an XML element; then, you declare one or more actions in the event element. The code encapsulated by each action is executed in response to the event.

The code has a `click` element in the `button` tag. This element represents the `click` event raised by the `Button` control. In the `click` element, you declare a `setPropertyAction` element, which represents a `SetProperty` action. The `target` attribute specifies the ID of the client component that exposes the property you want to set. The `property` attribute holds the name of the property you're interested in. The `value` attribute is set to the value you want to assign to the property. As a consequence, the text "Hello XML-script!" is displayed in the label.

With the `SetProperty` action, you can also access the properties of the DOM element associated with a control. Add the following markup in the `click` node in listing 11.5, just after the first `setPropertyAction` tag:

```
<setPropertyAction target="msgLabel"
                   property="element"
                   propertyKey="style.backgroundColor"
                   value="#FFFF00" />
```

In this case, you have an additiona `propertyKey` attribute that contains the path to the `backgroundColor` property of the `span` element associated with the `msgLabel` control. Let's compare the markup code with the equivalent imperative code:

```
$find('msgLabel').get_element().style.backgroundColor = '#FFFF00';
```

The `property` attribute, in this case, refers to the `get_element` method, which returns the associated DOM element. The value of the `propertyKey` attribute is appended to the object returned by `get_element`, and the result is the property to set. This causes the background color of the `span` element to become yellow. Figure 11.4 shows the example in listing 11.5 running in Firefox.

Did you see any JavaScript code in listing 11.5? With actions, you can wrap any kind of JavaScript code and execute it

Figure 11.4 The `SetProperty` action lets you set properties of client components without writing a single line of JavaScript code.

declaratively. The next built-in action we'll examine is `PostBack`; it's used to trigger a postback of the page.

11.2.2 *PostBackAction*

ASP.NET pages use a JavaScript function called `__doPostBack` to post form data back to the server. The `PostBack` action wraps the call to `__doPostBack` to trigger the postback of the page from XML Script code. Let's change the behavior of the button declared in listing 11.5. If you replace the `button` tag with the following code, you can make it trigger a postback when it's clicked:

```
<button id="greetButton">
    <click>
        <postBackAction target="myButton" eventArgument="" />
    </click>
</button>
```

The `target` and `eventArgument` attributes set the corresponding arguments in the `__doPostBack` function. The previous markup code executes the following JavaScript code:

```
__doPostBack('greetButton', '');
```

Another typical task performed by event handlers is invoking an object method. The Microsoft Ajax Library provides the `InvokeMethod` action to invoke a method declaratively in XML Script.

11.2.3 *InvokeMethodAction*

The `InvokeMethod` action is powerful because it invokes a method exposed by a client component and makes it possible to process the results using only declarative code. To demonstrate the `InvokeMethod` action, we'll introduce a built-in client component called `Sys.Preview.Net.ServiceMethodRequest`. You can use this class to invoke a web method and process the results in a callback function. To add some spice, you do so using only XML Script code. In listing 11.6, you declare the Web Service used in the example. The only web method, `GetTimeAsString`, returns the current date and time on the web server. In the example, you retrieve this information and display it in a label.

Listing 11.6 Code for the `DateTimeService` class

```
<%@ WebService Language="C#" Class="DateTimeService" %>

using System;
using System.Web;
using System.Web.Services;
```

```
using System.Web.Services.Protocols;
using Microsoft.Web.Script.Services;

[WebService(Namespace = "http://tempuri.org/")]
[WebServiceBinding(ConformsTo = WsiProfiles.BasicProfile1_1)]
[ScriptService]
public class DateTimeService  : System.Web.Services.WebService {

    [WebMethod]
    [ScriptMethod(UseHttpGet=true)]
    public string GetTimeAsString() {
        return DateTime.Now.ToShortTimeString();
    }
}
```

The `DateTimeService` class represents an ASP.NET web service configured for
ASP.NET AJAX. As usual, the class is decorated with the `ScriptService` attribute,
which instructs ASP.NET AJAX to generate a JavaScript proxy for the web service.
The `GetTimeAsString` web method returns a string with the current date and
time. The `ScriptMethod` attribute that decorates the web method is used to
change the way it's invoked. Because the `ServiceMethodRequest` class uses GET as
the default HTTP verb for making the request, you set the `UseHttpGet` parameter
to `true` in the `ScriptMethod` attribute. You can find all the information needed
to access Web Services with ASP.NET AJAX in chapter 5.

The Web Service is configured, so we can move on to the XML Script code.
Listing 11.7 shows how to make a declarative call to the web method defined in
the Web Service and access the returned string.

Listing 11.7 Making a declarative Web Service call

```
<h2>
    <span>Time on Web Server: </span>
    <asp:Label ID="DateTime" runat="server"></asp:Label>
</h2>

<script type="text/xml-script">
  <page xmlns:script="http://schemas.microsoft.com/xml-script/2005">
    <components>

        <label id="DateTime" />          ❶ Label
                                            control

        <serviceMethodRequest id="timeServiceMethod"     ❷ ServiceMethod-
                              url="DateTimeService.asmx"    Request component
                              methodName="GetTimeAsString">
```

```
<completed>
    <setPropertyAction target="DateTime"
                       property="text"
                       >                            Handle          ❸
                                              completed event
        <bindings>
            <binding dataContext="timeServiceMethod"
                     dataPath="result"
                     property="value"
                     />
        </bindings>
    </setPropertyAction>
</completed>
</serviceMethodRequest>

<application>
  <load>
    <invokeMethodAction target="timeServiceMethod"   ❹  Call invoke
          method="invoke" />                              method
  </load>
</application>

</components>
</page>
</script>
```

The HTML markup contains a span element associated with a Label control ❶. You use the label to display the string returned by the web method. The service-MethodRequest element is used to set up the call to the web method ❷. The url attribute contains the path to the ASP.NET web service, and the methodName attribute specifies the name of the web method to invoke. The string returned by the web method is stored in the ServiceMethodRequest instance. You need to assign it an id in order to be able to access the instance in XML Script.

The ServiceMethodRequest class raises a completed event when the result of the web method call is available. This is a good occasion to handle the event declaratively ❸ and access the result property, which stores the returned string. You use a SetProperty action and a new tag (a binding) to extract the value of the result property and display it in the label. We'll introduce bindings in section 12.3. For now, it's enough to say that a binding can be used to synchronize the value exposed by two properties. In this case, you're synchronizing the result property with the label's text property. As soon as the result property is set, the same happens with the text property.

The InvokeMethod action ❹, which is the action you're interested in, is used to handle the load event of Sys.Application. As soon as the load event is raised,

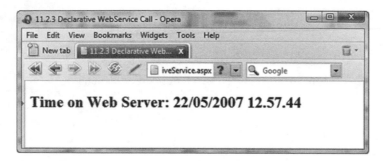

Figure 11.5 Result of the example in listing 11.7. The `InvokeMethod` action invokes a method on a client object that, in turn, calls a method defined in a local Web Service.

the `InvokeMethod` action calls the `invoke` method on the `ServiceMethodRequest` instance ❹. Note that the instance can be referenced because you assigned it an id. Figure 11.5 shows the date string displayed in the label.

The built-in actions provided by the Microsoft Ajax Library enable you to perform the most common tasks in declarative event handlers. But the real fun begins when you encapsulate the JavaScript code in custom actions. This can dramatically decrease the amount of JavaScript code you write, while expanding the number of tasks that can be accomplished with XML Script code. Before we discuss the base classes for creating custom actions, we need to talk briefly about how to set complex properties using the XML Script syntax.

Complex properties

Suppose you have a client component that exposes a property whose value is a simple JavaScript object (represented by an object literal) or an array. A good question would be whether you can expand the simple object or add elements to the array declaratively, using XML Script. The answer is positive.

Consider the example of a declarative web service call, from listing 11.7. You know the `ServiceMethodRequest` class can be used to call a method defined in a Web Service and process its results. It's a client component, and it exposes a type descriptor. As a consequence, you can use the class in XML Script. But what happens if the web method that you want to invoke accepts parameters? How can you pass them using XML Script code?

If you look at the type descriptor exposed by the `ServiceMethodRequest` class, you'll see that the class has a property called `parameters`, which is of type `Object`. Here's the property descriptor we're talking about:

```
{name: 'parameters', type: Object, readOnly: true}
```

The property is marked read-only because it returns a reference to a simple object that you can further expand. Whenever you add a property to this object, you add a parameter that will be passed to the web method. The name of the property represents the name of the parameter, and the property's value is the value of the parameter. For example, let's say you've rewritten (or overloaded) the GetTimeAsString method as follows:

```
[WebMethod]
[ScriptMethod(UseHttpGet=true)]
public string GetTimeAsString(string formatString) {
    return DateTime.Now.ToString(formatString);
}
```

The method accepts a single parameter called formatString, which is used to customize the format of the string with the current date. If the instance of the ServiceMethodRequest class is called instance, you can write the following imperative code to pass the formatString parameter:

```
instance.get_parameters().formatString = 'ddd MMM yyyy hh:mm:ss';
```

The previous imperative code can be obtained from the following declarative code:

```
<serviceMethodRequest id="timeServiceMethod"
                      url="DateTimeService.asmx"
                      methodName="GetTimeAsString">
    <parameters formatString="ddd MMM yyyy hh:mm:ss" />
</serviceMethodRequest>
```

You've added a parameters element with the same name of the property that returns the parameters object. At this point, each attribute that follows is added as a property of the exposed object, and its value becomes the value of the property. You can also declare multiple parameters elements, each with attributes that are parsed as properties of the parameters object.

> **NOTE** In the case of the ServiceMethodRequest class, the names of the properties added to the parameters object must match the names and the case of the parameters declared in the web method. Otherwise, an exception will be raised at runtime.

Arrays

A similar notation is used for properties that return arrays. In XML Script, the property is represented, as usual, by a tag with the same name as the property. The difference is that every child element is parsed as an instance of a client object and then added to the array. For example, suppose the client component exposes a property called someArray, which returns a simple array literal. In XML Script, you can write the following code:

```
<someComponent>
    <someArray>
        <label id="myLabel" />
        <textbox id="myTextBox" />
    </someArray>
</someComponent>
```

When this code is parsed, the array returned by the someArray property contains two items: an instance of the Label control and an instance of the TextBox control.

Now, we'll again focus on XML Script features. Our goal was to leverage client actions. So, let's have some fun with them.

11.2.4 *Custom actions*

Creating a custom action is a straightforward process. First, you have to create a client class that derives from the base Sys.Preview.Action class. Then, you must override the performAction method. In this method, you insert the JavaScript code that the action encapsulates.

Let's examine two examples of custom actions. The first example is an action called AlertAction, which wraps a call to the JavaScript alert function that displays a string in a message box onscreen. In listing 11.8, the AlertAction class not only overrides the performAction method but also exposes a custom message property and a type descriptor.

Listing 11.8 Code for the `AlertAction` class

```
Type.registerNamespace('Samples');

Samples.AlertAction = function() {
    this._message;
}
Samples.AlertAction.prototype = {
    performAction : function() {
        return alert(this._message);          ❶ Code to
    },                                            execute

    get_message : function() {
        return this._message;
    },                                         ❷ message
                                                 property
    set_message : function(value) {
        this._message = value;
    }
}
```

```
Samples.AlertAction.descriptor = {
    properties: [  {name: 'message', type: String} ]
}
Samples.AlertAction.registerClass('Samples.AlertAction',
    Sys.Preview.Action);
```

❸ **Type descriptor**

The performAction method ❶ contains the call to the alert function. The string passed to the function is returned by the message property. Because every action is a client component (because the base Sys.Preview.Action class derives from Sys.Component), you need a type descriptor ❸ to use the custom action in declarative code. You only need to describe the unique message property ❷ exposed by the class.

Now, look at listing 11.9, which shows an example use of the Alert action. The example displays a greeting message as soon as the Application object raises its load event.

Listing 11.9   Using the Alert action in XML Script

```
<script type="text/xml-script">
    <page xmlns=http://schemas.microsoft.com/xml-script/2005
          xmlns:cc="javascript:Samples">
      <components>
        <application>
          <load>
              <cc:alertAction message="Hello Xml-script!" />
          </load>
        </application>
      </components>
    </page>
</script>
```

As we explained in section 11.1.5, if the custom component is located in a different namespace than those listed in table 11.1, you should declare a new XML namespace. In the page element, you associate the cc prefix with a URI that contains the namespace to which the component belongs.

The next custom action you'll create extends the existing PostBack action and prompts the user with a confirmation message before triggering the postback of the page. If the user answers Yes, the postback is performed; otherwise, it's aborted. The code is shown in listing 11.10.

Listing 11.10   Code for the `ConfirmPostBack` action

```
Type.registerNamespace('Samples');

Samples.ConfirmPostBackAction = function() {
    this._message;
}
Samples.ConfirmPostBackAction.prototype = {
    get_message : function() {
        return this._message;
    },

    set_message : function(value) {
        this._message = value;
    },

    performAction : function() {
        if(window.confirm(this._message)) {
            return Samples.ConfirmPostBackAction.callBaseMethod(
                ➡this, 'performAction');        Code to
        }                                          execute
    }
}
Samples.ConfirmPostBackAction.descriptor = {
    properties: [ {name: 'message', type: String} ]
}
Samples.ConfirmPostBackAction.registerClass(
    ➡'Samples.ConfirmPostBackAction',
        Sys.Preview.PostBackAction);
```

The `message` property sets the text to display in the confirmation window. The `performAction` method contains the JavaScript code to execute when the action is triggered. You ask the user whether to perform a postback of the page. If the user agrees, you fire the base `PostBack` action by invoking the `performAction` method on the base class. As you learned in chapter 3, this can be done with the `callBaseMethod` method.

Let's write some code to test the new `ConfirmPostBack` action. Listing 11.11 shows how to use the custom action to handle the click of a button element.

Listing 11.11   Using the `ConfirmPostBack` action in XML Script

```
<div>
    <input type="button" id="myButton" value="Click Me" />
</div>

<script type="text/xml-script">
```

```
<page xmlns="http://schemas.microsoft.com/xml-script/2005"
        xmlns:cc="javascript:Samples">
  <components>
    <button id="postBackButton">
        <click>
            <cc:confirmPostBackAction target="postBackButton"
                message="Do you want to perform a postback?" />
        </click>
    </button>
  </components>
</page>
</script>
```

Note that in the `confirmPostBackAction` element, you set the `target` attribute that belongs to the base `PostBackAction` class. Then, you set the `message` attribute, which is mapped to the `message` property of the custom action class. The result is shown in figure 11.6.

Actions are useful to encapsulate and reuse the imperative code needed to perform common tasks in response to events raised by client components. The ability to execute multiple actions in sequence makes it possible to execute big portions of JavaScript code without writing a single line of imperative code.

The next feature we'll introduce is *bindings*, a powerful mechanism for synchronizing the value of two properties. A binding is a relationship between two properties of the same object or of different objects. This relationship is encapsulated by a specialized binding object, which has a fundamental mission: It detects when the value of one property changes and automatically reflects the change on the other property. You saw a binding in listing 11.7, which was about the

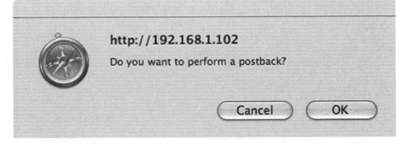

Figure 11.6 The `ConfirmPostBack` action displays a confirmation message onscreen before performing the postback of the page.

`InvokeMethod` action. In the code, a binding was used to synchronize the result property of a `ServiceMethodRequest` instance to the text property of a Label control. You didn't have to write all the JavaScript code required to access one property and set the value of the other one. This is interesting functionality, so let's take a deep breath and examine bindings.

11.3   *Bindings*

Suppose you have a text box and a label in a page, and you want to synchronize the text of the label with the text in the text box. With JavaScript, you would intercept the change event of the text box, and then retrieve its text and set it as the text of the label. This requires writing all the logic for subscribing to the event and accessing the DOM elements involved.

With a binding, the synchronization between the two properties is performed automatically. This is possible because a binding can detect changes in the values exposed by properties. To do that, a binding object relies on a mechanism called *property change notification*, which we discussed in chapter 8.

You can use bindings to create relationships between the properties exposed by client components. As we'll demonstrate in this section, bindings add expressiveness to declarative languages and make it possible to perform complex tasks using only declarative code.

11.3.1   *A simple binding*

To take your first steps with bindings, you'll use one to synchronize the text of a text box with the text of a label. Listing 11.12 has a text box and a `span` element, both associated with the corresponding wrapper controls. Whenever you change the text typed in the text box, the binding automatically updates the text displayed in the label.

> **Listing 11.12   Binding between a text box and a label**

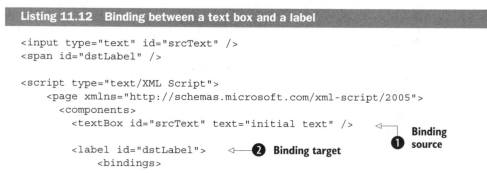

```
<input type="text" id="srcText" />
<span id="dstLabel" />

<script type="text/XML Script">
    <page xmlns="http://schemas.microsoft.com/xml-script/2005">
      <components>
        <textBox id="srcText" text="initial text" />              Binding source ❶
        <label id="dstLabel">       ❷ Binding target
          <bindings>
```

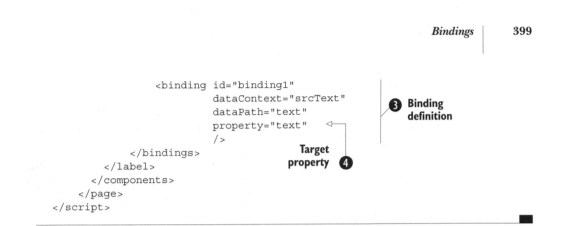

```
               <binding id="binding1"
                        dataContext="srcText"
                        dataPath="text"
                        property="text"
                        />
            </bindings>
          </label>
       </components>
     </page>
  </script>
```

In the code, the binding is declared in a ❶ bindings tag, which is a child node of label. Client components expose a property called bindings, which returns an array with all the bindings hosted in the component. Later, you'll see that bindings can also be defined outside of any components.

NOTE   Client components support bindings only in the Futures CTP. The Sys. Component class as defined in the Microsoft Ajax Library 1.0 doesn't offer support for bindings at the moment.

Bindings are supposed to have a *source* and a *target*. The source is a component that provides some data, and the target is a component that receives the data. Once you've defined the source and the target of a binding, you have to choose which property of the source and which property of the target you want to bind. Whenever the value of the source property changes, the binding takes it and assigns it to the target property. In this way, the two properties remain always synchronized.

In listing 11.12, you declare the binding in the target component ❷, the label. The source component is determined by assigning its id to the dataContext attribute, and the name of the source property is the value of the dataPath attribute ❸. The property attribute ❹ specifies the name of the target property.

If you run the example, the text of the label is set to the text in the text box. This means the binding has been *evaluated* to keep the two properties synchronized. If you modify the text in the text box and then press the Tab key, the binding is re-evaluated because a change in the source property has been detected.

However, life isn't so simple. Bindings in XML Script can be declared outside of any components. They're also able to work the opposite way by swapping the source and the target. They can even work in a bidirectional way. In the following sections, we'll clarify these concepts one by one.

11.3.2 *Binding direction*

In the first example, you saw how to define a binding between the text of a text box (the source of the data) and the text of a label (the target of the data). By doing that, you implicitly defined a *direction* for the binding. Every time the source property is modified, the binding is evaluated and the target property is updated; the data involved in the binding goes from the source property to the target property. Now, let's try the following experiment. In listing 11.12, replace the binding declaration with this one:

```
<binding id="binding1"
        dataContext="txtSource"
        dataPath="text"
        property="text"
        direction="Out" />
```

The declaration is almost the same, but you add a `direction` attribute and set it to `Out`. To complete the experiment, add the following JavaScript block after the XML Script code:

```
<script type="text/javascript">
<!--
    function pageLoad() {
        $find('dstLabel').set_text("Label's text");
    }
//-->
</script>
```

The JavaScript code programmatically sets the label's text when the page is loaded. If you run the example again, you'll discover that this time, the text in the text box is synchronized to the text in the label. Setting the `direction` attribute to `Out` swaps the source and target components of the binding. The `direction` attribute determines the *direction* in which the binding is evaluated.

If `direction` is set to `In` (the default value), the binding listens to changes in the value of the source property. When the value of the property changes, the target property is updated automatically. If `direction` is set to `Out`, the binding listens to changes in the value of the target property and updates the source property accordingly.

The `direction` attribute can be set to a third value, `InOut`, which is called *bidirectional mode*. In this case, the binding listens for changes in both the source and target properties, and updates the other one correspondingly.

Because things have become more complicated, you need a clear view of the other properties of bindings. In the next sections, we'll shed some light on the data path and target properties.

11.3.3 *Target and data path*

When you declare a binding in XML Script, the `dataContext` attribute determines the source component for the binding, assuming the binding direction is set to `In`. The counterpart of the `dataContext` attribute is the `target` attribute, which determines the target component for the binding. If a binding is declared "in" a component—as a child node of the `bindings` element—the component automatically becomes the target of the binding. This is what happens, for example, in listing 11.12, where you declare the binding in the `label` element.

> **NOTE** Data context lets child elements inherit from their parent elements information about the data source used for binding, as well as other characteristics of the binding such as the path. If you bind the parent element to a data source, the child elements automatically inherit the data-source information from the parent control. We'll present an example of declarative data binding in chapter 13.

A binding can also be declared outside of any components. To declare a stand-alone binding, you have to explicitly set the `target` attribute. For example, you can move the binding defined in listing 11.12 outside the `label` and declare it under the `components` node, as shown in listing 11.13.

Listing 11.13   A stand-alone binding

```
<binding id="binding1"
        target="dstLabel"
        dataContext="srcText"
        dataPath="text"
        property="text"
        />
```

Once you've specified the source component of a binding, you use the `dataPath` attribute to reach a particular property in the source component. This can be one of the properties exposed by the source component, but it can also be a property exposed by a child object of the source component. If the child object is a DOM element, you can also reach one of its properties.

To reach a property exposed by a child object of the source component, you can use the traditional dotted notation, as follows:

```
dataPath="childObject.childProperty"
```

The binding object can interpret the previous value in two ways. If `get_childObject` returns a component, then the data path is evaluated as follows:

```
var propertyValueToBind =
    sourceComponent.get_childObject().get_childProperty();
```

If `get_childObject` returns a JavaScript object, the remaining parts are interpreted as properties of the object, and the data path is evaluated like so:

```
var propertyValueToBind =
    sourceComponent.get_childObject().childProperty;
```

The same reasoning applies to the target component. In this case, you obtain the data path for the target component by concatenating the values of the `property` and `propertyKey` attributes. Then, it's evaluated the same way as the value of the `dataPath` attribute.

As a quick example, add the following binding to the `bindings` element in listing 11.2. It binds the background color of the text box to the background color of the `label`:

```
<binding id="binding1"
         target="dstLabel"
         dataContext="srcText"
         dataPath="element.style.backgroundColor"
         property="element"
         propertyKey="style.backgroundColor"
         />
```

In this case, the data paths of both the source and target components are evaluated as follows:

```
var valueToBind = component.get_element().style.backgroundColor;
```

The behavior of a binding changes if you reference a property of a client object or DOM element rather than a property exposed by a client component. Properties exposed by client components can raise the `propertyChanged` event. We discussed this event in chapter 8. Shortly, you'll see that a binding relies on this event to perform the automatic synchronization of two properties.

If the data path references a property of a simple object or of a DOM element, then the binding must be evaluated explicitly to synchronize the values. To better understand the concept of binding evaluation, we need to take a quick look at how bindings work.

11.3.4 *Bindings as components*

Bindings are client components like controls and actions. Specifically, a binding is an instance of the `Sys.Preview.Binding` class. As a consequence, bindings can be instantiated programmatically without necessarily using them in XML Script.

One of the powerful features of bindings is that they can keep two properties synchronized automatically, without the need for you to explicitly evaluate the binding. This can be done thanks to the property notification mechanism discussed in chapter 8. A binding uses the `property-Changed` event exposed by client components to track changes in the values exposed by properties. If a property involved in a binding calls the `raiseProp-`

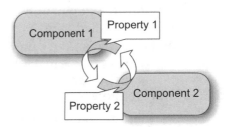

Figure 11.7 Bindings can synchronize the values of two properties of the same or different components.

`ertyChanged` method, the `propertyChanged` event is raised and the binding can detect a change in the value of the property. As a consequence, the change can be propagated to the target property, as shown in figure 11.7. When a property involved in a binding doesn't implement the notification mechanism, the binding must be explicitly evaluated.

Evaluating a binding means synchronizing the values of the bound properties. The evaluation is performed by two methods of the Binding object: `evaluateIn` and `evaluateOut`. The `evaluateIn` method synchronizes the value of the target property to the value of the source property; the `evaluateOut` method does the opposite job. To evaluate the binding in a bidirectional way, you call both the `evaluateIn` and `evaluateOut` methods.

Let's see what JavaScript code is generated when the markup code of a binding is parsed. The following code shows the imperative code corresponding to the stand-alone binding declared in listing 11.13:

```
var binding = new Sys.Preview.Binding();

binding.set_id('binding1');
binding.set_target($find('dstLabel'));
binding.set_dataContext($find('srcText'));
binding.set_dataPath('text');
binding.set_property('text');
binding.set_direction(Sys.Preview.BindingDirection.Out);
```

It's easy to translate the declarative code into imperative code, because of the correspondence that exists between attributes in the markup code and properties of the client component. The `direction` property receives one of the values defined in the `Sys.Preview.BindingDirection` enumeration; this value can be `In`, `Out`, or `InOut`.

So far, we've presented the evaluation of a binding as a process that synchronizes the values of two properties. But the value of the source property can be transformed to obtain the value of the target property. This is done with special functions called *transformers*. A transformer is a function that takes an input value and uses it to produce the output value. As you'll see, bindings can use transformers to obtain the actual value that will be bound to the target property.

11.3.5 Transformers

To illustrate the concept of transformers, look at listing 11.14, which shows an example of a counter built using XML Script. To display the value of the counter, you use a simple Label control. Interestingly, to update the counter's value, you bind the text property of the Label control to itself. Then, you use a transformer that takes the current value of the text property and computes the next value of the counter. Finally, you assign the new value back to the text property.

Listing 11.14   A counter built with XML Script

```
<div>
    <span id="myLabel"></span>
</div>

<script type="text/xml-script">
    <page xmlns:script=
             "http://schemas.microsoft.com/xml-script/2005">
        <components>
          <label id="myLabel" text="0">
              <bindings>
                  <binding id="lblBinding"
                           dataContext="myLabel"
                           dataPath="text"
                           property="text"            ❶ Binding
                           transform="Add"              in label
                           automatic="false"            control
                           />
              </bindings>
          </label>

                                                       ❷ Timer
                                                         component
          <timer id="theTimer" enabled="true" interval="1000">
              <tick>
                  <invokeMethodAction target="lblBinding"  ❸ Evaluate
                                      method="evaluateIn"     binding
                                      />                      manually
              </tick>
          </timer>
        </components>
    </page>
</script>
```

The HTML markup contains a span element, which is associated to the label control in the XML Script code. In the label is a binding ❶ in which the source and the target property are the same. Because the binding is added to the bindings collection of the label, the target is the label itself. In addition, the data context is set to the label control.

The transformer to use is specified in the transform attribute of the binding tag. It's a JavaScript function that handles the transform event that a Binding object raises before setting the value of the target property. This event gives external objects a chance to modify the value of the target property based on the value of the source property. The function that handles the transform event is called the *transformer*.

In listing 11.14, you use the Add transformer, which is one of the built-in transformers available as methods of the Sys.Preview.BindingBase.Transformers object. The Add transformer returns the value of the source property incremented by one. Note that in the binding tag, the automatic attribute is set to false. This means the binding is evaluated only when you explicitly call the evaluateIn or evaluateOut method. The default value for the automatic property is true, which means the binding is evaluated automatically every time a change in one of the properties is detected. In this case, the evaluation method to call is determined by the value of the direction property.

The code introduces a new and useful component: a timer ❷. The timer is an instance of the Sys.Preview.Timer class. The interval attribute specifies the timer's interval, and the enabled property specifies whether the timer should be started as soon as the instance is created. When the timer's interval elapses, a tick event is raised. In listing 11.14, you handle the tick event with an InvokeMethod action ❸ that calls the evaluateIn method of the binding. The new value of the counter is explicitly computed on every tick and then displayed in the label.

The Add transformer is just one of the many built-in transformers available. In the next section, we'll look at the other transformers and show you a couple of tricks and tips. We'll also explain how to create custom transformers and leverage them in XML Script.

11.3.6 *Playing with transformers*

In general, a transformer can behave differently based on the value of two different parameters:

- *The transformer argument*—A parameter you can supply to generate the output value. For example, in the Add transformer, this argument is used to specify the increment value.

- *The binding's direction*—For example, if the direction is set to Out, the Add transformer subtracts the increment value instead of adding it.

To understand how you can tweak a transformer, let's try to replace the binding declared in listing 11.14 with the following one:

```
<binding id="lblBinding"
        dataContext="myLabel"
        dataPath="text"
        property="text"
        transform="Add"
        transformerArgument="2"
        automatic="false"
        />
```

If you run the counter again, you'll see that its value is incremented by 2 on every tick.

Now, let's introduce another built-in transformer called Multiply. In listing 11.14, set the text attribute of the label to 1 and replace the binding with this one:

```
<binding id="lblBinding"
        dataContext="myLabel"
        dataPath="text"
        property="text"
        transform="Multiply"
        transformerArgument="2"
        automatic="false"
        />
```

If you run the example, the counter multiplies the current value by 2, and the factor is determined by the transformerArgument attribute. Like the Add transformer, Multiply behaves differently if the direction of the binding changes. Add the following attribute to the previous binding declaration:

```
direction="Out"
```

Now, the current value is divided by 2 instead of multiplied. The same thing works for the Add transformer. If the binding's direction is set to Out, the input value is decremented by 1 or by the quantity specified in the transformerArgument. Table 11.2 lists the built-in transformers available in the PreviewScript.js file.

Table 11.2   Built-in transformers available in the ASP.NET Futures

Name	Description	Transformer argument	Binding direction
Invert	Performs a Boolean NOT of the input value.	-	In
ToString	Formats the input value into a string. The input value replaces the {0} placeholder.	The format string with a {0} placeholder.	In
ToLocaleString	Same as ToString, but the input value is formatted using the toLocaleString method.	The format string with a {0} placeholder.	In
Add	Adds a number to or subtracts a number from the input value.	The number to add or subtract.	If the direction is In, performs an addition. If the direction is Out, performs a subtraction.
Multiply	Multiplies a number by or divides a number from the input value.	The factor or divisor.	If the direction is In, performs a multiplication. If the direction is Out, performs a division.
Compare	Returns the result of the comparison between the input value and the transformer argument using the identity operator.	The comparand.	In
CompareInverted	Same as Compare, but the comparison is performed with the !== operator.	The comparand.	In
RSSTransform	Parses an XmlDom object with an RSS feed into a DataTable.	-	In

Transformers become powerful when you start creating custom ones. With a custom transformer, new scenarios open, such as performing data binding with declarative code. In chapter 13, you'll see an example of declarative data binding with XML Script. In the next section, you'll learn how to create custom transformers.

11.3.7 *Custom transformers*

A custom transformer is a JavaScript function used to handle the `transform` event raised by a binding object. When the `transform` event is raised, the transformer is called, and the event arguments contain an instance of the `Sys.Preview.Binding-EventArgs` class. This instance contains all the properties you need to compute the transformed value and pass it to the binding. The `BindingEventArgs` class exposes the following methods:

- `get_value`—Returns the value to transform, which is the value of the source property
- `set_value`—Sets the transformed value, which is the value of the target property
- `get_direction`—Returns the value of the binding's `direction` property
- `get_targetPropertyType`—Returns the type of the `target` property
- `get_transformerArgument`—Returns the transformer argument

Creating a custom transformer is straightforward. A transformer retrieves the input value with the `get_value` method and then computes the transformed value based on the binding's direction and the transformer argument. Finally, it calls the `set_value` method, passing the transformed value as an argument.

The code in listing 11.15 shows a custom transformer called `ScrollMessage`, which simulates a simple scroll effect on a string displayed in a label. Believe it or not, you use the transformer from the counter example, thus turning the counter into a scrolling message.

Listing 11.15 A custom transformer that simulates a simple scroll effect

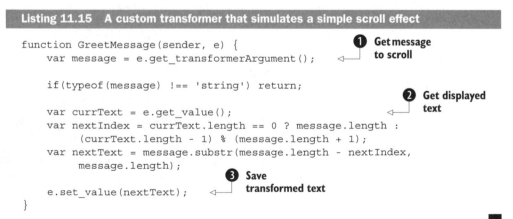

```
function GreetMessage(sender, e) {                    ❶ Get message
    var message = e.get_transformerArgument();  ◁─┘      to scroll

    if(typeof(message) !== 'string') return;
                                                  ❷ Get displayed
    var currText = e.get_value();               ◁─┘    text
    var nextIndex = currText.length == 0 ? message.length :
        (currText.length - 1) % (message.length + 1);
    var nextText = message.substr(message.length - nextIndex,
        message.length);
                             ❸ Save
                               transformed text
    e.set_value(nextText);  ◁─┘
}
```

The `GreetMessage` function is declared with the `sender` and `e` parameters, because it's a handler for the `transform` event. In the code, you retrieve the message to scroll through the `get_transformerArgument` method ❶ and the input value through the `get_value` method ❷. Then, you trim the first letter to obtain the transformed text. The transformed text is saved ❸ by passing it to the `set_value` method.

If you replace the binding in listing 11.14 with the following one, and add the `ScrollMessage` function in a JavaScript code block in the test page, you can see the new transformer in action:

```
<binding id="lblBinding"
         dataContext="myLabel"
         dataPath="text"
         property="text"
         transform="GreetMessage"
         transformerArgument="2"
         automatic="false"
         />
```

11.4 Summary

In this chapter, we introduced XML Script, a powerful declarative language for creating instances of client components. In a manner similar to what happens with ASP.NET markup code, the Microsoft Ajax Library can parse the XML Script contained in a web page, instantiate the client components, and wire them together. With XML Script, you can benefit from many features available to declarative languages and dramatically decrease the quantity of JavaScript code you have to write.

Among the features provided by XML Script are actions, which are objects that encapsulate a portion of reusable JavaScript code. You can use actions to handle events in declarative code without writing a single line of imperative code.

In XML Script, you can also declare bindings. A binding is an object that can synchronize the values of two properties of the same object or of different objects. The synchronization can be performed automatically when a change in the value of a property is detected. Bindings can use transformers to change the value that will be bound to the target property. A transformer is a function that takes an input value and uses it to produce the transformed value.

In the next chapter, we'll talk about the drag-and-drop engine.

Dragging and dropping

12

How many times a day do you move files from one folder to another, between windows, or even directly into the recycle bin, using only your mouse and one of your fingers? Every time you perform these actions, you complete a *drag-and-drop* operation, which is the visual representation of a set of commands. For example, if you move (or *drag*) a file icon from your desktop and release (*drop*) it over the recycle-bin icon, you're visually "throwing away" the file and marking it for deletion (but remember to restore it if you aren't going to delete it!).

Drag and drop is a powerful mechanism that enhances UIs. The introduction of the browser's DOM gave JavaScript developers a chance to implement drag and drop in web pages using CSS and dynamic HTML.

In this chapter, we'll analyze the drag-and-drop engine included in the ASP.NET Futures package. Your goal is to master the client classes used to add drag-and-drop capabilities to DOM elements of web pages. By the end of the chapter, you'll have the skills to develop a drag-and-drop shopping cart using both the client-centric and the server-centric development models. As part of the ASP.NET Futures package, the features illustrated in this chapter aren't currently documented or supported by Microsoft.

12.1 The drag-and-drop engine

The *drag-and-drop engine* is a set of client classes and interfaces for performing drag and drop in web pages. When we say *drag and drop in web pages*, we mean moving DOM elements around the page. You can also simulate the events and effects typical of drag and drop in the operating system. What you can't do with the drag-and-drop engine is interact with external applications or move data between them. But adding drag-and-drop capabilities to DOM elements can improve the user experience and take the web application to the next level.

Before we look at the drag-and-drop engine provided by the Microsoft Ajax Library, you need to enable it in a page. The JavaScript code is located in the PreviewScript.js and PreviewDragDrop.js files, both embedded as web resources in the Microsoft.Web.Preview.dll assembly. Listing 12.1 shows how the ScriptManager control looks after the script files are referenced in the `Scripts` section.

Listing 12.1 Enabling drag and drop in an ASP.NET page

```
<asp:ScriptManager ID="TheScriptManager" runat="server">
  <Scripts>
    <asp:ScriptReference Assembly="Microsoft.Web.Preview"
                         Name="PreviewScript.js"/>
```

```
  <asp:ScriptReference Assembly="Microsoft.Web.Preview"
                       Name="PreviewDragDrop.js"/>
  </Scripts>
  </asp:ScriptManager>
```

The PreviewScript.js file contains the base components needed to use the features of the ASP.NET Futures package. The PreviewDragDrop.js file is the script file that contains the components of the drag-and-drop engine. Once the script files are properly referenced, you're ready to code against the drag-and-drop API.

The elements involved in drag and drop have specific names, depending on their role in a drag-and-drop operation. In general, you have the following:

- *Draggable items*—DOM elements that can be dragged around the page
- *Drop zones* (or *drop targets*)—DOM elements that allow draggable items—that is, other DOM elements—to be dropped onto their area

For example, think of dragging a file over a folder in order to copy or move it. The file icon is the draggable item, and the folder icon is the drop target. Now, let's focus on the architecture of the drag-and-drop engine.

12.1.1 *How the engine works*

Enabling the drag-and-drop engine is just the first step. The engine is responsible for coordinating a drag-and-drop operation and providing information about the elements involved, but you must write part of the logic needed to interact with it. For example, you must inform the engine which elements act as the draggable items and where the drop zones are on the page. You're also responsible for detecting the start of a drag-and-drop operation and taking actions when it ends.

Have no fear: We'll guide you through the process to successfully set up a drag-and-drop–enabled UI. The first step is to represent the draggable items and the drop targets with client components. These components encapsulate the logic needed to deal with the drag-and-drop engine. You associate them with the DOM elements involved in the drag-and-drop operation; so, we'll use the terms *draggable item* and *drop target* to refer to the client components (either controls or behaviors) as well as to the associated DOM elements.

All the components involved in drag and drop must deal with the DragDrop-Manager, a global JavaScript object that is created during the loading of the page and stored in a global variable called `Sys.Preview.UI.DragDropManager`. Although you access the DragDropManager through the same variable, the underlying instance is different depending on the browser that is rendering the page. In

Internet Explorer, the DragDropManager is an instance of the `Sys.Preview.UI.IEDragDropManager` class; in the other supported browsers, you get an instance of the `Sys.Preview.UI.GenericDragDropManager` class. The reason for this difference is that Internet Explorer for Windows, starting with version 5.0, includes a group of drag-and-drop events in its DOM implementation. The `IEDragDropManager` class takes advantage of this API to implement the drag-and-drop engine. Does this mean you face new incompatibilities on the road to drag and drop? No. Despite the browser-specific implementations, the drag-and-drop engine offers the same features on all the browsers supported by ASP.NET AJAX.

Engine overview

To perform a drag-and-drop operation, you need at least a draggable item and a drop target. As we said before, both are DOM elements of a web page. They're also both associated with a client component that encapsulates the logic needed to deal with the DragDropManager.

The first thing a drop target does is register itself with the DragDropManager. It does so by invoking the `registerDropTarget` method of the DragDropManager instance. This way, the drop target tells the DragDropManager that it must consider the associated element a valid drop zone.

Usually, drag and drop in a web page starts when the user holds down the left button (Click on a Mac) on a DOM element and starts moving the mouse. When this happens, the draggable item invokes the `startDragDrop` method of the DragDropManager, signalling that a drag-and-drop operation has started and that the associated element is the source of the operation. This communication is illustrated in figure 12.1.

When the DragDropManager recognizes the draggable items and drop targets involved in drag and drop, it opens a *communication channel* with them. The purpose

Figure 12.1   Draggable items and drop targets communicate with the DragDropManager to participate in a drag-and-drop operation.

is to provide feedback about the progress of the operation. Receivers can use this feedback to determine the status of the operation and to enhance the user experience based on the current state. For example, a draggable item may want to display a semitransparent copy of the element being dragged, near the mouse pointer. A drop target may decide to highlight its area when an element is dragged over it.

To receive feedback from the DragDropManager, draggable items must implement the `Sys.Preview.UI.IDragSource` interface. Drop targets have to implement the `Sys.Preview.UI.IDropTarget` interface. Figure 12.2 shows the bidirectional communication established between the DragDropManager, draggable items, and drop targets.

Without the ability to access data, a drag-and-drop operation would remain just a visual effect. The goal is to obtain a visual representation of a particular *elaboration*. The `IDragSource` and `IDropTarget` interfaces define methods to process the data associated with a drag-and-drop operation, so you can process the data during the phases of the operation. For example, if you drag a file icon over the recycle-bin icon, you want the file marked for deletion. Similarly, if you drag a file over a folder, you expect the file to be copied or moved in that particular folder. You must be able to access and process the file involved in the drag-and-drop operation. The possibility of accessing data during a drag-and-drop operation gives you the entire picture of the drag-and-drop engine, illustrated in figure 12.3.

Now that you know the overall workings of the drag-and-drop engine, it's time to sit at a keyboard and start writing some code. In the next section, you'll implement your first drag-and-drop operation by simulating a basic drag-and-drop shopping cart.

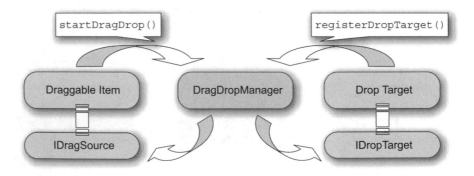

Figure 12.2 Draggable items and drop targets can receive feedback from the DragDropManager through the `IDragSource` and `IDropTarget` interfaces.

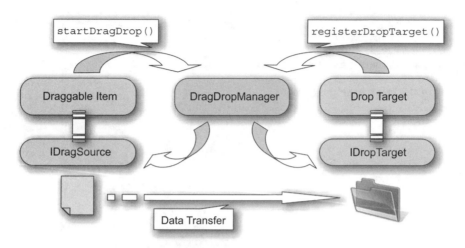

Figure 12.3 **Diagram of the Microsoft Ajax drag-and-drop engine**

12.1.2 *A simple scenario for drag and drop*

Suppose that recently you were promoted to IT Director at your company (it's about time!). As new developers come aboard, you want to make sure they have access to the right tools. To start, you create a shopping list of essential books that each individual needs. This concept is illustrated in figure 12.4, which shows images of a book and a shopping cart. You want to be able to drag the book over the cart to have it added to the list of books to buy. The data transferred can be represented by the book's ISBN code, which is its unique identification number.

Needless to say, you want to implement this scenario with the Microsoft Ajax drag-and-drop engine. To reach this objective, you have to apply what you learned in the previous section about the drag-and-drop engine. You need to code the following:

- *A client control that represents the draggable item, in this case a book*—The associated DOM element can be either the book image or a `div` element that contains the image. The control implements the logic needed to deal with the DragDropManager and receives its feedback by implementing the `IDrag-Source` interface. The control also encapsulates the data that you need to access: the ISBN number.

- *A client control that represents the drop target, in this case the shopping cart*—Again, the associated DOM element can be either the cart image or a `div` element that contains the image. By implementing the `IDropTarget` interface, you can receive the feedback provided by the DragDropManager.

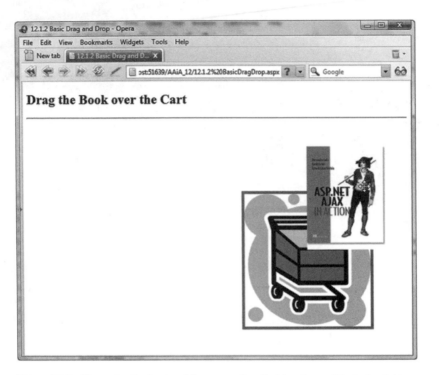

Figure 12.4 Example of a drag-and-drop operation that involves adding a book to a shopping cart

In the following sections, we'll show you how to build these controls and explain the nuts and bolts of the drag-and-drop engine. In the process, you'll write the code in a manner in which it can be reused for different scenarios. Let's start learning how to create a draggable item.

12.1.3 *Creating a draggable item*

When you want to perform drag and drop, you always click an item onscreen—for example, an icon—with the left mouse button (Click on a Mac). Then, you move the mouse and begin dragging. This behavior is also reasonable for DOM elements, and it's the reason you always trigger a drag-and-drop operation by hooking the mousedown event of the draggable DOM element. A draggable item triggers a drag-and-drop operation in the following way:

- It hooks up the mousedown event of the associated DOM element.
- In the event handler, it calls the startDragDrop method on the DragDrop-Manager.

In the following example, you'll create a client control whose associated element can be dragged around the page. The control is called BookItem, and it represents the book in the scenario outlined in the previous section. The code in listing 12.2 contains the logic that every draggable item must implement to deal with the DragDropManager.

Listing 12.2 Code for the BookItem control, which represents a draggable item

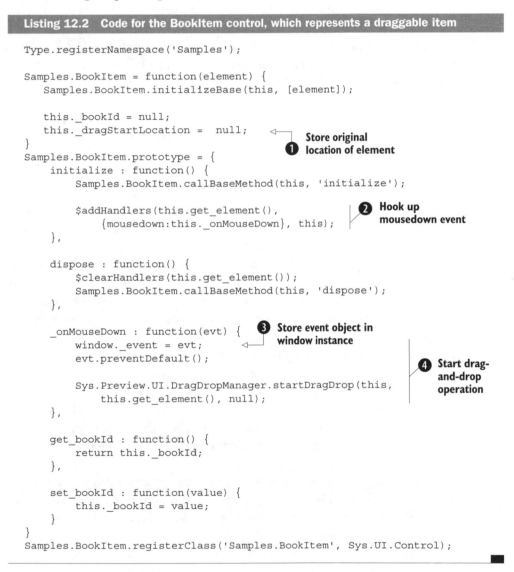

```
Type.registerNamespace('Samples');

Samples.BookItem = function(element) {
    Samples.BookItem.initializeBase(this, [element]);

    this._bookId = null;
    this._dragStartLocation =  null;    ◁─┐   Store original
}                                          ❶  location of element
Samples.BookItem.prototype = {
    initialize : function() {
        Samples.BookItem.callBaseMethod(this, 'initialize');

        $addHandlers(this.get_element(),          ❷  Hook up
            {mousedown:this._onMouseDown}, this);      mousedown event
    },

    dispose : function() {
        $clearHandlers(this.get_element());
        Samples.BookItem.callBaseMethod(this, 'dispose');
    },

    _onMouseDown : function(evt) {   ❸  Store event object in
        window._event = evt;         ◁─    window instance
        evt.preventDefault();
                                                        ❹  Start drag-
        Sys.Preview.UI.DragDropManager.startDragDrop(this,   and-drop
            this.get_element(), null);                       operation
    },

    get_bookId : function() {
        return this._bookId;
    },

    set_bookId : function(value) {
        this._bookId = value;
    }
}
Samples.BookItem.registerClass('Samples.BookItem', Sys.UI.Control);
```

The mousedown event of the associated element is hooked up ❷ in the initial-ize method. In the event handler ❹, _onMouseDown, you call the startDragDrop method of the DragDropManager, passing a reference to the current instance and the associated element as arguments. Note that you store the event object in the window._event property ❸. This is required by the DragDropManager in order to access the event object for the mousedown event.

The _dragStartLocation field ❶ stores the x and y coordinates of the loca-tion of the associated element before it starts being dragged. You save the original location of the element because you may need to restore it if the drag-and-drop operation fails. Later, you'll see how you can establish whether a drag-and-drop operation succeeded or failed.

The key to start a drag-and-drop operation is to call the DragDropManager's startDragDrop method. For this reason, it's important to understand the various parameters accepted by this method.

12.1.4 *The startDragDrop method*

The first argument passed to the startDragDrop method is the drag source, which is the draggable item itself. You'll pass the this keyword, which always points to the current instance of the control.

The second argument is called the *drag visual*, and it's the element that follows the mouse pointer during the drag phase. In the Microsoft Ajax Library, you imple-ment the drag movement by dynamically changing the element's location so it fol-lows the mouse pointer as soon as it's moved in the page area. Typically, the draggable element follows the mouse; this way, you can simulate a dragging effect. It's also possible to specify a different element as the drag visual; this approach is useful if you don't want to drag the associated element but instead drag a semitrans-parent clone. This happens, for instance, when you start dragging one of the icons in your desktop. The icon remains at its original location, and an alpha-blended copy is used during the dragging phase. To keep things simple, in listing 12.1 you pass the associated element as the drag visual; this is the element dragged around the page.

The last argument accepted by the startDragDrop method is a context object. This object is shared by the draggable item and all the registered drop targets. It's supposed to contain references that can be accessed by all the objects involved in a drag-and-drop operation.

Once you make the call to the startDragDrop method, the control officially acquires the role of draggable item. If all goes well, this is all you need to do to drag the associated element around the page. But you want some feedback from the DragDropManager, because it's fundamental to determine the current status of the drag-and-drop operation. Therefore, you need to introduce the IDrag-Source interface. In the next section, you'll implement the interface in the Book-Item control.

12.1.5 *The IDragSource interface*

Draggable items implement the Sys.Preview.UI.IDragSource interface to receive feedback—from the DragDropManager—about the status of a drag-and-drop operation. Table 12.1 lists the methods it defines, along with their descriptions.

Table 12.1   Methods defined in the IDragSource interface

Method	Description
get_dragDataType	Returns the type of data associated with the drag-and-drop operation
getDragData	Returns the data associated with the drag-and-drop operation
get_dragMode	Returns the drag mode
onDragStart	Called when the drag-and-drop operation begins
onDrag	Called whenever the drag visual is dragged
onDragEnd	Called when the drag phase ends

The first method, get_dragDataType, returns an identifier for the type of data you're carrying. When a draggable item is dragged over a drop target, the identifier is passed to the drop target. Based on its value, the drop target can decide whether the draggable item can be dropped. If the dropped item isn't allowed, the drag-and-drop operation fails.

The second method, getDragData, returns the carried data. Usually, the data is encapsulated by the control. As a consequence, a draggable item can return a reference to itself or to its associated element. You can access the component associated with a DOM element through the properties of the element, as we explained in chapter 8. Note that the getDragData method receives the context object that the draggable item passed to the startDragDrop method of the Drag-DropManager, as illustrated in section 12.1.4.

> **NOTE** In the Windows drag-and-drop engine, as well as in the IE's DOM API, drag-and-drop data is stored in a special data object called dataTransfer, which accepts only certain types of data. The Microsoft Ajax drag-and-drop engine mimics this behavior with the concept of data type, although the data object can be a generic JavaScript object. To learn more about the dataTransfer object, browse to: http://msdn2.microsoft.com/en-us/library/ms535861.aspx.

The `get_dragMode` method returns one of the values of the `Sys.Preview.UI.DragMode` enumeration: `Move` or `Copy`. These values define the current *mode* of the drag-and-drop operation, but they aren't associated with a default behavior. It's up to you to write the custom code needed to take concrete actions based on the current mode. As an example, let's consider again a file being dragged over a folder icon. When you drop the file over the folder, the file can be moved or copied depending on the drag mode. In Windows, you can make a choice by using the right mouse button to perform the drag and drop.

The remaining methods, `onDragStart`, `onDrag`, and `onDragEnd`, take actions during the drag phase. Figure 12.5 shows that the `onDragStart` method is invoked as soon as an element begins being dragged. The `onDrag` method is called repeatedly every time the element moves. Finally, the `onDragEnd` method is invoked when the user releases the mouse button. As we'll explain in section 12.1.6, the `onDragEnd` method is the right place to determine whether the drag-and-drop operation succeeded or failed.

Listing 12.3 shows an implementation of the `IDragSource` interface. Add the code to the prototype object of the BookItem control created in listing 12.1. This way, you can participate in the drag-and-drop operation and customize the behavior of the draggable item.

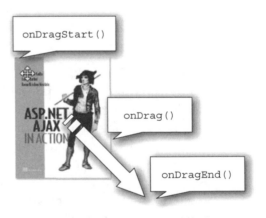

Figure 12.5 You can override the `onDragStart`, `onDrag`, and `onDragEnd` methods of the `IDragSource` interface to take actions during the drag phase.

Listing 12.3 `IDragSource` **interface implementation**

```
get_dragDataType : function() {        ❶ Data
    return '__bookItem';          ◁──    type
},

getDragData : function(context) {  ❷ Drag
    return this.get_element();     ◁──┘ mode
},

get_dragMode : function() {
    return Sys.Preview.UI.DragMode.Move;
},

onDragStart : function() {
    Sys.Debug.trace('Drag and Drop started');

    this._dragStartLocation =                                    ❸ Original
        Sys.UI.DomElement.getLocation(this.get_element());         location of
},                                                                 element

onDrag : function() {
},

onDragEnd : function(cancelled) {
    Sys.Debug.trace('Drag and Drop ended');

    var element = this.get_element();
                                                    Restore
    if (cancelled) {                     original location ❹
        Sys.UI.DomElement.setLocation(element,
            this._dragStartLocation.x, this._dragStartLocation.y);
    }
    else {
        alert('Item dropped! ISBN code: ' + this.get_bookId());
    }
}
}
```

You return __bookItem ❶ as the data type exposed by the BookItem control. You also return the associated element ❷ as the drag data. Because the element is associated with a BookItem instance, you need to access the control property of the DOM element to retrieve a reference to the client control.

In the onDragStart method, you store the original location of the associated element ❸ in the _dragStartLocation field that you declared in the BookItem class. This way, you can restore the original position ❹ if the drag-and-drop operation fails.

The onDragEnd method is the right place to determine the status of the operation. The DragDropManager calls the method with a cancelled parameter that tells you whether the drag-and-drop operation failed. If it did, the cancelled parameter is set to true; otherwise, it's set to false. Based on the value of the cancelled parameter, you can take the appropriate actions. In the example, you display a message with the book's ISBN code if the drag-and-drop operation succeeds. In real-life scenarios, you'll probably invoke a web service or a page method that takes the book's ISBN code and adds the article to the user's shopping cart. In section 12.2, you'll take a similar approach to build a more complex drag-and-drop shopping cart with ASP.NET.

As soon as you embed the code in listing 12.3 in the BookItem's prototype, you must remember to register the IDragSource interface by modifying the call to the registerClass method in the following way:

```
Samples.BookItem.registerClass('Samples.BookItem', Sys.UI.Control,
    Sys.Preview.UI.IDragSource);
```

We're halfway done, so feel free to take a pause before proceeding. The next step is to create a client control that behaves as a drop target. This will be the shopping cart, and it will give us the chance to talk about drop zones and the IDropTarget interface.

12.1.6 *Creating a drop target*

Having a draggable item would be useless without a place to drop it. To complete the implementation of the basic drag-and-drop shopping cart example outlined in section 12.1.2, you need a drop zone. The next task is to create a control that turns the associated DOM element into a drop target. To do that, the control must accomplish a simple task: registering itself as a drop target with the DragDrop-Manager. The registration is usually done in the initialize method, with a call to the DragDropManager's registerDropTarget method. This method accepts a reference to the drop target as an argument and adds it to an internal list held by the DragDropManager.

In the drag-and-drop scenario, the shopping cart will be the drop target. In figure 12.4, the cart is represented by an image element. The client control associated with the image element is called CartZone, and its code is shown in listing 12.4.

Listing 12.4   Code for the `CartZone` class, which represents a drop zone

```
Type.registerNamespace('Samples');

Samples.CartZone = function(element) {
    Samples.CartZone.initializeBase(this, [element]);
}
Samples.CartZone.prototype = {
    initialize : function() {
        Samples.CartZone.callBaseMethod(this, 'initialize');

        Sys.Preview.UI.DragDropManager.registerDropTarget(this);
    },

    dispose : function() {
        Sys.Preview.UI.DragDropManager.unregisterDropTarget(this);

        Samples.CartZone.callBaseMethod(this, 'dispose');
    }
}
Samples.CartZone.registerClass('Samples.CartZone', Sys.UI.Control);
```

As anticipated, the `registerDropTarget` method is called in the `initialize` method, where you perform the control's initial setup. Its counterpart is the `unregisterDropTarget` method, which is used to remove the control from the list of drop targets held by the DragDropManager. It's usually invoked in the `dispose` method, where the cleanup of the current instance is performed.

To receive feedback from the DragDropManager, a drop target must implement the `IDropTarget` interface. Following the same approach we took with the BookItem control, we'll first introduce the interface and then implement it in the CartZone control.

12.1.7 *The IDropTarget interface*

The `Sys.Preview.UI.IDropTarget` interface is implemented by drop targets to receive feedback from the DragDropManager. By implementing this interface, a drop target can determine whether a draggable item can be dropped over its area. You can also take actions based on the position of the draggable item with respect to the drop zone. Table 12.2 lists the methods defined by the `IDropTarget` interface along with their descriptions.

The `get_dropTargetElement` method returns the DOM element that acts as the drop zone. Usually, this is the associated element of the client component that represents the drop target. When an element is being dragged, the DragDropManager calls this method on every registered drop targets. Then, it performs

Table 12.2   Methods defined in the `IDropTarget` interface, which is implemented by drop targets to receive feedback from the DragDropManager

Method	Description
`get_dropTargetElement`	Returns the DOM element that acts as the drop zone
`canDrop`	Returns a Boolean value that tells whether a draggable item can be dropped over the drop zone
`drop`	Called when an element is dropped over the drop zone
`onDragEnterTarget`	Called when an element enters the drop zone
`onDragLeaveTarget`	Called when an element leaves the drop zone
`onDragInTarget`	Called whenever an element is dragged over the drop zone

some calculations to determine whether the element being dragged is overlapping the area occupied by a drop-zone element.

If there is overlap with a drop zone, the DragDropManager calls the `canDrop` method on the drop target to determine whether the draggable item can be dropped over it. The `canDrop` method returns `true` if the drop operation is permitted; otherwise it return `false`.
Typically, the drop target checks whether the data-type identifier passed by the DragDropManager to the `canDrop` method is one of its accepted data types. The value returned by the `canDrop` method affects the status of the drag-and-drop operation. The operation succeeds if the `canDrop` method returns `true`. In turn, this information is propagated to the draggable item through the `cancelled` parameter, as we discussed in section 12.1.5.

As shown in figure 12.6, the `onDragEnterTarget`, `onDragInTarget`, and `onDragLeaveTarget` methods are called when a

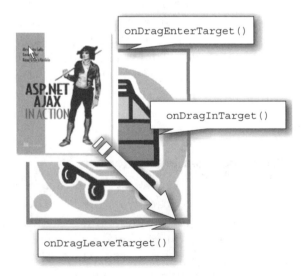

Figure 12.6   The `onDragEnterTarget`, `onDragInTarget`, and `onDragLeaveTarget` methods of the `IDropTarget` interface are called by the DragDropManager when a draggable item overlaps with a drop target.

draggable item enters a drop zone, is dragged in a drop zone, or leaves it, respectively. The drop method is called when an element is dropped over the drop zone, in a manner independent of whether the drag-and-drop operation succeeded or failed.

Listing 12.5 shows an implementation of the IDropTarget interface. As you did for the BookItem class, insert the following code in the prototype object of the CartZone control that you created in listing 12.3.

Listing 12.5 IDropTarget interface implementation

```
get_dropTargetElement : function() {      ❶ Return drop-
    return this.get_element();            zone element
},

canDrop : function(dragMode, dataType, dragData) {
    return dataType == '__bookItem';
},                                        Determine whether draggable
                                          ❷ item can be dropped

drop : function(dragMode, dataType, dragData) {
    Sys.Debug.trace('Item dropped');
},

onDragEnterTarget : function(dragMode, dataType, dragData) {
    this.get_element().style.backgroundColor = '#808080';
},

onDragInTarget : function(dragMode, dataType, dragData) {
},

onDragLeaveTarget : function(dragMode, dataType, dragData) {
    this.get_element().style.backgroundColor = '#FFFFFF';
}
```

In the previous code, the drop zone is the associated DOM element of the CartZone control ❶. A valid drop also happens when a draggable item carries data of type __bookItem. In this case, the canDrop method returns true ❷, and the drag-and-drop operation succeeds.

In the implementation, you also change the background color of the drop zone element as soon as a draggable item enters it. In a similar way, you change the background color to white when the draggable item leaves the drop zone.

When you embed the code in listing 12.5 in the CartZone prototype, don't forget to register the IDropTarget interface by modifying the call to the register-Class method as follows:

```
Samples.CartZone.registerClass('Samples.CartZone, Sys.UI.Control,
    Sys.Preview.UI.IDropTarget);
```

You're nearly done. Implementing drag and drop requires some effort, but in the end you'll have written code that can be easily modified and adapted to the majority of drag-and-drop scenarios. The final step is to wire together DOM elements and client controls to obtain a working example. That's what you'll do in the next section.

12.1.8 *Putting together the pieces*

Drum roll, please: You're ready to test the shopping-cart example. In the code downloadable at http://www.manning.com/gallo, we created an ASP.NET AJAX CTP-enabled website and copied the code for the BookItem and CartZone controls in two separate JavaScript files stored in the ScriptLibrary folder. Then, we created a new ASP.NET page named BasicDragDrop.aspx and referenced the two script files in the `Scripts` section of the ScriptManager control. Finally, we copied the code shown in listing 12.6 in the page's `form` tag.

Listing 12.6 ASP.NET page for testing the drag-and-drop example

```
<img id="imgBook" src="Images/book.gif" alt="" />

<div id="cartZone" class="dropzone">
    <img src="Images/shopping_cart.jpg" alt="" />
</div>

<script type="text/javascript">
<!--
    Sys.Application.add_init(pageInit);

    function pageInit(sender, e)
        $create(Samples.BookItem, {bookId: '1-933988-14-2'}, null,
            null, $get('imgBook'));
        $create(Samples.CartZone, null, null,
            null, $get('cartZone'));
    }
//-->
</script>
```

The code consists of some HTML markup and a JavaScript code block. The markup code contains the DOM elements used to represent the book and the shopping cart. The JavaScript code block contains the `$create` statements needed to instantiate the BookItem and CartZone controls. As you can see, the two controls are wired to the HTML elements that represent the book and the shopping cart. You also set the `bookId` property of the `BookItem` instance to the ISBN code of the book.

As soon as the page is run, you can drag the book image over the shopping cart. If you try to drop the book outside the cart, it returns to its original position. If, on the other hand, you drop the book over the shopping cart, the operation succeeds, and you get a message box displaying the drag data.

You now possess the necessary skills—and code—to add drag-and-drop capabilities to web pages using ASP.NET AJAX. Let's take the drag-and-drop scenario a step further. In the next section, you'll see how to leverage it to take advantage of the ASP.NET server-centric model and data-binding capabilities.

12.2 A drag-and-drop shopping cart

In the previous section, you built the client controls needed to perform drag and drop with DOM elements in a web page. Now, you need to put together client components and server controls to leverage the server-centric development model offered by ASP.NET. With the server-centric model, you can build server controls that are associated with client components. This way, you obtain ASP.NET controls with rich client capabilities. With the techniques studied in chapter 9, it's easy to create an extender or a script control that programmatically instantiates in the page the client component it needs and loads the necessary script files.

In this section, you'll combine server controls and client components to leverage the drag-and-drop scenario introduced in the previous section. The result, shown in figure 12.7, will be a shopping cart system with drag-and-drop support, built with the ASP.NET AJAX Extensions.

The shopping-cart application features a catalog control that lists the books available and a shopping cart control that displays information about the articles you add. The user can add a book to the cart by clicking the Add To Cart button displayed under the corresponding article. The button causes the shopping cart to be updated and to display the title and quantity of each article. You can also drag books from the catalog and drop them in the shopping cart. Once an article is dropped, the shopping cart is updated accordingly. The final touch is using an UpdatePanel control to update the shopping cart asynchronously, without needing to reload the whole page.

The full source code for the example is available for download at http://www.manning.com/gallo, and it's provided as an ASP.NET AJAX-enabled website. We recommend that you look at it and, even better, follow the discussion with the solution opened in Visual Studio. In the following sections, we'll focus on the

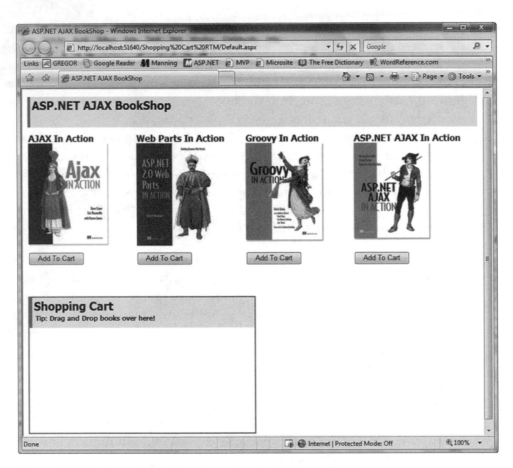

Figure 12.7 The drag-and-drop shopping cart running in Internet Explorer

application design strategies and the drag-and-drop implementation. For these reasons, the listings contain only the relevant portions of the code.

Let's start with an overview of the logical layers that make up the ASP.NET web application. Then, we'll focus on some modifications you need to make to the BookItem and the CartZone controls in order to take advantage of the server-centric model. Finally, we'll concentrate on the Ajax-enabled controls that you'll use to represent the catalog and the shopping cart.

12.2.1 Server-side design

The shopping-cart application is designed as a three-tier application. This means server objects are organized into three logical layers that communicate with one another, as shown in figure 12.8. The presentation layer, at the top, contains the controls responsible for rendering the UI and handling the user's input and interactions. The business layer consists of the server classes that represent the entities involved in the application. In the shopping-cart application, for example, you have a `Book` class that represents a book article. The business objects manipulate and process the data obtained through the data access layer.

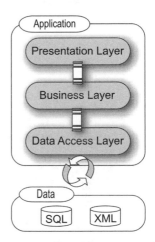

Finally, the data access layer is used to access the data store and to query, retrieve, and update the data. In the example, the data store is an XML file, and the data access layer is responsible for building business objects from the raw XML data. These layers have a uniform view of the data.

Figure 12.8   Structure of a typical layered application. Layers form a chain and can communicate with one another.

NOTE	Designing an application using layers allows for modularity and code reuse. You can find more information about this design pattern by browsing the following URL: http://msdn2.microsoft.com/en-us/library/ms978496.aspx.

Let's see in more detail how we decided to implement the three layers that make up the shopping-cart web application. We made some design decisions with simplicity in mind, because our main goal is to focus on concepts. In real life, production-quality code might require different and more complex strategies.

Data access layer

To keep things simple, we decided to use an XML file as the data store. The XML file contains the catalog's data as a set of book nodes contained into a root book element. Listing 12.7 shows an excerpt from the BookCatalog.xml file, contained in the App_Data folder of the sample website.

Listing 12.7   The XML file used as the data store

```xml
<?xml version="1.0" encoding="utf-8" ?>
<books>
  <book>
    <id>0001</id>
    <title>AJAX In Action</title>
    <imageUrl>~/Images/crane_3d.gif</imageUrl>
  </book>
  <book>
    <id>0002</id>
    <title>iBATIS In Action</title>
    <imageUrl>~/Images/begin_3d.gif</imageUrl>
  </book>
</books>
```

Each book node contains an `id` element with the book ID, a `title` element that contains the book's title, and an `imageUrl` element with the path to the image used in the catalog. Pretty simple, but it's enough for our purposes.

Business layer

The business objects used in the example are a `Book` class and a `Shop-pingCart` class. The `Book` class implements an interface called `IArticle`, which defines a set of properties common to generic articles or the catalog. The `ShoppingCart` class implements the `IShoppingCart` interface, which defines a single method called `Add`, used to add an article to the cart. Figure 12.9 shows the hierarchy of business objects used in the example.

Figure 12.9   Hierarchy of business objects used in the drag-and-drop shopping cart example

To keep things simple, the business objects provider is implemented with a class called `BusinessLayer` that exposes some static methods for accessing the XML file. The `GetBooks` methods returns all the books in the catalog, and the `GetBooksById` method returns the `Book` object corresponding to the given book's ID.

Presentation layer

The presentation layer consists of two web user controls called Shopping-Cart.ascx and BooksCatalog.ascx. The first control encapsulates the HTML and the logic for the shopping cart. In it, a Repeater is bound to a collection of IArticle objects to display the articles in the user's shopping cart. The ShoppingCart.ascx control is an Ajax-enabled control because it's associated with a client component, the CartZone control that you coded in section 12.1.6. It implements the `IScriptControl` interface.

The other control, BooksCatalog.ascx, encapsulates the logic for the catalog. It contains a DataList control bound to the catalog through the `BusinessLayer` class. It's also an Ajax-enabled control because it associates an instance of the client BookItem control built in section 12.1.4 with each item of the DataList. Each item in the catalog becomes a draggable item. For this reason, the BooksCatalog control implements the `IScriptControl` interface.

The application design on the server side is completed, and the next step is to work on the client side. You need to modify the JavaScript code for the BookItem and CartZone controls to take advantage of the ASP.NET data-binding capabilities.

12.2.2 *Client-side design*

The client components used in this example are the BookItem and CartZone controls you built in the first part of the chapter. To take advantage of ASP.NET's data-binding capabilities, we slightly modified the source for the BookItem control and removed the `bookId` property. Because the book's data can be bound to the DataList control that renders the catalog, there's no need to propagate it to the client side. Instead, you need only a reference to the Add To Cart button. Then, all you have to do is click the button programmatically using JavaScript. You don't need to duplicate the code needed to update the shopping cart.

In the BookItem.js file contained in the ScriptLibrary folder, we replaced the `bookId` property with a `_addToCartElement` member that stores a reference to the Add To Cart button. Then, we exposed its value through an `addToCartElement` property:

```
get_addToCartElement : function() {
    return this._addToCartElement;
},

set_addToCartElement : function(value) {
    this._addToCartElement = value;
}
```

The implementation of the `onDragEnd` method changes slightly because you want to programmatically click the Add To Cart button as soon as a book image is dropped over the shopping cart area. The new implementation of the `onDragEnd` method always restores the original location of the book image, because you don't need to leave it over the shopping cart area. The code becomes the following:

```
onDragEnd : function(cancelled) {
    var element = this.get_element();
    Sys.UI.DomElement.setLocation(element,
        this._dragStartLocation.x, this._dragStartLocation.y);

    if (!cancelled) {
        this._addToCartElement.onclick();
    }
}
```

Now that we've discussed the design strategies for the shopping-cart application, it's time to go deep into the code and focus on the server controls and on the data-binding logic. The main objective of the following discussion is to help you understand how the BookItem and CartZone client controls are wired to the catalog and the shopping-cart controls in order to enable drag-and-drop support.

12.2.3 *The ShoppingCart control*

The ShoppingCart control represents a shopping cart. Its purpose is to display a list of the articles added by the user during shopping. This is done with a Repeater control that is bound to a list of IArticle objects, each one representing an article added to the shopping cart. To provide drag-and-drop support, the shopping cart control is wired to an instance of the CartZone client control. It becomes a drop zone where you can drop books dragged from the catalog. Listing 12.8 shows the markup code for the control, stored in the ShoppingCart.ascx template file.

> **Listing 12.8   Code for the ShoppingCart.ascx file**

```
<asp:Panel ID="shoppingCart" runat="server" CssClass="cart">      ◁ ┐  Shopping
    <div class="header">                                              │  cart
        <span>Shopping Cart</span>                                  ❶  container
        <div>Tip: Drag and Drop books over here!</div>
    </div>
    <asp:Repeater ID="repArticles" runat="server">
        <ItemTemplate>
            <div id="article">
                <asp:Label ID="lblQuantity" runat="server">       ❷  Article
                <%# Eval("Quantity") %></asp:Label>                   quantity

                <asp:Image ID="imgArticle" runat="server"
                        Height="32" Width="32"
                        ImageUrl='<%# Eval("ImageUrl") %>'         ❸  Article
                        ImageAlign="AbsMiddle" />                      image
```

```
            <asp:Label ID="lblDescription" runat="server">
                <%# Eval("Description") %></asp:Label>
        </div>
    </ItemTemplate>
  </asp:Repeater>
</asp:Panel>
```

Article description ❹

The `ItemTemplate` of the Repeater contains a Label ❷ that displays the quantity of each book, an Image control ❸ with a thumbnail of the book, and another Label ❸ with the book's title. The containing control, a Panel ❶, defines the layout of the shopping-cart control.

As we said previously, the Repeater is bound to a list of IArticle objects, specifically instances of the Book class. The list is stored in a Session variable which is accessible from the Cart property declared in the ShoppingCart.ascx.cs code-behind file, as shown in listing 12.9. For simplicity, we decided to use a Session variable to store the articles in the shopping cart. In a production scenario, a more robust approach would be to serialize the collection and store it in a database. Nonetheless, using a public property is a good choice to encapsulate the logic that accesses the shopping-cart list, because it can be changed at any time without affecting other parts of the code.

Listing 12.9 Storing shopping-cart articles in a `Session` variable

```
private List<IArticle> Cart
{
    get
    {
        List<IArticle> cart = Session["Cart"] as List<IArticle>;

        if (cart == null)
        {
            cart = new List<IArticle>();
            Session["Cart"] = cart;
        }

        return cart;
    }
}
```

As we anticipated in section 12.2.2, the ShoppingCart class implements the IShoppingCart interface, which defines a single method, Add. This method is used to add an item to the cart, and its implementation is shown in listing 12.10.

Listing 12.10 IShoppingCart interface implementation

```
public void Add(IArticle article)
{
    foreach (IArticle art in this.Cart)
    {
        if (art.Id == article.Id)
        {
            art.Quantity++;
            this.DataBind();
            OnArticleAdd(this, EventArgs.Empty);
            return;
        }
    }

    article.Quantity++;
    this.Cart.Add(article);
    this.DataBind();

    OnArticleAdd(this, EventArgs.Empty);
}
```

The Add method is called with an instance of IArticle as an argument (a Book object in the example). If an article with the same ID is found, the article's quantity is incremented by one. Otherwise, the new article is added to the list and the Repeater control is data-bound again to reflect the latest changes. In the last statement, you call the OnArticleAdd method, which fires an event called ArticleAdd. As you'll discover later, this event is useful when you want to use an UpdatePanel control to refresh the shopping cart without having to embed it in the user control.

IScriptControl implementation

Being an Ajax-enabled control, the ShoppingCart control implements the IScriptControl interface. In chapter 9, we explained that this is required in order to provide a list of script descriptors and script references to the ScriptManager control. In turn, the ScriptManager uses them to load the necessary script files and to generate the $create statement that instantiates the client components associated with the server control. In listing 12.11, you can see how the IScriptControl interface is implemented by the ShoppingCart control.

Listing 12.11 ShoppingCart: `IScriptControl` interface implementation

```
public System.Collections.Generic.IEnumerable<ScriptDescriptor>
    GetScriptDescriptors()
{
    ScriptBehaviorDescriptor desc = new
      ScriptBehaviorDescriptor("Samples.CartZone",
        shoppingCart.ClientID);

    yield return desc;
}

public System.Collections.Generic.IEnumerable<ScriptReference>
    GetScriptReferences()
{
    ScriptReference scriptRef = new
      ScriptReference(Page.ResolveClientUrl(
        ➥"~/ScriptLibrary/CartZone.js"));

    yield return scriptRef;
}
```

In the `GetScriptDescriptors` method, you return a single `ScriptControlDe-scriptor` instance. This instance generates the `$create` statement that wires an instance of the client CartZone control to the shopping cart's `container` element. The ID of the container element is returned by the control's `ClientID` property. Then, the ID is passed as an argument to the constructor of the `ScriptControl-Descriptor` class.

The `GetScriptReferences` method returns an instance of the `ScriptRefer-ence` class that points to the CartZone.js file, located in the ScriptLibrary folder of the sample website. This file contains the code for the CartZone client control and is loaded in the page by the ScriptManager without the need to reference it manually in the markup code.

Now, let's focus on the remaining control: the BooksCatalog user control. The BooksCatalog control is the web user control responsible for rendering the catalog with the available books. You code it as a user control because you can define a template for the UI using declarative code.

12.2.4 *The BooksCatalog control*

The catalog is represented by a Repeater control bound to a collection of Book objects. The list of books is extracted from the XML file that acts as the local data store. As we'll explain in a moment, every item rendered by the Repeater is associated with an instance of the client BookItem control. As a consequence, every catalog item becomes a draggable item and can be dropped over the shopping cart. Listing 12.12 shows the markup code for the control, stored in the BooksCatalog.ascx template file.

Listing 12.12 Markup code for the BooksCatalog user control

```
<asp:DataList ID="listBooks" runat="server"
              RepeatDirection="horizontal"
              CellPadding="5"
              OnItemCommand="listBooks_ItemCommand"
              OnItemDataBound="listBooks_ItemDataBound"
              >
    <ItemTemplate>
        <div class="article">
            <asp:Label ID="lblTitle" runat="server"
              CssClass="title"><%# Eval("Title") %></asp:Label>

            <div class="image">
                <asp:Image ID="imgBook" runat="server"
                           ImageUrl='<%# Eval("ImageUrl") %>'
                           CssClass="draggable" />
            </div>

            <asp:Button ID="btnAddToCart" runat="server"        Add To Cart
                        Text="Add To Cart"                       button
                        CommandName="AddToCart"
                        UseSubmitBehavior="false" />
        </div>
    </ItemTemplate>
</asp:DataList>
```

The Add To Cart button's CommandName property is set to AddToCart. By subscribing to the ItemCommand event of the Datalist, you can intercept the Click event of the button and execute the logic for adding the corresponding article to the shopping cart. To retrieve the book's ID, you store it in the CommandArgument property of the Button control. This lets you retrieve the information about the book on the server side, in the event handler for the ItemCommand event, as shown in listing 12.13.

Listing 12.13   Handling the `ItemCommand` event

```
protected void listBooks_ItemCommand(object sender,
    DataListCommandEventArgs e)
{
    if (e.CommandName == "AddToCart")
    {
        Button btnAddToCart =
            e.Item.FindControl("btnAddToCart") as Button;

        Book book =
            BusinessLayer.GetBookById(btnAddToCart.CommandArgument);

        shoppingCart.Add(book);
    }
}
```

The `GetBookById` method returns the Book object corresponding to the book with the given ID. The book's ID is stored in the `CommandArgument` property of the Add To Cart button.

Note that the BooksCatalog control encapsulates an instance of the Shopping-Cart control. Because the ShoppingCart control implements the `IShoppingCart` interface, the BooksCatalog knows how to call the `Add` method of the shopping cart instance when a book must be added to the cart.

The BooksCatalog control is an Ajax-enabled user control. Therefore, it implements the `IScriptControl` interface. The implementation in listing 12.14 shows how you wire an instance of the client BookItem control to each one of the book images rendered by the DataList encapsulated in the BooksCatalog control.

Listing 12.14   BooksCatalog: `IScriptControl` interface implementation

```
public IEnumerable<ScriptDescriptor> GetScriptDescriptors()
{
    List<ScriptBehaviorDescriptor> descriptors = new
        List<ScriptBehaviorDescriptor>();

    foreach (DataListItem item in listBooks.Items)
    {
        if (item.ItemType == ListItemType.Item ||
            item.ItemType == ListItemType.AlternatingItem)
        {
            Image imgBook = item.FindControl("imgBook") as Image;
            Button btnAddToCart = item.FindControl("btnAddToCart")
                ➥as Button;
```

```
        ScriptBehaviorDescriptor desc = new
          ScriptBehaviorDescriptor("Samples.BookItem",
            imgBook.ClientID);                          ◁─────┐   Client control's
                                                               │   associated
        desc.AddElementProperty("addToCartElement",          ❶  element
          btnAddToCart.ClientID);       ◁────────┐
        descriptors.Add(desc);                    │
      }                                    Client ID of Add
    }                                      To Cart button ❷
    return descriptors.ToArray();
  }

  public IEnumerable<ScriptReference> GetScriptReferences()
  {
    ScriptReference scriptRef = new
    ScriptReference(Page.ResolveClientUrl(
        ➥"~/ScriptLibrary/BookItem.js"));

    yield return scriptRef;
  }
```

The `GetScriptDescriptors` method wires an instance of the BookItem control to
each of the DataList's items, through a `ScriptBehaviorDescriptor` object ❶.
The book image becomes the associated element of the client control, and the client ID of the Add To Cart button ❷ is set as the value of the `addToCartElement`
property of the `BookItem` instance. As usual, the `GetScriptReferences` method
returns the URL of the BookItem.js file, which is saved in the ScriptLibrary folder
of the sample website and holds the code for the BookItem client control.

With the BooksCatalog control, we've completed our overview of the shopping-cart application. We examined its architecture and the client components
that provide the support for drag and drop. Then, we explained how to Ajax-
enable the catalog and the shopping-cart user controls to wire them to the Book-
Item and CartZone client controls. What remains is putting it all together in an
ASP.NET page in order to obtain a full working example.

12.2.5 *Piecing it together*

The Default.aspx page of the sample website is where all the server controls are
wired together. The page hosts the BooksCatalog and ShoppingCart user controls.
Notably, the controls are wrapped by two UpdatePanels declared in the page. This
way, the partial rendering can be controlled globally from the hosting page.

Furthermore, you have a central place to enable or disable the partial-rendering feature. Even if partial rendering is disabled, the shopping cart continues to work by making full postbacks instead of partial ones. The relevant code is contained in the Default.aspx.cs code-behind file and is shown in listing 12.15.

Listing 12.15 Code for the Default.aspx page, which hosts the Ajax-enabled controls

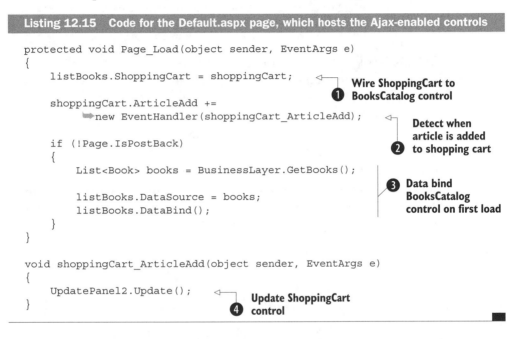

```
protected void Page_Load(object sender, EventArgs e)
{
    listBooks.ShoppingCart = shoppingCart;          ◁─┐  Wire ShoppingCart to
                                                      ❶ BooksCatalog control
    shoppingCart.ArticleAdd +=
        ➡new EventHandler(shoppingCart_ArticleAdd);  ◁─┐ Detect when
                                                          article is added
                                                      ❷ to shopping cart
    if (!Page.IsPostBack)
    {                                                    ┌─ Data bind
        List<Book> books = BusinessLayer.GetBooks();  ❸  BooksCatalog
                                                          control on first load
        listBooks.DataSource = books;
        listBooks.DataBind();
    }
}

void shoppingCart_ArticleAdd(object sender, EventArgs e)
{
    UpdatePanel2.Update();    ◁─┐ Update ShoppingCart
}                             ❹ control
```

In the Page_Load method, you wire the BooksCatalog control ❶ with the ShoppingCart control. This enables the BooksCatalog control to call the Add method of the ShoppingCart instance when needed. Then, you subscribe to the ArticleAdd event ❷ raised by the ShoppingCart control whenever an article is added to the cart, as shown in listing 12.8. In the event handler ❹, you manually update the UpdatePanel that wraps the ShoppingCart control, to display the updated cart. This is necessary because the Repeater in the ShoppingCart control is automatically data bound every time an article is added to the shopping cart. Finally, when the page is loaded for the first time, you initialize the catalog by getting the list of books and binding it to the BooksCatalog control ❸.

12.3 Summary

The ASP.NET Futures CTP provides a drag-and-drop engine that you can use to add drag and drop to web pages. Typically, drag and drop in web pages is implemented with draggable items (DOM elements that can be dragged around the page) and drop targets (elements that allow draggable items to be dropped onto their area).

You can easily implement draggable items and drop targets as Microsoft Ajax components that implement the IDragSource or IDropTarget interface in order to receive feedback from the DragDropManager, a global JavaScript object that coordinates a drag-and-drop operation.

In this chapter, you've seen how to implement a scenario involving a drag-and-drop shopping cart. In the first example, you implemented it using a pure client-centric model. Then, you took advantage of the data-binding capabilities of ASP.NET server controls and implemented the scenario using a server-centric model.

In the next chapter, you'll see how to implement common Ajax patterns with ASP.NET AJAX.

Part 4

Mastering ASP.NET AJAX

You've come to the end of the book, and you possess a deep knowledge of ASP.NET AJAX. It's time to apply your skills to implement some of the most common Ajax patterns. Part of chapter 13 is dedicated to implementing development patterns, such as writing debug versions of JavaScript files. The rest of the chapter shows how to implement patterns such as unique URLs, widgets, and client-side data binding. In this chapter, you'll combine the client-centric and server-centric models and use both the ASP.NET AJAX 1.0 features and the ASP.NET Futures.

13

Implementing common Ajax patterns

In this chapter:

- Guidelines for developing debug and release versions of script files
- Helpers for automating the creation of client properties and events
- Unique URLs and logical navigation
- Declarative data binding
- Declarative widgets

Ajax applications have changed the way users interact with web pages. With Ajax, you can process a form in the background and eliminate page refreshing. In this way, the user interface remains responsive while input is being processed. Eventually, developers realized that Ajax introduced the need to handle new development scenarios. For example, how do you keep the user informed about what's happening in the background? What's the best strategy to perform data access on the client side?

To use Ajax, we need to develop new design patterns for web pages. Many patterns have been defined and catalogued, and many are being defined every day, as developers continue to experiment with Ajax and use it in production scenarios.

Covering every Ajax pattern would require a dedicated book, but we discussed some patterns in previous chapters. In this final chapter, we've picked some more patterns and implemented them with ASP.NET AJAX. The first half of the chapter explores coding patterns and how they help you write JavaScript code that is easier to debug and maintain. Then, we'll address the problem of the broken Back button. Finally, we'll show you how to implement client-side data binding and how to build draggable widgets using features available in the ASP.NET Futures package.

13.1 Script versioning

Embracing Ajax as your primary development technique for web applications involves writing a lot of JavaScript code. Many tasks that were previously accomplished on the server side can now be performed using JavaScript on the client side. As a consequence, the script files get bigger as you add functionality to a web application. In addition, client objects are often responsible for performing data access, as well as elaborating the results and displaying data to the user. For this reason, debugging the client code becomes a necessary and fundamental task for every Ajax developer.

In chapter 2, we discussed client-side debugging and mentioned a feature of ASP.NET AJAX called *script versioning*. Thanks to script versioning, you can have debug and release versions of the same JavaScript file. In the following sections, we'll present guidelines for how to write the JavaScript code in the debug version of a script file. This will greatly improve your debugging experience and let you easily debug client code using one of the tools available, such as those discussed in appendix B.

13.1.1 *Getting informative stack traces*

When you want to define a method in a JavaScript object, you usually do so by assigning a function to a property of the object. Recall from chapter 3 that functions assigned to properties of an object can be invoked using the name of the property. For this reason, there's no need to specify a name for the function, which can be declared anonymous. You can see this in listing 13.1, which defines a Person class using the Microsoft Ajax Library:

> **Listing 13.1   Using anonymous functions to declare methods of an object**

```
function Person() {
    this._name = '';
}
Person.prototype = {
    get_name : function() {
        return this._name;
    },

    set_name : function(value) {
        this._name = value;
    }
}
Person.registerClass("Person");
```

In this listing, the functions assigned to the get_name and set_name properties have no name: They're anonymous functions. This isn't a big deal, because you can invoke the function through the name of the property:

```
var person = new Person();
person.set_name('Joe');
```

As a consequence, omitting the function names reduces the code size and makes it more readable. On the other hand, there's a price to pay. For example, a debugger can't prompt an informative stack trace if the code fails in an anonymous function. As a consequence, the stack trace will show a series of calls to functions with blank names, as in figure 13.1. This isn't what we would call a helpful debugging experience.

To work around this problem, you can take advantage of the script-versioning technique provided by the Microsoft Ajax Library. You need to build a debug version of the script file where all the functions are declared with a name. This makes

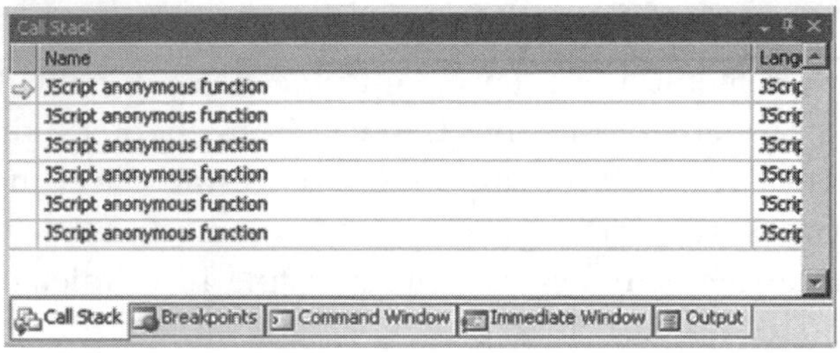

Figure 13.1
**The Call Stack window of
the Visual Studio Debugger**

the code more verbose and less readable, but you can inspect the stack trace in your favorite JavaScript debugger with a simple two-step process:

1 Declare all the functions as global named functions in the debug version of the script file.

2 In the `prototype` object, define an alias for the corresponding function.

Listing 13.2 shows how the client `Person` class looks if you take this approach.

Listing 13.2   A debug version of the `Person` class

```
function Person$get$name() {
   return this._name;
}

function Person$set$name(value) {
   this._name = value;
}

function Person() {
   this._name = '';
}
Person.prototype = {
   get_name : Person$get$name,

   set_name : Person$set$name
}
Person.registerClass("Person");
```

The instance methods are first defined as global named functions. To better recognize the constructor to which they belong, you concatenate the constructor name with the name of the method, using a $ character. This is the same approach used in the debug versions of the Microsoft Ajax Library files, but you're free to leverage your preferred naming technique. Finally, the functions are referenced

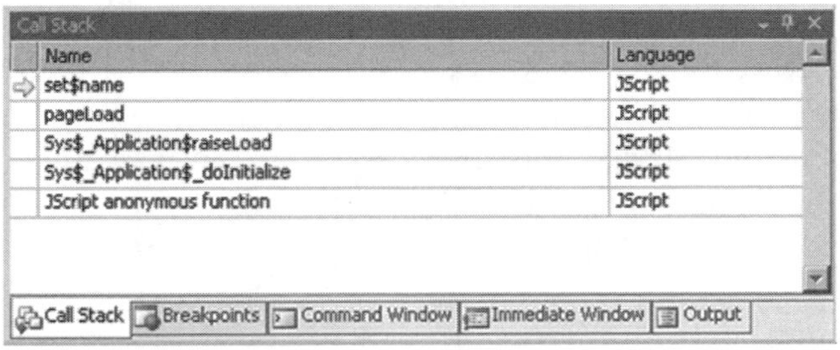

**Figure 13.2
Using named functions in the
debug version of a script file
lets you display a more
informative stack trace.**

in the prototype object of the Person constructor by assigning them to the
get_name and set_name properties. Methods are invoked in the same way as
before, but a debugger can display a more informative stack trace, as shown in figure 13.2.

> **NOTE** You may wonder why you need to declare the instance methods as global
> functions. Couldn't you assign a name to the functions in the prototype
> object? Although the majority of ASP.NET AJAX supported browsers
> would be happy, at present the Safari browser would complain and refuse
> to parse the code.

Now that you know how to obtain a more informative stack trace, the second technique that we'll illustrate involves adding comments to the code. As we'll see, the
Microsoft Ajax Library allows commenting the JavaScript code using a syntax similar to the one supported by the C# and VB.NET languages.

13.1.2 *XML comments in JavaScript code*

Often, you can distinguish between good and poorly written code by looking at
comments. If code is well commented, developers who consume it get a clearer
vision of the coder's work. As result, they can read, use, and maintain it without
much effort. Shipping uncommented code can reward developers—even those
who wrote the code—with daily headaches.

Beside the good old inline comments, languages such as C# and VB.NET let
you document classes and their properties, methods, and events. You do so with
an XML syntax that can be added before the declaration of a class or one of its
members. Tools can then generate documentation based on these comments. For
example, the IntelliSense tool in Visual Studio can use this documentation system
to generate documentation on the fly, as soon as you type the code.

The Microsoft Ajax Library provides a similar technique on the client side, letting you add comments to JavaScript classes, properties, and methods. In a way

similar to what happens with server-side classes, XML comments enable the use of the IntelliSense tool even in custom Java-Script files, with custom JavaScript objects. Figure 13.3 shows how the new IntelliSense works in a JavaScript file, in the new version of Visual Studio (code-name Orcas).

To see how XML comments work in JavaScript, listing 13.3 shows how you can add comments to the Person class defined in listing 13.1, with the help of the Microsoft Ajax Library.

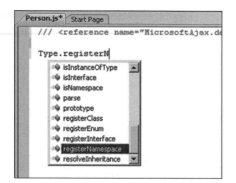

Figure 13.3   The IntelliSense tool in Visual Studio Orcas can show properties of JavaScript objects.

Listing 13.3   Adding XML comments to a JavaScript client class

```
function Person() {
    ///<summary>
    ///This class describes a person.
    ///</summary>

    this._name = '';
}
Person.prototype = {
    get_name : function() {
        ///<summary>
        ///Returns the name of the person.
        ///</summary>

        return this._name;
    },

    set_name : function(value) {
        ///<summary>
        ///Sets the name of the person.
        ///</summary>
        ///<param name="value" type="String">
        ///The name of the person.
        ///</param>

        this._name = value;
    }
}
Person.registerClass("Person");
```

Notice that you can add XML comments in a constructor, a property, or a method declaration. This is different from what happens on the server side, where XML comments are added outside an entity declaration. Other than this difference, the syntax used for the client-side comments is similar to that leveraged by the .NET framework on the server side.

NOTE You can find a description of the XML tags available in the .NET framework documentation engine at http://msdn2.microsoft.com/en-us/library/b2s063f7.aspx.

The example uses the `summary` tag to provide a description of the client class and its method. The `get_name` and `set_name` methods are the getter and setter for the client `name` property. Note that in the setter, a `param` tag describes the parameter accepted by the `set_name` method. The attributes of the `param` tag are the same as those used in parameter descriptors, which we'll discuss in section 13.1.4.

Figure 13.4 shows how the XML comments added to the `Person` class enhance the coding experience thanks to the new IntelliSense features available in Visual Studio Orcas.

Before we complete our discussion of how to take advantage of script versioning, let's see how you can enhance the debug version of a script file by performing validation on the parameters passed to JavaScript methods.

13.1.3 *Validating function parameters*

JavaScript doesn't perform any kind of validation on the parameters passed to a method. Despite what happens in strongly typed languages like C# or VB.NET, where checks are performed at compile time, there's no guarantee that the parameters you receive in a method are of the expected type. There could also be fewer or more than the expected number.

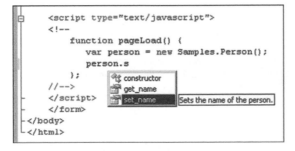

Figure 13.4
XML Comments added to custom JavaScript objects are used by the IntelliSense tool in Visual Studio Orcas.

For example, consider a JavaScript function called add, which is supposed to return the sum of the two arguments it accepts:

```
function add(a, b) {
    return a + b;
}
```

If the parameters a and b are numbers, everything goes as expected. But what happens if you pass strings instead of numbers? In this case, the + operator is interpreted as the string-concatenation operator, and the function returns the string resulting from the concatenation of the strings passed as arguments. The function's code doesn't raise any errors; it just returns an unexpected result. Finally, if you pass arbitrary arguments to the function, such as a Boolean and a string, a JavaScript error is raised at runtime.

Even if you can't prevent runtime errors from being raised, you can detect errors in the method and avoid returning unexpected results. An interesting feature introduced by the Microsoft Ajax Library is the ability to validate the parameters passed to a method. You can perform parameter validation through a method called Function._validateParams.

WARNING   Because Function._validateParams is declared as a private method, we feel the need to add a disclaimer that says "use at your own risk." Used properly, this method can be a great help in some scenarios. We hope that the Function._validateParams method will become a publicly accessible method in the next release of the Microsoft Ajax Library.

To illustrate how the method works, let's rewrite the add function to ensure that you operate on the right parameter types (see listing 13.4).

Listing 13.4   Validating the parameters passed to a JavaScript function

```
function add(a, b) {
    var e = Function._validateParams(arguments,
      [
        {name:"a", type:Number, mayBeNull:false, optional:false},
        {name:"b", type:Number, mayBeNull:false, optional:false}
      ]
    );

    if(e) throw e;

    return a + b;
}
```

The `Function._validateParams` method is called just after the function declaration, and its result is stored in the e variable. The first argument passed to the method is a variable called `arguments`; This is a special variable defined by JavaScript and accessible only in a function. The `arguments` variable holds a list of all the arguments passed to the function.

The first argument passed to `Function._validateParams` is the list of method parameters to validate; these are the parameters passed to the add function when it's called. The second argument passed to `Function._validateParams` is an array containing two objects that act as parameter descriptors. Note that parameter descriptors are associated with method parameters in the same order they're stored in the `arguments` variable: The first descriptor is associated with the first parameter passed to the function, and so on.

Each descriptor describes a particular parameter by specifying a list of requirements that it must meet. These requirements are represented by properties of the object. For example, look at the first parameter descriptor supplied:

```
{name:"a", type:Number, mayBeNull:false, optional:false}
```

The `name` property contains a string with the parameter name. If the validation fails, you can access the name of the parameter through the `Error` object. The second property, `type`, puts a constraint on the type of the parameter. In this case, you mandate that the a parameter is of type `Number`. The third property, `mayBeNull`, determines whether you can pass `null` as the value of the argument. If the property is set to `false`, you can't pass `null` as the value for the a parameter. The last property, `optional`, specifies whether the parameter is mandatory. If you set the property to `false`, the caller must supply at least one parameter, because you're dealing with the first parameter descriptor.

The properties illustrated in the previous example aren't the only ones available. Table 13.1 lists the properties you can declare in a parameter descriptor.

Table 13.1   Properties used in parameter descriptors

Property	Description
`type`	The expected type of a parameter. The possible values are `String`, `Number`, `Array`, `Function`, and `Object`.
`mayBeNull`	If `true`, the parameter can be `null`.
`optional`	If `true`, the parameter can be omitted.
`integer`	If the parameter is a `Number`, specify if it must be an integer.

Table 13.1   Properties used in parameter descriptors *(continued)*

Property	Description
elementType	If a parameter is an `Array`, specify the expected type for its elements. The possible values are the same as for the `type` property.
elementMayBeNull	If a parameter is an `Array`, specify if it can contain `null` elements.
elementInteger	If a parameter is an `Array`, specify if its elements are integers.
domElement	If `true`, the parameter must be a DOM element.

As we said previously, the return value of `Function._validateParams` is stored in the e variable. If the validation fails, the e variable contains an Error object with the information about the parameter that caused the error. The second statement in the add function in listing 13.4 raises a client exception if the validation fails:

```
if(e) throw e;
```

If the validation succeeds, `Function._validateParams` returns `null`, and the code in the body of the method is executed normally.

The `Function._validateParams` method is considered private because the name of the function starts with an underscore, which is a convention used by JavaScript developers to denote a function or member with private scope. The method is used internally by the Microsoft Ajax Library to help debug script files by validating the parameters passed to a method on every call. All calls to the `Function._validateParams` method are present only in the debug versions of the Microsoft Ajax Library files and are removed when in release mode.

This is done because the validation procedures are expensive in terms of statements executed. For example, validating the parameters of a method that is 5 statements long can result in 100 statements being executed at runtime, due to the execution of the internal validation routines. Abusing this function can result in a significant performance drop.

However, the `Function._validateParams` function and all its associated internal methods are defined in the release version of the library files. In the next section, we'll discuss a couple of scenarios for using parameter validation in production code.

13.1.4 *Parameter validation in production code*

Using the `Function._validateParams` method to validate parameters whenever a function is called is expensive in terms of performance. You should use this method only in the debug versions of script files; but in a couple of scenarios, this method can be useful in production code.

The first scenario involves type checking at runtime. Suppose you want to create a dynamic array that accepts only strings. On the server side, you have strongly typed collections to accomplish this task. On the client side, you can achieve something similar is by using `Function._validateParams` as shown in listing 13.5.

Listing 13.5 A StringCollection object in JavaScript

```
Type.registerNamespace('Samples');

Samples.StringCollection = function() {
    this._innerList = [];
}
Samples.StringCollection.prototype = {
    add : function(value) {
        var e = Function._validateParams(arguments,
          [
            {name: "value", type:String, mayBeNull:false,
              optional:false}
          ]);

        if(e) throw e;

        this._innerList.push(value);
    }
}
Samples.StringCollection.registerClass("Samples.StringCollection");
```

You create a StringCollection object that wraps a JavaScript array. You want to allow only strings to be added to the array. To do that, call the `Function._validateParams` method in the `add` method, which is used to add an element to the collection. The parameter descriptor for the `value` parameter mandates that it's of type `String`, and not `null`; and the `value` parameter can't be omitted. This ensures that only strings are added to the inner array. For simplicity, the code in listing 13.5 contains a single `add` method, but you can add more methods to simulate strongly typed collections in JavaScript.

Another interesting use of the `Function._validateParams` method ensures that required references are set before the initialization of a client component. In listing 13.6, the `Function._validateParams` method is used in the `initialize` method of a SomeControl control that is supposed to hold a reference to a DOM element called `childElement`. You ensure that the reference has been set correctly (for example, through a property) before the control is initialized.

Listing 13.6 Validating references in the initialization code

```
Samples.SomeControl.prototype = {
  initialize : function() {
    Samples.SomeControl.callBaseMethod(this, 'initialize');

    var e = Function._validateParams(
      [this._childElement],
      [
        {name:"childElement", mayBeNull:false, optional:false,
          isDomElement:true},
      ]);

    if(e) throw e;

    // Initialization code continues here.
  }
}
```

The reference stored in the _childElement field is validated using the Function._validateParams method. To validate a DOM element, the corresponding parameter descriptor has the isDomElement property set to true. If the validation succeeds, you can safely execute the initialization code for the control.

Let's continue discussing production code. In production, the script files are usually served to browsers using various kinds of network connections. To achieve a reasonable loading time even with slow clients, you need to minimize the size of the script files downloaded by the browser. Even if the browser can cache script files, you must seriously take into account first-time loading and empty caches. There's no point in forcing users to wait while a script file is being downloaded just because you added 10 KB of XML comments that users will never see. In the following section, you'll learn how to reduce the loading times of script files served using the ASP.NET AJAX ScriptResource handler.

13.1.5 Compressing and crunching script files

With ASP.NET AJAX, you can take advantage of the compression and crunching capabilities provided by the ScriptResource.axd HTTP handler. This handler is responsible for serving the JavaScript files embedded as web resources in separate assemblies. When a script file is requested through the handler (for example, by loading it through the ScriptManager control), the file is compressed and crunched before being sent to the browser. *Crunching* is the process of stripping all the comments and whitespace from the script file, to reduce its size. With compression, size is further reduced thanks to compression algorithms.

To activate compression and crunching, you have to modify some attributes in the website's web.config file. You do this by inserting the following code in the system.web.extensions element of the web.config file:

```
<system.web.extensions>
  . . .
  <scripting>
    <scriptResourceHandler enableCompression="true"
      enableCaching="true" />
  </scripting>
  . . .
</system.web.extensions>
```

You need to set the enableCompression attribute of the scriptResourceHandler element to true if you want to activate compression of script files served through the ScriptResource.axd HTTP handler. You can also set to true the enableCaching attribute if you want to cache the served script files in the browser.

The techniques illustrated so far should be used when you're developing debug and release versions of script files. In a debug configuration, it's a good choice to pay the price of an increased file size and slower performance to take advantage of stack traces, XML comments, and parameter validation. When you're dealing with production code, your goals should be obtaining the fastest possible code and decreasing file sizes as much as possible.

Let's move to other kinds of coding patterns. Our next objective is showing what you gain and what you lose when you decide to tweak the Microsoft Ajax Library to automate common programming tasks.

13.2 *Helpers, help me help you!*

Ajax applications usually need to download a significant number of kilobytes of JavaScript code to the browser. Even if the browser's cache can speed up the loading time of an Ajax-enabled web page, size matters for script files. Shorter script files lead to faster loading times, especially when you visit a website for the first time.

In the previous section, we explained how to take advantage of compression and crunching when you use ASP.NET AJAX to serve script files. In this section, you'll further decrease the size of your JavaScript files by extending the Microsoft Ajax Library. The objective is to reduce the quantity of JavaScript code needed to perform common tasks when creating client objects. You'll write two *helpers* (methods that help you perform a particular task) for declaring properties and events in JavaScript objects using a single statement. The rewards will be increased productivity, shorter script files, and a lot of saved keystrokes.

13.2.1 *Automating the declaration of properties*

If you read chapter 3, you should be aware that you can expose properties in Java-Script objects. Properties are nothing more than methods that act as the getter and setter for a particular value stored in an object. If you look at some of the listings in this book, you'll notice that declaring a property is expensive in terms of lines of code written. This is true especially when you use properties to expose the value of private members without performing any additional logic. This situation is shown in listing 13.7, which reports the code for a property called `someProperty`, declared in the prototype of a client class called `someClass`.

Listing 13.7   A simple property declared in a client class

```
someClass.prototype = {
    get_someProperty : function() {
        return this._someMember;
    },

    set_someProperty : function(value) {
        this._someMember = value;
    }
}
```

Although declaring a single property has no impact on the size of a script file, in some situations an object exposes many properties. This can be a concern because the size of the script can increase significantly.

Let's automate the process of declaring a simple property like the one shown in listing 13.7. The goal is to both reduce the size of the resulting script and save precious keystrokes. Listing 13.8 shows the code needed to declare a helper method called `createProperty`, which performs this task.

Listing 13.8   Code for automating the creation of a simple property

```
Type.prototype._createGetter = function(fieldName) {
    return function() {
        return this[fieldName];
    }
}

Type.prototype._createSetter = function(fieldName) {
    return function(value) {
        this[fieldName] = value;
    }
}
```

```
Type.prototype.createProperty = function(propName) {
    var fieldName = '_' + propName;

    var getter = this._createGetter(fieldName);

    var setter = this._createSetter(fieldName);

    this.prototype['get_' + propName] = getter;
    this.prototype['set_' + propName] = setter;
}
```

The previous code extends the Microsoft Ajax Library by adding functions to the Type.prototype object. As we explained in chapter 3, Type is an alias for the built-in Function object. Because client classes are JavaScript functions, you're providing new static methods to all the client classes.

The first two methods, _createGetter and _createSetter, are supposed to be private methods used by the createProperty helper. Their purpose is to return a closure with the code for the property's getter and setter. *Closures* are functions that can be bound to the local variables of the parent functions in which they're declared, as we explained in section 3.1.3.

You declare a property with the createProperty method. It calls the _createGetter and _createSetter methods and assigns the returned functions to the prototype of the client class from which you call createProperty. Note that it's not necessary to declare a private field in the constructor; the helper creates the field by adding an underscore character to the property name. Finally, the getter and setter methods are added as properties of the prototype object using the naming convention for properties introduced in section 3.3.3.

With the new createProperty method, adding properties to a class is easy. Listing 13.9 demonstrates by declaring a class called Samples.Customer that exposes three properties: fullName, address, and city.

Listing 13.9 Creating client properties with the `createProperty` method

```
Type.registerNamespace("Samples");

Samples.Customer = function() {
}
Samples.Customer.createProperty("fullName");
Samples.Customer.createProperty("address");
Samples.Customer.createProperty("city");

Samples.Customer.registerClass("Samples.Customer");
```

Properties are declared after the `Samples.Customer` constructor by calling the `createProperty` method on the constructor. The `createHelper` method accepts a string with the name of the property as an argument. As we mentioned previously, an interesting side effect of `createProperty` is that private fields are implicitly created by the `_createSetter` function when the following statement is executed:

```
this[fieldName] = value;
```

In this case, trying to access the `fieldName` variable on the current instance causes the field to be created if it doesn't exist. By convention, private fields are created by prefixing the name of the property with the underscore character.

You've reached your first goal toward reducing the number of statements in a JavaScript file. With the `createProperty` method, you can declare a private field and the corresponding property with a single statement. Now, it's time to automate the creation of client events.

13.2.2 *Automating the creation of events*

In section 3.7, we explained how to expose events in client objects. Recall that exposing an event requires writing methods for adding and removing an event handler, as well as a method for raising the event. This significantly increases the number of statements required to declare a single event in a client object. In chapter 3, you mitigated this issue by declaring a single method that can raise a generic event, given the event name and the event arguments.

In this section, you want to expose a client event using a single JavaScript statement. You'll create a helper method called `createEvent`, in a manner similar to what you did in the previous section with the `createProperty` method. Let's start by looking at the code, which is shown in listing 13.10.

> **Listing 13.10   Automating the creation of a client event**

```
Type.prototype._createAddHandler = function(eventName) {
    return function(handler) {
        this.get_events().addHandler(eventName, handler);
    }
}

Type.prototype._createRemoveHandler = function(eventName) {
    return function(handler) {
        this.get_events().removeHandler(eventName, handler);
    }
}
```

```
Type.prototype.createEvent = function(eventName)
{
    var addHandler = this._createAddHandler(eventName);
    var removeHandler = this._createRemoveHandler(eventName);

    this.prototype['add_' + eventName] = addHandler;
    this.prototype['remove_' + eventName] = removeHandler;

    if(!this.__events) {
        if(!this.inheritsFrom(Sys.Component)) {
            this.prototype.get_events = function() {
                if (!this._events) {
                    this._events = new Sys.EventHandlerList();
                }

                return this._events;
            }
        }

        this.prototype._raiseEvent = function(
                      eventName, eventArgs) {
            var handler = this.get_events().getHandler(eventName);

            if (handler) {
                if (!eventArgs) {
                    eventArgs = Sys.EventArgs.Empty;
                }

                handler(this, eventArgs);
            }
        }

        this.__events = true;
    }
}
```

1 Add methods for managing event handlers

2 Set up events for generic objects

3 Add method for raising generic event

The code is structured in a manner similar to listing 13.8 for client properties. The functions declared in the code act as static methods that can be called from the client object that wants to expose an event. The first two methods, `_createAddHandler` and `_createRemoveHandler`, return the functions responsible for adding and removing an event handler. The code for these functions is the same that you wrote in section 3.7.1, when we discussed how to expose an event in a JavaScript object.

The `createEvent` method uses `_createAddHandler` and `_createRemoveHandler` to inject the returned functions in the prototype of the object. **1** The injected methods follow the naming convention for events that we introduced in section 3.7.1.

Then, the `createEvent` method checks whether the client object is a client component created with the Microsoft Ajax Library or just a JavaScript object. As you know, client components come with an instance of the `Sys.EventHandlerList` class stored in a private `_events` member. This instance, which is needed to manage event handlers, is returned by a public method called `get_events`, exposed by the base `Sys.Component` class. If you're dealing with a simple JavaScript object, you need to ❷ declare the `_events` variable as well as the `get_events` method.

Finally, ❸ `createEvent` injects the `_raiseEvent` method in the `prototype` object. As you know from section 3.7, this method can raise a generic event exposed in the client object. All you have to do to raise an event is pass in the event name and the event arguments to the `_raiseEvent` method.

With the new `createEvent` helper, exposing client events is fast and easy. For example, you can create a `customerInitialized` event in the `Samples.Customer` class with the following code:

```
Type.registerNamespace("Samples");

Samples.Customer = function() {
    // Declare class members.
}
Samples.Customer.createEvent("customerInitialized");

Samples.Customer.registerClass("Samples.Customer");
```

The `createEvent` method is called just after the constructor as a static method of the `Samples.Customer` class. To raise the `customerInitialized` event, you can call the `_raiseEvent` method anywhere in an instance method, like so:

```
this._raiseEvent("customerInitialized");
```

Finally, an external object can subscribe to the event as usual, by passing an event handler to the `add_customerInitialized` method:

```
var customer = new Samples.Customer();
customer.add_customerInitialized(myEventHandler);

function myEventHandler(sender, e) {
    // Handle the event.
}
```

In the same manner, you can call the `remove_customerInitialized` method to remove an event handler added with `add_customerInitialized`. The nice thing is that all these methods are automatically created by the `createEvent` helper based on the name of the event passed as an argument to the method. You save plenty of keystrokes while decreasing the number of statements and the size of the script file that hosts the client object.

Now, we'll abandon coding patterns and implement some of the most common Ajax design patterns. We'll start with an implementation of the logical navigation and unique URLs patterns. Then, we'll examine client-side data binding and draggable widgets.

13.3 *Logical navigation and unique URLs*

Ajax applications are frequently praised for the richness they provide. Users have come to expect pages that are interactive, fluid, and more responsive than traditional websites. Now that these pages have become a reality, a few of the features you've taken for granted in traditional web applications are missing or perceived as broken.

A frequent remark about Ajax applications is that the browser Back and Forward buttons no longer function as expected. Take, for example, the Google Maps (http://maps.google.com) and Windows Local Live (http://local.live.com) sites. Each of these web applications provides an interactive map, which the user can manipulate by clicking and dragging the mouse over the surface. As data is retrieved seamlessly in the background, the UI is dynamically updated to reflect the movements made with the mouse. Changes are made to the page and its appearance, but no items are entered into the browser's history record—so the next time the user clicks the Back button, they aren't taken to an earlier version of the map (before the dynamic updates began). Instead, they're redirected away from the map page to the page or site that was previously viewed in the browser.

Another missing or broken characteristic that is often observed with Ajax applications is the inability to bookmark a version of a page after making significant updates to its state and appearance. Imagine going through the steps of finding your home or work address on Google Maps and then bookmarking the page in the browser. The next time the bookmark is restored from the browser, you understandably expect the state of the page to be similar to the way it was when you added the bookmark. The reality is that the page is rejuvenated to its original state, before any user interactions user began.

Ajax applications inherently behave differently than traditional applications because they don't perform the same actions. They don't perform a full page refresh when application updates are made, so no entry is made in the browser history. They also don't provide unique URLs when a page is updated, so bookmarks aren't aware of changes made to the application and its state. These intrinsic qualities present challenges for Ajax developers. Providing support for such innate browser activities will enhance your Ajax applications.

13.3.1 Logical navigation

The term *logical navigation* refers to the possibility of associating multiple logical *views* with the same page. Consider the UpdatePanel server control in ASP.NET AJAX: With its support on a page, you can show variations of the same interface without the price of reloading the entire page. Each page variation can be perceived as a separate logical view. Implementing logical navigation means offering the user the ability to navigate between views (or variations) with the browser's Back and Forward buttons.

Support for the logical navigation pattern, often referred to as Back button support, is presented in the form of a History control.

History control

Debuting in the May 2007 release of ASP.NET Futures is a control called History. This control, which provides server-side and client-side support, lets you manage browser history during asynchronous updates on a page. We'll begin our exploration of this control by investigating how you can apply it in a server-centric solution.

> **NOTE**   The previous two chapters, and the third part of the book, are solely dedicated to features in the ASP.NET Futures CTP. We're discussing the History control here instead because its use is more applicable to Ajax patterns and the topic of this chapter.

To use the controls in ASP.NET Futures, first create a new website and select the ASP.NET Futures AJAX Web Site option in the New Web Site dialog (see figure 13.5) in Visual Studio.

Selecting this option adds a reference to the Microsoft.Web.Preview.dll assembly that contains the controls and other features in the library. In addition, an update to the web.config file includes the tag mappings to the new controls:

```
<pages>
 <controls>
  <add tagPrefix="asp" namespace="System.Web.UI"
     assembly="System.Web.Extensions,
     Version=2.0.0.0, Culture=neutral,
     PublicKeyToken=31BF3856AD364E35"/>
  <add tagPrefix="asp" namespace="Microsoft.Web.Preview.UI"
     assembly="Microsoft.Web.Preview"/>
  <add tagPrefix="asp"
     namespace="Microsoft.Web.Preview.UI.Controls"
     assembly="Microsoft.Web.Preview"/>
  ...
```

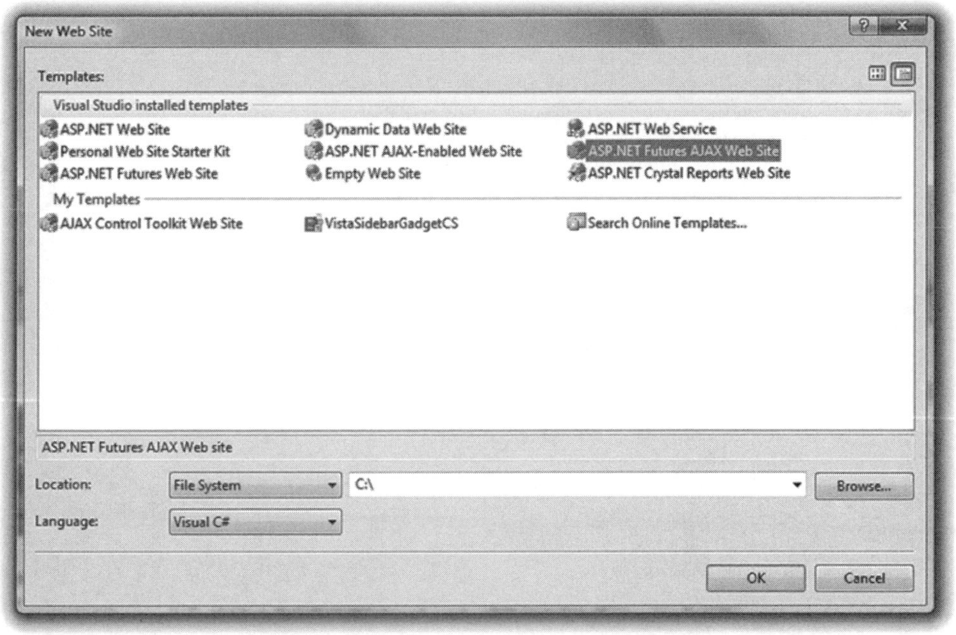

Figure 13.5   Installing ASP.NET Futures adds a website template for preconfiguring sites.

For this exercise, you'll update an application that uses the UpdatePanel control to dynamically render the page with different views of RSS feeds. Listing 13.11 illustrates the markup portion of the application prior to any updates made with the History control.

Listing 13.11   A simple RSS aggregator that uses the UpdatePanel to update the page

```
<%@ Register Assembly="RssToolkit, Version=1.0.0.1, Culture=neutral,
    PublicKeyToken=02e47a85b237026a"
    Namespace="RssToolkit" TagPrefix="rssToolkit" %>
...

<asp:ScriptManager ID="ScriptManager1" runat="server" />
<div>

 <rssToolkit:RssDataSource ID="RssDataSource1"
    runat="Server" MaxItems="7">
 </rssToolkit:RssDataSource>

 <asp:UpdatePanel ID="UpdatePanel1" runat="server"
  RenderMode="Inline">
  <ContentTemplate>
```

```
<asp:DropDownList ID="Blogs" runat="server" AutoPostBack="true"
  OnSelectedIndexChanged="Blogs_Changed" >
  <asp:ListItem Text="ASP.NET Weblogs"
    Value="http://weblogs.asp.net/MainFeed.aspx" />
  <asp:ListItem Text="MSDN Blogs"
    Value="http://blogs.msdn.com/MainFeed.aspx" />
  <asp:ListItem Text="DotNetSlackers Community"
    Value="http://dotnetslackers.com/community/blogs
      ➥/MainFeed.aspx" />
</asp:DropDownList>
<hr />

<asp:DataList ID="Posts" runat="server"
 DataSourceID="RssDataSource1">
 <ItemTemplate>
  <asp:HyperLink ID="TitleLink" runat="server"
      Text='<%# Eval("title") %>'
      NavigateUrl='<%# Eval("link") %>' Target="_blank" >
  </asp:HyperLink>
 </ItemTemplate>
</asp:DataList>

  </ContentTemplate>
 </asp:UpdatePanel>
</div>
```

To accompany the markup portion of the solution, listing 13.12 shows the code-behind portion of the application that updates the feeds on the page.

Listing 13.12 Code-behind solution for a simple RSS reader application

```
protected void Page_Load(object sender, EventArgs e)
{
    if (!String.IsNullOrEmpty(Blogs.SelectedValue))
        RssDataSource1.Url = Blogs.SelectedValue;
}

protected void Blogs_Changed(object sender, EventArgs e)
{
    RssDataSource1.Url = Blogs.SelectedValue;
    Posts.DataBind();
}
```

The application uses an RSS component called the ASP.NET RSS Toolkit. You can download the source and binaries for this component from CodePlex (just like the Ajax Control Toolkit) at http://www.codeplex.com/ASPNETRSSToolkit. Also note that each time a selection is made from the DropDownList, a postback occurs because the control's `AutoPostBack` property is set to `true`. Wrapping this region of the page and the DataList in an UpdatePanel replaces the traditional postback with an Ajax or asynchronous postback.

If you run the application in its current state, the feed content refreshes but no updates are reflected in the browser history. If this is the first page you load in the browser, then the Back and Forward buttons remain disabled even after updates to the page are made. The first step in resolving this situation is to add the History control to the page:

```
<asp:History ID="History1" runat="server"
    OnNavigate="NavigateHistory" />
```

Similar to the ScriptManager, only one instance of the control can exist on a page. It can also be placed on a master page to extend its reach to multiple pages. The `Navigate` event is raised on both the client and server and includes data about the state of the page in the URL. Handling this event and using the data appended to the address lets you re-create the state of the page for a specific logical view. Let's examine these events more closely to add the functionality you're looking for.

The History control has a method called `AddHistoryPoint` that adds an entry in the browser's history repository. It's important to note that the page and all the postback information aren't placed in memory (that would be inefficient): Only the URL of the page and the appended variables that reflect its current state are added to the browser history. This will make more sense after you examine listing 13.13, which illustrates how to use the `AddHistoryPoint` method when the selected blog feed has changed.

Listing 13.13   Using the `AddHistoryPoint` method

```
protected void Blogs_Changed(object sender, EventArgs e)
{
    History1.AddHistoryPoint("blogState", Blogs.SelectedIndex);
    RssDataSource1.Url = Blogs.SelectedValue;
    Posts.DataBind();
}
```

You pass in two parameters to the `AddHistoryPoint` method. The first parameter is the key for an item in a dictionary called `blogState`. (You can name this key anything you'd like—`blogState` seemed descriptive.) The second parameter represents the value you want to associate with the key. Because you want to restore the page to its original state before the postback occurred, you store the index of the selected feed in history. You can then retrieve this value to restore the page when the Back or Forward button is clicked (more on this soon).

This time, when you run the application and select a different feed from the list, the URL is updated along with an entry in the browser history (see figure 13.6).

WARNING At the time of this writing, the history state is unencrypted. This means a user could tamper with the state directly. You should implement measures to validate the data on both the client and server.

This is the first half of the pattern: adding an entry in the history repository. The second half is reading that entry and restoring the state of the page. Listing 13.14 shows how you can accomplish this in the `Navigate` event handler for the page.

Listing 13.14 Retrieving the state of the page and restoring it to completes the logical navigation

```
protected void NavigateHistory(object sender, HistoryEventArgs e)
{
    int index = 0;
    if (e.State.ContainsKey("blogState"))
        index = int.Parse(e.State["blogState"].ToString());

    Blogs.SelectedIndex = index;
    RssDataSource1.Url = Blogs.Items[index].Value;
    Posts.DataBind();
}
```

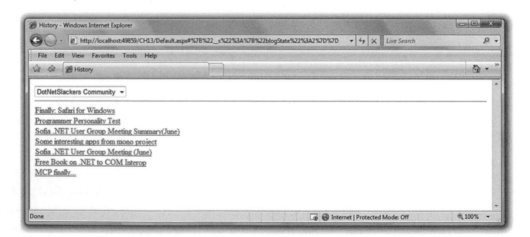

Figure 13.6 Calling `AddHistoryPoint` updates the URL with the state of the page and adds an entry to the history log.

When the `Navigate` event is thrown, that is your opportunity to retrieve the state of the page and restore it. Passed in to the event is a set of arguments of type `History-EventArgs` (declared in the `Microsoft.Web.Preview.UI.Controls` namespace). The arguments include a `State` variable that contains the key/value pairs for the state of the page. With this information, you can retrieve the last state of the page and update the UI accordingly.

The logical navigation pattern can also be implemented from the client. You can add entries to the browser history as well as restore the page, all from JavaScript. To demonstrate, consider a page with three buttons. The click of each button updates an element on the page that displays which button was clicked. Listing 13.15 shows the complete solution for how you can manage history from JavaScript.

Listing 13.15 Managing the History control and the `Navigate` event from JavaScript

```
<form id="form1" runat="server">
 <asp:ScriptManager ID="ScriptManager1" runat="server" />      ❶ Add History
 <asp:History ID="History1" runat="server" />                       control
 <div>
  <p>
   <input type="button" id="button1" value="Button 1"
     onclick="handleClick(1);" />
    <input type="button" id="button2" value="Button 2"
     onclick="handleClick(2);" />
    <input type="button" id="button3" value="Button 3"
     onclick="handleClick(3);" />
  </p>
  <p>State: <span id="currentState"></span></p>
 </div>
</form>

<script type="text/javascript" language="javascript">           ❷ Add handler
                                                                  for navigate
 Sys.Application.get_history().add_navigate(onNavigate);           event

 function pageLoad(sender, args){
   $get("currentState").innerHTML = 0;     ❸ Initialize
 }                                            current state

 function handleClick(state){
  $get("currentState").innerHTML = state;
  Sys.Application.get_history().addHistoryPoint(    ❹ Add to browser
    ➡{pageState: state});                              history
 }
```

```
function onNavigate(sender, args){
  var state = args.get_state().pageState || 0;        ⊲─┐   Retrieve
  $get("currentState").innerHTML = state;              ➎   state
}

</script>
```

The declaration of the ➊ History control is placed immediately after the Script-Manager. Next, you declare the markup for the buttons and the element on the page (currentState) that displays the current state.

Now, let's check out the script. To handle the Navigate event that is raised when the user clicks the Back or Forward button, you need an instance of the client-side History class. You can retrieve this from Sys.Application by calling ➋ get_history. Registering the event is accomplished by calling add_navigate (a global event handler named pageNavigate is also available, just like pageLoad). What follows are the handlers for the events on the page.

First, the ➌ pageLoad function initializes the default state of the page (see chapters 2 and 7 for more about pageLoad and the client-side page lifecycle). By default, the state is 0, signifying that no button has been clicked. When a button is clicked, an instance of the client-side History class is retrieved so you can call the ➍ addHistoryPoint function and pass in a dictionary object with the current state. Last, in the onNavigate event handler, you retrieve the state arguments ➎ and restore the page by updating the currentState element.

This sums up how you can manipulate and work with the browser history to fix the Back button. Next, we'll take a look at unique URLs and how you can add richer bookmark support to your sites.

13.3.2 *Unique URLs*

The ability to link from one site to another, together with the capacity to bookmark a page and return to it later, are key to the success of the web. Earlier, we demonstrated how appending content to a URL provides a mechanism for retrieving the state of a page. This technique addresses the issue of the Back and Forward buttons in the browser but leaves you short of a solution to bookmark pages that have been updated dynamically. You still need a means of retrieving and sharing the state of a page across browser instances.

The term *permalink* was first coined to describe how users could bookmark a blog post that would otherwise be difficult to find later. The idea was that the *permalink link* would represent an unchanged connection to a page or some content that would otherwise be broken or become irrelevant over time—a process also known as *link rot*. Ajax applications frequently suffer from similar symptoms. For instance, many times, users would like to bookmark a page after investing a significant amount of time adjusting its state and appearance. Unfortunately, what commonly happens is that the bookmark or link they end up adding doesn't hydrate the same version of the page they wished to capture.

For a *permalink-like* solution, the History objects on the client and server provide a function that retrieves the state string on the page. Using this formatted state string, you can bookmark and share a link that you can rely on. For server-side code, you can retrieve the link by calling the getStateString method:

```
Permalink.NavigateUrl = "#" + History1.getStateString();
```

In JavaScript, you can accomplish this by calling the get_stateString function:

```
plink.href = "#" + Sys.Application.get_history().get_stateString();
```

In both instances, the state string is prefixed with the # character so it can be formatted correctly in the browser. The formatted link can then be made available for the user. Listing 13.16 offers a JavaScript solution for providing a unique URL for the page.

Listing 13.16 Retrieving and formatting the state string to get a unique link to a page

```
function handleClick(state){
    ...
    updatePermalink();
}

function onNavigate(sender, args){
    ...
    updatePermalink();
}

function updatePermalink(){
    var plink = $get("permalink");
    plink.href = "#" +
     Sys.Application.get_history().get_stateString();
    if (plink.href !== "#")
        plink.innerHTML = "Permalink: " + plink.href;
    else
        plink.innerHTML = "Permalink";
}
```

Although this seems like a trivial task, this minor addition to a web application can greatly improve the user's experience.

Now, let's move to another design pattern. In the following sections, we'll discuss client-side data binding and show you how to perform it using XML Script declarative code and a client control called the ListView.

13.4 *Declarative data binding*

In a web application, controls are often bound to data. The data coming from a database—or other kinds of data storage—is displayed in the UI of one of the web pages that make up the application. For example, a Label control might be in charge of displaying the description of one of the products contained in a store's catalog. Similarly, a HyperLink control could be used to redirect the user to the details page for a specific product. In this case, the URL of the HyperLink would contain a reference to the product ID.

The process of displaying data through controls in the page is called *data binding*. With ASP.NET, data binding typically occurs on the server side, thanks to the many server controls available for this purpose, such as the Repeater, Grid-View, and DataList. In this section, you'll perform data binding on the client side using ASP.NET AJAX and a client control contained in the ASP.NET Futures package. This control, ListView, is a templated control similar to the Repeater server control. Through the ListView, you can define a global layout as well as templates for the items to display, and also a template to display in case the data source is empty.

In the following example, you'll use the ListView control to display a list of products extracted from the AdventureWorks database. (You can download this database for free from the Microsoft website and use it as a test database during the development phase. Appendix A contains instructions on how to set up the AdventureWorks database.) To make things more interesting, you'll write the client-side logic using XML Script, the client declarative language that we discussed in chapter 11. As usual, you can download the complete code for the example from the book's website, www.manning.com/gallo. Figure 13.7 shows the example up and running in Internet Explorer.

13.4.1 *Setting up the Web Service*

Because the ListView control operates on the client side, the first thing to do is get the data to bind to the client control. To do that, you'll create an ASP.NET Web Service that connects to the database and returns a list of Product objects. Each Product

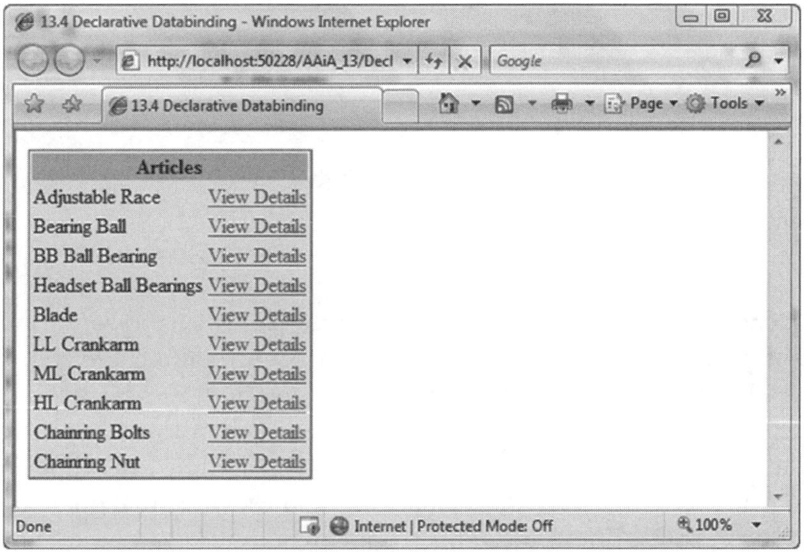

Figure 13.7 A ListView bound to a list of products using XML Script. The data, stored in the AdventureWorks database, is accessed through a Web Service.

instance contains the ID and the description of a product extracted from the AdventureWorks database.

The Web Service is called ProductsService, and you create it in the root directory of an ASP.NET Futures-enabled website. The Web Service class is located in a file called ProductsService.asmx. The Web Service is configured for ASP.NET AJAX, following the procedure explained in chapter 5. The only web method exposed by the Web Service is called `GetTopTenProducts`. The web method returns the first 10 products extracted from the Product table of the AdventureWorks database. The relevant code for the Web Service is shown in listing 13.17.

Listing 13.17 Code for the ProductsService Web Service

```
[WebService(Namespace = "http://tempuri.org/")]
[WebServiceBinding(ConformsTo = WsiProfiles.BasicProfile1_1)]
[ScriptService]
public class ProductsService : WebService {

    [WebMethod]
    public Product[] GetTopTenProducts()
```

```
{
    return GetProducts();
}

private Product[] GetProducts()
{
    // ADO.NET code for accessing the AdventureWorks database.
}
}
```

The `ProductsService` class is decorated with the `ScriptService` attribute. This instructs ASP.NET AJAX to generate a client proxy for calling the web methods from the client side. The `GetTopTenProducts` method uses a private method called `GetProducts` to access the database and return an array of `Product` objects. The code for the `GetProducts` method has been omitted for simplicity, but it opens an ADO.NET connection to the database and uses a textual query to retrieve the products records. Then, the returned records are used to build instances of the `Product` class, which is declared as shown in listing 13.18.

Listing 13.18　Code for the `Product` class

```
public class Product
{
    private int id;
    private string name;

    public int ID
    {
        get { return id; }
        set { id = value; }
    }

    public string Name
    {
        get { return name; }
        set { name = value; }
    }
}
```

The `Product` class exposes two properties: `ID` and `Name`. These properties hold the ID and the product name, respectively. Because the `GetTopTenProducts` web method returns an array of `Product` instances, the `Product` type is automatically proxied on the client side by the ASP.NET AJAX engine. As a consequence, Product instances are serialized to JSON and sent to the browser after the web method returns.

The next step is to set up the ASP.NET page that contains the client ListView control. This page contains the code for calling the web method, retrieving the list of products, and binding it to the ListView. Before we show the code, let's introduce the ListView and its main features and properties.

13.4.2 *The ListView control*

The ListView is a templated client control for displaying data, similar to the Repeater and DataList controls provided by ASP.NET. The main difference with a server control such as the DataList is that whereas the DataList renders static HTML in the page, the ListView is rendered using dynamic HTML on the client side. The ListView control is defined in the Sys.Preview.UI.Data.ListView class and supports the following templates:

- *Item template*—Defines the appearance of a data item.
- *Layout template*—Defines the layout of the data container. For example, the layout template could be a table and the item template could be row of the table.
- *Empty template*—Contains the HTML to display when no data is available.

The templates are defined in the page using static HTML. Then, the IDs of the templates are passed to the ListView instance. Finally, the ListView control takes care of instantiating the templates to obtain the final layout of the control. Listing 13.19 shows the templates you use in the data-binding example.

Listing 13.19 Templates for the ListView control

```
<div id="myListView">                              ←──❶ Associated element
    <table id="listView_layoutTemplate">   ←──┐
        <thead>                                       ❷ Container for
            <tr>                                         layout template
                <th colspan="2">Articles</th>
            </tr>                                     ❸ Container
        </thead>                                         for items
        <tbody id="listView_itemTemplateParent">  ←──┘
```

```
            <tr id="listView_itemTemplate">
                <td><span id="nameLabel"></span></td>
                <td><a id="detailsLink"
                        href="#">View Details</a></td>           4   Item
            </tr>                                                     template
        </tbody>
    </table>
</div>
```

The templates are declared in a **1** container element, which becomes the associated element of the ListView control. In the container element, the layout template is declared as a **2** table element with the ID listView_layoutTemplate. (The layout template is a portion of HTML that is always displayed on the page, even if there's no data to bind to the control.)

Don't forget to specify a container element for the item template **3**. This element is used by the ListView as the container for all the data items. You obtain the HTML for each data item by cloning the item template. In this case, the item template is represented by a table row **4** that contains a span element and an anchor tag. These elements are bound to the ID and the Name properties of each Product object returned by the web method.

The entire job of instantiating the ListView and wiring it to the templates is straightforward if done using the declarative XML Script language. The declarative code for the example, shown in listing 13.20, should be embedded in an XML Script block in the ASP.NET page.

Listing 13.20   XML Script code for the declarative data-binding example

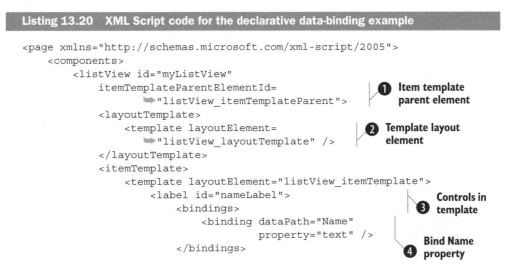

```
<page xmlns="http://schemas.microsoft.com/xml-script/2005">
    <components>
        <listView id="myListView"
            itemTemplateParentElementId=                    1   Item template
                "listView_itemTemplateParent">                  parent element
            <layoutTemplate>
                <template layoutElement=                     2   Template layout
                    "listView_layoutTemplate" />                element
            </layoutTemplate>
            <itemTemplate>
                <template layoutElement="listView_itemTemplate">
                    <label id="nameLabel">
                        <bindings>                           3   Controls in
                                                                 template
                            <binding dataPath="Name"
                                     property="text" />
                        </bindings>                          4   Bind Name
                                                                 property
```

```
            </label>
            <hyperLink id="detailsLink">
                <bindings>
                    <binding dataPath="ID"
                            property="navigateURL"
                            transform="ToDetailsUrl"
                            />
                </bindings>                    Use transformer to    ❺
            </hyperLink>                        bind ID property
        </template>
      </itemTemplate>
    </listView>
  </components>
</page>
```

The ListView control is declared in the components node, with the ID myListView. The itemTemplateParentId attribute ❶ is set to the id of the HTML element that will contain the data rows. As we said before, each data row is obtained by cloning the elements in the item template and adding them in the parent element.

In the listView tag, you associate the HTML for the templates with the List-View control. You do so with the layoutTemplate, itemTemplate, and emptyTemplate tags. Each tag has a child node called template, with a layoutElement attribute ❷. Its purpose is to specify the id of the HTML element that acts as the template container. In each template element, you can map the DOM elements to the corresponding controls ❸, as you do with the nameLabel label and the detailsLink hyperlink.

Because you want to bind the controls in the item template, you declare bindings for the label and the hyperlink. When you bind the ListView control by setting its data property (you'll do so in a moment), each control in the current data row can access the corresponding data item through its dataContext property. This is also true for the bindings declared in the code, because they inherit the same data context as the containing control. In this example, each data item is a Product instance. Therefore, you have to set the dataPath attribute of each binding to a property of the current Product instance. The label's text is bound to the Name property ❹ and the hyperlink's URL is bound to the ID property, through a transformer called ToDetailsUrl ❺. The transformer turns the value of the ID property into a valid URL.

To complete the example, you have to add a JavaScript code block to the ASP.NET page. This block contains the code for the transformer, together with the other imperative code used in the example, as shown in listing 13.21.

Listing 13.21 Imperative code used in the declarative data-binding example

```
<script type="text/javascript">
<!--
    function pageLoad() {
        ProductsService.GetTopTenProducts(onGetComplete);      ❶ Invoke web
    }                                                              method

    function onGetComplete(result) {            ❷ Bind
        $find('myListView').set_data(result);       ListView
    }

    function ToDetailsUrl(sender, e) {
        var productId = e.get_value();                          ❸ Format
        var formatUrl = "catalog.html?product_id={0}";             URL for
                                                                   details
        e.set_value(String.format(formatUrl, productId));   ◀    page
    }
//-->
</script>
```

In the `pageLoad` function, you invoke the web method defined in the `ProductsService` service ❶ through the client proxy created by ASP.NET AJAX when you configured the Web Service. For simplicity, you pass only one callback, `onGetComplete`, which is called as soon as the web method returns.

In the `onGetComplete` function, you call the `set_data` method of the ListView ❷ to pass the array of `Product` instances returned by the web method. As soon as the `data` property is set, the ListView generates the data rows and performs the data binding defined in the XML Script code.

Finally, the `ToDetailsUrl` function is the transformer used to bind the ID property of each `Product` item to the `navigateURL` property of the `HyperLink` control. The transformer ❸ appends the value of the ID property of the current `Product` instance to the base URL of the details page for the current product.

13.5 Declarative widgets

If you've ever visited Live.com, PageFlakes.com, or the Google personalized home page (http://www.google.com/ig?hl=en), then chances are great that you've encountered draggable items commonly known as *widgets*. These items are self-contained portions of the interface that the user can customize and drag around the page. Each widget, in turn, can be dragged from its original location and *docked* into a new area on the screen.

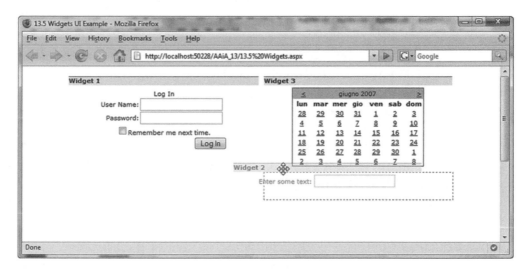

Figure 13.8 Example of widgets with drag-and-drop support, realized using the `DragDropList` and `DraggableListItem` behaviors.

In this example, you'll leverage two client components shipped with the ASP.NET Futures—`DragDropList` and `DraggableListItem` behaviors, to create a similar pattern. To build the example, you'll take advantage of the XML Script declarative language discussed in chapter 11. Figure 13.8 shows what you'll put together with these behaviors.

Before we explain the steps needed to build the example, let's do an overview of the `DragDropList` and `DraggableListItem` behaviors. These behaviors work together to create a list of draggable DOM elements. The `DragDropList` behavior lets you turn a DOM element into a container that hosts a group of draggable elements. In the container, you define the draggable elements—the widgets—as portions of static HTML. Then, you associate an instance of the `DraggableListItem` behavior with each widget to turn it into a draggable item.

To better clarify the concept of a drag-drop list, let's examine the behaviors and their main features. We'll discuss components that take advantage of the drag-and-drop engine, so you may want to review the concepts presented in chapter 12 before proceeding.

13.5.1 *The drag-drop list*

The `DragDropList` behavior can turn a DOM element—usually a `div` or a `span`—into a container of draggable elements. In the container, which is called the *drag-drop list*, a portion of static HTML can become a draggable item by being associated with a `DraggableListItem` behavior.

The `DragDropList` and `DraggableListItem` behaviors are shipped with the ASP.NET Futures package, which is available for download at the official ASP.NET AJAX website (http://ajax.asp.net). Appendix A provides instructions on how to install the package. The client classes relative to the behaviors are located in the PreviewDragDrop.js file, which is embedded as a web resource in the Microsoft.Web.Preview assembly. Specifically, the `DragDropList` behavior is defined in the `Sys.Preview.UI.DragDropList` class. The `DraggableListItem` behavior is defined in the `Sys.Preview.UI.DraggableListItem` class.

The following is a list of the main features offered by the `DragDropList` behavior:

- List items can be dragged outside the list or dropped in it. If the accepted data type is set to `HTML`, dropping an item in the list causes the automatic rearrangement of the remaining items to accommodate the dropped item (reorder-list functionality).

- The list can be rendered horizontally or vertically.

- You can specify a drag mode (`Move` or `Copy`). If you specify `Move`, the dragged element becomes the current drag visual. If you specify `Copy`, an alpha-blended clone of the element is used as the drag visual.

- You can declare an HTML template for the drag visual.

- You can declare an HTML template for the drop cue. The drop cue is used to highlight the area where an item can be dropped.

- The list can be data bound.

The `Sys.Preview.UI.DragDropList` class exposes the following properties:

- `acceptedDataTypes`—The accepted data types
- `data`—The data bound to the list
- `dataType`—The data type associated with the list
- `emptyTemplate`—The template to display when the list is empty
- `dropCueTemplate`—The template used to highlight the drop zone
- `dropTargetElement`—The element associated with the `DragDropList`
- `direction`—Specifies whether the list should be rendered horizontally or vertically
- `dragMode`—The drag mode (either `Move` or `Copy`)

To make the `DragDropList` behavior work, you need to create a block of *structured markup*. You must declare a portion of static HTML in the proper way. Usually, you start with a container element that becomes the DOM element associated with the `DragDropList` behavior. In the element, you declare a set of child nodes that become the list items. For example, the following HTML markup is suitable for use with a `DragDropList` behavior:

```
<div id="listContainer">
    <span id="listItem1">Item 1</span>
    <span id="listItem2">Item 2</span>
    <span id="listItem3">Item 3</span>
</div>
```

The `div` element is the list container and becomes the element associated with the `DragDropList` behavior. Each `span` element represents a list item and can have child elements. To create the drag-drop list, the container element is associated with the `DragDropList` behavior, and each item element must be associated with an instance of the `DraggableListItem` behavior.

The `Sys.Preview.UI.DraggableListItem` class works in conjunction with the `DragDropList` behavior to provide a list with drag-and-drop capabilities. The `DraggableListItem` class exposes the following properties:

- `data`—The data bound to the current item
- `handle`—The ID of the HTML element that acts as the handle for the draggable item
- `dragVisualTemplate`—A template to display while the item is being dragged

To become more confident with the `DragDropList` and the `DraggableListItem` behaviors, you'll now learn how to implement the scenario illustrated in the introduction to section 13.5 using the XML Script declarative code. We covered the XML Script declarative language in great detail in chapter 11.

13.5.2 *Widgets and XML Script*

Finally, it's time to put together the declarative widgets example. Let's start by configuring the ASP.NET page that will host the widgets. Because you'll use the `DragDropList` and `DraggableListItem` behaviors, you need to work in an ASP.NET Futures enabled website. Instructions on how to set up such a website can be found in appendix A. Then, you need to load some script files using the Script-Manager control that you'll declare in a new ASP.NET page. You'll write the client code using the XML Script declarative language, so you need to enable it in the page together with the drag-and-drop components. The ScriptManager control looks like this:

```
<asp:ScriptManager ID="scriptManager" runat="server">
    <Scripts>
        <asp:ScriptReference Assembly="Microsoft.Web.Preview"
                Name="PreviewScript.js" />
        <asp:ScriptReference Assembly="Microsoft.Web.Preview"
                Name="PreviewDragDrop.js" />
    </Scripts>
</asp:ScriptManager>
```

After the ScriptManager control, you have to define the static HTML that will become the drag-drop list. To obtain the kind of layout shown in figure 13.8, you style two div elements as the two columns that host the draggable widgets. This is done in a CSS file referenced in the ASP.NET page, which isn't included in the following listings. (You can access and run the complete source code for this example after downloading it from www.manning.com/gallo.) Listing 13.22 shows the static HTML to add to the ASP.NET page.

Listing 13.22   Static HTML for the declarative widgets example

```
<div class="widgets">

  <%-- Left List --%>
  <div id="leftArea" class="left_col">

      <%--  Widget 1 --%>
      <div id="widget1" class="widget">
          <div id="widget1_Handle"
              class="widget_handle">Widget 1</div>
          <div class="widget_content">
              <asp:Login ID="myLogin" runat="server"
                          CssClass="centered"></asp:Login>
          </div>
      </div>
```

❷ Widget

Left-side list ❶

```
      <%-- Widget 2 --%>
      <div id="widget2" class="widget">
          <div id="widget2_Handle"
              class="widget_handle">Widget 2</div>
          <div class="widget_content">
              <span>Enter some text:</span>
              <asp:TextBox ID="TextBox1"
                          runat="server"></asp:TextBox>
          </div>
      </div>

  </div>
```

```
<%-- Right List --%>
<div id="rightArea" class="right_col">

    <%-- Widget 3 --%>
    <div id="widget3" class="widget">
        <div id="widget3_Handle"
             class="widget_handle">Widget 3</div>
        <div class="widget_content">
            <asp:Calendar ID="Calendar1" runat="server"
                          CssClass="centered"></asp:Calendar>
        </div>
    </div>

</div>

<%-- Templates --%>
<div class="templates">
    <%-- Drop Cue template --%>                        ❸ Drop Cue
    <div id="dropCueTemplate" class="drop_cue"></div>  ←┘   template
    <%-- Empty template --%>
    <div id="emptyTemplate"
         class="emptyList">Drop widgets here.</div>    ❹ Empty
</div>                                                      template

</div>
```

The static HTML includes two div elements, both containing two widgets. The outer div elements ❶ act as drop zones for the widgets and will be associated with instances of the DragDropList behavior. The div elements that act as the widgets ❷ will become items of the containing list and will be associated with instances of the DraggableListItem behavior.

At the bottom of the markup code, you define templates used by the DragDropList behavior. The drop-cue template ❸ highlights a valid drop zone for the widget being dragged. The empty template ❹ displays some text when a list doesn't contain any items. Because the templates are used by the DragDropList, you don't need to show them in the page; you just need to declare the HTML and wire it to a DragDropList instance. For this reason, templates are hidden by the templates CSS class, which sets the display mode of the child elements to false.

To turn the static HTML into dynamic HTML, you write some XML Script code in the page. The HTML Script code contains the declarative markup that wires the DOM elements to instances of the DragDropList and DraggableListItem behaviors. The entire XML Script block to embed in the ASP.NET page is shown in listing 13.23.

Listing 13.23   Declarative XML Script code for the widgets example

```
<script type="text/xml-script">
    <page>
        <components>

            <!-- Left Area -->
            <control id="leftArea">
                <behaviors>
                    <dragDropList dragDataType="HTML"
                                  acceptedDataTypes="'HTML'"
                                  dragMode="Move"
                                  direction="Vertical">
                        <dropCueTemplate>
                            <template layoutElement=
                                "dropCueTemplate" />
                        </dropCueTemplate>
                        <emptyTemplate>
                            <template layoutElement=
                                "emptyTemplate" />
                        </emptyTemplate>
                    </dragDropList>
                </behaviors>
            </control>

            <!-- Right Area -->
            <control id="rightArea">
                <behaviors>
                    <dragDropList dragDataType="HTML"
                                  acceptedDataTypes="'HTML'"
                                  dragMode="Move"
                                  direction="Vertical">
                        <dropCueTemplate>
                            <template layoutElement=
                                "dropCueTemplate" />
                        </dropCueTemplate>
                        <emptyTemplate>
                            <template layoutElement=
                                "emptyTemplate" />
                        </emptyTemplate>
                    </dragDropList>
                </behaviors>
            </control>

            <!-- Draggable items -->
            <control id="widget1">
                <behaviors>
                    <draggableListItem handle="widget1_Handle" />
                </behaviors>
            </control>
            <control id="widget2">
                <behaviors>
```

**DragDropList
declaration** ❶

❷ **Drop Cue
template**

❸ **Empty
template**

❹ **Widget**

Widget handle ❺

```
                    <draggableListItem handle="widget2_Handle" />
                </behaviors>
            </control>
            <control id="widget3">
                <behaviors>
                    <draggableListItem handle="widget3_Handle" />
                </behaviors>
            </control>

        </components>
    </page>
</script>
```

The approach followed in the code is to encapsulate the relevant DOM elements into generic client controls. You do so by declaring a control tag with the id attribute set to the ID of the associated DOM element. In the XML Script code, you create controls for the two drag-drop lists ❶ and the widgets ❹. Because the two drag-drop lists are declared in a similar manner, let's focus on the one that occupies the left portion of the page area.

Each DragDropList behavior is added as a behavior of the corresponding control. You do this by adding a dragDropList element in the behaviors element of the control. As a consequence, the control associated with the container div of the left list has a DragDropList behavior whose attributes are set as follows:

- The dragDataType attribute must be set to HTML to make the list automatically rearrange its items when a widget is dropped over the list's area.

- The acceptedDataType attribute lets you specify a comma-separated list of accepted data types. Each data type is a string enclosed in single quotes. The dragDataType is set to HTML, so the acceptedDataTypes attribute contains at least the HTML data type.

- The dragMode attribute is set to Move. Copy mode has no effect on the DragDropList behavior.

- The direction attribute is set to Vertical to specify that the list has a vertical orientation.

The dropCueTemplate ❷ and emptyTemplate ❸ tags wire the HTML for the templates to the DragDropList instance. This is done by specifying the ID of the DOM element that contains the HTML for the template in the id attribute of the template tag.

Widgets ❹ are declared as generic client controls with an associated `Dragga-bleListItem` instance. Each widget has a handle ❺ that is used to drag it around the page. The handle is represented by a `div` element rendered at the top of the widget, as shown in figure 13.8. To specify that this element is the widget's handle, you set the `handle` attribute of the `draggableListItem` element to the ID of the handle element. All the remaining widgets have similar declarations.

Note that you don't have to wire the widgets to the drag-drop list in the XML Script code. The list items are considered child elements of the DOM element associated with the drag-drop list, as specified in the static structured HTML.

13.6 Summary

In the final chapter of this book, you have used the ASP.NET AJAX framework to implement some of the many Ajax patterns available. A large portion of the chapter has been dedicated to coding and development patterns. Due to the role of JavaScript as the main client development language for Ajax applications, we showed how to implement some patterns that make JavaScript files shorter and easier to debug. We provided patterns on how to provide informative stack traces, comment the JavaScript files (in order to also take advantage of the IntelliSense tool in Visual Studio Orcas) and performing parameters validation in the debug version of a script file.

Since in JavaScript size matters, we provided two helper methods for creating client properties and events using a single statement. These helpers, which extend the Microsoft Ajax Library itself, allow writing less client code and saving a lot of keystrokes, while decreasing the size of JavaScript files sent to the browser.

Then, we moved to examine the implementations of some design patterns. We started with logical navigation and unique URLs. Logical navigation fixes the "broken Back button" problem by allowing access to different views of the same page. Unique URLs is a pattern that allows bookmarking the state of a page, to realize a sort of permalink-like solution.

The last two patterns are related to drag and drop widgets (ala PageFlakes) and data binding. To implement these patterns, we used some of the features available in the ASP.NET Futures package, such as the declarative XML Script language and the drag and drop engine. For performing data binding on the client side, we took advantage of the client `ListView` control to display a list of products from the AdventureWorks database.

Appendices

Appendix A contains instructions for installing ASP.NET AJAX, the ASP.NET Futures package, and the Ajax Control Toolkit. It also shows you how to set up the AdventureWorks database, in order to run some of the examples presented in the book.

Appendix B is dedicated to debugging tools. It contains an overview of the main features provided by Firebug for Firefox and Web Development Helper for Internet Explorer. The final section shows you how to debug JavaScript files using the Visual Studio Debugger.

appendix A: Installing ASP.NET AJAX

In this appendix, you'll learn how to install ASP.NET AJAX and the additional packages available on the official website, such as the ASP.NET Futures, including the ASP.NET AJAX source code. We'll also explain how to install the Ajax Control Toolkit and how to interact with the Toolkit homepage hosted at the CodePlex website. Because some of the examples presented in the book take advantage of the AdventureWorks database, the last section shows how to use this database in an ASP.NET website.

A.1 Downloading and installing ASP.NET AJAX

You can download the ASP.NET AJAX Extensions installer from the official website at http://ajax.asp.net. Figure A.1 shows the Downloads page of the official website. To reach it, click the Downloads button at the top of the page. From this page, you can download the latest release of ASP.NET AJAX as well as additional packages and resources such as the official documentation.

Once you've downloaded the ASP.NET AJAX Extensions installer, you can launch it by double-clicking the executable file. This starts the installation wizard, shown in

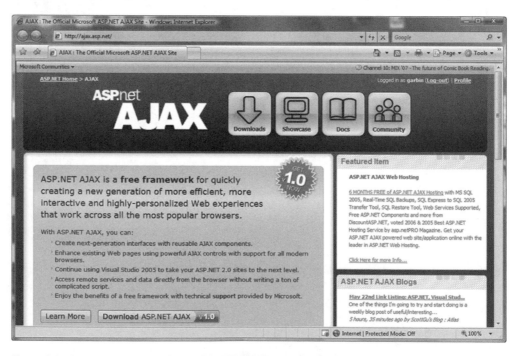

Figure A.1 You can download all the ASP.NET AJAX packages from the Downloads page of the official website.

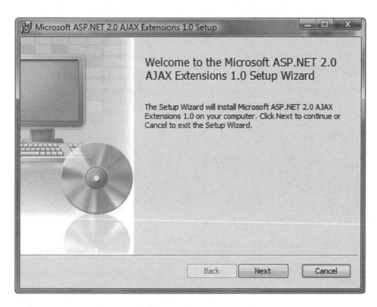

Figure A.2   The ASP.NET AJAX Extensions installer

figure A.2. The installer copies the necessary files to the default installation directory, which is the following:

```
C:\Program Files\Microsoft ASP.NET\
     ➥ASP.NET 2.0 AJAX Extensions\v1.0.61025
```

The installation folder has the same name as the current version number, which will vary for subsequent releases.

If you browse to the installation folder, you'll find the following files:

- The Microsoft Ajax Library files, stored in the MicrosoftAjaxLibrary folder
- The `System.Web.Extensions` and `System.Web.Extensions.Design` assemblies, which contain the ASP.NET AJAX server framework
- A web.config file already configured for ASP.NET AJAX

The `System.Web.Extensions` assembly is automatically added to the Global Assembly Cache (GAC) by the installer. For this reason, there's no need to reference it in a website's bin folder. The Microsoft Ajax Library files are also embedded as web resources in the `System.Web.Extensions assembly`. To configure an ASP.NET AJAX-enabled website, the only thing you have to do is use the web.config file found in the installation directory. If you're upgrading an existing website,

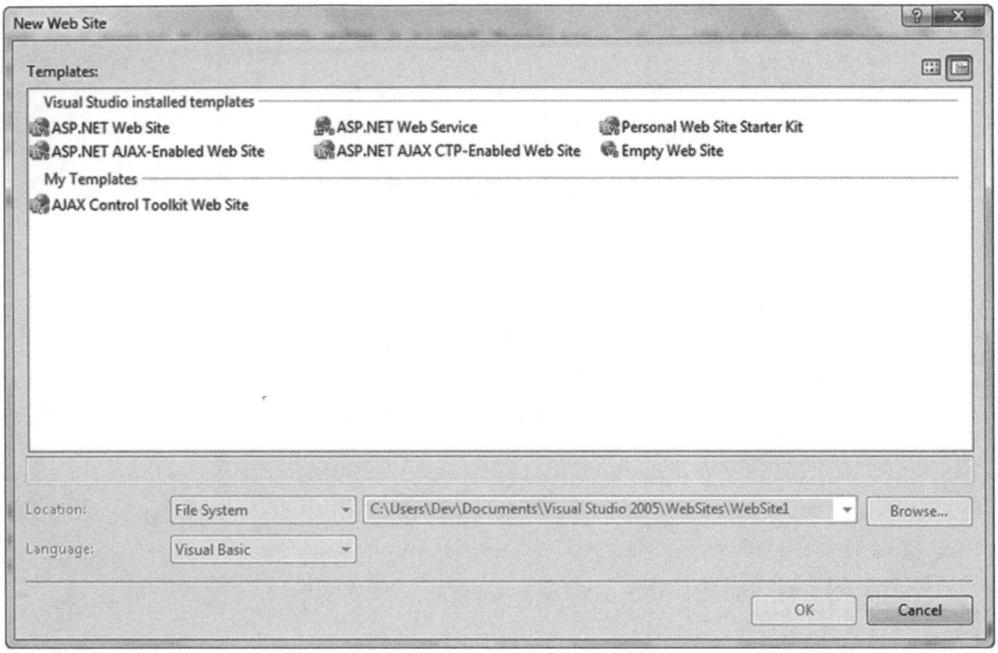

Figure A.3   Templates installed by the ASP.NET AJAX installers

you have to copy all the settings of the web.config file found in the installation directory to the web.config file of the website to upgrade.

To make it easier starting with ASP.NET AJAX, the installer configures also a Visual Studio template that sets up an ASP.NET AJAX-enabled website. To select the template, open Visual Studio 2005 and choose New Project from the File menu to open a window similar to the one shown in figure A.3.

The ASP.NET AJAX-Enabled Website template creates the following files:

- A Default.aspx page with the ScriptManager control in it
- A web.config file already configured for ASP.NET AJAX

To take advantage of the Visual Studio Designer while developing for ASP.NET AJAX, you may want to add the ASP.NET AJAX controls to the Visual Studio Toolbox. The next section explains how to do it.

A.1.1 Adding the ASP.NET AJAX controls to the Toolbox

To add the ASP.NET AJAX controls to the Visual Studio Toolbox, proceed as follows:

1 Right-click (CTRL-Click on a Mac) the Toolbox, and choose Add New Tab. Name the new tab `ASP.NET AJAX Extensions` or give it whatever name you prefer.

2 Right-click the new tab, and click Choose Items. A Browse dialog opens, where you can choose which assembly to add. Browse to the System.Web.Extensions.dll file, and double-click it. Now all the Toolkit controls are in the new tab in the Visual Studio Toolbox, as shown in figure A.4.

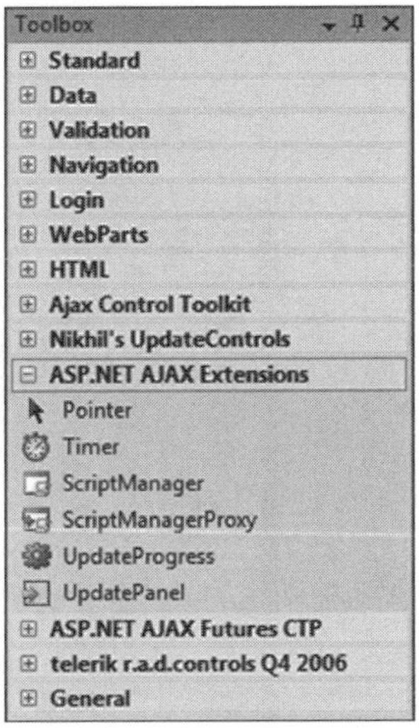

The Downloads page of the official ASP.NET AJAX website contains additional packages available for download. The following sections will guide you through the installation process.

Figure A.4   The ASP.NET AJAX controls added to the Visual Studio Toolbox

A.1.2 Installing the ASP.NET Futures CTP

The ASP.NET Futures CTP is a package containing additional features that are supposed to be included in the next releases of ASP.NET AJAX. These features aren't supported by Microsoft and are provided as Community Technical Preview (CTP) code for evaluation purposes.

You can download the Futures CTP installer from the official ASP.NET AJAX website. When you run it, a wizard will guide you through the installation process, as shown in figure A.5. The installation directory contains the following:

- The Microsoft Ajax Library script files, stored in the ScriptLibrary folder
- The Microsoft.Web.Preview.dll assembly
- A web.config file already configured for ASP.NET AJAX CTP

To configure a new website for ASP.NET AJAX CTP, the only thing you have to do is use the web.config file found in the installation directory. If you're upgrading an existing website, you have to copy all the settings of the web.config file found in the installation directory to the web.config file of the website to upgrade.

The installer also configures a Visual Studio template to create an ASP.NET AJAX CTP-enabled website. To select the template, open Visual Studio 2005, and choose New Project from the File menu.

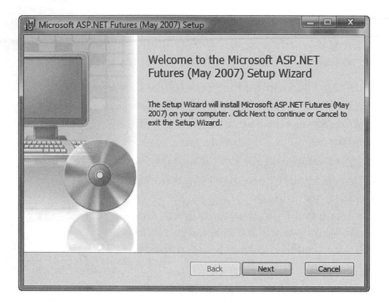

Figure A.5   The ASP.NET AJAX CTP Installer.

The ASP.NET AJAX CTP-enabled Website template creates the following files:

- A Default.aspx page with the ScriptManager in it
- A web.config file already configured for the Futures CTP
- A bin folder that contains the Microsoft.Web.Preview.dll assembly

The script files embedded in the Microsoft.Web.Preview.dll assembly as web resources need to be explicitly referenced in the page using the ScriptManager control. Chapters 11 and 12 explain how to reference the Futures CTP files in an ASP.NET AJAX CTP-enabled page. Finally, you can add the ASP.NET Futures CTP controls to the Visual Studio Toolbox by following the same steps explained in section A.1.1. The only difference is that you have to select the `Microsoft.Web.Preview` assembly in the Browse dialog. The result is shown in figure A.6.

Figure A.6   The ASP.NET Futures CTP controls added to the Visual Studio Toolbox

A.1.3 Additional ASP.NET AJAX downloads

In addition to the main ASP.NET AJAX package and the ASP.NET Futures CTP, you can download the following files from the Downloads page of the official ASP.NET AJAX website:

- *ASP.NET AJAX Extensions Source Code*—The source code for ASP.NET AJAX, written in C#. The code can be modified and re-compiled to generate the `System.Web.Extensions` assembly. You can also use the source code to debug ASP.NET AJAX applications and step into the code.

- *Microsoft AJAX Library*—The JavaScript files needed to enable the Microsoft Ajax Library in a non-Windows system. For example, the package enables development with a PHP server.

- *Sample Applications*—A collection of samples written with the ASP.NET AJAX Extensions.

- *Ajax Control Toolkit*—A collection of Ajax-enabled controls provided as an open-source project hosted at CodePlex (http://www.codeplex.com).

The following section gives detailed instructions on how to install the Ajax Control Toolkit.

A.2 Installing the Ajax Control Toolkit

The Ajax Control Toolkit is hosted at CodePlex, which is Microsoft's open-source project hosting website. The project homepage is at http://www.codeplex.com/AtlasControlToolkit; see figure A.7.

By clicking the Current Release tab in the homepage, you can choose whether to download the compiled binaries or the source code. In the first case, you get an archive that contains a sample website with demos of all the controls and a Visual Studio template to create a new Extender. If you want to use the Toolkit in your website, you only need to browse to the bin folder of the sample website and copy the AjaxControlToolkit.dll assembly into the bin folder of your website. Figure A.8 shows the Toolkit's sample website, which you can browse online at http://ajax.asp.net/ajaxtoolkit/.

If you download the source code, you gain the advantage of being able to study it or modify it to accommodate your needs. As usual, you must compile the source code to generate the AjaxControlToolkit.dll assembly to add to your website's bin folder.

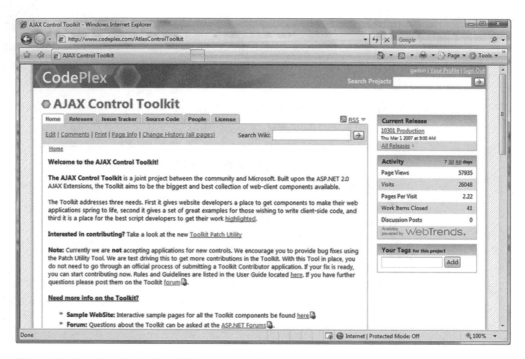

Figure A.7   The Ajax Control Toolkit homepage at CodePlex

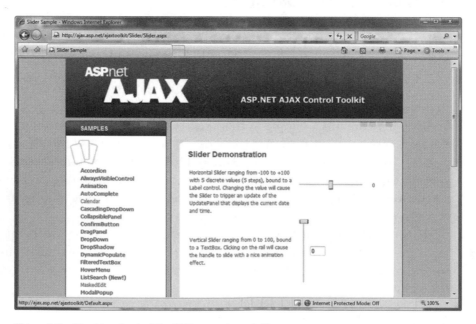

Figure A.8   The Ajax Control Toolkit's sample website

A.2.1 Adding the Toolkit controls to the Visual Studio Toolbox

To add the Toolkit controls to the Visual Studio Toolbox, follow these steps:

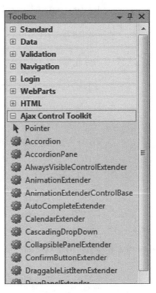

1 Right-click (CTRL-Click on a Mac) the Toolbox,
and choose Add New Tab. Name the new tab
`Ajax Control Toolkit` or give it whatever name
you prefer.

2 Right-click the new tab, and click Choose Items.
A browse dialog opens, where you can choose
which assembly to add. Browse to the installation
directory, and double-click the AJAXExtensions-
Toolbox.dll file. Now all the Toolkit controls are
in the new tab in the Visual Studio Toolbox, as
shown in figure A.9.

A.2.2 Using the Ajax Control Toolkit controls

To use the controls contained in the AjaxControlTool-
kit.dll assembly, you need to register them in an ASP.NET
page. Usually, you do this by adding a `@Register` directive at the top of the ASP.NET page in which you declare

**Figure A.9 The Ajax Control
Toolkit's controls added to
the Visual Studio Toolbox**

one or more Toolkit controls. This directive specifies which assembly and
namespace contain the controls, as well as the tag prefix to use in declarative code.
In the following example, the tag prefix has been set to `ajaxToolkit`, but you can
choose the one you prefer:

```
<%@ Register Assembly="AjaxControlToolkit"
       Namespace="AjaxControlToolkit"
       TagPrefix="ajaxToolkit" %>
```

If you added the Toolkit controls to the Toolbox, you need to drag one onto the
Visual Studio Designer to have the `@Register` directive automatically added to the
web page. As an alternative, to avoid registering the `AjaxControlToolkit` assembly in every page, you can register it globally by adding the following code to your
website's web.config file, under the `system.web` element:

```
<pages>
  <controls>
    <add Assembly="AjaxControlToolkit"
         Namespace="AjaxControlToolkit"
         TagPrefix="ajaxToolkit" />
  </controls>
</pages>
```

Finally, when you're dealing with the Toolkit controls programmatically, be sure to import the `AjaxControlToolkit` namespace:

```
using AjaxControlToolkit;
```

A.2.3 *Interacting with CodePlex*

The CodePlex website offers a nice interface to deal with hosted projects. For example, from the Ajax Control Toolkit homepage, you can download the recent builds of the source code, which are created as soon as the source code is modified by one of the team members. Figure A.10 shows the page you can access from the Source Code tab in the project's tab strip.

If you think you've found a bug or want to signal a feature that you wish would be included in one of the next releases, you can do that on the page accessible from the Issue Tracker tab, as shown in figure A.11. You can also vote for the issues you think should get high priority. The Toolkit team takes votes into consideration for determining the priority of bug fixes.

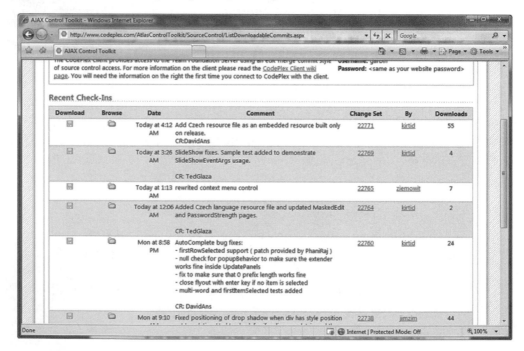

Figure A.10   You can download recent builds of the Ajax Control Toolkit from the CodePlex website.

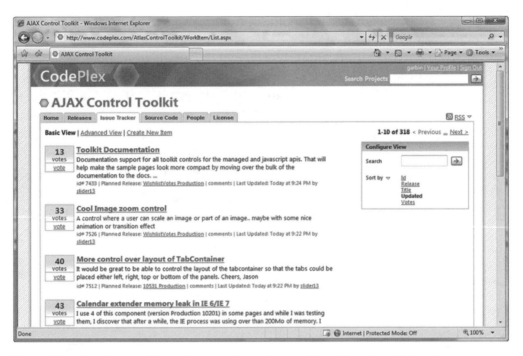

Figure A.11   CodePlex provides an issue tracker to signal and track bugs found in the Ajax Control Toolkit.

Finally, remember that the Ajax Control Toolkit is an open-source project open to contributions from the community. If you think you've developed a cool Ajax-enabled control, check the homepage for instructions on how to submit your creation and enter the project as a Toolkit contributor.

A.3   *Installing the AdventureWorks database*

Some of the examples in the book require access to the AdventureWorks database. Using the AdventureWorks database requires that SQL Server 2005 or SQL Server Express be installed on your machine.

The AdventureWorks database is provided free by Microsoft as an example corporate database to be used in development and testing scenarios. You can download the database from the following URL: http://www.microsoft.com/downloads/details.aspx?FamilyId=E719ECF7-9F46-4312-AF89-6AD8702E4E6E&displaylang=en.

Follow these steps to use the AdventureWorks database in an ASP.NET website:

1 Download and install the AdventureWorks database with the AdventureWorksDB.msi installer. This creates two files—AdventureWorks_Data.mdf and AdventureWorks_Log.ldf—in the installation directory.
2 In Visual Studio, select New Website from the File menu, then choose the ASP.NET Website template or the ASP.NET AJAX-Enabled Website template. Visual Studio sets up the new website for you and adds the App_Data folder.
3 Right-click (CTRL-Click on a Mac) the App_Data folder, and choose Add Existing Item. Then, browse to the AdventureWorks installation folder, and choose the Adventure- Works_Data.mdf file.

Finally, you need to add the connection string to the web.config file. Open the web.config file, and add a `connectionStrings` section under the `configuration` element:

```
<connectionStrings>
    <add name="AdventureWorks" connectionString="Data
        ➥Source=.\SQLEXPRESS;AttachDbFilename=
        ➥|DataDirectory|\AdventureWorks_Data.mdf;
Integrated Security=True;User Instance=True" />
</connectionStrings>
```

Now you're ready to use the AdventureWorks database in a web application. Figure A.12 shows the AdventureWorks database added to a website's App_Data website.

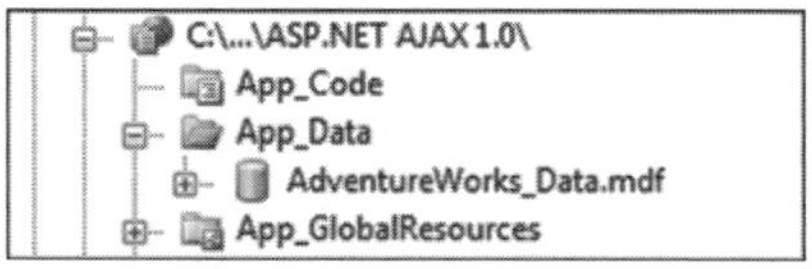

Figure A.12 The AdventureWorks database added to an ASP.NET website

To reference the connection string in declarative code, you can use the following substitution expression:

```
<%$ ConnectionStrings:AdventureWorks %>
```

You can also reference the connection string programmatically in the code-behind file. To do that, you need to import the `System.Configuration` namespace. The following code stores the connection string for the AdventureWorks database in the `connString` variable:

```
string connString =
 ConfigurationManager.ConnectionStrings["AdventureWorks"].ConnectionString;
```

appendix B:
Tools for debugging Ajax applications

This appendix gives you a tour of some of the tools most frequently used by Ajax developers. It explains how to install web tools like Firebug and Web Development Helper and provides an overview of their main features. A section is also dedicated to Fiddler, a tool for debugging HTTP traffic. Finally, the last section explains how to debug script files using the Visual Studio debugger and the Script Explorer window.

B.1 Using Firebug for Firefox

Firebug is a web tool shipped as an add-on to the Firefox browser. It can monitor HTTP traffic, inspect the DOM of a page, and debug JavaScript code. When run in the browser, Firebug lets you change the look and behavior of a web page in real time.

You can install Firebug from the official website at http://www.getfirebug.com, which also contains an online guide to the features provided by this web tool. Figure B.1 shows the Firebug homepage. Let's examine the installation procedure for Firebug before diving into a tour of its features.

Figure B.1   The homepage of the Firebug add-on for Firefox

B.1.1 Installing Firebug

Installing Firebug is straightforward. On the homepage, click the Install icon located at upper right. Firefox prompts you for the permissions to perform the installation and then restarts the browser, as shown in figure B.2.

Once the browser has restarted, you access Firebug by clicking the little green icon on the status bar at the bottom of the browser. You can also open and close the tool by pressing the F12 key and selecting View > Firebug in the Firefox menu bar. Doing so opens the Firebug's console shown in figure B.3.

Let's do a general overview of the features available in Firebug, starting from the logging console.

Figure B.2 Firefox prompts you before installing the Firebug add-on.

Figure B.3 The Firebug tool up and running in Firefox

B.1.2 *Quick Overview of Firebug*

Clicking the Console tab switches to the console window, where messages are logged. As we explained in chapter 2, the Microsoft Ajax Library lets you send messages to the browser's console by calling the `Sys.Debug.trace` method anywhere in the application's code, passing a string with the message to display as an argument. Figure B.4 shows a message logged in Firebug's console using `Sys.Debug.trace`.

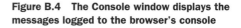

Figure B.4   The Console window displays the messages logged to the browser's console

Selecting the HTML tab switches to a tree-view of the HTML elements of the browsed page, as shown in figure B.5.

In the left window, you can expand or collapse each node of the DOM tree, relative to a particular HTML tag in the page, and inspect the entire markup code of the page. For each node, the right window lets you inspect the element's style, the layout properties (displayed using with the box-model view shown in figure B.5), and all the properties of the corresponding DOM object.

Figure B.5   Firebug lets you inspect the entire DOM tree of a web page.

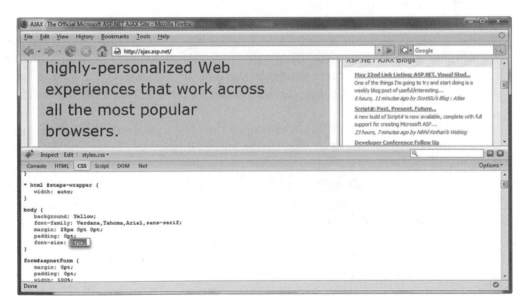

Figure B.6   The CSS tab lets you inspect the CSS files loaded by the browser.

The CSS view lets you explore the style-sheets loaded by the browser. You can choose one from the drop-down list located above the CSS tab, as shown in figure B.6.

Interestingly, you can modify the style of a page in real time. If you click a CSS selector in the CSS view, you can edit its properties and add new ones. As soon as you modify a selector, the changes are reflected on the page. For example, in figure B.7, we've modified the background color of the page and changed the font size of the body element by adding a font-size property.

The Script tab opens one of the most interesting windows. In the Script window, you can inspect the script files loaded by the browser and debug them by setting breakpoints. Figure B.8 shows the Script view, which is split into two windows.

Figure B.7   With Firebug, you can modify the CSS of a web page and see the results in real time.

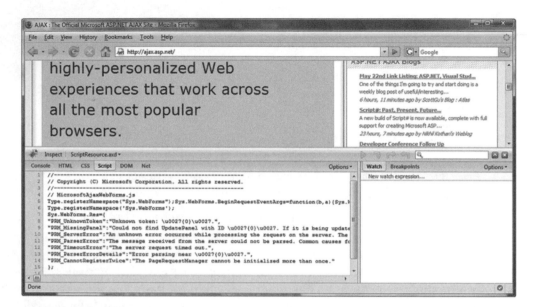

Figure B.8   The Script window lets you inspect and debug script files.

The left window shows the code for one of the JavaScript files requested by the browser during the page load. The right window is the Watch window, which lets you monitor client variables.

You can select script files from the drop-down list located above the Script tab. To debug a JavaScript file, you set a breakpoint by clicking the left zone near the line numbers. You can use the Watch window on the right to examine the values of all the variables and references in the current statement. In addition, you can step into the code, add new watch expressions, and examine all the breakpoints by clicking the Breakpoints tab.

Next, in the DOM tab, you can inspect the page's entire DOM tree. In the same way that the HTML window offers a tree view of the markup code, the DOM window offers a tree view of the DOM objects. This means you can access every element in the page as well as all the JavaScript objects created by your client code. Just as you did in the CSS window, you can change the values of client objects' properties at runtime and immediately see the results. Figure B.9 shows the DOM window.

Finally, you can select the Net window to debug HTTP traffic. The window reports all the requests made to the web server—either synchronous or asynchronous—with the corresponding round-trip time. By expanding the node relative to a particular request, you can inspect the HTTP request and response and their

Figure B.9   The DOM window lets you inspect client objects and modify their properties in real time.

headers and payload, as shown in figure B.10. HTTP requests can also be filtered based on categories. The top toolbar lists all the available categories: HTML, CSS, JS, XHR, Images, and Flash.

Firebug is a premium tool for debugging applications from the Firefox browser. Next, let's examine a similar tool for Internet Explorer: Web Development Helper.

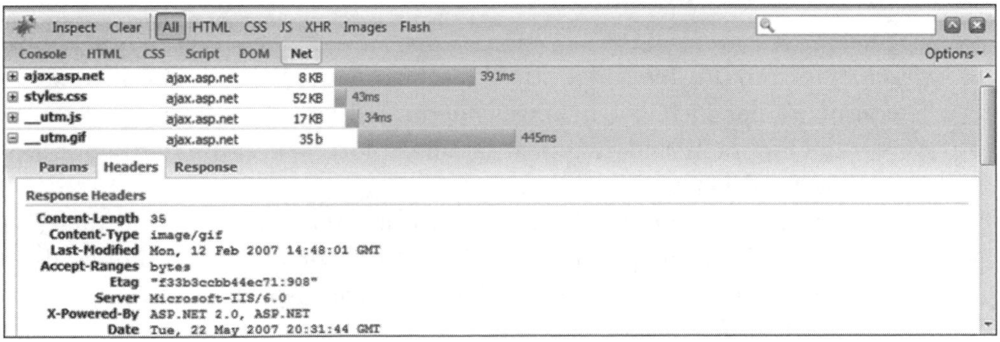

Figure B.10   You can use the Net window to debug HTTP traffic.

B.2 *Using Web Development Helper*

In this section, we'll examine a powerful tool called *Web Development Helper.* Provided as a browser extension (also referred to as a *browser helper object*) for IE, Web Development Helper is useful in JavaScript, Ajax, and ASP.NET development. Features of the tool include HTTP tracing capabilities; an in-process script debugger; and the ability to view items like ViewState, trace messages, and cache information, all from within the browser. Web Development Helper also gives you the ability to view HTTP traffic between the browser and server, get a live snapshot of the DOM, and inspect script errors from an immediate window.

The richness of this tool and its awareness of ASP.NET AJAX make it a must-have for ASP.NET developers. Let's get started by looking at how you can download and install this valuable tool.

B.2.1 *Installing Web Development Helper*

Web Development Helper was created by Nikhil Kothari, an architect on the Web Platform and Tools team at Microsoft. You can find releases, documentation, links, and other relevant information about the tool at http://projects.nikhilk.net/Projects/WebDevHelper.aspx. Requirements include the Microsoft .NET 2.0 framework and Internet Explorer 6 and above.

Installation is clear-cut and simple. After downloading and uncompressing the zip file, launch the utility by running the WebDevHelper.msi application. You'll be prompted with a license agreement and a few quick steps through a wizard, and then the tool is installed and ready for use.

B.2.2 *Launching Web Developer Helper*

You can activate Web Development Helper several ways. A common approach is to select it from the Tools menu in the IE menu bar. You can also invoke it from the command bar in IE by clicking its dedicated icon or selecting it from the Tools menu. Once launched, it appears as an explorer bar at the bottom of the browser (see figure B.11).

For clarity, commands in the tool are separated according to their logical feature areas: Page, Script, HTTP, and ASP.NET. For instance, commands for HTTP include the ability to enable HTTP logging for inspection of traffic. Some of the ASP.NET features include examining the ViewState, trace information, and cache.

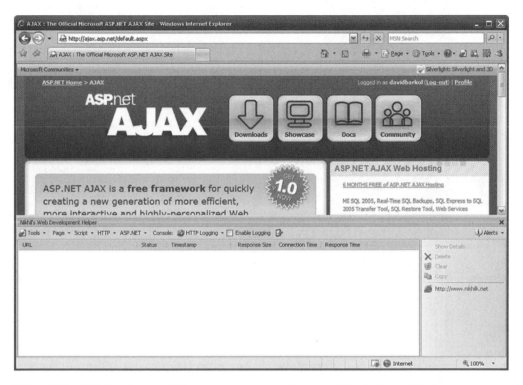

Figure B.11   Web Development Helper appears as an explorer bar at the bottom of the browser.

B.2.3   Inspecting HTTP traffic

You configure Web Development Helper for HTTP logging by selecting HTTP Logging from the drop-down list in the command bar and selecting the Enable Logging check box. The next time an HTTP request is executed, information about the request and its response from the server are appended into a log window. Figure B.12 shows the initial captured requests from a sample application in chapter 5.

You can view additional details about a single request by double-clicking an item in the list. Figure B.13 shows the details of a request made after the Submit button on the form has been clicked.

Details about a request are divided into two sections. The top section displays the request header and body information from the transaction. The bottom section details the response payload from the server by providing header and content data, respectively. Selecting the Response Content tab provides UpdatePanel-related

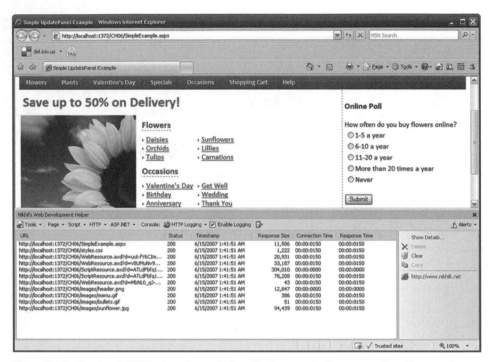

Figure B.12 Captured HTTP requests made from the browser to the server when the page is initially loaded

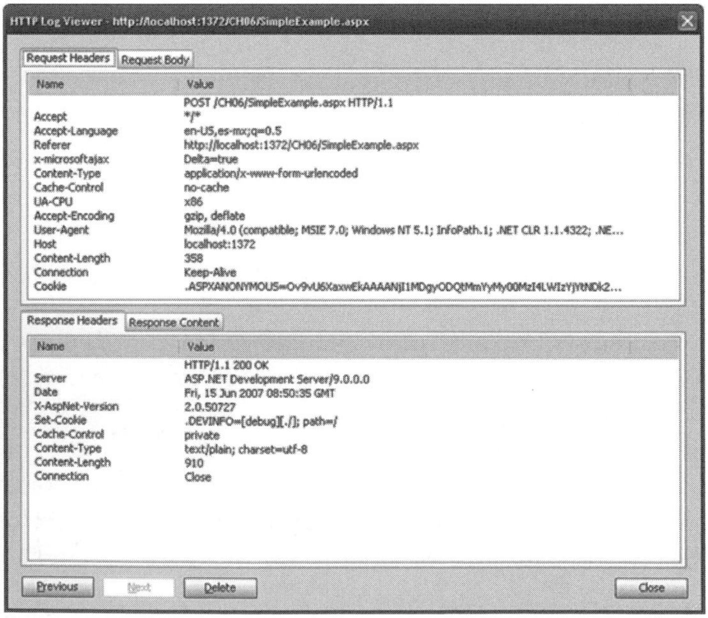

**Figure B.13
The HTTP Log Viewer splits information about an HTTP transaction into two windows: request information and response information.**

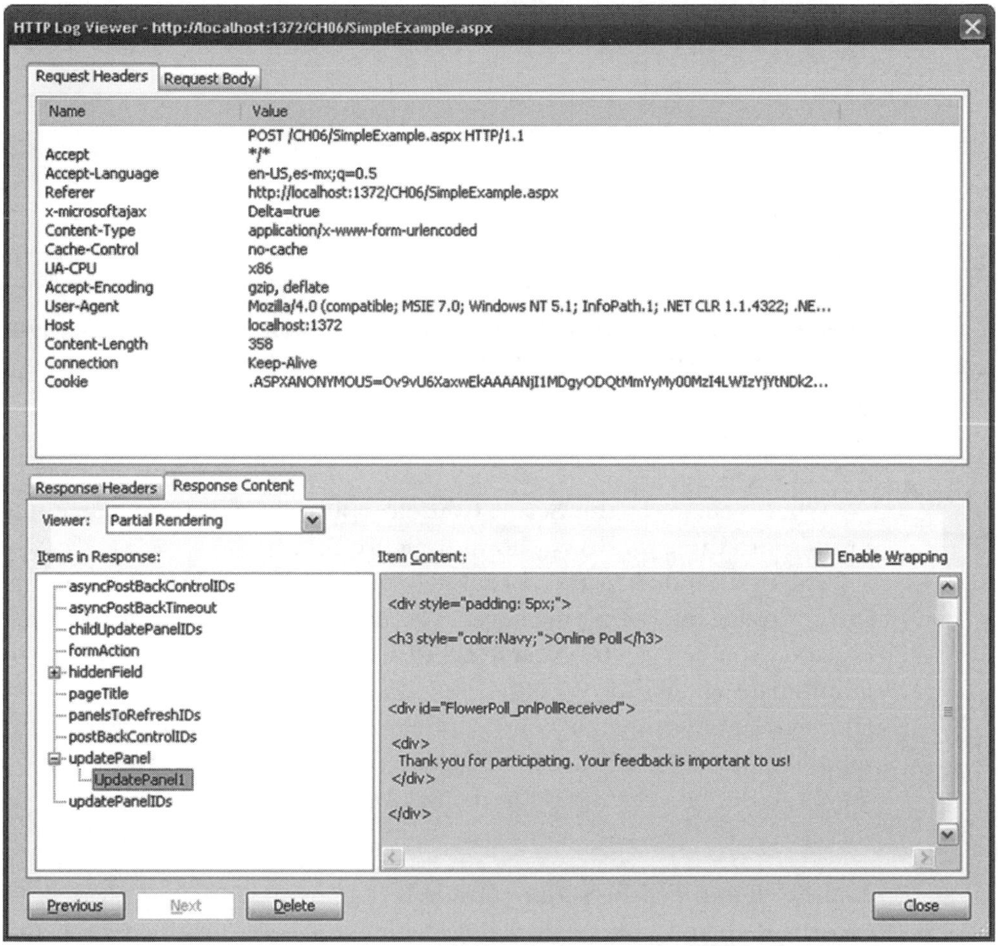

Figure B.14   Web Development Helper offers UpdatePanel-sensitive data on the Response Content tab.

information about the response from the server. Figure B.14 shows some of the ASP.NET AJAX postback-aware data.

B.2.4   Script debugging and tracing

To date, the best debugging experience for JavaScript is available in Visual Studio, which we'll cover later in this appendix. Web Development Helper offers some in-place debugging support that can be helpful as well. To enable script debugging select Script Console from the command bar, and select the Enable Debugging

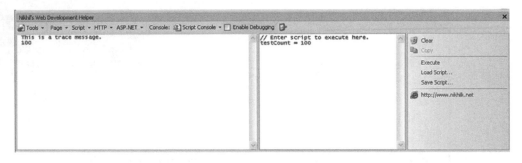

Figure B.15 **The Script Console divides Web Development Helper into three useful windows: output messages (messages log), immediate window, and commands.**

check box. (You don't need to select the check box if all you want to do is view trace messages.)

When you select the Script Console option, the bottom portion of the tool divides into three windows, shown in figure B.15.

The first window in the console is dedicated to displaying output information such as trace and debug messages. The middle window acts as an immediate window that you can use to execute client script on the fly; with this feature, you can manipulate client-side variables and execute logic at runtime. The last window contains links to shortcuts and commands in the tool, such as clearing the messages log or executing code from the immediate window. To output a trace message, call the `trace` function in the Sys.Debug object:

```
Sys.Debug.trace("This is a trace message.");
```

Another feature of the script console is rich error reporting. By default, when an error is detected, you see a dialog containing helpful information that includes the location and callstack of the exception, as shown in figure B.16.

In the Script Error dialog box, you can examine the steps that led to the exception and try to determine its cause. Settings for the error dialog and other features in the tool are available on the Tools menu or by clicking the Console Options button in the command bar. (The Console Options button is the last button on the command bar and has no text associated with it.)

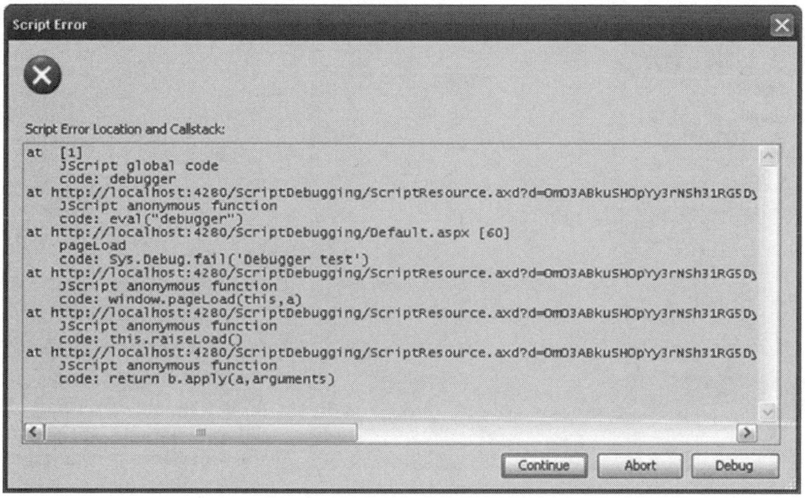

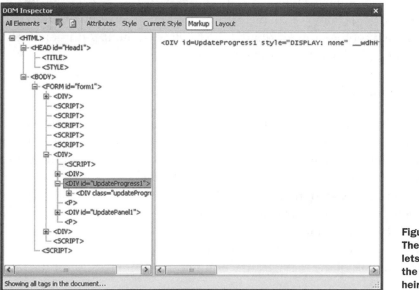

Figure B.16 Web Development Helper offers rich error reporting that includes location and callstack information.

B.2.5 Page and ASP.NET diagnostics

Selecting Page > DOM Inspector brings up a window in which you can view the current DOM on the page. Figure B.17 shows the DOM Inspector in use.

**Figure B.17
The DOM Inspector
lets you navigate
the page's DOM
heirarchy.**

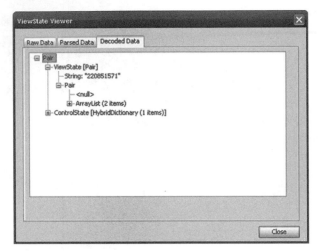

Figure B.18
The ViewState Viewer
grants us a number of
different options for viewing
the ViewState on the page.

With the DOM Inspector, you can observe the attributes, styles, markup (currently selected), and layout of the page. This tool can be a useful alternative to viewing the source generated by the browser.

Next up is the ASP.NET menu, which offers options for viewing the ViewState, trace information, and cache used by the current application. When ViewState is selected, the ViewState Viewer window appears. You can use the viewer to navigate between different versions of the data, as shown in figure B.18.

Web Development Helper is rich and easy to use. Because of its integration with ASP.NET AJAX and its many features, we highly recommend that you make it part of your toolbox for Ajax and ASP.NET development. Additional documentation is available from the tool's home page.

B.3   *Debugging HTTP with Fiddler*

Fiddler is a tool for debugging the HTTP traffic between the browser and the Internet. Unlike Firebug and Web Development Helper, Fiddler is a stand-alone program that can monitor all HTTP traffic. You can download it from the Fiddler homepage, located at http://www.fiddlertool.com. Figure B.19 shows the Fiddler logo that appears as soon as you run the program.

Once you launch the executable file, Fiddler begins capturing network packets with HTTP requests and responses. The main window is split into two parts: The left side lists all the captured HTTP requests and responses, and the right side contains the details of the HTTP transaction selected from the list on the left.

Figure B.19
Logo of the Fiddler tool for HTTP debugging.

You obtain information and statistics about the captured HTTP traffic by selecting one of the tabs on the toolbar at the top right of the main window. As shown in figure B.20, the first tab reports various statistics about the network-time performance of the selected HTTP request and the associated response.

Figure B.20   The Performance Statistics window provides statistics about network times of the HTTP request selected in the left window.

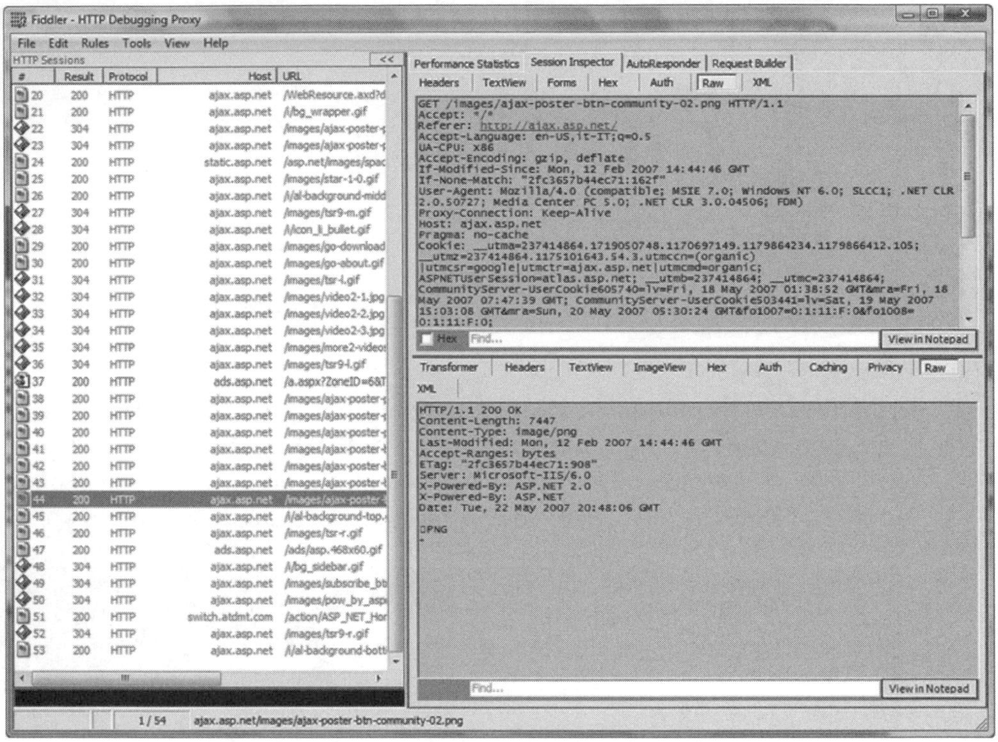

Figure B.21 In the Session Inspector window, you can examine the contents of the HTTP messages in various formats.

The Session Inspector tab switches to the details of the selected HTTP request and the associated response. In this window, you can examine the headers as well as the contents of the HTTP messages in various formats. Figure B.21 shows the Session Inspector window.

The third tab from the left opens the AutoResponder window, shown in figure B.22, which lets you use a previously received response to respond to requests made to a particular URI. This way, you use a predefined response instead of making a connection to the web server.

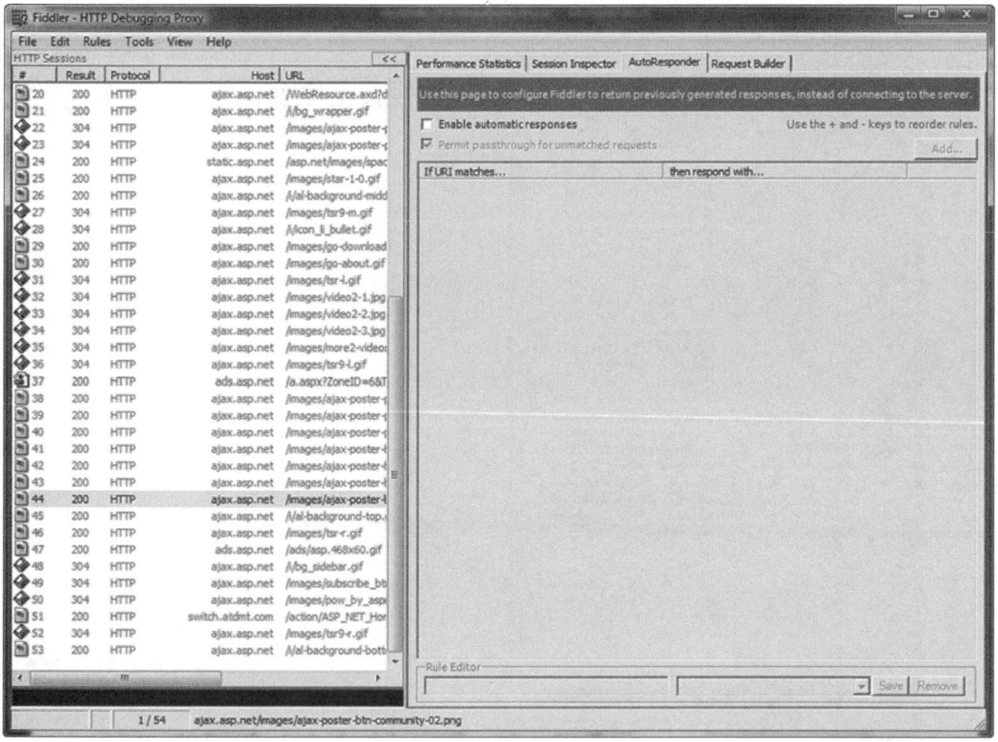

Figure B.22   The AutoResponder window lets you configure a predefined response for HTTP requests directed to a specific URL.

One of the nice features of Fiddler is that it lets you test a network connection by building and sending custom HTTP requests. Figure B.23 shows the Request Builder window, where you can use an editor to build the headers and the payload of a HTTP request and send it to the specified URL. Then, you can monitor the results using the other windows as you do with normal traffic.

The next section will explain how to set up IE and Visual Studio 2005 for debugging JavaScript files.

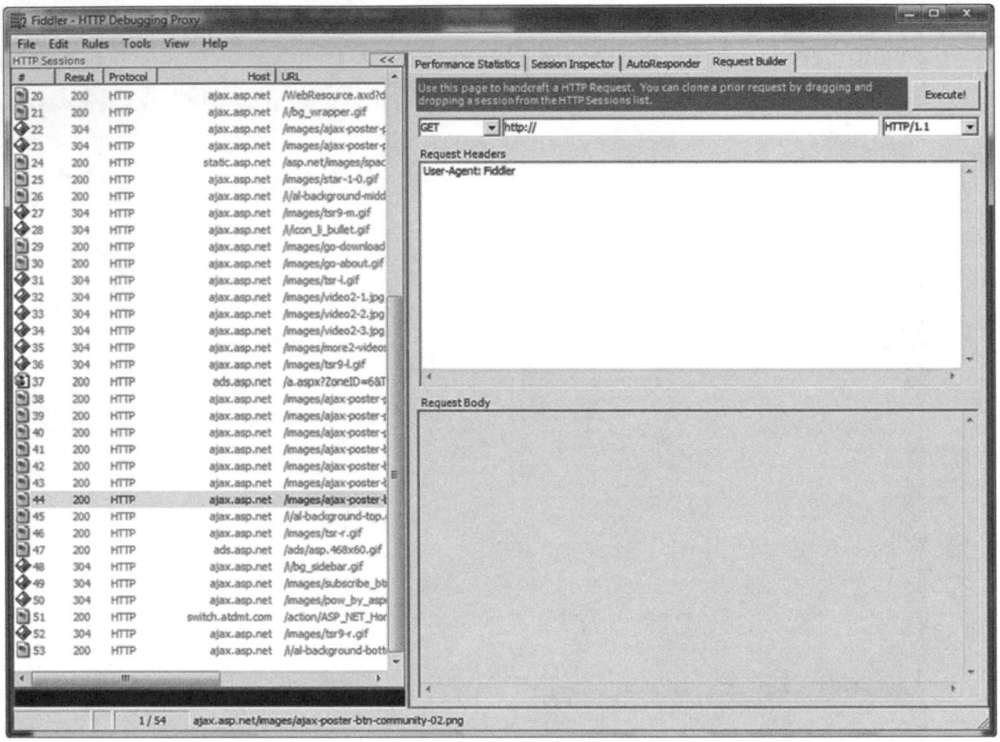

Figure B.23   With Fiddler, you can build custom HTTP requests and send them to the specified URL. The editor lets you specify the headers as well as the payload of the custom HTTP request.

B.4   Debugging JavaScript in Visual Studio 2005

With Visual Studio 2005, you can debug ASP.NET applications using the integrated debugger. To take advantage of the Visual Studio debugger, ASP.NET applications must run in debug mode. The compilation mode can be set by modifying the web.config file of the website accordingly.

Visual Studio also lets you debug script files loaded by the browser at runtime. First, let's see how to configure IE for web-page debugging. Then, we'll explain how to set breakpoints in JavaScript files through the Script Explorer window.

B.4.1   Enabling script debugging in Internet Explorer

To enable script debugging in IE, open the Internet Options dialog and ensure that the following items are deselected:

- Disable Script Debugging (Internet Explorer)

- Disable Script Debugging (Other)

Figure B.24 shows the Internet Options dialog in IE 7, but the same settings apply to IE 6.

Once script debugging is enabled in IE, you can set up the Visual Studio environment. Let's see how this is done.

B.4.2 Setting breakpoints

Normally, the client code loaded in a web page is contained both in script tags in the page as well as in separate files loaded by the browser. Visual Studio 2005 doesn't permit you to set breakpoints in the JavaScript code contained in an ASPX page. But setting breakpoints in separate script files (for example, JavaScript files with the .js extension) sometimes result in errors being raised by the Visual Studio debugger. Let's see what you can do to work around these limitations.

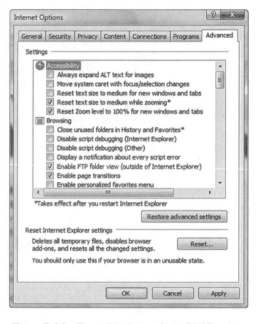

Figure B.24   To enable debugging with Visual Studio, you have to configure some options in IE.

To set breakpoints in the JavaScript code contained in an ASPX page, you must break into the debugger at a specific location in the code. You can do this by adding a statement with the `debugger` keyword at the specific location:

```
debugger;
```

The `debugger` keyword stops the execution of the program and enters the Visual Studio debugger. In the debugger, a new tab opens with the source code of the page you're currently browsing. Now, you can set breakpoints in the source code tab. Once you've set breakpoints, you need to reload the page in the browser in order to debug it.

Figure B.25 shows the source code tab with the `debugger` statement added to the `pageLoad` function. Note that you're setting breakpoints in the source code tab and not in the original ASPX page, which is the inactive tab in the figure.

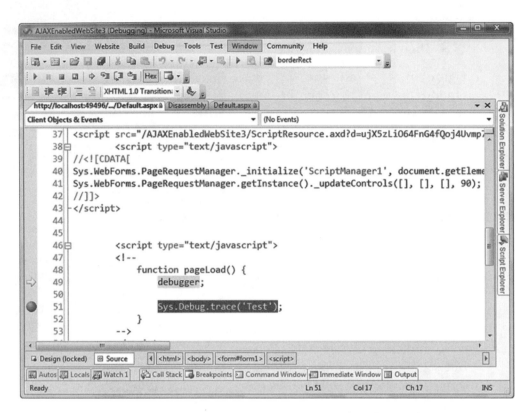

Figure B.25 In Visual Studio 2005, you can set breakpoints in an ASP.NET page after invoking the debugger.

Sometimes, when you set breakpoints in JavaScript files, the debugger complains at runtime, saying that "There's no source code available for this location" and displaying a warning dialog. This happens because script files are loaded dynamically in the page. In such cases, you have to rely on the Script Explorer window to set breakpoints in JavaScript files.

To open the Script Explorer window, choose Debug > Windows > Script Explorer. If you don't see the Script Explorer menu item, choose Tools > Customize. In the new window, select Debug > Script Explorer. You can also drag the Script Explorer icon to a Visual Studio toolbar to add it automatically.

The Script Explorer window lists all the script files loaded in the page you're debugging. If you double-click a file, the file opens in a new tab, and you can set breakpoints; see figure B.26. Once you set breakpoints, you have to reload the web page in order to debug the code.

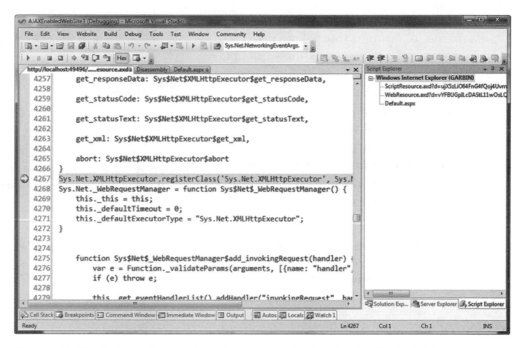

Figure B.26   The Script Explorer window lets you set breakpoints in script files loaded in the page.

In addition to using the debugger keyword, there are a couple other ways to break into the Visual Studio debugger.

B.4.3   Other ways to break into the debugger

Another way to enter the Visual Studio debugger is to raise a client exception. You can do this, for example, with the Sys.Debug.fail method provided by the Microsoft Ajax Library, as shown in the following code:

```
function pageLoad() {
    Sys.Debug.fail('Debugger test');

    Sys.Debug.trace('Test');
}
```

An alternate approach is Sys.Debug.assert, which takes a condition and a string with a message as arguments:

```
Sys.Debug.assert(0 > 1, 'Testing Visual Studio Debugger');
```

Because the condition is evaluated to `false`, IE prompts you, asking if you want to enter the debugger, as shown in figure B.27. Clicking OK stops the execution of the client code and enters the Visual Studio debugger.

Once the Visual Studio debugger is running, you can debug the client code in the same manner that you debug the C# or VB.NET code and take advantage of all the features provided by the Visual Studio debugger.

Figure B.27   Entering the Visual Studio debugger using the `Sys.Debug.assert` method

NOTE   If you want to know more about the Visual Studio debugger, check the MSDN documentation at http://msdn2.microsoft.com/en-us/library/sc65sadd.aspx.

Resources

ASP.NET AJAX framework

The ASP.NET AJAX site contains the latest information about the current status of the framework as well as upcoming news and changes. The forums are also a valuable resource for discussions and solutions to complex problems:

Documentation—http://ajax.asp.net/docs/.

Forums—http://forums.asp.net/default.aspx?GroupID=34.

Homepage—http://ajax.asp.net.

"How do I"—A collection of webcasts titled "How do I" with ASP.NET AJAX is available at http://www.asp.net/learn/videos/default.aspx?tabid=63#ajax. Many of the videos are dedicated to extenders shipped with the Ajax Control Toolkit.

Patterns—An exhaustive and frequently updated list of Ajax patterns and links to implementations is available at the AjaxPatterns.org website, http://ajaxpatterns.org.

ScriptManager—For a complete reference to the ScriptManager control's properties, methods, and events, as well as the other server controls in the ASP.NET AJAX framework, visit the Server Reference section of the online documentation at http://ajax.asp.net/docs/mref/R_Project.aspx.

Ajax miscellany

The term AJAX—The original post from Jesse James Garret of Adaptive Path that coined the term *AJAX* is located here: http://www.adaptivepath.com/publications/essays/archives/000385.php.

Ajax Control Toolkit—http://www.codeplex.com/AtlasControlToolkit. From the home page, you can download the binaries and the source code for the latest release. You'll find also the official bug tracker for the project and useful information about becoming a contributor.

Animations—A reference for all the animations defined in the animation framework is available in the Toolkit's sample website, which is also hosted online at: http://ajax.asp.net/ajax-toolkit/Walkthrough/AnimationReference.aspx.

PHP—Steve Marx, a Microsoft Ajax evangelist, has started a project called PHP for Microsoft Ajax Library aimed at providing support for using the Microsoft Ajax Library with PHP. The project is located on the CodePlex website, at http://codeplex.com/phpmsajax.

web.config—For a more detailed reference on the `customErrors` section in the web.config file, see http://msdn2.microsoft.com/en-us/library/h0hfz6fc(vs.80.aspx.

Widgets—Omar Al Zabir, one of the creators of the PageFlakes website (http://www.page-flakes.com) wrote an article that explains how to create a user interface that supports widgets in ASP.NET AJAX. The article can be found at: http://www.codeproject.com/Ajax/Making-GoogleIG.asp.

Tools

Firebug—An essential tool for debugging JavaScript applications in Firefox, available at http://www.getfirebug.com/.

Web Development Helper—For IE users, a tool developed by Nikhil Kothari (http://www.nikhilk.net) that you can use to debug HTTP traffic, log debug messages, and inspect scripts. It also includes an HTTP request/response viewer with support for partial rendering.

XMLHttpRequest

The ASP.NET AJAX framework abstracts away any use of the XMLHttpRequest object; however, you should have a basic understanding of how it works under the hood. These URLs offer more insight into the protocol and use of the control:

Wikipedia—http://en.wikipedia.org/wiki/XMLHttpRequest

W3C Working Draft—http://www.w3.org/TR/XMLHttpRequest/

Other items of interest

HTTP protocol specification—http://www.ietf.org/rfc/rfc2616.txt.

IntelliSense—IntelliSense in JavaScript files is a feature of the next version of Visual Studio, code-name Orcas. The Web Development Tools Team has a post with the details in its official blog: http://blogs.msdn.com/webdevtools/archive/2007/03/02/jscript-intellisense-in-orcas.aspx.

MSN Virtual Earth mapping engine online SDK—http://dev.live.com/virtualearth/sdk/.

YAHOO! Geocode service and other YAHOO APIs—http://developer.yahoo.com.

Yahoo! Design Pattern Library—Describes and shows various visual patterns that can be implemented with the Toolkit's animation framework. Check them at http://developer.yahoo.com/ypatterns/.

index

ASP.NET 2.0 Web Parts in Action
  Building Dynamic Web Portals
  by Darren Neimke
  ISBN: 1-932394-77-X
  344 pages
  $44.99
  October 2006

Ajax in Action
  by Dave Crane and Eric Pascarello
    with Darren James
  ISBN: 1-932394-61-3
  680 pages
  $44.95
  October 2005

For ordering information go to www.manning.com

MORE TITLES FROM MANNING

Ajax in Practice

by Dave Crane, Jord Sonneveld
and Bear Bibeault
with Ted Goddard, Chris Gray,
Ram Venkataraman and Joe Walker
ISBN: 1-932394-99-0
536 pages
$44.99
June 2007

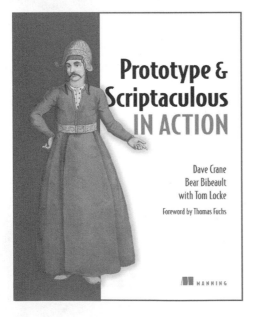

Prototype & Scriptaculous in Action

by Dave Crane and Bear Bibeault
with Tim Locke
ISBN: 1-933988-03-7
544 pages
$44.99
March 2007

For ordering information go to www.manning.com

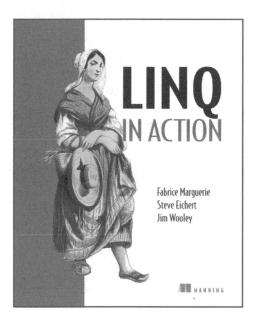
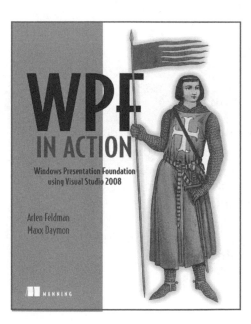

MANNING EBOOK PROGRAM

All ebooks are 50% off the price of the print edition!

In the spring of 2000 Manning became the first publisher to offer ebook versions of all our new titles as a way to get customers the information they need quickly and easily. We continue to publish ebook versions of all our new releases, and every ebook is priced at 50% off the print version!

Go to www.manning.com/gallo to download the ebook version of this book and have the information at your fingertips wherever you might be.

MANNING EARLY ACCESS PROGRAM

Get Early Chapters Now!

In 2003 we launched MEAP, our groundbreaking Early Access Program, to give customers who can't wait the opportunity to read chapters as they are written and receive the book when it is released. Because these are "early" chapters, your feedback will also help shape the final manuscript.

Our entire MEAP title list is always changing and you can find the current titles at www.manning.com